Broken Heartlands

Sebastian Payne is the award-winning Whitehall Editor for the *Financial Times*. At the 2019 British Journalism Awards, he was awarded Political Journalist of the Year in recognition of his work on the *FT*'s series 'The Corbyn Revolution'. Sebastian presents the *Payne's Politics* podcast, which was short-listed for News Podcast of the Year at the 2020 National Press Awards.

Broken Heartlands

A JOURNEY THROUGH LABOUR'S LOST ENGLAND

Sebastian Payne

PAN BOOKS

ISBN 978-1-5290-6739-2

Photography by Sebastian Payne
Map artwork by ML Design Ltd

Typeset by Palimpsest Book Production Ltd, Falkirk, Stirlingshire
Printed and bound by CPI Group (UK) Ltd, Croydon, CR0 4YY

MIX
Paper | Supporting
responsible forestry
FSC® C116313

Visit **www.panmacmillan.com** to read more about all our books
and to buy them. You will also find features, author interviews and
news of any author events, and you can sign up for e-newsletters
so that you're always first to hear about our new releases.

Contents

Conversative Party possible gains in 2019

	Uniformed National Swing (UNS)	Red Wall	UNS Gains / Possible	Red Wall Gains / Possible	Total: Gains / Possible
North West	Barrow and Furness Bury North City of Chester Crewe and Nantwich Lancaster and Fleetwood Warrington South Wirral West	Blackpool South Bolton North East Burnley Bury South Chorley Heywood and Middleton Hyndburn Leigh* Oldham East and Saddleworth Wirral South Workington	4 / 7	8 / 11	12 / 18
Yorkshire and the Humber	Colne Valley Dewsbury Keighley	Batley and Spen Bradford South Don Valley Great Grimsby Halifax Hemsworth Penistone and Stocksbridge Rother Valley Scunthorpe Wakefield	3 / 3	6 / 10	9 / 13
North East	Darlington Stockton South	Bishop Auckland Blyth Valley Newcastle upon Tyne North North West Durham Redcar* Sedgefield Tynemouth	2 / 2	5 / 7	7 / 9
West Midlands	Warwick and Leamington Wolverhampton South West	Birmingham Northfield Coventry North West Coventry South			

Region	Constituencies			
East Midlands	**Derby North, High Peak, Lincoln** · **Stoke-on-Trent Central, Stoke-on-Trent North, West Bromwich East, West Bromwich West, Wolverhampton North East** · **Ashfield, Bassetlaw, Bolsover,** Chesterfield, Gedling	1 / 2	8 / 10	9 / 12
London	Battersea, Brentford and Isleworth, **Carshalton and Wallington****, Croydon Central, Enfield Southgate, Ilford North, **Kensington**	3 / 3	4 / 5	7 / 8
South East	Brighton Kemptown, Canterbury, **Eastborne****, Portsmouth South, Reading East	2 / 7 1 / 5		2 / 7 1 / 5
Eastern	Bedford, **Ipswich**, **North Norfolk****, Peterborough	3 / 4		3 / 4
South West	Bristol North West, Plymouth Sutton and Devonport, **Stroud**	1 / 3		1 / 3
Total Tory gains		19	33	52

Notes: (Bold – Conservative gains) * missed by the Kanagasooriam model; ** missed by the Kenagassooriam model due to collapse in Lib Dem vote

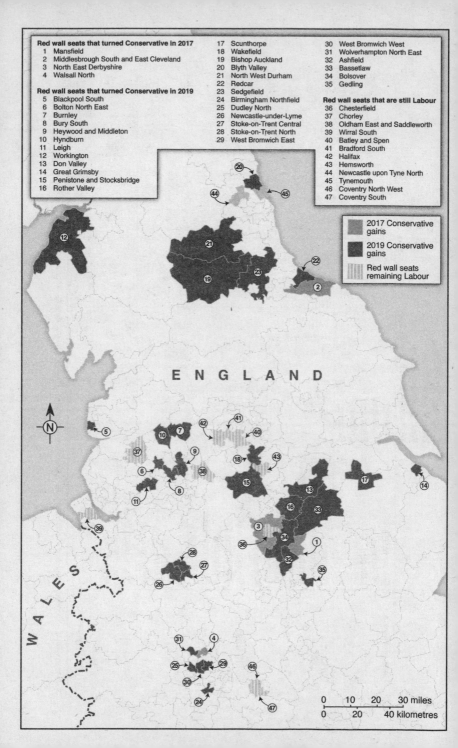

Red wall seats that turned Conservative in 2017
1. Mansfield
2. Middlesbrough South and East Cleveland
3. North East Derbyshire
4. Walsall North

Red wall seats that turned Conservative in 2019
5. Blackpool South
6. Bolton North East
7. Burnley
8. Bury South
9. Heywood and Middleton
10. Hyndburn
11. Leigh
12. Workington
13. Don Valley
14. Great Grimsby
15. Penistone and Stocksbridge
16. Rother Valley
17. Scunthorpe
18. Wakefield
19. Bishop Auckland
20. Blyth Valley
21. North West Durham
22. Redcar
23. Sedgefield
24. Birmingham Northfield
25. Dudley North
26. Newcastle-under-Lyme
27. Stoke-on-Trent Central
28. Stoke-on-Trent North
29. West Bromwich East
30. West Bromwich West
31. Wolverhampton North East
32. Ashfield
33. Bassetlaw
34. Bolsover
35. Gedling

Red wall seats that are still Labour
36. Chesterfield
37. Chorley
38. Oldham East and Saddleworth
39. Wirral South
40. Batley and Spen
41. Bradford South
42. Halifax
43. Hemsworth
44. Newcastle upon Tyne North
45. Tynemouth
46. Coventry North West
47. Coventry South

2017 Conservative gains

2019 Conservative gains

Red wall seats remaining Labour

ENGLAND

WALES

N

0   10   20   30 miles

0   20   40 kilometres

In memory of Charles Trevor Payne, 1941–1998,
a fighter who taught me the importance of the forgotten man

Prologue –
The Fall of the 'Red Wall'

Election night 2019 was a leaden December evening marking the end of a frazzled political year. Walking through the deserted City of London to the *Financial Times*'s newsroom, my stomach and head were queasy. The fatigue from long months of political warfare was vying with anticipation for the long night ahead – and the possibility the UK may be on the cusp of finding closure.

That year began and ended with Brexit and the tortuous process of breaking ties with the European Union after a nationwide referendum. It began with Prime Minister Theresa May securing a withdrawal agreement to extract the UK from the bloc after four years of rancorous bickering. But in successive late-night votes, the deal failed to find a majority in the House of Commons. The governing Conservative Party was tearing itself apart and the Labour opposition was adrift, uncertain whether to back a deal or campaign for another Brexit referendum to overturn the first.

MPs fiercely opposed to crashing out of the EU without a trade deal inflicted two extensions to the withdrawal on the Government, forcing the country into the absurd position of holding elections for the European Parliament while on the cusp of leaving it. As a consequence of May's parliamentary failures, a pop-up political party led by long-time Eurosceptic campaigner Nigel Farage emerged and won those elections. The Tories were embarrassingly pushed into fifth place. The Brexit Party's success prompted a series of dramatic events that led to May's departure from Downing Street and the rapid rise of Boris Johnson, the former foreign secretary who led the campaign for the UK to break with the EU. His victory in that summer's leadership contest was followed by a revised exit deal with the EU. The parliamentary deadlock made an election inevitable and that winter, Johnson went to the country to ask for a mandate to 'get Brexit Done'.

It was my third general election campaign in ten years as a political journalist, my second at the *Financial Times* and my first as a front-line political reporter. My rituals for polling day were well developed. All reporting that could impact the result is forbidden, so there is no news. After a year of running ragged, rising late out of bed, exercising and casting my vote at a local primary school in north London, it was an opportunity to have a long lunch with an old friend followed by a luxurious afternoon nap. The working day began at 9 p.m.

Inside Bracken House, the *FT*'s historic home opposite St Paul's Cathedral, the newsroom was abuzz. The desks were groaning with sweet treats and cafetières. Among the gaggle of editors and data and graphics experts were my three political reporting colleagues. All of us had spent time on the road and were losing our lucidity after the travails of Brexit, the Tory leadership contest and finally the election campaign. There was a consensus among the team that a solid Johnson victory was the most likely outcome, but I was especially bullish about his chances of pulling off a substantial win. Yet we all wondered whether this could be 2017 again, the previous snap Brexit election when the Labour Party surprised the nation by coming close to governing. Much had changed in the intervening two years, especially the declining standing of opposition leader

Jeremy Corbyn, but I sensed something was brewing beyond the polls and voxpops that could boost Johnson's chances.

As winter closed in through late November and December, I had zigzagged across England to figure out whether Johnson was indeed on course for a big win. Across the post-industrial north of England and the landlocked Midlands, the message from voters, activists and campaigners was loud. People were fed up with Westminster, fed up with Brexit and fed up with stagnation. They wanted politics to go away. In large numbers, they appeared to rather like Boris Johnson – particularly his carefully honed optimistic persona. This Old Etonian, Oxford-educated figure was finding purchase in Labour's traditional working-class heartlands in a way that seemed implausible for someone with his backstory. But in seat after seat, it was hard to conclude anything but that Labour was in deep, deep trouble.

In the newsroom, as the BBC's election coverage ramped up and the minutes ticked down to the polls closing, the *FT*'s video crew were trained on me for an instant reaction. Hyped up with coffee, this was the moment where I'd discover whether the thousands of words I had written were accurate or utter rubbish. Anchorman Huw Edwards declared at 10 p.m., 'Our exit poll suggests there will be a Conservative majority.' My reaction was a little less studied: 'Oh my God! they've smashed it.' And by it, I meant the 'red wall': whole parts of England that had always supported the Labour Party since its arrival in national politics almost a century ago. Until that night.

Boris Johnson scored the Conservative Party's first decisive election victory since the 1980s and the days of Margaret Thatcher thanks to parts of the UK that had never voted for his party before. Constituencies in England that were devoted to Labour for generations had shed their voting traditions to return the prime minister back to Downing Street with a mandate to conclude Brexit and reshape the country in his image. It was the most potent and transformative election outcome since 1979. Westminster was agog. But had they paid more attention to voters, they would have realized those who felt disenfranchised were finding their disruptive voice again, just as they had in the 2016 referendum and again in the 2017 election. Their anger did not suddenly erupt. The groundwork had been laid by Theresa May two years previously, but it was chiefly the culmination of years and decades of neglect by successive governments and politicians.

At 4.35 a.m., when Johnson was clearly heading back to Number 10 with a thumping mandate, the *FT*'s editor Lionel Barber reminded me via text that I had spotted the fragility of Labour from the start of the campaign: 'You called the red wall.' But no one had predicted the sheer scale of Labour's collapse. The party had suffered its worst election result since 1935. Maybe it was Brexit. Maybe it was Jeremy Corbyn. Or maybe it was something deeper. There was more to this story and the only way to find out was to hit the road, returning to Labour's former heartlands to find out why so much of the country had decisively broken with the party. And where better to start than the town I still call home, Gateshead.

As well as travelling the country to better understand the people and places that voted Tory for the first time, I wanted to speak to the key political players about the big questions: Boris Johnson and his personal connection to working-class voters, Keir Starmer's enormous challenges in reshaping Labour, Tony Blair on where his New Labour project succeeded and failed, Nigel Farage on how he personally reshaped British politics and Michael Gove's views on the future of conservatism. From Alan Johnson to John McDonnell, Norman Tebbit to Michael Heseltine, David Miliband to Ed Miliband, these people are all part of the journey.

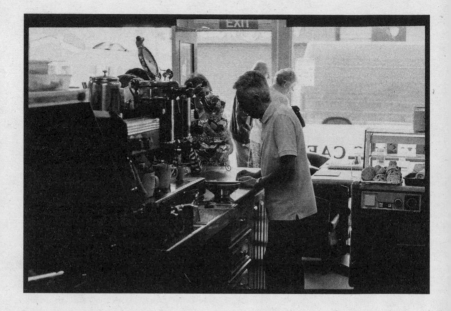

Introduction – Gateshead

'No true civilisation could have produced such a town, which is nothing better than a huge dingy dormitory'

J. B. PRIESTLEY,
AFTER VISITING MY HOME TOWN IN 1934

There is a sense of pride to growing up in Gateshead. It is not the prettiest town in the north-east of England, nor the most economically buoyant. The continual deprivation and poor education in some areas are a national disgrace. But there is a sensitivity about people in other parts of the region peering down at us, never mind the rest of the country. For some residents, part of that psyche is resentment: a feeling that the town's best days are behind it and prosperity is too often found elsewhere. For others, it is a comforting insularity: many of those I went to school with were cheerfully proud that they would spend their lives in the town. There may be bitterness too. My friend Pooja Kumari, who grew up a few streets away from my family, told me she felt that the intensity of local pride was powerful enough to trump any negative feelings. She and I moved away at roughly the same time a decade ago – both down to the capital London for jobs and a different life – yet we are still filled with an affection for our home town, especially its high-spirited people. We both return regularly.

Gateshead has long suffered from a perception that it embodied life being 'grim up north'. Samuel Johnson described the town in the eighteenth century as the 'dirty back lane leading to Newcastle'. That lane has been widened into a dual carriageway that slices through the town centre, so most visitors are not even aware they've been through the town. When the writer J. B. Priestley made his *English Journey* ninety years ago, his report of Gateshead painted a harsh picture. 'No real town', he stated, had such a 'lack of civil dignity and all the evidences of an urban civilisation'.[1] Even in 1933, he felt it was in decline. The then 125,000 people of Gateshead owed their existence to 'Britain's famous industrial prosperity' that was, he felt, waning rapidly. Much has thankfully changed since his visit, and Gateshead has forged a new image thanks to the redevelopment of the riverside. The images most Britons now have of the town are of the Baltic contemporary art centre, the eye-shaped Millennium Bridge and the modern Sage music venue – the legacy of the New Labour era and Tony Blair's reign from 1997 to 2007. But beyond the glossy waterfront, it faces the same struggles of many English towns. Priestley recommended that 'every future historian of modern England should be compelled to take a good long slow walk round Gateshead. After that, he can at his leisure fit it into his interpretation of our national growth and development.' Where better to start my journey – a road trip to examine the political upheaval of the last decade.

This is not a book about me, but I hope a potted biography will explain why I care about this story – the events of 2016 to 2019 were the first political events of my lifetime that affected those I knew and grew up with. I was born in 1989 to an intensely caring and hardworking mother, Bronwen, a secondary school teacher. My father Trevor was a local character, a 'small business owner' or Del Boy without the sidekicks. My mother stoically supported our household while dedicating herself to the classroom for forty-five years. My father's pursuits ranged from selling slush machines to rolling garage doors, to building computers and visiting auction houses. She was born in Carlisle to a middle-class, well-read family; he was brought up in the working-class slums in Gateshead town centre and did not experience an indoor toilet until his teenage years. After brief periods in the RAF and working at the British Library, he returned home and lived there until he passed away at the age of fifty-seven. Both of my parents benefited from secondary education at grammar schools.

The home I grew up in to the south of the town, Ferndene Lodge, was salubrious for the area: an attractive gatekeeper's cottage covered in ivy, built in the mid-nineteenth century, to a long-ago demolished mansion. It stands opposite the fifty-five-acre Saltwell Park, known as the People's Park for the greenery offered to the hundreds of nearby flats without gardens. It has everything a child could desire: a boating lake, maze, ice cream and chip shop, and a bizarre tiny zoo – home to a handful of disorientated exotic birds. When I returned during the autumn of 2020 ahead of this road trip, I was delighted to find none of the park's childhood appeal has waned. My education zigzagged across the north-east: beginning in the state sector at Sacred Heart Primary in Newcastle and St Thomas More High out to the west side of Gateshead. I yearned to study politics and computing, so my mother took the tough decision to invest our limited finances – with no holidays for several years – in sending me to a private school, Dame Allan's, for my final two years. I was fortunate to have this opportunity, which few can enjoy and, as I wrote in the *Spectator* in 2015, I owe much of my career to 'the teaching, advice and encouragement of a small independent school'.[2]

My earliest memories of Gateshead town are of Saturday-morning shopping trips to the high street: the Halifax building society, bargains in the Kwiksave supermarket, clothes and household goods in Woolworths. Like many of England's towns, Gateshead suffered from an appalling mid-century concrete redevelopment, the Trinity Centre, an effort to compete with the larger shops across the river in Newcastle. My recollections are of a deserted indoor market and empty shops. The most notable landmark in the town centre was the multi-storey brutalist car park, which had all the elegance of a sagging sponge cake. Michael Caine made the structure famous in 1971 when he threw his nemesis off its roof in *Get Carter* – the gritty gangster flick that captures the harsh realities of north-eastern life at the time. The car park was thankfully torn down in 2009, and the town centre redeveloped with an even bigger Tesco, plus a cinema, gym and student accommodation. If those parts of Gateshead life sound depressing, none of it blighted my childhood – spent in a loving family, a community of kindly neighbours, in the company of sparky family friends and exploring the wonderful landscape. When I first brought my now-wife Sophia – an accomplished social researcher – to visit Northumberland, I fell in love with the area all over again, with the curiosity and distance of a tourist.

Gateshead's politics have barely budged during my lifetime, which is why it is not part of the *Broken Heartlands* tour. Even with a ten-point surge in the Conservative vote in the 2019 election, it returned a 19 per cent majority for Labour. My upbringing was not party political; no one around us was actively involved in party politics. But current affairs were knitted into the fabric of home life. The maternal side of the family were assuredly middle class – teachers and solicitors – and culturally and politically conservative. The *Daily Telegraph* was, and still is, delivered every day to the doormats of my mother and her relations. The paternal side was more working class: Catholicism first, instinctively attuned to Labour second.

This divide presented itself in my earliest political memory. On 1997 election day, when Tony Blair's resounding landslide delivered the first Labour government in decades, my mother, father and I walked to the primary school around the corner so they could vote. My father was eagerly voting Blair – 'he's clearly on our side' – while my mother refused to engage in any conversation, sheepishly still intending to vote Tory. Into the ballot box I went with her, I saw the cross go into the box for the Conservative candidate, who had not a slightest hope of victory. As we meandered home, my father badgered her about which way she had voted. She never relented. It was the last election he would vote in. My greatest sadness is that my father did not live until I was at an age where we could talk politics, so I cannot say for certain how he would have felt about the events of 2016 and 2019 – but my gut says he would have backed Brexit and Boris Johnson due to his maverick appeal. Thankfully, my mother's interest in the news remains strong, and we frequently chat about Westminster's ups and downs. In recent years their politics would have been united for the first time.

Growing up in a politically divided household was unusual for Gateshead, and I hope it has offered me a vague ability to look in a balanced way at the left–right divide, particularly on Brexit. On both sides of my family, almost everyone voted Leave. I was deeply torn: my northern hinterland and instincts pulled me towards Brexit, but after twenty minutes in the polling booth, my head put a tick in the Remain column. In the Gateshead seat, 56 per cent of the constituency backed Leave. (According to Professor Chris Hanretty of Royal Holloway University in London, whose calculations for each constituency's Brexit vote are the gold standard and will be used throughout my travels.)[3] The referendum marked the first moment when voters broke en masse with their tribal ties to Labour, when the logic that everyone voted Labour 'because my father/grandfather would turn in their grave if I don't' was shattered. Among those voters, I suspected, were some close friends, who I took the opportunity to catch up with before setting off.

The Black Horse is a five-minute drive from my family home in Low Fell, a middle-class enclave on the outskirts of Gateshead. On a not-especially-warm Saturday afternoon – the north-east weather is always tepid at best – the indoor bar was shut off due to the coronavirus pandemic, so I nursed a pint outside. First to arrive was Frank Tatoli, sixty-eight, one of my father's best friends and still a close family figure in my life. Slight, moustached with slicked-back half black/half grey hair, if there was ever a modern Gateshead legend, he is it: second-generation Italian, Geordie, cafe owner and guitarist. His band, Frankie's Cafe, have toured the north-east for twenty years, playing energetic blues and soul to packed pubs and clubs. Guesting with them on bass guitar in a vague effort to impress my wife is one of my proudest life achievements (she may remember the evening differently). And the highlight of my stag weekend was taking a dozen London friends out of their media and political bubbles to a rural pub outside of Newcastle to see the band perform.

Frank's father arrived in the north-east after being taken as a prisoner of war in North Africa. He was shipped to Northumberland and sent to work on farms. After the war, his wife joined him in England and Dominic's Cafe was opened in 1962 thanks to some (dubious-sounding) connections. 'There was an Italian bloke in Hexham called Big Tony, Tony was a fixer. He used to introduce people in the Italian community to different people, to try and make it easier for you to get used to the place." Frank had no desire

---

* Minor edits have been made to interview quotes throughout for concision and readability, but I've endeavoured to preserve my interviewees' own words as closely as possible.

to work in the cafe and lined up several jobs after school: an apprentice mechanic; working in TV production but his father was taken ill. 'Sorry, you're going to have to run the shop now,' he was told. The cafe remains a beacon for the local community: I visited weekly as a child for a nutritious lunch of sausage, beans and chips. The cafe was a meeting place for my father and his associates, with workmen flowing in and out. Frank retired in 2006 after thirty years on his feet, taking orders and brewing coffee. Behind the counter, he had a unique view of how Gateshead and its people have changed. From the 1960s to the 1990s, when he lived in a flat above the cafe with his wife Irene, he has fond memories of the people and the community. But, without wanting to disparage, he regretted that, 'unfortunately nothing stays the same.'

The Gateshead of Frank's youth was dominated by heavy engineering. 'I can remember at half past four, down at Armstrong Street which runs under the bridges, it was packed with people walking up from the factories. For an hour, you couldn't get through. They all lived locally, it's different now. People are not working in big factories, they're not in a trade union.' Those tight-knit communities were shattered by the fragmentation of the economy, but also the rise of the car-based society. The Gateshead town centre of his youth was dominated by pubs and Shepherd's department store, which he said rivalled those across the river in Newcastle. 'When Shepherd's closed, you could see the writing on the wall for Gateshead, and they built Trinity Square. That was a disaster, there was a restaurant that never opened.' The empty restaurant is also fatefully seen in *Get Carter*.

As with many of Gateshead's people, Frank does not call himself as political, but, when you probe, strongly held views emerge. 'During every general election in the cafe, there were a lot of miners, a lot of engineering people used to come in,' he recalled. 'If you were brought up in Gateshead, you voted Labour.

That was it.' He rebelled by voting for the Liberal party in his younger days: 'I never used to vote Conservative or Labour, I always voted Liberal not expecting them to get in, just as a protest.' He liked Labour's Harold Wilson, had little time for the Tories' Ted Heath, respected Margaret Thatcher, but was turned off by the 'pomp' associated with the Tory Party. He felt Tony Blair was a 'breath of fresh air' for Labour and voted for him in 1997.

Frank was one of the 32 per cent of Liberal Democrat voters who endorsed leaving the EU in the 2016 referendum and, went on to enthusiastically back Boris Johnson in the 2019 election, due to the parliamentary chaos that followed the plebiscite.[4] 'It was a bad time, everybody felt the same way whether you voted to leave or stay. When Boris won the general election, he sealed it good and proper.' He was not surprised that Geordies backed the Tories in droves for the first time, due to Jeremy Corbyn. 'Plenty of people were saying if it hadn't been for that bloke, I would never have voted for Boris.'

By this point, my next family friend had arrived with further pints: Mark Brown, who took over Frank's cafe with his wife Pam in 2006. Mark left school at seventeen and began his career with an apprenticeship in a Gateshead foundry in the early 1980s. He won national apprentice of the year – beating rivals from Rolls-Royce and British Aerospace – and spent most of his career in a series of small manufacturing firms. He was made redundant following the financial crash and set up his own logistics company, working closely with the NHS.

Mark also fondly remembered the Gateshead of his youth: the sturdy men in the factories, the comradeship of guiding young ones through apprenticeships. But he isn't consumed by nostalgia. 'Communities, the clubs, that social gathering of people from the same community, that's all gone. And it's a shame that we've lost that. You'll have the hard left who still cry on for the days of the unions. But the world changes, we've got to learn to adapt and move forward.'

His politics were typically Labour until 2019. 'Did I think about voting for another party before? No, because of how tough things have been for the area. But also, what have Labour really done for people here?' In his heart, Mark thought of himself as a social democrat who 'wants to see a little bit more fairness, of distribution of wealth at the top.' He was buoyed by how society changed during the pandemic – especially the focus on 'everyday people' driving buses and working on supermarket tills.

A year on from the election, he was pessimistic for Labour's future. 'I don't see a way back for them. It's a broken party. What's the future? How can they make a comeback? Tax the rich more?' Mark put the blame on Labour's Brexit stance. 'I really found out about the true feeling of staunch Labour supporters – of how disgusted they were with Labour for sitting on the fence about Brexit. It really opened my eyes.' Nor does he make much of how the party has changed under Keir Starmer's leadership. 'I just don't think people really connect with him either.'

For Mark, the political events of 2016 to 2019 broke his ties with the party for good. 'I couldn't genuinely see myself voting Labour – not just because I run my own business. I just don't think that the party has a coherent strategy, the way they went about themselves over the last few years.' And how did he vote? 'I voted Conservative, which was the first time since I was old enough to vote. Broken Heartlands indeed,' he laughed.

The last addition to the drinking session was one of my school friends. Richard Bruce attended Dame Allan's school, making the arduous hour-long commute from Durham daily, and we have remained close pals over the past fifteen years. In my first politics class, he introduced himself simply as Bruce, and thus he has remained since. He lives in Durham, working for the university's student union as their policy supremo, and has a keen eye on politics locally and nationally. He agreed with Frank that Corbyn was the driving factor in the Tories' 2019 victory, along with Brexit.

'With some people who were "I will vote Labour until I die", Corbyn pushed them away. In other areas they didn't agree with Labour's stance on Brexit.' Among his older relations, Bruce spoke of a fatalism stirred by memories of the past. 'There was a lot of more genuine fear of Corbyn, especially those remembering the 1970s in particular. At the younger end of the spectrum, there was a lot on the pro-Corbyn side of things. But those people in their forties and fifties I can think of, there was a lot of "Well, I'm not really a fan of Corbyn even though I voted Labour all my life,"' he said.

Bruce did much soul searching in 2019. He was fed up with Brexit and wanted it resolved. 'I was quite frankly sick of the Brexit story. But by the same token, I was still fearful about the impact of it. This slightly jingoistic line of "it'll be fine, because we're British" was quite worrying to me.' Like Frank, he was inclined towards the Liberal Democrats and ultimately stuck with the party, without enthusiasm, based on their local candidate. Bruce agreed that anti-Conservative feelings were dominant during our childhoods, particularly whenever Margaret Thatcher's name was mentioned. 'That visceral hatred was very, very palpable and real. It seemed to have crossed generations, even to people who weren't born when Thatcher was in power. Partly because there was that general cultural feeling of "we hate Thatcher", which had originated in the mines and all of that economic upheaval,' he said. Frank was not surprised by the 2019 election, but Bruce was. 'I was quite stunned. If I think of some of those areas, the working men's clubs and the miners' clubs, I just can't imagine a victory party in there for a Tory candidate.'

I was keen to know if Bruce's early political memories chimed with mine and how he felt about the north-east's regeneration. 'That cultural investment is really interesting because earlier in the nineties, my memory of Newcastle is dereliction and empty docksides, and bare concrete spaces. And then not too many years after that, you're talking Millennium Bridge, Baltic, Sage and the renovation of some of the other galleries. Durham gets a little bit missed out of that but Newcastle changed enormously between the mid-nineties and the mid-two thousands.' Like me, he felt there was pride mixed with insularity, which fed into anti-establishment feelings on the EU question. When the national political orthodoxy was Remain, the north-east went in the opposite direction. 'The idea that Westminster was behind staying, there was a contrarianism. There is something in the north-east of "We don't like Mr Southerner, whatever that is", whether that's convenience, coffee, or the EU.' An earlier example of that sentiment was the 2004 referendum of regional assemblies. In Dominic Cummings' first political campaign, 78 per cent of the north-east voted against further devolution. The concept was judged as too remote from voters, too expensive and too orientated around cities.

This attitude is partly due to decades of government neglect. Bruce had recently spent much time in the north-west of England and reckoned this feeling spreads across the whole of the north. 'If you look at what London gets from central government, it's very easy to see why there's that resentment. If you look at the quality of the roads and railway stations, there's a long-term feeling of neglect. If you live in some of these pit villages, you can understand why people would just hate Westminster.'

These feelings made much of the north-east prime targets for

Boris Johnson's boosterism. 'When Johnson came along with his optimism and being so ebullient about everything, you can see how that speaks to people. Because they want some positivity,' Bruce said.

Did the trio think the Tories can cling on in the north-east, or even make more gains? 'If it looks like there is not only physical and financial, but also emotional investment by Westminster in the north-east. If people in Westminster genuinely seem to value the opinions and lifestyles of people in the north-east, then yes, I can see it sticking.' Frank and Mark nodded vigorously, agreeing with what Bruce said. With three rounds sunk and the cold setting in, it was off to pick up my first road-trip companion to better understand what the 'red wall' is.

That same autumnal weekend was one of James Kanagasooriam's first visits to Gateshead. As I took him around Saltwell Park, he remarked, 'This is really middle class, this could and should be a Tory area.' After I showed him the town centre and the urban housing streets, he acknowledged that the Tories would have some way to go. Kanagasooriam is one of the most interesting minds in British politics. He arrived in Westminster from banking, working for the pollsters Populus – including on the Scottish Conservatives' successful campaigns in 2016 and 2017. We met soon after his first front-line success and bonded over a nerdy enthusiasm for numbers. I have an affection for political data, a hangover from my days as a computer scientist. Whereas I am not especially good at it, he is excellent.

As the 2019 election geared up, Kanagasooriam called me up and asked to visit the *Financial Times* to present a model he built for the upcoming campaign. 'You're going to want to see this,' he urged. In a presentation to senior editors, he produced a table (see p. vi–vii) ahead of a potential winter election, on which seats the Conservative Party could potentially gain. The multitude of articles, features and columns I researched during that campaign on the red wall phenomena suggested his model was accurate.

The first column contained UNS, or 'uniformed national swing', seats which are those that could go Tory, based on the fact the party was significantly ahead in the opinion polls. The far more interesting column was the one titled 'red wall', which Kanagasooriam named after the Brian Jacques children's fantasy novels. In his explanation, this is what they are:

'There are two buckets of red wall seats. The first is what most people refer to the red wall as: a series of contiguous seats stretching from North Wales, through to outer Merseyside, Lancashire, dipping into the East Midlands and going into South Yorkshire. Fundamentally there's a bit of Britain that, going back to 1997, 2001, 2005, is a massive band of red. It crosses about eight different counties but those areas, despite having completely different histories and dynamics, have something shared, in that they're all traditionally Labour areas. The second bucket is a series of clustered seats around the north-east.'

With hindsight after the campaign, Kanagasooriam and I sat down at my family kitchen table in Gateshead to review the data over dinner and figure out what was right and how the model coped with real-world anomalies. For the first time, he was eager to explain and discuss his work publicly. His model was a success, omitting just two red wall seats: Redcar in the north-east and Leigh in the north-west (the former has a volatile voting record, while he had deemed the latter too urban to go Tory). There were also three swing seats that went Conservative in London and the south-east due to the collapse of the pro-Remain Liberal Democrat vote. Reviewing the 2019 election results, we agreed four criteria that define red wall constituencies:

1. *Never returned a Tory MP since 1997, with a subset that had not returned a Conservative since the Second World War*
2. *Significant vote to leave the EU. On average, red wall seats returned a 63 per cent vote for Brexit compared to the national average of 52 per cent*
3. *A substantial Labour majority during the 1990s*
4. *A substantial minority Tory vote that never threatened Labour but never fully waned either*

Not all constituencies that are sometimes described as 'red wall' meet these criteria. Many, for example, are more demographically middle class and returned a Conservative MP during the peak of Margaret Thatcher's years in power. Darlington, a railway town in the north-east, is often cited as red wall but returned a Conservative MP in the 1950s and again from 1983 to 1992. There are also four constituencies that meet the core characteristics that went blue for the first time in the 2017 election, two years prior to Boris Johnson's victory: Mansfield and North East Derbyshire in the East Midlands, Middlesbrough South and East Cleveland in the north-east, and Walsall North in the West Midlands. Why these fell in 2017 and the others did not will be explored in chapter seven. In total, there are forty-eight seats we can confidently define as red wall, with the Tories winning thirty-four of them in 2019. That leaves fourteen others as likely targets in the next campaign. I put this to a senior Labour figure involved in the 2019 election, who confirmed their strategists feared the result could have been much worse. 'We looked at the north and Midlands and thought the whole thing could just go, it could have been another Scotland for us,' the aide said, referencing the near total wipeout the party suffered north of the border in 2015.

What sets the red wall seats apart from typical marginals is the intersection between their heavy Brexit support and their strong Labour support over the last two decades. Kanagasooriam said, 'You've got the recipe for mass switching; overlaid on top of that is the fact that they are all from an identifiable area that is contiguous, where there is a series of common analyses and common reasons why they've ended up Conservative.' He explained that the Tory vote is very modellable for strategists. 'There are common features of why certain areas vote Conservative: people who tend to own cars, live in detached houses, live in un-dense areas, the countryside or hamlets.' I pointed out that Conservative campaigners used to note where to find their likely voters based on whether there was a hanging basket, which he flagged as something that has disappeared with the red wall, as the Conservative voting coalition has become less prosperous.

Kanagasooriam spotted early in his 2019 work that the demographics of the red wall seats meant they 'should be slightly more Tory than they are'. If many of the first-time Tory constituencies were situated in, say, Kent or Essex, they would have returned Conservative MPs long ago. Some stereotypes have emerged about these old Labour heartlands – that they are poor, small failing towns and all white. None of them are accurate. Thanks to the unique moment of 2019 – the combination of Brexit and Corbyn's abysmal ratings – Kanagasooriam predicted from a purely statistical viewpoint that they would flip as a batch.

Brexit broke the dam of traditional Labour voters abandoning the party and flipping Conservative. David Cameron's pledge in the 2015 election for a referendum on EU membership was widely criticized by other political parties for destabilizing Britain's political system – and abruptly ended his own career. But, it can also be seen as a Tory masterstroke that commenced the decoupling of certain older voters from Labour – mostly white (plus a strong part of the Asian population in places like the Midlands), mid-level education, mortgage-free, medium levels of private wealth and healthy pensions. The process continued in 2016 with the referendum, and again in 2017 when Theresa May called an election to settle the issue of Brexit, and once more in 2019, when Boris Johnson repeated the same trick, albeit much more successfully.

But that process goes beyond the last five years. Kanagasooriam argued there has been a long-term drift of Labour's traditional voters as the party has become increasingly metropolitan in its nature, something most pronounced under Ed Miliband's leadership of the party from 2010 to 2015. 'He set politics on its current course. In policy terms he is a classic interventionist. But the fact that he was an MP parachuted into Doncaster; the fact that he looks less authentic than many of the local Tory candidates; that chipped away at what Labour was.' When Jeremy Corbyn succeeded Miliband in 2017, a whole new group of voters – younger, urban ethnic minorities, middle-class public-sector professionals – flocked to the party, which masked what was happening in its traditional heartlands. 'The reality of the red wall was hidden by the fact that the Labour Party picked up almost equal countervailing votes, but had swapped its electorate.' While Corbyn was very popular in some parts of the country in 2017, the picture had changed drastically two years later, thanks to his much-criticized response to the Skripal poisoning in Salisbury, struggles with anti-Semitism, his ineptitude on the Brexit question and the overall steady decline in his standing. Corbyn did not cut through in the same way in 2019, or as my dinner guest joked, 'You can't reinflate a balloon'.

Having worked in polling since 2014, Kanagasooriam has seen first-hand the dramatic upheaval in the electorate. In most elections prior to 2017, the Tories retained 90 per cent of their vote and Labour around 80 per cent. In 2017, the first election following the referendum, one in four voters changed sides. But Theresa May's success, which went mostly unnoticed due to her abysmal campaign, was to maintain 85 per cent of the Conservative party's vote from David Cameron's last election – and then improve upon it. The shift away from Labour was therefore much more gradual than the dramatic outcome of 2019 would suggest.

'Boris then kept that coalition, so the change is more modest. The Tory vote in the red wall was already at 30 per cent and had increased significantly over the prior decade. There has been a huge change in the political landscape, but those singular events hide the fact that actually this is a more gradual process. I would estimate that seventy per cent of the Cameron coalition were probably the same individuals who subsequently voted for Boris Johnson,' he said.

The party's victories in 2010 and 2015 were described by the new places Cameron won: Putney and Battersea in south-west London. Kanagasooriam put this down to the nature of those commenting on politics. 'Journalists who are London-dwelling live precisely in the areas that are the hardest edge of voter flows. If you live in south-west London, you would have seen three different parties take control in the last ten years, so you might lead yourself to the conclusion that politics is incredibly volatile.' He dryly noted that, 'The Conservative Party does revolution often by stealth and slower than people think. It creeps up. Something is deemed a revolution when people don't notice and then suddenly do.'

Were it not for the fall of the red wall, Kanagasooriam thinks Boris Johnson would have won a majority similar to David Cameron in 2015, of around ten to twenty seats. The emergence of the red wall concept is a 'game changer' for the party because it offers a smoother path to much bigger parliamentary majorities – and in turn more power over how the UK is governed. The prime minister's personal appeal in the Labour heartlands is part of that, as Frank Tatoli highlighted for Gateshead's residents: 'He's a politician that many in these areas want over for tea, they want to talk to him, they laugh. It's the ability to connect, be human and self-deprecating while at the same time making people feel that it is within their gift and their opportunity to better themselves.' Some people decry Johnson's appeal as mere celebrity or Trumpian, but neither is wholly correct. Celebrities struggle to win more than one-off elections; Johnson has never lost one; London mayor twice, the Brexit referendum and the 2019 election. And whereas Trump's Make America Great Again campaign was about stoking anger and grievances, Johnson promotes optimism and sunlit uplands.

Whether Labour can rebuild its red wall will be established at the ballot box. The arrival of Keir Starmer as Labour leader in 2020, with his 'new management' slogan to distance himself from Corbyn, has picked the party up from its 2019 defeat. However, there is no clear indication of whether he is making the necessary gains in the red wall to have any chance of forming a future government. Kanagasooriam reckoned that the Tories' hold on these former heartlands was strong. 'I think once you've broken the link about voting for a particular party you have a historical legacy with, it can be very hard to reattach it.' The rise of the Scottish National Party affirms this: once the historical link between the Labour Party and working-class voters is broken, it takes something new to win them back. The party has yet to find an answer for Scotland, never mind in England.

The 2019 election campaign began in late October that year, after MPs acquiesced to ending the parliamentary stalemate over Brexit. The six-week campaign was shorter than those of recent years, with few dramatic moments. Isaac Levido and Michael Brooks have worked on successive conservative campaigns in the UK and Australia under the tutelage of Sir Lynton Crosby, the Australian 'Wizard of Oz' who masterminded David Cameron's 2015 victory. The 2019 campaign was the Conservative's first under the duo's command. Levido is carefully and softly spoken, never someone to use ten words when two will suffice. He was the Tories' campaign director, gaining his own chant of 'Oh, Isaac Levido!' to the tune of the White Stripes' 'Seven Nation Army' whenever a victory was scored. Brooks is chatty, unusual for a pollster and data scientist. They always do business as a pair. Back around my family dinner table they began by explaining the huge relief when the results confirmed their data and modelling was accurate. Did they expect the majority to be as big as it was?

'We were pointing towards that sort of result for the last sort of ten days. You saw it reflected in the public numbers that it was a relatively stable picture for the final week,' Levido said. 'We got the framing right at the start and we held it. That is no mean feat. You need an incredibly disciplined effort from the whole team and obviously the boss [Boris Johnson] and the other guys on the front line.' Despite his confidence, nerves were fraught on polling day at Conservative Party HQ after a short campaign where pundits second-guessed the polls throughout.

Since Johnson entered Downing Street in the summer of 2019, Westminster had talked up the possibility of a snap election to resolve Brexit. Levido acknowledged it was on the cards soon after Johnson become prime minister due to the 'arithmetic problem inside Parliament', the fact there was no majority for delivering Johnson's formulation of Brexit. Another senior Tory official involved in the campaign told me this framing was also driven by Dominic Cummings, Johnson's chief strategist who freelanced on the campaign. 'Dom told us "We go so hard to get out [of the EU], whatever it takes. And in order to stop us, they're going to have to do something really unreasonable. And they're going to have to do something that will be very, very unpopular in the country. And if they do that, we'll smash them in the election."' The decision of MPs to force a third Brexit extension on Johnson while rejecting his reworked Brexit deal became that unreasonable act.

Levido said, 'every effort' was made not to result in an election. 'I didn't want to run a general election campaign in December in the UK. But that was what came to pass. Ultimately, the key strategic imperative that we needed to have demonstrated to the British people was that there was no other way to resolve the parliamentary deadlock over Brexit.' Brooks and Levido were hired by the party in August 2019 to lay the groundwork in case a poll became inevitable. Millions of pounds were poured into research, with a particular focus on the red wall constituencies which the Tories came very close to taking in the 2017 election. Brooks chimed in that this was not a fluke: 'We went looking for the voters open to supporting us: what are the issues they were facing, and what were their hesitations in supporting us. Then we went through very methodically in trying to mitigate any hesitations they might have. It wasn't just like, which seats are of interest or open to voting for us?' Another party aide summed up what the campaign was about: 'If we held on to the Tory voters while bleeding to the Brexit Party, then we aimed to get a bunch of the Labour leavers over.' That official recalled the struggles of planning an election during the summer of 2019 when the party had little sense of the battleground. 'It all sounds very obvious now, but at the time it was so uncertain on whether there's going be a deal or not.'

In polling and practical terms, the 2019 election was uneventful. One campaigner who had served the Tories in several elections described the whole six weeks as 'very smooth, especially compared to the past'. On 6 November, the night Parliament voted for an election, YouGov put the Tories eleven points ahead of Labour.[5] The last poll on election night by Survation also put the Tories eleven points ahead.[6] And on election night, the Conservatives emerged 11.7 points ahead. There was only one major wobble, insiders said, when Labour released its manifesto chock-full of spending pledges. Increasing the health budget, ramping up the minimum wage, nationalizing the big six energy firms, the railways, Royal Mail, National Grid, scrapping universal credit, building 100,000 council homes a year. All those pledges proved popular, while the Conservative manifesto risked looking dull in comparison. In the following weeks, the Tory lead sank to six points, according to ICM.[7] Levido confirmed that Conservative HQ briefly lost its crucial campaign framing on Brexit. 'I did not adequately foresee how focused the media treatment of our manifesto was going to be as a comparison to the 2017 general election. A lot of the content had been previously announced during the campaign and the overarching story was a cautious platform without the nasty surprises of last time.' While Johnson and his party were telling the country they represented change – by resolving the EU question and investing in public services – their manifesto felt like more of the same. Levido insisted their policy plan was a 'fundamentally transformational document' but had been presented as a safety-first manifesto given the scars of the last campaign.

Brooks and Levido worked on Theresa May's 2017 campaign, which suffered from an overcrowded manifesto and a campaign that struggled to find a narrative. Dominic Cummings summed up the Johnson platform in simple terms, telling aides their aim was to sell: 'Blairism without caring about the causes of crime', a hint towards the electoral coalition they were seeking to rebuild. Brooks said the biggest transformation since 2017, however, was not the mechanics of the campaign but their opponent. 'People knew more about Corbyn. There was just greater awareness of him and what he stood for. The critical thing that was different was that in 2017 there was no risk with Labour, because nobody believed Corbyn could win. And in 2019, because 2017 had happened and it had turned into a hung Parliament, we were therefore able to infuse a vote for Labour with the risk of Corbyn actually becoming prime minister. Whereas if you said to someone in 2017 that Jeremy Corbyn was going to become prime minister they would have laughed you out of the room.' The chaos of the 2017–19 Parliament, which resulted from Theresa May's failure to gain a majority in the election, helped make the case that Corbyn as PM was a real possibility. 'That gave a lot more sharpness to the choice that [voters] were facing,' Brooks said.

The other crucial message the Tories put to the country was that they could simply make politics go away. The series of knife-edge Brexit votes in the House of Commons that I endured night after night from the press gallery were joyous for political pundits and constitutional experts, but exhausting for ordinary voters. Speaking to that emotion, through the lens of resolving Brexit, helped the Tory team win over many disgruntled Labour voters. Brooks said, 'They wanted politics to go away, they knew they were sick of politicians arguing, they wanted politicians to focus on fixing things like the NHS, crime, schools, all the things that they perceived have been neglected over the last few years.' All of the things, in fact, people had voted for Brexit to change. The Tory campaign had to convince the public the Conservatives were best placed to do that – most clearly articulated in their party political broadcast titled 'End the argument. Get Brexit done. Vote Conservative.'[8] To the choral strings of 'Zadoc the Priest', bickering politicians with rolled-up order papers were seen 'arguing about arguing' over dinner tables, bus stops and living rooms. With almost four million views on YouTube, the ad encapsulated the campaign's motivation. Brooks said, 'It was almost, at times, a quite mechanical message about "here is how you can use your vote to achieve the outcome that you want." We weren't trying to persuade voters of the outcome that they wanted – they already knew that – but rather we were telling them how to get there.'

The pair also cited Boris Johnson's communication skills as important to the result. 'In what he says and how he says it, the PM has an authenticity which is incredibly important in modern politics,' Levido said. 'What voters really don't like is someone who they can transparently see is pretending to be something they are not. People can just sense things about politicians and with Boris Johnson they sense that what you see is what you get from him. When you see him out on the road, people just warm to him.' Voters also warmed to Johnson because of his views on spending, heavily influenced by Dominic Cummings. One Conservative HQ staffer at the time said, 'Dom is the anti-austerity person. He was saying this election is going be very difficult for him because it's a change election and we're not change.'

Of course, not everything went to plan for the Conservatives. Candidate selection proved a challenge, with the unpalatable views of several prospective MPs flagged up in the media and resulting in rapid deselections. Levido said, 'A campaign is only ever one fuck-up away from cataclysmic disaster, or events that can knock you completely off course if you don't respond correctly. Anything could happen at any point: Donald Trump came to town, there were floods, a fire in a university dormitory, all manner of things could have gone wrong.' Another campaign insider told me that there was widespread concern over whether the party had made the wrong decision on avoiding a set-piece interview between Johnson and the BBC's Andrew Neil. 'There was constant wobble over that,' the person said.

The other major election event was the terror attack on London Bridge on 29 November, where five people were stabbed, including two fatally.[9] Campaigning was briefly suspended and the prime minister's aides were engaged in how to respond. One recalled that 'Dom [Cummings] basically said we lock them up and throw away the key. The Justice Secretary said "That's going to cost quite a lot of money" and he responded, "Don't worry, we'll pay for it." We then came up with a policy which was essentially very, very tough on terrorists and obviously you can't be too tough on terrorists.' When Jeremy Corbyn was faced with that question on TV, he said terrorists should not be locked away forever.[10] The team had navigated a tragedy and returned the framing to Brexit and their plan for the general election in the final few days.

Far away from another election, the framing of the next campaign is tough to decipher. Levido said the issue of the cultural divide between Labour's London success and its tradi-tional working-class voters is likely to cause problems. 'I would be worried if I were Keir Starmer because he will get dragged to the left on some very uncomfortable issues.' Brooks said it would be a test of Starmer's convictions, whether these issues will dominate and if he can assert his will. 'One of the key things when you look at the PM, he makes difficult decisions. He has always been very clear in standing up for his convictions' – not something everyone will agree with – 'and I think that's a critical test that voters set for prime ministers. It's one that Starmer will have to pass.'

Brooks pressed the case that every election is a unique 'confluence of events' and the role of people like himself and Levido is to direct. He remained uncertain whether the red wall collapse was a generational shift or a simple one-off event. 'The way someone will vote should never be taken for granted. Voters look to the future and say, "Given the circumstances I'm facing today and the things that I think need to change or need to be reinforced in my life, who is the best placed to do that?" It's our job as campaigners to convince them it's our side.' Levido called it a 'purchasing decision', adding, 'the best predictive factor if you're going to vote for a party is if you voted for them before. But there will still be a lot of people that voted for [a party] for the first time that are reserving judgement for now.' He also noted that some of the red wall seats turned Tory because Labour voters stayed at home. In Bassetlaw, Nottinghamshire, the Labour vote dropped 25 percentage points in 2019 and the overall turnout was down 3 per cent. Without that change in turnout, it would not have gone blue.

Our dinner took place as the UK's vaccination programme actually proved world-beating – unlike other aspects of the nation's fight against Covid-19. At that moment, Levido predicted that voters would be unforgiving on jabs: if the roll out went well, the government would be highly praised; if it goes badly, they would be punished. 'Voters vote on the future not the past,' he said. Brooks added, 'This is a really important distinction that politicians always get wrong. They think "I have delivered, therefore voters should reward me." It is important to remember the voters [in 2019] are the ones who took the chance the first time around. They were the ones who bet on changing to a different government, and they're the ones who bet on the government delivering.'

As our long evening came to a close, Levido and Brooks mulled over how the next campaign might look and the challenges the Tory Party will face in making itself feel fresh – while fulfilling the promise to its first-time supporters to deliver tangible differences during a global pandemic. Both agreed a second Johnson term would require convincing voters that change had been delivered and more would come down the tracks. The prime minister has set about trying to do this through his 'levelling-up' agenda, which remained an amorphous concept a year after his election victory.

Rachel Wolf, a long-time advisor to Boris Johnson who co-wrote the 2019 manifesto told me that 'tangible differences' were necessary for the Tories to keep those voters onside. 'They need to be able to show quick, tangible change to how places look and feel, and that means things like cleaning them up, more police on the streets, security guards returning to markets, shops re-opening, cultural events, bus services people can get on.' She also thought that progress would need to be made on the bigger infrastructure projects that would eventually produce jobs and 'make other parts of the country more productive.'

In her view, the phrase 'levelling up' was akin to a slogan people can project whatever they want onto – see also, 'one nation' or 'progressive'. When pushed to define it, Wolf thought it captured an effort to show to the first-time Tory voters that 'their lives will be tangibly different and better than they were two years ago, five years ago.' Through her focus groups, she revealed not everyone likes the concept. 'Most people haven't heard it because most people are terribly proud of where they live and are happy to insult it themselves, but don't really like other people saying that it needs to be upped from down.'

Levelling up has been set back significantly by the pandemic. At best, Johnson has two or three years after the pandemic to deliver that tangible change after the worst of coronavirus. The government has spent significant sums of money on dealing with lockdown – almost £300bn by May 2021 – which has left many of England's towns in a worse state than in 2019. 'If we take the high street as an example, people still really want towns where they can shop and there are places to meet and things to do for their families. Those places were already really suffering. You saw shops closed. You saw graffiti on the Cenotaph and they're now on their knees, and it's not at all obvious how rapidly retail, the high streets and cultural events are going to be able to reappear.'

The reinvention of town centres is not about turning them into mini replicas of London, in her view, but about making them 'nice places to live. It's a pleasurable existence, a huge proportion of what people want are safe clean streets, local museums, weekly or monthly markets. This is not about creating or putting Deloitte or a big manufacturer into the middle of a town.' The small, tangible changes will be the most important. 'People compare their place to towns they like going to. They always talk about things like if it's clean, there are hanging baskets, the shops are open, there's a local football club. These sound incredibly simple, but they actually give people both pleasure and pride. They are symbols that these are places that people look after because they have ownership of them. I am absolutely not saying that doing these things suddenly makes you richer. I'm saying that they are a very reasonable thing to do to make people's lives better.'

Another ally of Dominic Cummings recalled that his hopes for the future were even simpler. 'I remember chatting to Dom two days before the election and asking what's the strategy for getting re-elected. He said, literally, "Build shit in the north." But they have been delayed in building because of everything that has happened with Covid.' Cummings' vision has morphed into Johnson's 'levelling-up' agenda, to tackle long-standing regional inequalities and equalize opportunities in England's less prosperous regions.

From my first conversations in Gateshead, some early themes emerged about why the Conservatives won over Labour working-class heartlands in 2019. The first contingent factor is Brexit: much of northern England is inherently Eurosceptic and found itself falling out of step with the party during the 2016 referendum. Although Jeremy Corbyn proclaimed to be 'seven and a half' out of ten on his enthusiasm for the EU, the majority of the party and wider trade union movement were avowedly Remainers.[11] Despite some notable Leave voices in Labour, voting for Brexit was a break with orthodoxy. The second contingent factor was the leader himself: a combination of his personality and what he stood for. Jeremy Corbyn entered the 2019 campaign as the most unpopular opposition leader since polling began.[12] The hope and optimism he inspired during the 2017 snap election had disappeared by the start of the 2019 election, with just 16 per cent of voters voicing approval of his leadership. His economic pitch did not speak to the increasingly middle-class make up of Labour's traditional heartlands: the dichotomy that Britain was a country of billionaires and the homeless did not chime with most people's lived existence. His persona and ideas harked back to an era that many people concluded was long forgotten.

The road trip was about exploring the extent to which both of these contingent factors gave Boris Johnson his victory, alongside other, longer-term structural factors. As per Frank Tatoli's recollections, northern England is no longer the industrial workshop of the world, nor has it been for many decades. The communities have changed, their jobs and economies unrecognizable from old stereotypes. One of the achievements of Tony

Blair was to paint New Labour as the political force embracing and shaping that change, yet his successors have chosen to jettison. Part of the journey is to explore the legacy of the New Labour project, which had its roots in northern England but detractors claim did little of substance to improve the region. I confess to setting off with some scepticism: the cultural regeneration of Gateshead was clearly a boon, but the shaky jobs market and societal challenges for those who live there raise the question of whether those efforts were misguided.

Pinning the 2019 result on just Brexit and Corbyn is the easiest rational explanation. Before setting off, it was something I had been guilty of doing, convincing myself these two contingent factors were responsible for half of the outcome each. But the consequences of that election were so great that I felt this simple dichotomy needed probing. Labour's collapse was significant and the journey was about exploring that.

Based on James Kanagasooriam's modelling and the election results, I picked ten constituencies that fit the red wall criteria in different regions of England. The red wall extends into Wales, but I have decided to focus on England due to Wales's devolved Parliament and distinct cultural hinterland. The electoral upheaval in Scotland and Northern Ireland deserve their own books. On each stop, I sought out key members of the communities, residents, businesses owners, local politicians, and MPs past and present in an effort to answer a question: was 2019 a fluke, or a realignment? Along the way, I brought in national political figures who are relevant to the particular themes of each stop.

This is not a comprehensive examination of every inch of the red wall, but all regions of England where the Conservatives made gains are covered: from Blyth Valley in the north-east to Burnley in north-west; Don Valley and Wakefield in Yorkshire, to Coventry suburbs and Derbyshire countryside in the Midlands. At each stop, I dug into policy themes of the past and present: deindustrialization, ailing infrastructure, austerity, devolution and the rise of green manufacturing to name a few – all while keeping in mind the key question of whether the collapse of the red wall was a one-off event or a structural shift. The journey wraps up in Westminster, where I spoke to senior political figures about the trip and their views on whether Labour can win back the red wall, or if the Tories can make it theirs.

No road trip is complete without a suitable vehicle. In my first political journey across the UK during the 2015 election, I purchased an old-style red Mini, nicknamed Ruby by my flatmates for her bright paint job – which later turned out to be a respray, and not a very good one. 'One lady owner, it's had a new clutch and clean as anything,' went the patter. Never have I been so conned – as one mechanic told me, 'You've got yourself a lemon, son.' For this much longer trip, I was sensible, adopting a reliable and much more comfortable modern Mini Cooper – all bright red, deep exhaust and boy-racer stripes. The car was some loose metaphor for British industry: designed and built in Oxford, sold around the globe as a symbol of Britain, German owned. It's nippy and a joy to drive. The less you hear about the car in any road trip book, the better it is going.

My travels took place from autumn 2020 to spring 2021, when the Covid-19 pandemic had ended normal life. Politics was essentially frozen – much like me, as most encounters took place in inclement climes while observing social distancing. Despite my best efforts, I managed to catch the coronavirus during my travels, but thankfully recovered without long-term effects. This book is not about coronavirus, so I will only dwell on the pandemic when it affects the red wall story, even if it made the logistics rather tedious.

The first stop, Blyth Valley, is a mere thirty minutes from Gateshead on the Tyne and Wear Metro. I set off to meet someone who had kindly offered to take me around their home town as a starting point on my journey exploring the England that Labour has lost.

1. Blyth Valley

So join the union while you may.
Divvin't wait till your dying day,
For that may not be far away,
    you dirty blackleg miner!

'BLACKLEG MINER', A NINETEENTH-CENTURY
FOLK SONG HEARD IN THE MINERS' STRIKE

Dan Jackson waited patiently outside West Monkseaton Metro station, after my train decided to break down. The rolling stock on the north-east's light railway was forty years old and its replacement long overdue – a victim of successive cutbacks to local transport budgets. The sullen exodus of afternoon commuters, from Newcastle to their homes on the coast, confirmed they are well used to this hindrance. Ready in his sleek black BMW, Jackson ushered me into the passenger seat for a trip up the north-eastern coast to the border country of Northumberland (the Mini was parked for now). Forty-year-old Jackson is an NHS executive with a charming young family, but he is also one of England's finest local historians. Our acquaintance began through his worldly @northumbriana Twitter account, serving up north-east history with sharp dry English humour. His expertise spawned a bestselling book, *The Northumbrians*, the most beguiling guide to Geordie history, character and culture you can find.

Our first stop was Earsdon, a small village at the southern tip of Northumberland. Departing the leather comfort for the autumn drizzle, we trudged into St Alban's church – dark, weather-beaten stone surrounded by long tree branches sagging under the weight of the rain. Jackson took me to a commanding obelisk in the middle of the graveyard, commemorating one of England's most tragic mining disasters. On the morning of 16 January 1862, at the nearby Hartley Colliery, the beam propping up the pit's steam engine snapped, fell, and blocked the shaft down to the mine.[1] Five men in a lift to the surface died instantly. Without the steam engine, the pit was flooded, and by the time the shaft was reached six days later, 199 were dead. The names Jackson pointed to on the monument were chillingly young: J. Foster, aged fifteen; J. Ford, aged twelve; J. Armstrong, aged ten. 'It devastated a tight-knit community like this. Some families lost several generations of men,' he said. 'This' – he gestured across at the graves of all the men who had perished in successive industrial disasters or had seen their lives end early due to the uncompromising work – 'was the hard reality of mining life in Northumberland'. Beyond the graves lay rolling countryside: much of it slag heaps that have now been reclaimed by nature and grassed over. I squinted to see Blyth town itself in the distance, with not a single spot of heavy industry visible.

Back in the warmth of the car and motoring to Blyth, Jackson described the area as 'urban and rural at the same time'. Somewhere that has 'always been underestimated' in the shadow of the city of Newcastle as well as the larger towns and the surrounding countryside. Northumberland is one of England's best tourist spots, with stunning beaches, breathtaking countryside and only occasionally intolerable weather. Blyth, along with the town of Cramlington, sits awkwardly on the tip of urban Tyneside while overlooking beautiful vistas. Throughout the twentieth century, its economy was dominated by heavy industry: mining, but also manufacturing and shipping. As the mines entered rapid decline in the 1960s, so did the surrounding community. Blyth's railway station was closed in 1964 during the Beeching cuts, and since then the economic news has been almost relentlessly downbeat. The last pit closed in 1986, the vast coal power station in 2002.

Blyth town centre supported thousands of workers who lived in the terraced houses around the shopping streets and further afield in small dormitory villages. On my first visit, it was a rather sorry sight: the town square *had* received a £9 million redevelopment, which included a swish open-air market but with no protection from the northern elements.[2] Jackson said it was barely half full at the best of times. Another redevelopment effort, the Keel Row Shopping Centre, opened in 1991 during the peak of the town's struggles. It brought more new shops, but with the growth of private housing estates and car ownership, most residents I encountered said they preferred the larger out-of-town outlets where parking is easier and choice more plentiful.

Blyth's new marketplace had metal artwork and a lovely water feature, but on that gloomy day, it felt anything but fresh. The streets were deserted. Too many of the shops were closed, the shutters defaced with coarse graffiti. Those still trading were predominantly chains aimed at less well-off demographics found in many of England's small towns: Greggs the baker, retailers Poundland, frozen specialists Heron Foods. Blyth still had a complement of banks, but its biggest amenities were long gone. The only recent addition was a series of vape shops. The cinema is now a Wetherspoons pub, complete with the original projector. Impressively, the Art Deco interior is intact – the screen had become the bar, with the black and silver pillars framing bottles of Jägermeister. There was a hollowness to the town. 'I used to come here for shopping, or go to the cinema on a Saturday. Now the only reason I come is to get the dog's hair trimmed,' Jackson said.

On the waterfront, the impression is similar. The vast warehouses were dilapidated or soon to be cleared away. Some new housing has emerged, but the large green patches of wasteland added to the sense of desolation. Opposite the seafront car park were storage vessels from the Alcan aluminium smelter, which was opened in 1974 as part of a scheme to bring jobs to the area. But the dual pressures of environmental regulation and the end of coal mining led to its closure in 2012, with 515 jobs lost.[3] Jackson reeled off the major employers that had deserted Blyth in recent decades: the Officers' Club clothing company, 500 jobs lost in 2011; the Wilkinson Sword factory grinding out razor blades, 350 jobs gone.

The Port of Blyth has existed in one form or another since the twelfth century. But as mining and manufacturing declined, so did the cargo. One iteration of its management at least had the foresight to retool the port for roll on/roll off traffic, meaning millions of tons still flow through every year. It also diversified into packing. But the economic value of the goods is a fraction of what it was in the past, as is the employment base. The harbour is now more popular for pleasure pursuits: the Royal Northumberland Yacht Club has its base here.

As we drove out of Blyth town, past the vast General Electric cable reels waiting for shipment abroad, Jackson pointed out the names of the streets of tight terraced houses: Balfour Street, Salisbury Street, Disraeli Street, the grandest of Tory names. Blyth highlighted the two disparate nations Britain has become – precisely what Benjamin Disraeli warned of and fought to avoid during his time as prime minister. Towns such as this were emotionally and geographically far away from the prosperous cities that voted Remain in the 2016 referendum and continue to back the Labour Party. Blyth, and towns like it, voted for change: first through Brexit and then with the Conservative Party under Boris Johnson. Dan Jackson was a Labour man by heart and tradition – he once worked for Alan Campbell, the Labour MP for Tynemouth, also on the coast, yet he can't hide his thrill at the political prominence of his home turf. He read many of the infamously long blog posts by Dominic Cummings, Johnson's chief advisor and the architect of the Vote Leave campaign, and found much of interest and relevance. 'I have to say, I was quite excited by it,' he smiled, as we temporarily parted company. He still voted Labour, if only because his local MP is a long-standing friend.

On 2019 polling night, Huw Edwards could barely hold back his disbelief. An hour or so after the polls closed, the BBC election night anchor declared, 'It's neck and neck we are told between Labour and the Conservatives in Blyth Valley, which is a sentence I never thought I would utter on an election night programme.' Ten minutes later, this southern corner of Northumberland elected its first ever Conservative MP. The constituency is formed around Blyth but includes Cramlington: a village designated as one of England's 'new towns' after the Second World War as part of a national plan to grow the industrial base and encourage fresh investment into some of the struggling regions. Such towns were part of a vision for rebuilding the country and turning it into a paradise based on the National Health Service, private gardens, and solid sources of employment. Many of the red wall seats were home to new towns, although few fulfilled that halcyon vision.

Mining dominated Blyth Valley until the mid-twentieth century, when a consolidation programme saw the smallest pits close and jobs coalesce around the bigger collieries that could be modernized to improve productivity. Until that first wave of closures, there were at least six collieries in the area, all substantial sources of employment by modern standards. Cambois employed 1,261 at its peak, closing in 1968. Cowpen was smaller, but still had employment for 802 when its last coal was dug up in 1969. North Seaton had work for 927 in the early 1950s, which had fallen to 340 when it closed in 1961. New Delaval colliery only had a workforce of 225 when it shut down in 1955. During this era, Blyth was the busiest port in Europe, shipping six million tons of coal every year.[4]

The mine that held out the longest was Bates. As the smaller pits closed, employment at this colliery remained high. Almost 2,000 miners worked there during its 1964 peak. Bates was earmarked for closure and became a local fixture during the 1984–85 miners' strike. When it closed a year after the strike ended, 1,735 jobs were lost – including those of two future Labour MPs: Ian Lavery and Ronnie Campbell. There are no physical remains of the pit today, only a plaque at the Morpeth Road Primary School reminding pupils of where their forebears worked.

Another major employer that has been lost is shipbuilding. The Blyth Dock and Shipbuilding Company folded in 1966, when thirty other shipyards in the region had closed due to greater economic competition abroad. HMS *Ark Royal*, the UK's first aircraft carrier, was constructed here. Sixty-two ships came out of its shipyards during the First World War, twenty-four in the second. Most of the shares in the Blyth Company were owned by a Hong Kong based firm, which inflicted much pain on the town when the decision was made to shut it down. Eddie Milne, the town's idiosyncratic Labour MP from 1960 to 1974, said to the House of Commons that Blyth was 'stunned' when the yards were closed and the decision made on the other side of the world. Not least as most of the workforce was on annual leave. The first they heard of the news was in the local newspaper, *Blyth News*.

Milne told MPs:

Workers on holiday received the news from newspaper reports, and many returned from their holidays to receive the news in envelopes marked Hong Kong . . . As anybody in the House will appreciate, it is a matter of great sadness to watch a great industry die. The method of announcing the closure was criminal. No other word could fit the act. Men who had given a lifetime of service to the Blyth Company, in good times and bad, were entitled to treatment better than this.[5]

That same sense of mistreatment by far-away forces was felt as Blyth Valley gradually shed its traditional political affiliation. In the 1997 election, when New Labour won its first landslide victory, Ronnie Campbell was returned with an immense 17,736 majority – over three times the votes the Conservatives won in a distant third place. His majority dwindled over the subsequent two decades, yet never sunk into difficult territory. In the 2017 snap election, seventy-four-year-old Campbell was re-elected almost 8,000 votes clear of his rivals. While the Liberal Democrats and UKIP had been the runners-up, it was a local NHS mental health nurse called Ian Levy who added fifteen points to the Tory vote. Two years on, Levy squeaked in with a 712 majority – no doubt in part thanks to Campbell's retirement, as well as hoovering up the votes of the UK Independence Party, who came second in the 2015 election. The new electoral mood was set in the 2016 referendum, when 60 per cent of Blyth Valley voted to leave the EU. The memories of lost industries, a weakening jobs base and a struggling town convinced its people to vote for change. Jackson had dropped me off, so it was back to the port on foot to meet the man who benefited from that desire for change and created a defining moment in modern British political history.

New MPs' constituency offices share a soullessness: their incumbents are often shocked at finding their livelihoods upturned, uncertain of what facilities and staff they need to serve their new constituencies. The nakedly political ones paint their signs in party colours; the more restrained opt for neutral colours with the portcullis emblem that confers parliamentary authority. Ian Levy has neither: he picked the modern Blyth Workspace, on Commissioners Quay, for his local base. The fifty-five-year-old genially welcomed me into the clean, open-plan space for a strong cup of tea. Smartly dressed in suit, tie and hoodie – typically for Blyth, it is not a warm day – his closely cropped hair was typical for a man of his vintage. In demeanour, he is more Geordie than Conservative. Before we talk about 2019, he launched into his personal journey.

'I'm born and bred in Blyth, as is my wife,' he explained in eager tones. 'Our family has farmed the land in the realm of Blyth that can be traced back 500 years.' Levy did not farm though, working instead for the health service before politics entered his consciousness. With grown-up children at university, he could have retired and taken his pension. Instead, something snapped about five years before his election. 'We would often go out for a meal or a drink, me and my wife Maureen. On the wander back, when I'd had a few beers, I would start complaining about the state of the town centre: the state of the bus shelters, the feeling of despondency there was in the town where people feel really, really let down, and that their vote is taken for granted,' he said.

'I think she was happy to hear this, once, twice, maybe thirty times. But once it got to forty or fifty, she'd absolutely had enough. I remember this one night in particular she said, "Either do something about it or shut up." And I said, "Right, OK then."' The next day, Levy woke his wife with tea and toast and informed her he was going to run for Parliament. She suggested he should try to become a local councillor first, but Levy insisted that such a position would only bring change on a small scale. He told her, 'If I want to tidy up the high streets, if I want to try and eradicate crime, if I want to get poverty down, if I want to bring businesses into the area, and I want to bring wealth for people to the area, and training for kids, then I've got to be the MP.'

His 'gut feeling' took him towards the Tories. 'The Conservatives will give you the tools to live your life, they don't want you to live on benefits. Some people will always need to have support, and that is what we're there for. But having a good, strong economy helps look after the people that need it.' Levy discovered there was no party association in Blyth Valley and he was uncertain what to do. 'If I was looking to get a job as, say, a wagon driver and I didn't know who to contact, I'd write to the boss.' So, remarkably, he opened up a computer to write the first formal letter of his life (Levy is dyslexic). He addressed it to David Cameron, explaining his passion for Blyth, the problems he had identified and how he intended to fix them. Much to his, and Maureen's, surprise, he received a positive response. Levy was invited to Conservative Party HQ in 2016 for an interview to become a prospective parliamentary candidate.

'I was sat with people who had massive amounts of political experience, had all these high-paid jobs with lots of responsibility, and I was thinking, I've done a great job that I've enjoyed for many years working for the NHS and in mental health and it's been really fulfilling. But I haven't managed staff, I haven't done the things that a lot of these people have done.' He left feeling that he was on the back foot, but was ultimately accepted onto the candidate's list. And when the snap election was called in 2017 by Theresa May, he was duly installed as the party's pick in Blyth Valley.

His first political campaign was run on £500 donated by Matt Ridley, the aristocratic science writer and libertarian campaigner based in Northumberland, and supported by Levy's daughter and her friends. 'A lot of the kids turned up and I would bribe them with a pot of broth to put the leaflets out in the morning,' he said. 'People got really involved in it.' On that mere £500, with little assistance from Tory headquarters, he doubled the Conservative vote to 16,000 – a similar rise to the other red wall seats. Two years later, the next election arrived, and the party unsurprisingly chose him to stand for Blyth Valley again.

As soon as Levy started knocking on doors during the winter days of the 2019 campaign, he felt something had shifted, even among those who did not ultimately vote for him. 'Some of them were chasing us from the door', but others welcomed his efforts. He recalled one voter saying, 'Look, son, I'm sorry. I'm still going to vote Labour, my dad voted Labour, my granddad voted Labour, but you're doing a cracking job.' Labour was the incumbent party not just in the area's Westminster representation but across local government: town councillors, county councillors were almost universally of the left. But as the campaign continued, voters became more receptive. 'One elderly guy in Cowpen [village] said, "I hear you're standing as the Conservative." And then he asked "Have you got some more of these leaflets?" I gave him some and he said, "No I want a pile!" I thought he was going to burn them because he was telling us he'd been a pitman at Bates pit.' But the old fella wanted to take them down to his working men's club. 'I thought, whoa, this is massive. This is huge, absolutely huge.' Levy joked, 'I'd woken Blyth up, it was like the Sleeping Giant.'

After a 'horrible, wet and cold' campaign, Levy felt there was a perfect storm brewing in Blyth Valley, starting with Brexit. Although he backed Remain in the 2016 referendum – 'I was very concerned that Nissan would be offered a really good deal to move [the company's plant in Sunderland] to Europe' – his constituency was Leave and he felt a democratic impulse to support that result. He also knew that the opposition led by Jeremy Corbyn, a character who would not chime in Blyth Valley. 'They felt very disillusioned with Jeremy Corbyn, they didn't like what he stood for. They didn't personally like the guy.' The personal animus towards the Labour leader may have been born of character, but also his policies too, which I examined later in the trip. He described the typical Blyth Valley first-time Tory voter as a family person, who feels 'very let down, very despondent, and they're looking for more.' Although there was a strong loyalty to Ronnie Campbell, Levy sensed that voters felt the MP and his party had taken the area for granted.

With such a thin majority, Levy has had to provide real change. His focus was securing funding for the reopening of the Northumberland Line railway, which lost its passenger services in the Beeching cuts of 1964. Shovels hit the ground from 2022 and, handily, trains will run again from Ashington to Newcastle around the time of the next general election in 2024.[6] As with many of his colleagues, Levy has made a plethora of applications for money from the pots the Johnson government has set up to help the red wall – the towns fund, the levelling-up fund, the future high streets fund. For Blyth, he is hopeful of a new hotel, a three-screen cinema, a visitor centre and a branch of Primark. He acknowledged that the town is never going back to its industrial prime, but signs of investment will boost morale.

The most exciting project is another factory, but of a more modern kind. Britishvolt, a battery start-up, announced plans in 2020 for a £2.6 billion 'gigafactory' to produce batteries for electric cars.[7] If the plan is successful, it is projected to create 3,000 jobs and another 5,000 in the supply chain. Situated on the site of Blyth's old coal power station, it could transform the area – and Levy's electoral prospects. Improving the physical environment of Blyth Valley's towns is important to create that sense of change voters wanted, but Levy believes lasting change flows from job opportunities. 'People have given us an opportunity to prove what the Conservatives can do for the area, and we'll be judged on the merits,' he said.

His first 'bloody hard year' as an MP was dominated by the pandemic and Levy is acutely aware he had little time left to deliver tangible benefits to sustain the trust of his voters. But he noted one positive from the year of successive lockdowns and fears about health and livelihoods: 'Communities have come together. We started binding and rallying together. People have worked together. People are acknowledging their neighbours, they're acknowledging their friends and the good work that's been done in the community.' From a politician representing a party that has long put the emphasis on the individual, Levy is an embodiment of how red wall success is challenging recent notions of conservatism.

On a sun-kissed afternoon, Middleton Street on the other side of town felt the most contented part of Blyth. Plonked in the middle of this middle-class neighbourhood was a large detached house. Ten minutes' walk across town from Levy's office, Ronnie Campbell was waiting contentedly on the patio with a mug of tea. Now seventy-seven and retired after thirty-two years in the House of Commons, his welcome was as warm as the afternoon light. Campbell spoke with a hint of sadness that his exit from politics may have precipitated a first-time Tory victory in his home town. 'It got to me because I thought, I should have maybe stood. Maybe I could have won it on my reputation.'

He disparaged Tony Blair's years leading the party, arguing voters were not satisfied with his leadership and his landslide majority was 'wasted'. Jeremy Corbyn instead received his qualified praise. 'You have some good policies there that would have been great for working-class people.' Although his time on the doorstep in 2019 was limited due to a heart complaint, his wife Deirdre canvassed and the pair agreed there was a real issue among his traditional supporters. 'There were more Labour votes in the posh areas than there were in the council estates last election. The canvassing returns were horrible and yet on some of the private estates it was pretty good.' Conveniently, Deirdre returned from shopping in time to join us in the garden, after first scolding Ronnie for not offering me a drink. 'The first couple of nights I'd been out, when I came in I said to you, "We're not going to win this election." I knew. I've been canvassing over thirty years, and you can tell.' On the council estates, she was told to go away. Can she imagine the voters coming back? 'I don't know what it'll take,' she sighed.

Although Ronnie thought Boris Johnson is 'daft as a brush', he put the Conservatives' success down to 'the best candidate they could have got' in Ian Levy, who he described as a 'nice, quiet lad' although he curtly criticised Levy for taking credit for improvements begun under his watch. 'I never bragged about anything I did, I just did the bloody thing. This guy's in the newspapers, he's standing like this.' (Campbell gave an exaggerated thumbs up at this point.) Campbell cited the Port of Blyth, which he helped designate as an enterprise zone to encourage inward investment. After Bates pit closed, the land, along with the power station, harbour and shipyard, was repurposed. Now it employs over a thousand people. 'He can't take credit for that, that goes to me.'

Our conversation turned to Keir Starmer, who created a dividing line in the Campbells' marriage. Ronnie does not think much of his leadership so far. 'He's trying to go up the middle of the road.' But his wife liked and voted for him, telling her husband he was critical for Labour getting its act together and becoming credible again. Then a rather different Labour character entered the conversation: the mayor of Greater Manchester. 'I always say Andy Burnham is the best prime minister we never had.' Ronnie voted for him in the 2010 leadership contest but changed his allegiance when his old comrade Jeremy Corbyn ran five years later. Deirdre sighed. 'Oh, Andy. I wish we could bring him up here and let him loose.' Ronnie's face suggested he was a little unconvinced.

Ronnie was a true socialist Brexiter, campaigning against every EU treaty from Maastricht to Lisbon, and blamed the rise in the Tory vote on Labour's equivocal stance. 'I've been voting against it because it's undemocratic, I don't like the organization, look what they're trying to do. Heavens!' At his local working men's club, he grasped a feeling that 'people weren't happy' because they had voted Leave and 'the Labour Party wasn't taking any notice of it'. Oddly, Blyth Valley ejected its pro-Brexit MP for one that voted Remain simply based on the strength of party perceptions. Campbell made a point to his mates of his Brexit support, but he was no longer on the ballot paper. 'I was quite proud of the statement from a lot of people, saying they would have voted for me but I'm not standing so they're voting Tory.' Before returning inside, Deirdre agreed with Ronnie that 'Labour's whole picture on Europe really annoyed people', as did chucking too many spending commitments into its manifesto.

Before his time in Parliament, Ronnie Campbell spent three decades as a miner and trade union activist. He was born just down the coast in Tynemouth, where his mother 'jumped on the bus' to give birth, but has lived in Blyth all his life. He was first elected to the district council in 1969 and became the local mining union chairman in 1982 – putting him at the heart of the 1984–85 miners' strike. After his pit closed, he worked his connection with Arthur Scargill, then head of the National Union of Mineworkers, to be selected as the candidate for the Blyth Valley Labour Party.

During his life, Campbell noted two major changes to the area. First is more prosperity, seen in the growth of private houses, but also a decline in the town's facilities. 'What are you going to come into Blyth for?' he asked me (having visited, nothing came to mind). He agreed that the town centre is struggling: 'I knew people came into Blyth for the market when it was flourishing. Now the market is just dead. Once the pit went, Blyth subsided and never came back again.' He joked that his main occupation has turned into waiting at home to collect Amazon deliveries for his grandchildren.

The second is the end of mining, which 'smashed' the area. When he worked at the Bates colliery, 2,000 were employed there. He bemoaned not that the Northumberland coalfield was brought to an end but that the Thatcher governments did not offer replacement jobs. 'They said, "Well, the pits were wrong and the green people didn't like the dirty fuels." That's fair enough. But if you're going to close a pit then think of what you're going to put in its place.' The opening of the Nissan car plant further south in Sunderland in 1986 may have created 6,000 jobs in the region, but it didn't come close to replacing the 160,000 lost with mining. 'Blyth didn't recover from the closure of the pit. Never did.'

Campbell has devoted his life to the labour movement, but he laughed off the notion that mining was part of a national endeavour, deeming that a romantic view of a society that has gone. 'It was hard slog. The conditions could be brilliant if you knew the pit. But sometimes, when the water used to come in, oh my god! And the roof started to crack open, stone starting to fall, oh my god! You're in big trouble.'

Deirdre returned, and chipped in that she was also unconvinced by the Tories' arguments for major infrastructure projects. What Blyth needs is jobs and a better physical environment – clean streets, not piles of rubbish. 'You don't need to give them great big projects to say, vote for me, they're not interested in that. It's just a lot of people want decent schools, decent homes to live in, and have a job, and it doesn't have to be a great big job so long as they've got a job, and the environment's clean and tidy.'

There was a striking similarity in what the Campbells and Levy said about the collapse of traditional community life. The world Ronnie inhabited before politics was highly collectivized: work, life, community were all based around the pit. After the miners' strike was beaten by the Thatcher government and its successive electoral mandates for economic reform, that disappeared. Out of Blyth centre and into the suburbs and countryside, the recent prosperity is apparent. Few of the cars in the streets around the Campbell residence hold registration plates older than five years. New detached homes dwarf the terraced miners' cottages that Ronnie lived in as a pitman. This new side of the Labour heartlands has created a more individualistic culture, which in turn played into the increase in support for the Conservatives.

Who better to run this theory by than a man who devoted much of his working life to explaining the changing moral and philosophical shape of England. John Gray is a Tyneside lad, he grew up in South Shields and attended grammar school before growing into one of Britain's pre-eminent political philosophers. Despite his decades lecturing at Oxford and the London School of Economics, he has maintained a delightfully soft Geordie lilt; I could listen to him say 'bourgeoisification' all day. Typically for someone brought up in the industrial north-east in the 1950s and 1960s, his politics were Labour left. Along with many contemporaries, he made the journey to the new right in the 1970s after the industrial strife and Labour's failure in governing. He was closely associated with Thatcherism, yet today, his political views are fluid. He does not assign himself to the left or the right, Labour or Conservative, but he is fascinated by what may be emerging as Johnsonism.

Speaking from his home, the seventy-two-year-old eagerly agreed that what happened in the Labour heartlands in the early years of the twenty-first century was based on a deepening individualism and the dissolution of a traditional way of life. 'They were working communities, embedded in street life and human settlements in towns and terraces,' he said, recalling the homogeneity of his childhood. 'They were organized around work, most people walked to work. Crime of the kind you see these days was low. They were safe communities. But they could be repressive; the position of women was subordinated. There was a mixed attitude to people who were socially deviant or people who were known to be gay. To my knowledge they weren't harassed, I never saw anyone being beaten up or anything like that. On the other hand, they were not positively embraced.'

Gray described Tyneside society of the mid-twentieth century as cohesive but inhibited. 'I didn't see them as being notably racist. When I grew up there was very little, if any, anti-Semitism. But it could be repressive on individual aspiration both in men and women. And if you really felt that, you just left. The common way of leaving was to join the merchant or Royal Navy. Or move down south.' The ending of the patriarchal family structure prompted a 'colossal change' in how these societies were structured, as did the changing nature of work. 'It had partly gone because the wage structures had gone. The forms of steady industrial life too – not commuting for work, or not having to go long distances to find work. If you were a miner, you just had to walk down the bottom of the street and it would be there. If that's what you wanted to do, and most people did up to the sixties, they just accepted they went to the mines.'

Although the industrial decay can be traced back to the end of the war, Gray marked the liberalization of society in the 1960s as the turning point, which accelerated in the 1980s with deindustrialization. Gray was personally close to Margaret Thatcher, but reflected she made some major misjudgements. He said of that period, 'up in the north there was a profound sense of grievance, which has lasted to this day. There's also the issue of security for working people: they were kind of tossed on the scrapheap in the steel towns because of economic change. Telling them to "get on their bike" was just a further insult [a reference to Norman Tebbit's infamous remark that the unemployed should get moving to find work].'

But what defines the new culture of the English heartlands is not a sudden love for Thatcherite individualism – Gray wryly stated 'There's not much call in Blyth Valley for Friedrich Hayek or Ayn Rand'. The new spirit is not economically right-wing now, nor is it countercultural in the way Jeremy Corbyn attempted to pitch himself. 'Along with Corbynite collectivist economics, there was a kind of postmodernist individualism that you can be whoever you want to be, you can just create yourself, you can choose your identity. None of that meant anything to the people that I knew.'

Gray and I attempted for an over an hour to define exactly what this new societal view is. The nearest we came is describing an attitude that is flexible, commonsensical and tolerant of gradual change. 'To make your life as you go along,' as Gray summed up. This new outlook is not about moralizing, but it does treasure family structures. It is not about pursuing an ever smaller state, but nor is it welcoming of collectivist economics. It depends on a welcome physical environment and strong local services – many of which were wrecked during the Tory-led austerity years. Gray agreed municipal, local and health services are key but added there is also a coarse edge. 'It can be hard, mind you, hard on welfare cheats and stuff like that.'

First-time Tory voters, Gray felt, 'would be turned off by Thatcherism, naturally because of historical memories, but also because of its indifference to fairness. The suffering that was involved was forgotten by many of the Thatcherites. It's often terminal if you're cast out of work in your late forties, whether you're a man or a woman, in a town that was heavily dependent on a certain kind of industry. It's very difficult to get back into work at all.' Such a hard-nosed approach to employment created 'a lifetime of unhappiness and frustration and defeat' for these communities.

How does Boris Johnson fit into this? The prime minister wears his politics and ideology lightly, shifting from right-wing magazine editor, to metropolitan liberal mayor of London, to the voice of England's forgotten regions. On economics, Johnson is no neoliberal. He may have an instinct for lower taxes and thriving business but his love of *grand projets* and a desire to be liked by the electorate nudges him towards more spending. Gray reckoned all of Johnson's policies are based on intuition. 'I don't think he sits back and theorizes about anything.' During his first year in Downing Street, the prime minister drifted towards expansionist economics, as shown by the £300 billion pumped into the economy during the coronavirus lockdowns, despite ministers in his Cabinet holding opposing views. On the surface, Johnson was reverting to a pre-Thatcherite form of conservatism, more akin to Harold Macmillan's approach of the 1950s and 1960s (Gray pointed out that Macmillan was an early disciple of John Maynard Keynes). But that era was dominated by class politics – most of the Conservative cabinet was aristocratic – which has mostly disappeared from society: 'I remember there was something impossibly snooty about it,' Gray said simply.

Johnson, in his view, was combining the caring parts of middle-ground conservatism with aspects of 'Old Labour' that were eroded by Tony Blair's modernization project. 'It is the combination of a certain kind of instinctive patriotism with a big protective state. High spending and aiming for full employment, not letting the market do anything really important, and a non-dogmatic approach to personal freedom. And patriotism. That's actually what the centre ground is now. The closest you can get to it in English politics is Johnsonian Conservatism.'

If Johnson is as in tune with the new communities of the heartlands as Gray, it would suggest there is scant hope of Labour rebuilding itself. The charge Gray has laid in successive essays is that the party has gone in the opposite direction of the communities it was founded to support and has become middle class. It was therefore only a matter of time before a voting fissure emerged at the ballot box. He thinks Blair's efforts were necessary for the party to win the more prosperous south of England, but set the course for long-term decline in the heartlands.

'The Labour response under Blair was to bourgeoisify, which worked for a long time. He did do pretty much what he said he would do. So the question is, who now has the sense of this fluid, non-dogmatic, flexible, working class, individualism and is non-Thatcherite? Who has it? The only person that has any kind of instinctive grip on it is Johnson at the moment.'

Before returning to the streets of Blyth Valley, I wanted to delve a little more into Thatcher's legacy in the red wall. Even those on the left who are harshly critical of her efforts to modernize Britain's economy do not deny it was necessary, but I wanted to know whether this more individualistic society was a determined part of the project to reshape England – or a side effect of economic renewal. Few ministers of that era are still alive or active in politics, but I tracked down two. Norman Tebbit, who was in charge of industry and trade during the miners' strike, made a startling but little-noticed admission of failure about deindustrialization. Speaking to Francis Beckett and David Hencke in 2009 for their book on the strike, *Marching to the Fault Line*, he admitted that the destruction of the collectivized communities had a negative effect on British society:

> *Those mining communities had good working-class values and a sense of family values . . . [and they] were able to deal with the few troublesome kids. Many of these communities were completely devastated, with people out of work turning to drugs and no real work because all the jobs had gone . . . The scale of the closures went too far. The damage done to those communities was enormous as a result of the strike.*

Now eighty-nine, Lord Tebbit, speaking from his House of Lords office, admitted that his policies were driven by the hard economics of the UK's situation but also mentioned the Tories were eager to foster the spirit of small business that would not be dominated by troublesome trade unions. But Thatcher under-estimated the lack of alternative employment options. 'There were mining communities in rural areas where there was very little other work. Unfortunately we could have run those mines down much more slowly. We could have done more to help to bring jobs to those areas. There was a deep and profound economic and social change that went on, which was adverse to those local people.'

Tebbit cited again the success of Nissan as one example of bringing new employers to the north-east. He recalled a scheme where unemployment benefit could be drawn for twelve months while individuals tried to set themselves up in business. 'So for twelve months you've got the security of that income while you're setting up. A lot of people set up businesses, some of which have become reasonably large employers now. That type of scheme was successful, but it was limited.' But he admitted the miscalculation was the singular employment base. 'There's a much greater variety of employment available if you live in Essex as opposed to living in Durham for example, and so when people are given more choice they are more likely to find what suits them and what suits their kids.'

The other dominant figure in the 1980s debate about regeneration was Michael Heseltine, who served as environment and defence secretary. The eighty-seven-year-old, who was and is the political nemesis of Tebbit, was at the forefront of the Thatcher government's efforts to counter deindustrialization. From the grand study of his countryside residence in Oxfordshire, Lord Heseltine argued that the caricature of an uncaring government driven purely by economic force is false. Starting in 1979, the Conservatives pursued 'a very interventionist policy of restoring hope and opportunity to some of the most deprived parts of our economy'. Heseltine founded so-called development corporations to stimulate the struggling docks of Liverpool and London; he ordered grants to clear up toxic waste from coal mines – but only if public and private partnerships could be agreed.

Taken inspiration from the post-war *Bundesgartenschau* in Germany, Heseltine held five major garden festivals across the UK on derelict land to encourage tourism, generate employment and reclaim the toxic land. I have personal experience of Gateshead's 1990 festival: my family moved to a newly built home on Festival Park during my childhood. The 200-acre site near the River Tyne once housed a gasworks and coking plant.[8] Around 50,000 tons of discarded coal was heaved out and 5,000 workers created the festival. After the festival was over, new housing was built. According to the *Evening Chronicle* newspaper, Gateshead's festival marked the start of a cultural renewal in the urban Tyneside region that eventually led to the much-lauded Sage concert venue and Baltic contemporary art gallery. Heseltine believed this combination of public-private partnerships and strong local leadership was a formula for success: 'By the end of the decade, in the eighties and early nineties, we knew how to regenerate urban areas.' But he lamented the stalled progress on devolution, which he thought had 'died on the vine', leaving Whitehall fully in charge of policy-making. 'What they never do is go to local people and say, "What do you think is the best way to do it for you?"'

Where Tebbit said the Thatcher project was mostly economically driven, Heseltine disagreed and said there was a driving belief that 'you want to enthuse and encourage people to own a stake in their society'. The most striking example was his Right to Buy policy for council homes, which my paternal grandparents eagerly took up. 'That had a transformational effect on a generation of people who had missed out on the benefits of property ownership.' The much-made criticism of the scheme is that too many of the funds that flowed into the Treasury were not ploughed into new housing stock. Before Heseltine moved to the Ministry of Defence in 1983, he said 75 per cent went into new social housing. 'Look at the problem with social housing as a consequence! The criticism I have of the Thatcher government – and one I stressed constantly at the time in the Cabinet – is that we stimulated consumption at the expense of capital investment.' In other words, the Thatcher government was focused on getting people to spend instead of investing in infrastructure. Reflecting on the miners' strike, Heseltine acknowledged that more could have been done to carefully phase out the mining 'but it wouldn't have changed the outcome'.

Although he was booted out of the Conservative Party for advocating backing the pro-Remain Liberal Democrats in the 2019 European elections, he was intrigued by the collapse of the red wall and thinks the economic and social changes that started forty years ago have come to fruition. 'They're not the same communities, a lot of people have joined the electorate and a lot have gone, but that is a consequence, and I suspect one of the reasons is that the over-dependency on one union, one industry, has been broken up in those areas. People may be travelling further to work, but they've now retrained, regrouped, reskilled, and they've got different jobs in different industries.'

While the post-Thatcher economy is often criticized by the Tory left and Labour for its careless attitude towards strategic industries, Heseltine offered a recent counter example. When the Redcar steelworks in North Yorkshire closed in 2015, he was sent by David Cameron to investigate its impact on the local economy. What he found was not mass unemployment but resilience. 'It was extraordinary that despite the closure of this major employer, the unemployment figures hardly changed because the local people were absorbed into a very diverse economy. And I'm proud that I was part of a Conservative government that brought about those shifts, because they are shifts to higher standards of living.' The Redcar constituency went Conservative for the first time in 2019.

His advice to Boris Johnson was to focus on skills and education, combined with a major push on devolution. 'The Tories have it within their gift to transform these places . . . but to do that they have got to have ministers who are there, who sound like they know what the situation is, who sound like they have the experience to understand the problems and the concerns as well. The voice and tone is a very important part of the policy initiatives of devolution that are required.' But without Jeremy Corbyn and with the 'good sense' of the Labour Party to realign around Keir Starmer, he admits the next election will be 'much different' to the one just passed.

Finally, it was time to find Dan Jackson again for a pint in a unique pub. On the platform of Monkseaton Metro station, the Left Luggage Room offered six locally brewed beers. The pub was housed in the old parcel office and cheerily busy on a Friday afternoon. It was perfectly set up for the pandemic, with antiseptic and tables spaced out across the platform for watching the trains flow by. The atmosphere was markedly different from the declining, musty working men's pubs and clubs still in the area. As well as the pints, tables of women were enjoying large glasses of wine after work. The new culture, if you like, versus the old.

Over a couple of pints of Two by Two IPA, brewed in Wallsend, where my grandmother was born among the thriving shipyards and terraced houses around the turn of the twentieth century, we chatted more about Jackson's upbringing: he was born in the tiny village of New Hartley, one of the 'work camps' supporting the coal mines. His childhood was in step with the gradual decline of heavy manufacturing. I had passed through the village and seen the old terraced miners' cottages facing off with the more spacious 1970s housing estates (he grew up in the latter). Jackson's father still lived in the village and is a regular patron at the

Victory working men's club, built after the First World War. All of Jackson's forebears worked in heavy industry – he was the first in his family to go to university and the first to do white-collar work.

For his peers, most of the job options after school were in mining, oil rigs or the public sector. Further and higher education were not widespread. He agreed with my conclusion that the overall economy of Blyth Valley today was more diverse and had greater pockets of prosperity, even if much of it is still struggling. The upheaval is 'something we have been coming to terms with for fifty years,' he said. Although Ronnie Campbell did not recall his days in heavy industry with pure fondness, Jackson argued that something is missing from the area's new economic base in the small industrial parks. 'People had a sense of pride, of national purpose, working in the big industries. They were fundamental to Britain's role in the world. You don't get that from a production line.'

As Deirdre Campbell put it, what people care about is jobs, jobs, jobs, which Blyth Valley is still struggling with. Prior to the pandemic, the unemployment rate here was 7.8 per cent, above the national average. The median age is forty-four, again above the national average, and the median salary is below the average. For Ian Levy's hopes of re-election, better employment opportunities are as vital as a new railway line and new businesses in the town centre. Some of the folks I spoke to in the market-place insisted that a better physical environment would brighten their outlook. But much of that rests on improving personal prosperity.

If Britishvolt is successful with its battery plant project in Blyth Valley, it would revolutionize the local economy. At time of writing, construction was set to begin in the summer of 2021.[9] It feels almost too good to be true, but if it comes off there will be one marked difference from the days of heavy industry. The workforce will not have the same collectivism and community spirit of old. Society has moved on, families have two working parents and battery factories are not heavy mining. Those that look back on the salad days of manufacturing overlook women, who were stuck at home while their husbands were at work all day and down the pub at night. In his childhood home, Jackson said that his grandfather was insistent 'no wife of mine' would work. 'It was unsustainable, it was a way of life that was in decline since the 1950s. A very patriarchal society that was on its way out.'

After a second round of pints, Jackson returned to sort his family's dinner. I made my way to the Metro to head back to Gateshead. As the train rolled through Newcastle and across the River Tyne – not breaking down this time, thankfully – a wave of sadness flowed over me, only slightly related to the hops and days of travelling in the cold. I was thinking of Blyth's dilapidated town centre, the empty shipyards at Wallsend, and the long stretches of grass once dominated by industry. The work founded on the area's natural resources was tough, unforgiving and ultimately economically unsustainable. But it gave the region its pride. The communities were small, interwoven, but as John Gray set out, that era is gone. The pull of nostalgia is powerful, and I was struck at how Conservatives and socialists have both spoken of the desire to return to some of that togetherness. There was some panic buying, particularly of toilet paper, and ministers encouraged neighbours to report those who broke the lockdown rules. But the way communities supported each other during the lockdowns of 2020 and 2021 suggested individualism has its limits. Little I had seen on the first stop challenged my scepticism about just how much New Labour had actually done for its northern heartlands, although the successful remodelling of the Port of Blyth is a clear boon. The schools may have been improved and the housing stock better, but it did little to revive a town that gradually lost its purpose.

Maintaining some sense of community spirit is a crucial part of where English politics heads next. Jackson's departing remark circled in my mind. 'The north-east was about *big* industry, we never did small boutique firms. That's why the region was hit so hard when the heavy industry began to close.' Whatever comes in the years ahead, the future is unlikely to be *big*. Coming to terms with that is important for understanding both what has been lost and what can adequately replace it. In 2017 and 2019, Jeremy Corbyn offered a striking new vision for these communities. On my next stop, thirty miles south to County Durham, I wanted to find out why it was so heartily rejected.

2. North West Durham

'Here lies Consett Steelworks, born 1840, died 1980, not peacefully, but after a brave fight for life. Those who seek a true memorial should look about them at those who lost 3,700 jobs and at the community whose health and prosperity it sustained.'

NEWCASTLE EVENING CHRONICLE,
SEPTEMBER 1980

The bone-chilling wind from the Pennines smacked into every crevice of West Wylam: a former colliery village with commanding views of the Tyne Valley, on the edge of the North West Durham seat. Having picked up the car in Gateshead, I drove the ten miles west to meet Barry and Irene McElearney, recommended to me by a mutual friend as typical of the voters Labour has lost. Working-class retirees, they are deeply proud of the vibrant patch in front of their bungalow: full of ornaments, colourful bushes and knick-knacks. Over their fence – with a dog frequently interjecting, awaiting his lunch – Irene enthusiastically dived into politics. She was a lifelong Labour supporter. 'I came from a colliery village . . . no matter who stood as a Labour candidate, they got in.' Irene voted Conservative for the first time in 2019, driven by Boris Johnson, who she 'absolutely loves'. 'I love him because he seems straightforward, he's positive in his thinking, he doesn't give any negative waves off. There's no such thing as "no" in his vocabulary. It's "yes, we'll do it." Sometimes you think, *Well, will you?* But it's nice to know he's a trier.' His pro-Brexit stance also chimed with hers.

Barry's electoral history is more mixed: he was also originally tribally Labour but has flirted with the Tories. 'I voted for Margaret Thatcher, basically because she was a woman. Women generally do things quite well. Just watch *Last of the Summer Wine* [the BBC sitcom set in Yorkshire] . . . I voted for her because I thought she would do well. A woman's way of thinking, you know. But she made too many mistakes.' After flitting between the parties, he also voted for Johnson in 2019 and now sees himself as a Tory, despite feeling uncomfortable at the thought of telling his family and old friends. 'Oh, you'd be lynched,' he said. 'My Mam and Dad would be doing somersaults in their graves if they knew,' Irene adds.

The pair were both Labour Party members and fervent supporters of Tony Blair. Their membership cards were shredded when David Miliband failed to be elected leader in 2010 and his left-leaning brother Ed won instead. The final break came five years later. 'When Jeremy Corbyn took over the Labour Party, that was it . . . I didn't trust him with anything,' she said. Both were particularly put off by his attitude towards national security. 'I'm a big believer in defence, particularly Trident, which can launch a nuclear missile anywhere. He wanted to scrap all that and he wouldn't press the button. If somebody chucks a stone at me, I want to chuck it back,' Barry said. 'The thought of him actually leading the country. His principles were "Well, we're CND, ban the bomb", but leading the country you've got to look to the future, not what you think.'

Ahead of the last election, the Conservatives were twenty-five points ahead on the polling question of which party is best at handling defence and security.[1] Polling was similar on the economy and the health service, and Corbyn's perceived lack of trustworthiness on these three policy areas proved disastrous in Labour's traditional heartlands. During the 2017 election, his argument that 'you can't protect the public on the cheap' connected with voters.[2] But by 2019, he had almost nothing to say on security beyond staid arguments about reshaping foreign policy into what his fans call 'anti-imperialism' (in other words, anti-American).

I met Barry and Irene a year on from the election, just before the second nationwide lockdown hit England, and they both were full of sympathy for Johnson and his pandemic efforts. 'I feel so sorry for the prime minister and the government. They had all these aspirations when they got in and this has happened, which nobody anticipated. I think he must be so frustrated, because I would be,' she said. 'There were a lot of people, Labour people, who voted for him in the north of the country that had never had a Tory MP before and he said, "We're going to thank those people by delivering." But he can't because he's stuck with this virus.'

Given Corbyn's departure from frontline politics after his election failure and Johnson's travails in dealing with Covid-19, could the pair imagine voting for Keir Starmer? (Neither could actually name the opposition leader.) Barry was 'very, very doubtful'. Irene acknowledged that 'the leader is better than the one they had certainly, but he doesn't inspire any confidence'. With that, the McElearneys went inside for their lunch, and I hopped back in the Mini to drive through the lovely winding lanes to Consett, the heart of one of the most surprising seats to flip Conservative for the first time.

North West Durham, a large, mostly rural seat is a Petri dish of Jeremy Corbyn's political project and how it lost Labour one of its historically safest seats. The area is dotted with small villages like West Wylam, which once supported heavy industry. Its most notable attribute is the chill, blowing in from the North Pennine hills. The temperature adds to the area's sense of isolation: a local joke in Newcastle goes that you can tell someone travels in from County Durham if there's snow and skis on the back of their car.

This corner of North West Durham was once renowned for its mines and manufacturing. During its 1950s peak, the constituency had seventy-two mines, employing thousands of men who lived in the bracing colliery villages across the countryside. One of the lost pits, Eden in Leadgate, lasted until 1980. Even though its workforce had shrunk to just 194 by its closure, the loss was acutely felt. As a community historian reported, 'The last shift was on 18 July 1980, a sad day for many in Leadgate, not just for the mine workers but for the local economy which was greatly affected by the loss of traditional working in the area.'[3]

The major wave of closures in County Durham began in the 1960s, when the burden of the smaller uneconomical collieries became too much for the state to cope with. The decline in their employment was long and gradual. In the village of Chopwell, the pit employed 2,185 at its peak in 1921, which had fallen to 210 when it closed in 1966. When the colliery was shut down, the surrounding village was categorized as a place to be put into managed decline. Annfield Plain village is now most notable for the Tesco superstore and the Krazy Kingdom children's leisure centre, but was once dominated by the Morrison Busty Colliery. In the middle of the twentieth century, it employed almost 2,000 people, dwindling to 548 before it closed in 1973.

North West Durham's major town is Consett, the heart of the north-east's iron industry for 140 years. During its peak in the 1960s, 6,000 workers were employed at the steelworks. When the works closed in 1980, it still employed 3,700 people, and the ensuing poverty was called 'the murder of a town'.[4] Well over a century of steel-making along the River Derwent Valley had come to an end, and 20,000 people moved out of the area.[5] The plant was still profitable, but the decision was made by British Steel headquarters not to modernize and restructure its operations. Unemployment – which hit 36 per cent in 1981, quadruple the national average – did not return to normal levels until Tony Blair came to power.

Consett has undergone a major regeneration since the closure of the steelworks, impressively titled Project Genesis.[6] Launched in 1993, it had a brief across 700 acres of former industrial land. After £10 million was spent to decontaminate the steelworks site, hundreds of new homes were built, along with Derwentside College for further education, a McDonald's and scores of businesses and small manufacturing outfits. The sums invested in Consett have been significant: £45 million in total by 2006.[7] The new housing developments have made the area a popular commuter belt for the cities of Durham and Newcastle upon Tyne. These estates are palpably middle class. As Irene McElearney put it, 'You've got a lot more commuters going to Newcastle. The demographic is different now. All these new houses, all these new builds. People are living here and commuting to work. You're getting a different type of person coming in.' Consett has become such a draw that its population is now larger than in its manufacturing prime. Despite Project Genesis being part-funded by a grant from the European Union, 55 per cent of North West Durham voted for Brexit in the 2016 referendum.[8]

The area's jobs base is more diverse than when the steelworks were the main employer. International Cuisine, opened in 1988, prepares ready meals and employs 500 people. Erwin Hymer, the caravan and mobile-home manufacturer, employs a similar number. Lanchester Wines, one of the UK's largest wine importers, hit record turnover in 2019 and is another significant employer.[9] Elddis Transport, a family run firm, was started to shift steel around on flat trailers. The company reimagined itself when the works closed to focus on consumer goods and continues today, employing 330 people.

Consett's latter-day jobs story, however, is not entirely one of success. Phileas Fogg crisps was founded in the town in 1982, and gained international popularity due to its quirky marketing campaigns. But the company was sold to KP Snacks, who shut the factory in 2015. Some jobs were transferred, some were lost, but one of Consett's success stories came to an abrupt end. At the time, Suzanne Reid, a union organizer, said the closure of the factory was 'devastating', adding 'people have worked there for twenty, twenty-four, even twenty-six years – it's like family. They have been through so much together; marriage, children, even divorce. People are really lost.'[10] Much like the steelworks, it was a decision made by managers far away that deprived North West Durham of both an employer and a source of local pride.

Similarly to Blyth Valley, the train line into North West Durham closed during the Beeching cuts of the 1960s. Both the Lanchester Valley and Derwent Valley railways closed first to passengers and then to goods, in a pattern familiar to England's smallest branch railways. The natural beauty of the area was put to good use when the former tracks were turned into the Derwent Walk, an extremely popular country park and cycle way. Walking through the woods, along the river, underneath the old pedestrian bridges, showed me the 175 hectares reclaimed by the country-side have given County Durham an outstanding attraction.

While the area's dominant economic narrative is one of decline and depression, the overall picture of North West Durham is more nuanced – particularly among the new businesses that emerged in the post-industrial era. Before exploring Consett town centre, I drove ten minutes east to the sprawling factory of the Lanchester Group in the village of Anfield Plain, once home to several collieries. One of the UK's biggest wine importers is also one of the biggest employers here. Tony Cleary started the firm in his lounge in 1980, the year the steelworks closed. By 2020, Lanchester reached a turnover of £94 million. Cleary told me, as we wandered through the firm's sweet-smelling warehouse, he was hopeful of breaking £110 million in 2021. He was born and bred in the area, growing up just south of Durham city, and went to school in the village his company is named after. From an early age, he had no interest in working for a big organization and was happy to take risks. 'I've always wanted to work for myself. I'm in charge of my own destiny rather than other people, which was hugely important to me.' That motivation is behind many of the small businesses that have started in the wake of deindustrialization.

Lanchester Wines began with three vans. Wine was imported by Cleary and stored in a bonded warehouse. He would go around local off licences and pubs and do business cash in hand. From his house, the business soon moved to an office in Lanchester village. Then he leased his own bonded warehouse. The group expanded beyond wine to all sorts of produce – ciders, perries, spices, hampers and confectionary – and employs 550 people today.

Cleary's father worked for the National Coal Board, and he recalled Consett was 'a bit of hellhole' in its steel days. 'Red dust everywhere. I mean, god almighty it was filthy.' He also had no time for the unionized workforce. 'We used to have contractors who were really really good, but they were all unionized. At 12 o'clock they would head out and you would say, "Look, if you have two minutes we can finish that order and get it out today." They would respond, "Oh no, it's lunchtime, we've got to go." That used to really drain me, that attitude was not where I wanted to be.' Unsurprisingly, he has little time for the political party that once dominated the Consett area. 'Labour is yesterday's operation – all about unions, all about strikes. Lanchester is not about that, it's about people who look after people. We don't need any union on our side.'

Cleary has built a successful company and claimed to look after his workforce well, but many of the new industries that have emerged do not. How does he feel about the people of Consett who work in other warehouses on zero-hours contracts with no rights? He answered with Covid in mind. 'There's some good companies going to come out of this, I think we'll do well in the next two or three years. We'll lose a lot of zombie companies but we should have lost them anyway. Some of them should have gone ages ago, because they weren't making money and they just plod along.' He returned again to his management ethos. 'Employ good people and pay them well and give them interesting jobs. That is where people want to be.'

He recalled how Consett has changed during his lifetime: 'It's gone from an industrial area of miners and people working with their hands, going to workmen's clubs at lunchtime and drinking three and four pints then going back into steel furnaces, into different industries.' The transformation to these new industries is one Cleary welcomed but he argued the shift should have been 'quicker and better'. He is positive about the opportunities ahead: 'You've got all sorts of new industries coming into the north-east, but I think we've got a little bit of a chip on our shoulder, I think we could do with a bit more gumption. We've got some good people in the area who represent the area quite well.'

The most exciting development for Cleary is green energy,

where he thinks the government should be investing more in their efforts to rebalance the economy between the north and south. 'We've got some good industries and I think we're way ahead on sustainability in the north-east.' He is in the midst of building a larger 22,000-square-foot bottling plant which will be almost entirely powered by renewables. Outside Cleary's window, there is a tall white turbine spinning around that helps power the current plant. Boldly, he claimed, 'When we get this bottling building up, it'll be the most modern, sustainable building of its size worldwide. It's a big investment, we'll have a million watts of solar on the roof, we'll have the heat pumps and massive batteries.' He predicts that just 2 per cent of Lanchester's power will come from the electricity grid. Cleary thinks that the green message is important for giving the area a sense of optimism about the future. 'It's a positive message that you're sending out.'

For Lanchester's future, Cleary believes that having a sustainable business is going to be vitally important, and he wants to ensure his businesses do not go the same way as the steelworks. 'I believe we're future-proofing the business by doing what we're doing. It's number one on our agenda.'

The Conservative victory in the North West Durham seat was, in 2019, utterly unexpected. The seat was solid red since its inception in 1950, and its predecessors had a Labour heritage extending even further back. Prior to 2019, the Tories' most notable claim on the seat was as a pit stop for Tories on their way to occupying safer seats. Theresa May stood in 1992 before winning Maidenhead in Berkshire five years later. The Conservatives gradually increased their vote share through the New Labour years, and then in the 2017 election they jumped 11 percentage points and their vote share rose to 35 per cent.

Two years and another seven points later, the Tories won with a 1,144-vote majority. The loss was especially acute for Jeremy Corbyn and his project, because North West Durham's MP, Laura Pidcock, was a shadow minister, a wholehearted devotee of his leadership and a protégée frequently tipped as a successor. Alas, we struggled to arrange an interview.

Richard Holden did not expect to be North West Durham's first Tory MP. I knew Richard from the Westminster bubble: he was a well-known political advisor to the Conservative Party, served several Cabinet ministers, worked at Tory Party HQ and campaigned for Boris Johnson to become leader months before the election. His last job before the election was as an aide to the education secretary, Gavin Williamson. During my election travels, Holden spotted on social media that I was in County Durham and tried to entice me to go on the stump with him, his campaign little more than a tatty red van with his face sellotaped to the side. With limited time, I am afraid I missed out on his efforts and focused on covering apparently more winnable seats.

A year on, Holden had settled into his new life as an MP with a new constituency office in the heart of Consett, opposite the bus station and a few doors up from the working men's club. Before our appointment, I parked up in the town centre and took the opportunity to explore the high street and scoff a sausage roll for lunch. The town centre is small and most of the shops are discount outlets: Barry's Bargain Super Store was full of masked-up customers – my uncle Martin, a local resident, proudly purchased forty-eight small bottles of sauvignon blanc here for £24 – while one farmer was selling meat and fresh produce out of the back of his van. There were sadly many abandoned enterprises too: the Zone bar and nightclub had not welcomed dancers for many decades. But the basic amenities were still present:

opticians, cafes, clothing and sportswear. Between this and the new out-of-town shopping parks, my uncle reports Consett has everything you need (and much of it at great discounts too).

Lancashire-born Holden has adopted affectations as part of his embracing of the area, arriving in his office with a flat cap and football scarf for Consett FC. Over tea, he reflects on his nigh one-man campaign. 'Candidates can only swing a couple of hundred votes really, and, you know, they might be able to drive a little bit of turnout. But what really struck me about two weeks in, when postal votes were landing or people decided to post their postal votes, people were telling me, oh, I've already switched, I've already voted.'

Jeremy Corbyn was the primary motivator in his victory, he thinks, as red wall voters had realized he could actually be prime minister and saw him as a threat to their values. During the 2017 election, when Holden stood in the safe Labour seat of Preston in Lancashire, voters 'genuinely didn't think it was possible that Jeremy Corbyn could be prime minister', adding, 'Nobody liked him, but nobody thought it was a serious threat.' But in 2019, Laura Pidcock was a potent reminder of Corbyn's politics. 'Speak to people – this is not a sort of Marxist Socialist debating club, on the high street or in the pubs here in Consett, or in the former pit villages.' He also mentioned the significant swing rightward in next-door Bishop Auckland, which the Conservatives gained from Corbyn's Labour despite the presence of a more established, more centrist Labour candidate. 'For Labour's vote to collapse by nearly a third here, from 55 per cent vote share to under 40 per cent vote share, is very significant.'

Holden argued that the electorate was attuned to the cultural Toryism that has emerged under Boris Johnson, one that is rooted in family and community. 'And that doesn't mean necessarily very traditional two parents, two children,' he said. 'It's that broader family thing. It's the extended family: granddad and grandma might play a role in lives, or aunts and uncles. Community is such a vague term, but the sense of town, street, and village. Some little place like Tow Law [a small town near the Pennines] has got its own proper centre, its own little football club, its own community, councils, these are places with a real sense of their own identity as well.'

During the campaign, Holden identified two Labour policy pledges that struck a discordant note with residents abandoning the party. The first was the party's pledge to offer £58 billion of compensation to women born between 1950 and 1955 suffering from historic pension inequality, the so-called 'WASPI women'. The sheer scale of the pledge, after the manifesto was published, lost the party credibility, Holden said. 'I spoke to a woman in the prefabbed bits of Dipton [village] who said to me, "I'm a WASPI woman. Am I going to get thirty grand?" And then she was like, "He's not going to give us it if he gets in, is he? There's no bloody money there."' The second was Corbyn's pledge to deliver free fibre broadband to the whole country by 2030. 'In the Black Lion [pub] in Wolsingham, I heard two chaps talking about it. One was definitely Conservative, probably came over in 2017, and the chap he was talking to was going to be a first-time Conservative voter this time. "This free broadband thing," one said, "what's it all about? And where is the money coming from?" And their conversation became, "Why would we want go back to BT, a nationalized BT, it doesn't make any sense."' The nationalized BT of the 1970s is a far cry from the international private company today, which voters can appreciate.

Holden's first parliamentary term will be devoted to holding on to North West Durham. With such a slim majority, it will only take a minimal swing towards Labour for the seat to flip back. His infrastructure efforts are focused on transport. 'I was really unaware of how few seats didn't have any dual carriageway, didn't have any train line at all, those transport links are massive in the bottom of the constituency. The bus routes are a major issue for young people . . . I'm convinced that part of the drain away of that age group to other areas, as much as anything else, is that sense of rural isolation, that is a real problem.' He is also campaigning for a new rail line to transport passengers from Consett to Newcastle in thirty minutes, instead of the hour's drive during peak times, opening up further opportunities for the seat to become a home for commuters. 'It's got to be quicker and more convenient than the car.'

Corbyn's leadership will no longer be a first-order political issue come the next election, but Holden thinks a cultural divide will persist. What he calls Keir Starmer's 'pandering to certain political movements' that want to tear down historical statues will further exacerbate the divide, and he believes the bond between Labour and its heartland voters has been broken. Nor can it be simply repaired. 'They've broken it properly. A lot of what happened was a wife or husband voted Conservative in 2017, then the other one came across this time, or families switched over. You now have the Brexit vote, plus the Conservative vote,' he said.

'Are those people going to be convinced by Keir Starmer, who basically told these people he was sort of on the pro-EU side of the Labour Party? He was in the shadow cabinet, rammed it down their throats in 2019 that we are definitely going have a second referendum, meaning we'll ignore the votes of people in this area. Are they going to trust him?'

Jeremy Corbyn went into the 2019 election as the most unpopular leader of the opposition since polling began.[11] Before the election was called in September that year, his ratings were

-60, with just 16 per cent of voters expressing satisfaction with his leadership. For comparison, Ed Miliband scored -44 the year before he attempted to win a general election. In 1983, Michael Foot – another notable figure of the Labour left – scored -56. While Corbyn was unpopular across the whole country, it felt especially potent in Labour's former northern heartlands. Voters in the C2DE social economic group – defined by the Market Research Society as skilled and non-skilled working-class – had significantly worse perceptions of the leader than those in the wealthier ABC1 category, which includes upper- and middle-class voters, accounting for around 45 per cent of the population.[12]

Corbyn still has his followers, who believe that other factors broke down the red wall. The most prominent and boisterous voice of Corbynism can be found a little way up the coast, so a quick detour from North West Durham is required, back up to Northumberland to find Ian Lavery, in lieu of speaking to Laura Pidcock. A former miner and controversial leader of the National Union of Mineworkers, Lavery entered Parliament in 2010 for Wansbeck in Northumberland and initially garnered little notice. But the rise of Jeremy Corbyn led to the rise of Ian Lavery, as he became one of the leader's staunchest supporters – particularly in the broadcast media, where his sharp Geordie lilt and broad stature added diversity to the primarily southern, softer tones of Corbyn's front bench. Lavery was appointed Labour's election coordinator for the 2017 campaign. A rare ardent Labour Brexiter, he consistently warned that edging towards a pro-Remain position would cost Labour the next general election. He was proved right: Lavery clung onto his constituency in 2019 with a mere 814 votes, compared to a 10,435 majority two years prior. Wansbeck is already on the radar of northern Tories, who would love nothing more than to de-throne one of Corbyn's few remaining supporters in Parliament (although his constituency is likely to be subsumed into Blyth Valley in the upcoming boundary reviews).

Lavery is out of front-line Labour politics, one of the first casualties of Keir Starmer's efforts to refurbish the party's image and make a clean break with the Corbyn era. We met at his constituency office in a modern business park on the outskirts of Ashington. The first notable sight was a maroon Jaguar saloon, a car for the man of the people only in colour. Lavery was waiting in the boardroom, full of mining memorabilia and a tapestry for the NUM that is still paraded during the Durham Miners' Gala, the annual celebration of mining heritage. He is proud of his militant union background. 'I'd been on strike for a year . . . I was in a police cell on a regular basis,' he recalls of the 1984–85 miners' strike. 'I like to call myself an industrial leftie. I rarely call myself a socialist, it's just what I am, and I'm a product of the coal-mining industry, of this place where I grew up, I'm a product of fighting and supporting the people who I worked with all my life.'

Lavery is full of lyrical memories of the halcyon days of mining and how the pit communities were bound up in work. In a two-mile radius around his constituency office, 10,000 men worked in mining. Miners who found themselves in trouble on a Friday night would be put in their place by the men at the pit. 'All this fantastic stuff, gone,' he said of the days when the pit was the entire community. 'I'm a dying sort, but there were such things as sports days arranged by the community. You would have the big leek shows, the vegetable shows, flower shows – you'll remember from Gateshead [I do not] – there was the whippet sweeps, every week there was the pigeon racing. We still have that social culture here, but not to any degree like what it was.' Social indeed: there were more drinking establishments per head of population in the pit town of Ashington in its industrial prime than anywhere else in the country.

Lavery recalled his childhood, when there were five working pits that 'everything was based around' and you didn't need to think about education. 'We would never ever think of a future without the coal industry, because you would leave school, very few people went to university . . . you were lucky if you got an apprenticeship somewhere, but the lads were OK, because they would get a job in one of the pits or the supply chain for the pits, in engineering, mechanical, electrical engineering, fantastic stuff. There was always the understanding that things would be fine, because the pit was here. You had the unions that basically took up disputes for anybody, you didn't have to be a member of the NUM to get support from a union, the community looked after itself. Mainly the wages, terms and conditions at the pit were fairly good, there was free council housing. You got a house, and the miners paid for the swimming pool, the leisure facilities, libraries, and paid initially for schools.'

Now, in his constituency, that infrastructure and collectivized community has gone. 'What we've got now is a high street full of bookmakers, kebab shops, charity shops, and Ramsdens [pawn-brokers] . . . the industry is gone, there isn't any huge industry that's come in here despite many pledges of investment.' The working classes of England have become what Lavery calls 'the *Homes under the Hammer* brigade', the BBC's mid-morning home renovation programme watched by millions. 'They're in their house, they get up, they have their brekky, they haven't got a job. They'll watch *Homes under the Hammer*, they become secure in the knowledge that if things just continue the way they are, nothing drastic is going happen to them, therefore they'll think, whatever's to their advantage, whatever will keep their life in a stable direction, is best for them.'

Lavery is eager to stress that voters who left the Labour Party were not brainwashed by the Tories, but eager to find an alternative to their status quo. 'These aren't all daft people, it's not that they haven't a clue what they're talking about. A lot of these people have had a real rough ride over decades. They've lost their job, the community in which they've lived and loved has been systematically destroyed, there isn't anything there. They're seeing their clubs – social clubs, working men's clubs – close, libraries close, public services reduced, and they blame Labour.' It is curious that despite a decade of Conservative government, they do not blame austerity for these challenges. The sad truth is that that happened many years ago, we had the Blair years where we were allegedly really popular. We weren't popular in the red wall areas.' What happened in 2019 was 'all those people who had possibly abandoned politics, disenfranchised from politics, a lot of them then came back with a vengeance', and backed the Conservatives.

But Lavery refuted the suggestion that left-wing policies were to blame for Labour's troubles. Under Corbyn's leadership, the 2017 and 2019 manifestos were 'absolutely magnificent', full of what he describes as hope, aspiration and equality. 'Everything I've ever fought for since I was a little laddie in the playground, right the way through my time as a miner, right the way through my time as a trade union rep and an MP.' Those policy documents were 'political utopia' for Lavery and he 'naturally thought that it would be for many others'. When I pointed out that voters rejected them, he exploded. 'Listen, Sebastian, how many people read the manifesto?' I had to admit not many. 'The majority of people will not have a great idea of what the headline policies are of any party.' But what about Get Brexit Done? He was having none of it. 'We'll get Brexit done, we'll take control of our own finances, take control of the borders and take control of the judiciary system, Make Britain Great Again.' He slammed his hand on the table. 'It's Trumpism, man. It's the Trump playbook, but it worked so effectively.'

He takes particular affront at suggestions Jeremy Corbyn was to blame, even if he has concluded that he was not the best man to lead the party. 'I've got to tell you, Jeremy Corbyn is a very close friend of mine, he's one of the nicest individuals I've ever met, certainly one of the nicest politicians I've ever met. But he wasn't ruthless, he always tried to compromise with people in politics. You've got to be ruthless, you've got to strike at the right time, you've got to make decisions, can't dither.' Labour became one of the largest political parties in the Corbyn era but not many of those members were in places such as North West Durham. 'The majority of people are away from the heartlands, away from the broken heartlands' – it is nice to hear him embrace this book – 'away from the red wall areas, the majority of the membership are in the south, and a lot of them are . . . from left-wing backgrounds.' And all this plays into his conclusion: 'The Labour Party took northern heartlands for granted, "they'll not vote for anybody else", and I was of that view, right up to the last election. But Brexit broke all that.'

With Corbyn gone, Brexit delivered and Labour moving back towards a more moderate policy platform, how does Lavery feel about Labour's prospects in these heartlands? 'My view is that Labour can win back, but I think we've got to make sure that we are different, it isn't any good just continually saying we support the government.' But he is aware that the Tories will 'pour money' into the places they won for the first time. 'They'll deliberately starve my area, I'm telling you, because I'm a Labour MP and the only one in Northumberland now, and I've got the pincer movement around me.' But he acknowledges the events of 2016–19 have broken a bond between England and the Labour

Party. 'Brexit changed the world, Brexit changed British politics forever, and there's no going back on that, that's a fact of life, and it changed people's views on politics.'

Lavery concluded our ear-boxing chat with a prediction that has not come true. 'I'm not sure by the time you write your book that Boris Johnson will be leader of the Conservative Party.'

If Lavery is the working-class hero of the Corbyn project, now is a good moment to temporarily leave the North West Durham story and compare his views with a similar figure from an earlier Labour era. Alan Johnson took a similar path into politics: he became a postman after leaving school at fifteen, joined the trade union and rose up to become its general secretary. His memoir, *This Boy*, charts an extraordinary story of childhood poverty and is easily some of the best political writing of the last decade. He entered Parliament in 1997 for Hull West and served in the Cabinet as Home, Health, Business and Education Secretaries. He was one of the New Labour's most authentic working-class voices and one of Blair's closest allies. In an interview in 2013, Johnson said, 'I remember once talking to Tony Blair about family, as my youngest was around the same age as his son Leo. When I told him I was married and living in a council house with three children by the age of twenty, his response was, "Gosh, you really are working class, aren't you?"'[13] He exited front-line politics in 2010, reinventing himself as a lucid author and political commentator. On 2019 election night, he sat in ITV studios beside Jon Lansman, Jeremy Corbyn's key grassroots organizer, as the disaster unfolded for Labour. He told Lansman to 'go back to your student politics' and to take his 'little cult' with him. 'Corbyn was a disaster on the doorstep . . . everyone knew he couldn't lead the working class out of a paper bag.'[14]

Almost a year on from the election, Johnson was delighted to have a long chat about what went wrong for Labour, but also what went right. 'We would have lost all three Hull seats, as we would have lost all of Doncaster, if the Brexit Party hadn't stood candidates and split the votes.' But based on his experience, voters abandoned the party for one reason: 'Absolutely no question, they hated Corbyn.' His anger hadn't yet abated. 'They had sussed out his hard-left politics, his lack of patriotism, this view of the working class, a patronizing view, that we had no agency whatsoever, we have to be moulded and directed by middle-class people from Islington. They hated him on the doorstep. He was useless as a leader of the opposition.'

There is particular animosity between the pair over Brexit: Corbyn's self-confessed 'seven and a half' enthusiasm for remaining in the EU was less than welcomed by much of the party. Johnson led the 'Labour In for Britain' campaign during 2016 and had to spend much of it making up for Corbyn's lack of enthusiasm. 'Brexit was 95 per cent about immigration', he asserted, and he recalled during his tenure as Home Secretary 'being told we could never debate these things', especially the controversy over asylum seekers that successive New Labour governments struggled with. The governments implemented a system of dispersal of asylum seekers across the country that Johnson believes led to problems locally. 'So, in places like Hull, I likened it to being in London in the 1950s. It was happening fifty years later, but you could see the same tensions as suddenly lots of, particularly, Iraqi Kurds were walking round the streets of Hull, which was 98.9 per cent white, indigenous. But actually, to be fair to the people of Hull, they handled that quite well.'

Johnson could understand such tension, 'particularly when you got the odd story of an Albanian who murdered someone in Albania and then murdered someone over here, and no one knew about their criminal record. That was part of the problem,

European countries not giving us information about people coming over here. But we could say until we were blue in the face, "Look, it's not an open-door policy", but it was for the EU. You could go anywhere you wanted in the EU and live there with very few constraints, and that meant to the public, quite rightly, that's uncontrolled immigration.'

He believed that New Labour's reputation for economic competence, shattered during the financial crisis, helped to break down a 'blue wall' of traditional Conservative seats. 'Forty-seven successive quarters of growth, the lowest unemployment . . . in 2004 we were at 75 per cent employment rate, looking to go to 80 per cent, which is one of the reasons why in 2004 we had Polish workers, Czech workers and Hungarian workers and all that coming straight in at us, Ireland and Sweden, because we were the three most successful economies, and in a way that might be where our problems started.'

Despite his prominent role as a Labour Remainer, he agreed with Ian Lavery that there was a major missed opportunity for Labour to hold onto their heartlands. 'Oh, that's easy. It would have been supporting Theresa May's deal. The problem with Labour is on the other side of Corbyn, if you like. My good friends, Alastair Campbell, Tony Blair, Hilary Benn, were obviously holding out for a second referendum. Whether it was intended or not, they were saying "Look, you didn't know what you were voting for, you were too silly, there'll be another referendum and we'll stay in the EU.'

Johnson is optimistic that the English working class will return to Labour, unlike their defection to the SNP in Scotland. 'It doesn't feel like Scotland in 2015, when that was a definite, no return. It doesn't feel like that with the Tories, they've got no infrastructure up here, no councillors, it would have been interesting if those local authority elections had taken place this year that were put back because of Covid, to see whether their success in December 2019 translated. I doubt it will.' The results of May's 2021 local elections, where the Conservatives made significant net gains across England – including in County Durham and Northumberland – suggested his view was inaccurate. With Brexit subsiding as a major political issue, the challenge is to convince traditional supporters that 'Keir Starmer and Labour have recovered from Corbyn'. But Johnson is upbeat that the end of immigration issues will help the party. 'There won't be the same rancid atmosphere around free movement, that will have gone. And free movement, of course, went in Theresa May's deal, which is once again why it would have been so easy to sell, except she couldn't sell it herself.'

Unlike Ian Lavery, Johnson is not pining for a return to the collectivized communities that empowered the Labour movement. He recalled his organizing days for the union at the Post Office: 'It was easy to recruit when you had thousands of people in the same place. Now it's a much more diverse labour market and more difficult to keep recruiting. I think of BT. You had telephone exchanges, telephonists and telephone engineers who came in every day, that doesn't happen now, they work out of Openreach [the infrastructure subsidiary]. They're in their vans, they're almost self-employed. So yeah, it's a very profound change.'

Johnson, who has kept a diary since the age of twenty-six, found an entry from a trip he made to Consett during his postman days soon after the steelworks closed. 'The guy I went to, the local Post Office union rep, took me to his social club that evening. The solidarity was palpable, I recorded that in my diary because I'd never been anywhere like this club, a big club with the sense of community. Various things were announced throughout the evening about someone needing help somewhere;

there was a general raffle with proceeds all going back into the community fund; there were people, highly educated but self-educated, discussing all kinds of things about politics or whatever; they had all kinds of societies listed on the walls. I've never forgotten that evening in Consett in County Durham. But I bet that club's gone and I bet that, if the club hasn't gone, that sense of community has gone.' He mused on whether the return of community spirit we saw during the coronavirus pandemic would see people 'looking out for each other' to this old degree when normal life resumes. He welcomed the fact people have been doing each other's shopping while shielding from Covid, but wondered whether it will be the Conservatives that 'pick up some of the political capital from that.'

After these grandees, it was time to return to North West Durham for an evening of pints with someone who encapsulates its past and potential. The Steel Club in Consett is the only obvious reminder of the town's industrial heritage. A mix of pub, bar, and north-eastern working men's club, it frequently hosts live music and is the main social draw of the town centre. Dave Skelton stands out among the drinkers for his fedora and tweed jacket, but he is as authentically from North West Durham as the other patrons and their pints. The forty-two-year-old is a Tory, an ardent Brexiter and a citizen of the world: Google's head of global strategic planning. But he also feels an emotional pull back to his childhood. He left Consett after school – only 10 per cent of people in his class received five or more decent GCSEs – but returns often. 'There were very few opportunities in Consett, which makes me even more determined to create a country where people don't have to leave home to get by,' he said.

Both of his grandfathers worked in heavy industry: one in the steelworks and the other in the mines. The latter died in his fifties of a 'horrific lung problem' that many of his colleagues also endured. 'So many people kind of glamorize life in the pits, but it wasn't a very pleasant job for many people.' He was born in 1978, two years before the steelworks closed, and his childhood was overshadowed by its legacy. The old works were visible from his home, his school a couple of miles from the works. 'I saw when I was growing up what the social impact was of the steelworks closing.'

His family were all Labour people but also quietly religious. 'It was very much the thing that they believed in socialism and Methodism in equal measure. My grandma was one of the only people who bothered putting a Labour poster in her window when she knew that all of her neighbours were going to vote Labour. I think there was something about the mining villages where they lived, where being Labour was part of the identity.' He remembered that the party's heartlands formed a Labourism that was 'about the union, the pit, the community, the chapel, it was about all of these elements of working-class life and being Labour was part of that.'

As we further drained our pint glasses, he reflected on his childhood and how the values of his Labour-supporting family have fallen out of step with the party of today. 'I remember going to my grandma's house and seeing as many plates and tea towels of past monarchs of England as you possibly could want. And I think that there's a sense of a kind of working-class patriotism, and that real sense of Labourism, which has been lost in those communities. I had that sense when I was growing up, even though Tony Blair was to an extent "one of us". There was much pride when Tony Blair was elected in 1997, that he was a northeast MP, and he was from Sedgefield, but there's been a growing realization that the Labour Party was no longer the kind of party that came out of those communities, and represented those communities.'

On his mother's side of the family, which was especially Labour, they spoke of the prime minister as 'Our Tony, like a member of the family'. They all voted for Brexit in 2016 and 2019 and now speak of 'Boris' in the same way. He sees the transfer of the values of patriotism and self-reliance from the political left to the right as essential in the town's shift.

Skelton is the author of *Little Platoons*, a polemic inspired by philosopher Edmund Burke on how England's towns can be revived and given a new purpose. His vision speaks of his life experience, and he believes England's towns 'should not be places where you have to go to university and leave in order to have a successful career.' Consett is a case study for much of his book, owing to both Skelton's personal connection and its success in regeneration. 'It did recover better than a lot of places did. The community often said the impact in Consett was the biggest and the greatest of the industrial towns because it was probably the first of the major, major industrial towns to lose their base,' he said.

It was a particularly cold evening and our conversation turned to the isolated nature of Consett and how it has maintained its population despite the loss of its main industry. Skelton pointed out that the town started as a camp formed around the steelworks, morphing into a 'very settled' community with deep roots. 'It's partly isolated because of decisions that were made by government, because there was a railway that the government removed. There could have been better road links, but the government decided not to invest in them over many years. So yes, it is isolated, but no more isolated [in terms of physical geography] than some south-eastern places, which *do* have good transport links and have always had the right kind of investment.'

Much of Skelton's critique of how Westminster has failed

Labour's heartlands focuses on the centralization of decision-making, which reached its zenith in the post-war Labour governments that nationalized much of Britain's heavy industry. Prior to the Consett steelworks renationalization in 1967, Skelton argues 'a lot of decisions were made locally by people who understood what had to happen as opposed to guys in Whitehall who said that that can't be done. This needs to be saved, because we're talking about the British Steel budget as opposed to the Consett Steel Company. And so when it becomes a far-away town to someone in Whitehall, that's very different to the beating heart and soul of a local community.'

Despite his Tory leanings, Skelton is no fan of Margaret Thatcher. Her pursuit of growth rested on deindustrialization, resulting in the 1984–85 miners' strike that left psychological scarring on the area that took three decades for her party to overcome. Growing up in Consett, he concluded 'a free market left alone does not solve all problems'. When he moved to London, he was not only unimpressed with the dominant laissez-faire doctrine in Westminster but also the 'top-down socialism' espoused by Labour, which meant Consett did not receive the modernization needed to remain competitive.

Thatcher's use of the phrase 'the enemy within' to describe the striking miners was 'done unapologetically', in Skelton's view, and there was little thought 'as to what might follow in the wake of heavy industry' – something Norman Tebbit acknowledged during our chat in Blyth Valley.

'There was less thinking about how people could be properly reskilled, how you could maintain social capital, how you could have jobs that people could be proud of. And still when you speak to people who worked in the steelworks' – he pointed around the bar of the Steel Club – 'and sadly there's less of them every year, they're still very proud about what they did, very proud about the fact you could go all around the world and see things made out of Consett steel.' His grandfather did a skilled job in the mines, and he worries that these jobs were replaced with 'packing boxes of crisps' that may be 'important for the economy, but don't have the same dignity of labour.'

As our evening drew on, we returned to the theme of North West Durham, Jeremy Corbyn and his political project. Skelton thought that the party of today has moved beyond 'the Labour Party that my family almost brought me up in' and is not returning. The values he believes in are 'patriotic, relatively communitarian but with a streak of individualism', which I pointed out sounds very New Labour and Tony Blair. He acknowledged this matches New Labour's rhetoric, but not what it achieved. 'I certainly don't think New Labour made community stronger in the north-east of England.' He added, 'I think it's [Conservative values] an absolute belief in the potential of the region, an absolute belief that our economy is held back by so many parts of the economy not fulfilling their potential. This isn't just about Consett, this is, for me, about a failing political economy over the past forty years'.

This man of Consett has become a man of Big Tech and Silicon Valley, but Skelton's heart still yearns for a return to manufacturing in his personal heartland. His rhetoric was strikingly similar to that of many Jeremy Corbyn supporters, who argue that 'forty years of Thatcherism' have failed to create a sustainable economy. Skelton laughed, but rebutted: 'Jeremy Corbyn didn't believe in a thriving private sector. I do.'

Consett is one of the earliest examples of the deindustrialization that swept through England, and that brought along with it the gradual decline in support for and connection to the Labour Party. It is a similar story to that of Youngstown, Ohio, which was dominated by iron and steel works that closed at the same time as those here. Bruce Springsteen wrote a hymn to the town, charting how the rise and fall of its plant followed the contours of America's wars. Ohio supported Donald Trump in 2016, just as North West Durham supported Brexit. Consett's decline and resurgence has broken the historic bonds between its residents and the Labour movement.

The long legacy of deindustrialization made the Conservatives anathema to aspirational working-class voters. The events of 2016 changed that, but what many observers have failed to realize is that North West Durham has changed too. The mining and steel industry forged a bond between the workers and the labour movement, but now the area's economy is more fragmented. Communities may be less united but small-scale manufacturing continues. North West Durham's residents today are more likely to be commuters who have opted for the charm of the country-side over city life. As these wealthier residents have arrived, and the last generation of heavy-industry workers dies out, the area has naturally become more prosperous and therefore more likely to vote Tory. The town centre of Consett is hardly the most vibrant place, but the shoots of renewal elsewhere in the seat are real. Driving through the windy hills, with the sights of heavy manufacturing gone, the sense is of typical pastoral Tory England.

Again I was struck by the missed opportunity of 2017. Alan Johnson and Ian Lavery both noted the moment Theresa May lost her majority could have been Labour's opening. Had Jeremy Corbyn held his nose and done a deal with the Conservatives, Brexit would have been delivered on softer terms. As well as splitting the Tories – the hard-line Brexiters would have baulked at remaining in a customs union with the EU – it would have likely gone some way to propping up parts of the red wall. The Parliament of 2017 to 2019 was so fraught that nothing is certain.

Corbyn could not have saved all the seats, but the party may have clung on in the more marginal ones.

With its 1,144 majority, North West Durham will be one of the Conservatives' toughest fights come the next election. But the scale of change is astounding: in 1997, the seat's majority was almost 25,000 votes for the Labour Party. Now it has gone. Much of that may be down to politics, but so are the changing economies of the former heartlands. The question of what happened between 1997 and 2010 is the topic for our next stop, a forty-minute drive south through County Durham to Sedgefield. Richard Holden, David Skelton and Ian Lavery all think New Labour failed to deliver for their heartlands while they were in power. Are they right?

3. Sedgefield

'I have come back here, to Sedgefield, to my
constituency. Where my political journey began
and where it is fitting it should end.'

TONY BLAIR, ON THE DAY HE RESIGNED
AS UK PRIME MINISTER IN 2007

The Dun Cow Inn, on the main thoroughfare of Sedgefield, is
the ancient market town's most warming and traditional pub. A
drinking house, in fact, fit for a prime minister and a president.
It was here in 2003 that the local MP, Tony Blair, brought then
American premier George W. Bush for a traditional English
lunch of leek soup followed by fish and chips. In a visit costing
the taxpayer well over £1 million (for 1,300 police officers shipped
in from across the country), Blair and Bush's post-Iraq bromance
was sealed in Labour heartland country. The mythology of
Sedgefield and County Durham was always core to Blair's wide
appeal to the voters of middle England. The subtle influence of
Christianity, his Conservative-voting father, the north London-
dwelling liberal lawyer who was rooted in the north. As one
resident, Gary Forshaw, said during President Bush's visit, 'It is
good for him to come up here and not just see the highlights
of London, but to be shown the real world where Tony lives.'[1]

Seventeen years on from the visit, and thirteen years since

Blair lowered the curtain on his New Labour project, which modernized the party and brought it back from the electoral wilderness, Brian and Janine Lowes were supping late-afternoon glasses of red wine on the benches outside the Dun Cow. It was a crisp autumnal day during one of the looser moments of the Covid restrictions: socializing outside allowed, indoor mixing forbidden. The pair worked as teachers, had lived in Sedgefield for thirty-six years and taught in the nearby cathedral city of Durham. Their memories of Bush's visit were vivid. 'It was really exciting, the police cordons were up there,' Janine pointed at the crossroads. 'The marksmen up there,' at the church. 'For an afternoon, it was the safest place in the Western world,' Brian added. Despite the harsh memories of the Iraq war, which are especially potent in working-class England as they had a long tradition of supplying the armed forces with recruits, Blair remained a source of pride. 'To me, to all of us, he was really great,' Janine said. 'He put Sedgefield on the map. Even now, if I say to people that I'm from Sedgefield, they say "Tony Blair".'

Brian and Janine should be archetypal Labour supporters – public sector employees, staunch supporters of remaining in the EU, admirers of Blair and his New Labour project – but both backed Boris Johnson in the 2019 election. Janine had never voted Conservative previously, while Brian has done so occasionally, and both cited Jeremy Corbyn as the reason. 'Because of the finances, that really worried me, where is it coming from? Covid has changed the whole thing, but it hasn't changed my opinion about trusting a Labour government,' she said. Brian, who still regretted Brexit, said, 'Boris did well in the last election and it was mainly because of Brexit, because he was going to get the job done.' Almost a verbatim translation of the Conservatives' three-word election slogan: 'Get Brexit Done'.

Their retirement lives are comfortable, enough for frequent

afternoon glasses at the Dun Cow. Not least because the Sedgefield constituency has gentrified during their decades living here. Janine agreed the area was probably richer now than in its heavy-manufacturing prime. The secondary school has made its way towards the top of national best schools lists, while the primary schools are similarly highly ranked.[2] 'People move here for schools – there's a social feeling here too with nice pubs and restaurants,' she said. Brian concurs: 'Compared to the north-east, it has got more upmarket.'

Of all the verdant small towns and villages in County Durham, Sedgefield is one of the most affluent. Leafy, avowedly middle class, with a thirteenth-century church and rows of neat Georgian houses, the passing visitor may struggle to align it with their stereotypical imagination of northern coalfields past their industrial prime. Parking up the red Mini in the town centre, I saw there were another four already there, all less than three years old. Well-tended hanging baskets hung from the town hall – opened 1895 – and vivid flower planters lined the pavements. Despite the economic storm of 2020, the small boutique shops all survived and were trading well. The estate agent showed a healthy market for small cottages in the town centre, well above the average price for a small County Durham residence.

For the casual traveller to Sedgefield, the most appealing destination is the racecourse – one of the most renowned in England, described by its infamous patron Clement Freud as 'all field and not much sedge'. Richer, farming-dominated villages are dotted across the wider constituency, including the eponymous town, where foxhunting used to be popular. The South Durham Hunt was once frequently spotted throughout parts of Sedgefield, and residents claim that surreptitious meets continue as the police busy themselves elsewhere – years after the practice of chasing small animals for sport was outlawed by the area's most famous son. These leafy parts historically leaned Conservative, yet were always outweighed by the sheer bulk of the working-class Labour vote from elsewhere in the constituency.

Drive out of Sedgefield town to the neighbouring villages of Trimdon and Fishburn, both once dominated by coal mines, and the less well-heeled side becomes apparent. These isolated pit villages, once layered in dirt and soot, have minimal employment opportunities and stand as reminders of the decades when mining underpinned the whole economy. Wealth may not have been in abundance during their industrial heyday, but residents recall that the small intertwined communities had a deep sense of contentment. They lived, breathed and socialized their work. There was no need to consider life beyond the pit, or even the village, until the pits disappeared. The largest settlement is by far the new town of Newton Aycliffe, created in 1947 to be the model of William Beveridge's welfare state – where the safety net of the National Health Service, government-backed housing and low unemployment would be on show for all to see. Successful in its day, Aycliffe has latterly suffered its own decline, with the industrial park usurping heavy manufacturing. Labour's vote was strongest in these urban and poorest parts of the constituency. When they began to slide away, Sedgefield's days as a safe Labour seat were doomed. When Tony Blair's old seat fell to the Tories on 2019 election night, it was the greatest symbol of Labour's collapse in its traditional heartlands.

Mining and horse racing are important assets for Sedgefield, but they will forever be eclipsed by Blair, who represented the seat from 1983 to 2007: the politician who led Labour back to power and embodied the centrism that dominated British politics. It was here his political journey started, where the New Labour project to modernize the party's electoral offering was conceived and where it met an abrupt end.

In Trimdon village – the pit closed in 1925, employing 300 in its prime – the Labour Club hosted many key moments in his rise and fall.[3] Blair declared his candidacy for the party leadership from the concert room in 1994 and welcomed in successive New Labour election victories from the same location. On election night in 1997, the barmaid struggled to find the newly elected prime minister when 'someone called Clinton' rang on the club phone.[4] And it was St Mary Magdalene's Church in the next-door village that provided the backdrop for possibly his most famous soundbite. The morning after Princess Diana died in Paris, the prime minister peeled away from Sunday morning mass to tell the world of the British people: 'They liked her, they loved her, they regarded her as one of the people. She was the people's princess.'

Blair's arrival in this north-eastern 'real world' was almost by chance. The young socialist barrister had previously stood in the unwinnable southern Tory seat of Beaconsfield in the 1982 by-election, but was eager to find something more favourable four years on. Labour legally challenged the constituency boundaries during the 1983 campaign, meaning Sedgefield required a last-minute stand-in candidate. The constituency's Labour Party – which had mini-branches in each major village at that time – wanted a left-winger. But a gang of 'famous five' plotters had a better idea. Led by activist John Burton, who went on to become Blair's constituency agent, the group worked through the constituency's branches and cajoled him onto the shortlist. That glinting smile and easy charm were put to good use on the members of the Sedgefield Labour Party. He was duly chosen as its candidate and elected to Parliament at the age of thirty.

Blair's majority in Sedgefield never slid to below five figures. But as with all of the red wall seats, Sedgefield consistently returned a solid base level of several thousand Conservative votes that never posed a threat to Labour's supremacy. The Conservative vote share gradually increased over a decade, before a significant ten-point jump between the 2015 election and 2017.[5] The constituency had last returned a Tory MP for a brief period in 1931, during the Tory–Labour national government, and had been solidly red ever since. Just under 60 per cent voted to leave the EU.[6] Most of its heavy industry – and its thousands of blue-collar jobs – has long since shrivelled up, yet parts of Sedgefield are more prosperous than ever. One of the area's biggest employers is the North East Technology Park, or NETPark, where small businesses are working on advanced materials and medical research in partnership with Durham University. They are the kind of employees who Blair's policies appealed to – that dreaded word, 'aspirational' – but who now find themselves drifting towards the Conservatives. In short, Sedgefield's economic base is more diverse, more prosperous, and therefore more Tory.

Tony Blair has been out of front-line British politics for fourteen years, since he left Downing Street, stood down as an MP and dedicated himself to (sometimes controversial) international affairs. He has not, however, disengaged with domestic matters and continues to closely follow his party's ups and downs. He was harshly critical of his successors Ed Miliband and Jeremy Corbyn, and the party's historic loss in 2019 was, at least in part, an affirmation of his warnings about it becoming unelectable by veering too far from the centre ground. He was eager to talk through what has happened to his party and why it should listen to him again.

What did Blair feel, when the result was declared and his constituency went blue for the first time in his life? 'It was completely obvious,' he told me during our lengthy chat. 'You can do all sorts of complicated sociological and psephological theses as to what went wrong. But what went wrong was precisely what went wrong in 1983 [when left-winger Michael Foot led the party to a historic defeat], except worse, which is that we ended up with a party leadership that was completely alien to traditional Labour voters. I mean, it's really not complicated.'

Yet it is a little more complex than that: Blair admitted there has been a cultural change since he first stood in the seat. The mining traditions have drifted into history: the most you will see of them in Sedgefield now are abandoned minecarts filled with flowers and memorials to those who died in successive disasters. And with the end of heavy manufacturing, the diehard bonds with the Labour Party also loosened. As Blair recalls from the 2019 campaign, 'The only difference is that in 1983 I cannot tell you the number of people on the doorstep that said to me "I've always voted Labour, I'm voting Labour because my dad would just kill me if I didn't. He'd come back from the grave and kill me."'

The second, slightly more complicated reason the likes of Sedgefield slid away from Labour is Brexit. Blair was a fervent advocate of a second referendum, as was Phil Wilson, his successor as the MP for the area. Almost every figure central to the New Labour project campaigned hard to re-run the 2016 referendum. Their analysis of what went wrong duly focuses almost entirely on Jeremy Corbyn's leadership. In politics, there is possibly no greater loathing than that centrists hold for the hard left. It is a comfortable crutch for Blair's allies to dismiss the impact of calling for another referendum. But he admits the pair of issues are intertwined.

'Brexit was also a major problem, though I think Corbyn was at least as big a problem. Once those people voted for Brexit, they wanted it implemented. But the thing you've got to understand about this is you can't divorce people's feelings about Brexit from the absence of any Labour leadership on the issue,' he said. 'Brexit of course played a role in it, it would be bonkers to think otherwise. I think if you'd had David Miliband leading the Labour Party you would never have had the 2015 election result that we did, and you'd probably never have had Brexit.'

David Miliband, for those unaware of the former Foreign Secretary, was the golden boy of the Blair era – nicknamed 'Brains' during his time running the Downing Street policy unit. Born and bred in the intellectual milieu of north London academia, he entered Parliament in 2001 for the north-east fishing town of South Shields. His failed attempt to take the party leadership in 2010 – beaten by his more left-wing brother Ed – marked the end of New Labour. Blair sees him as the party's lost leader, the one who could have avoided the party's collapse in England. Miliband has long moved on from British politics, relocating to New York in 2013 to lead the International Rescue Committee. Yet every so often, he surfaces on Sunday political programmes and at ideas festivals to offer his thoughts on the status quo. What is less known is that he also continues to return to the UK to campaign for Labour in the north-east. He still owns a house in South Shields and visits at least once a year for a holiday with his family. He also hosts an annual lecture in the town, bringing celebrities from Gary Lineker to John Major to stir up deep thoughts in his old patch.

I took a break from my Sedgefield travels to speak to Miliband at his New York apartment, sadly not in person. He recalled doorstep memories from the 2019 campaign. 'I was up in Ronnie Campbell's former constituency, I was in Sedgefield. The campaigning that I'd done on the Thursday, Friday, Saturday before the election had given me a very strong sense that while there was some enthusiasm for Labour in London . . . you could see big problems for the party up there.' Similarly to Blair, he pinned the blame on Jeremy Corbyn's leadership, which 'was going to alienate a lot of voters', a situation he saw as 'a very large self-inflicted wound . . . People did not see Labour as credible, in terms of government, they were pretty repelled I'm afraid, so I think it was quite a simple story in some ways.'

But, digging a little deeper, Miliband agreed there has been both structural and contingent changes in these communities that fed into the party's collapse. The structural side, in his view, is significant: economic change that has disrupted the working-class demographics in these 'older communities' that now tilt away from the Labour Party. And he acknowledged that the decline in collectivism has also played a role. 'The mechanisms of collective organization have been changed, there's no point denying that,' he said. 'Then there are contingent things – who's running, what's the political issues and personalities of the moment. I think that, in general, the contingent are more important than the structural, and certainly the contingent are being given less credit or credibility or importance than the structural,' he added. Brexit is both of these factors in Miliband's analysis of what happened. 'Bill Clinton used to say it's better to be wrong and strong than weak and right, and Labour got the worst of all worlds, because its policy was hard to define, and late to be called, actually contradictory in various ways, and so I think that clearly Brexit was an issue.'

One of the issues that was raised previously at the Dun Cow pub, when several other customers joined the conversation after my drink with Brian and Janine, was carpetbagging candidates – MPs who are not born and bred in an area but represent it in Parliament. Blair was not from Sedgefield, nor was David Miliband from South Shields, whereas many of the newly elected Conservative MPs are from the areas they represent. 'I couldn't represent South Shields by claiming I was from South Shields,

I had to represent South Shields by arguing for it, and delivering for it,' he said. 'The sense of being rooted, I think, is important; being informed, being representative, you know, you can represent both by who you are and what you do.'

Through his odd mixture of being thousands of miles away but also with first-hand Labour doorstep experience, Miliband is optimistic that Labour can win back the red wall. 'They're in play, you've got to say they're in play, it would be foolish to say the vote's only been lent and the pendulum's bound to come back, but it would be equally foolish to say there's been a Damascene conversion and they'll never come back. The Sedgefields and the Blyth Valleys of this world are full of voters who want to know what politics is going to do for their lives, it's about relevance . . . about organizing.'

Miliband is hopeful that Keir Starmer has grasped the message that the party needs to change its message. 'We used to say in the nineties, if we'd been rejected four times, the electorate is sending us a message, the message is not "disappear", the message is "come back, but come back better, give us a proper choice". I mean, people don't want the Labour Party to disappear, they want it to be relevant and effective . . . if we don't understand what the electorate are saying then they'll do it again to us.'

There is one Labour figure whose local credentials can never be doubted. Phil Wilson was one of the 'famous five' who installed Blair in Sedgefield in 1983 (two members of that original gang, Paul Trippett and Peter Brookes, have quit Labour due to Corbyn). His story is intertwined with the Brexit tale that cost Labour its red wall seats. At the age of sixty-one, he has a kindly, earnest demeanour. Bespectacled and sometimes downbeat, he exudes the sense of being a politician who is in the game for the right reasons. Within minutes of encountering him, it is impossible to question his deep love for his party, his home town and his Tony. Or his aversion to leaving the EU.

No one knows Sedgefield or Blair better than Wilson. He has lived in the constituency all of his life and devoted his career to its former MP. When his icon exited politics in 2007, Wilson took over the seat from Blair to keep the New Labour flame alive. He duly won the seat again in 2010 and 2015, but difficulties had emerged by 2017. During that campaign, he took to the pages of the *Northern Echo* to decry and distance himself from Jeremy Corbyn's leadership, stating he had no confidence in him whatsoever.[7] Only thanks to Theresa May's appalling election campaign did he win again.

During the 2019 campaign, I visited Wilson at his home in the village of Heighington, one part of Sedgefield that leaned Tory. Most of my memories of that election are of cold, drizzling evenings: it is rare for the UK to hold a December poll for good reason. Labour and Conservative campaigners traipsed across the red wall seats with torches and oodles of scarfs and gloves while their canvassing return sheets disintegrated. There is nothing romantic about politics in such conditions.

That dreary winter evening with Wilson in his local, the Bay Horse Inn, was no exception. Over pints and crisps, his depression consumed our corner of the pub. Locals popped over to wish him well for polling day, but he could scarcely muster any optimism. He was dejected at the state of Brexit – Phil led the failed guerrilla campaign in Westminster to attach a 'confirmatory' referendum to Boris Johnson's Brexit withdrawal deal – and seething at Corbyn's leadership. His anger at the direction of Labour had grown further during the campaign. He could feel Sedgefield was slipping away and could not hide his despair at seeing his life's work vanish in one day.

Later, on a brighter day, Phil and I returned to the Bay Horse for lunch – for both of us, our first pub meal after they reopened after the first lockdown. We were the only patrons indoors and followed the awkward one-way system to a broad corner table. The Bay Horse is your typically northern rural pub, all red and black carpets and gothic lettering on the walls. Helpfully, the BBC News Channel was streaming prime minister's questions over our shoulders, with Keir Starmer making his latest attempt to cut through Boris Johnson's bluster. Wilson's demeanour was less resigned than the previous time we met, but the only rays of sunshine came in through the pub window.

Over fish and chips, Wilson admitted he hasn't recovered from election night. 'I just thought that it was inevitable really. You know, you didn't know how bad the shock was going to be.' He has campaigned for Labour in Sedgefield since 1979 but found the last election the worst campaign he had ever fought. Not because of the inclement weather, the Tories or Brexit, but the leader he blamed for losing his seat. 'You've seen it all before and you're just thinking: this is worse. And then you had the likes of Jeremy Corbyn as leader of the Labour Party: this great party led by somebody who's as incompetent and narcissistic as him.'

When we later decamped to Phil's garden overlooking the village green, he brandished a generic letter from Corbyn apologizing for his loss. Across the bottom, the outgoing opposition leader scribbled some personal thoughts. They were evidently written in a hurry, and neither of us can fully make out what he is trying to say. Squinty eyed, the best I could interpret, is 'so sorry for the election . . . we had . . . future . . . all the best, Jeremy'. Phil intends to frame it in his study – alongside the signed original text of Tony Blair's announcement he was standing for the Labour leadership.

While it is Corbyn's leadership that Wilson primarily blames for the Sedgefield electorate turning against him – 'we give them Jeremy Corbyn, they just thought we were taking the piss' – he stated the decline began much earlier, in the days of Thatcherism. Although Sedgefield's last mine closed in 1973, a full decade before Blair became its MP, he bemoaned the end of the 'communality' that bound people together. It is a trend that has been seen in the UK and many other Western countries through deindustrialization, but the end of community collectivism is especially potent in mining towns where lives were so closely interwoven. Wilson said, 'In the 1980s, everybody was in poverty when the pit shut so it was very easy to find someone who was prepared to speak out on it. But now people suffer their poverty in isolation. Back then you would know who your neighbours were, where they worked. Today you don't.' Thanks to social media, however, we in fact know more about each other's lives than ever before and we have our own networks that are not based on geographic proximity – something Labour has struggled to adapt to.

Wilson's decades of campaigning in the patch led him to the conclusion Labour's support was broad but not deep. In the southern part of the constituency, voters were naturally more willing to listen to the Conservatives. 'But the rest of the constituency was always able to absorb the vote and come out with a big majority.' When the red wall was firmly red, he knew where to focus canvassing efforts based on where the coal mines were. Those days have also passed. 'Only if you're brought up here do you know where the pit used to be.'

Wilson's father was a Durham miner who ordered his son never to go down the pit, although, he wryly noted, 'I didn't need any persuasion.' Heavy industry dominated his childhood, but the Sedgefield of today is a broadly wealthier, if more segregated, collection of towns and villages. 'My father wouldn't recognize this place today. Back in his day it was all mines, now one of the biggest employers is the science and technology park.' And it is these new residents who Wilson identified as having turned away from his party since the days of the Blair supremacy. 'We've got to not be ashamed of people who vote Labour being well off. I mean for god's sake, we want to keep them well off! That's the whole idea of the Labour Party.'

It was not only wealth. On the doorsteps, Wilson struggled with his community on Brexit. His arguments about needing to think again about leaving the EU fell on deaf ears. 'Even in the referendum we were saying "these are the things that are at risk", but they weren't listening to us anymore.' Why? The poorest residents in the former pit villages of County Durham could not be convinced life could get any worse. 'In some of these housing estates, you would say to voters, "You know you're going to be worse off?" And they would respond, "I can't be any more worse off than I am now, so I want Brexit." When the Tories came along with the slogan "Get Brexit Done", who are they going to vote for?'

The loss of Sedgefield was a dagger into Labour's heartlands. But it was possibly inevitable: the seat has changed; its voters typify those who fell into the Conservatives' arms. Wilson rejects generic labels about how the area has changed. 'I've always hated the phrase "left behind seats". It's not the seats that are being left behind, it was the Labour Party, and the party hasn't changed with [the voters].' While Brexit and Corbyn were the catalyst for Sedgefield returning its first Tory in modern times, he agrees with the notion that the rot began with Ed Miliband's leadership from 2010 to 2015. 'There was something sort of weird about Ed, they [voters] couldn't associate him as being the leader of the Labour Party. And so they thought we were having a joke and then we give them Jeremy Corbyn. If that bond between us and Labour supporters was starting to fray at the edges, it was just cut.'

Just south of the Sedgefield constituency lies Darlington, the large town that also flipped Conservative at the last election. It is not technically a red wall seat, having returned Conservative MPs in 1983 and 1987. Yet it shares many characteristics of the other County Durham Tory seats: a mixture of well-heeled and working class, culturally separate from any of the nearby cities. The further south you travel from urban Tyneside towards the greenery of Yorkshire, the more the Tory vote stacks up. Darlington is where Paul Howell, Sedgefield's new Conservative MP, calls home. Whereas Phil Wilson exudes raw Geordie passion, Howell is understated. The pair are the same age but their backgrounds are far apart. The new MP is a middle-class property developer, the sort of guy it is a struggle to love or loathe.

Over socially distanced tea in his back garden – the sun was thankfully out on that day – Howell was still elated at his election victory. 'How fabulous is this, this is my world these days!' he proclaimed. His analysis of what happened to Labour was 'a series of waves followed by a tsunami'. The Sedgefield constituency has changed, but the political parties too have been gradually reshaped. When Ben Houchen was elected as the mayor of the Tees Valley region in 2017, which included the seat, he became the first notable Conservative voice for the area in two decades. Brexit was another wave, when people split with the message of the Labour leadership (even if Corbyn was a low-key voice for the Remain cause). Howell campaigned in all of these elections but noted a striking mood change by the 2019 general campaign.

'I've campaigned many times in parliamentary, local councils . . .

I'd never seen responses on the doors like I was getting. They were giving very short messages, you know, can we please get Brexit done? Sedgefield was a pro-Brexit seat, as you know. They were very much wanting to know why that hadn't been delivered, they wanted to know why their MP was standing against that idea, because Phil was very much pro second referendum.'

While Howell reckoned that anti-Corbyn sentiment was the strongest element that flipped Sedgefield blue, locality and a sense of place were also in play. 'The other thing that I would get is: "Where are you from son? Are you from round here? Do you understand us?" It's about locality and things like that, isn't it? And as soon as you start talking . . . that discussion evolves fairly quickly.'

Sedgefield's political transformation was most decisively seen when Boris Johnson visited the constituency to drum up Tory support. He was videoed leaving a rugby club with Howell and outside the crowd was chanting 'Boris! Boris! Boris!' To witness this, in Tony Blair's former patch, pointed to Johnson's personal appeal – an odd thing for an Old Etonian educated at Oxford. 'He has a connection with people that is just beyond belief,' Howell recalled. 'It's a charisma thing, and people believe that they can relate to him, and he relates to them. It's strange given his background, I agree.'

Howell believed that the sunny optimism at the core of Johnson's schtick – which caused him so many headaches during the dire days of the coronavirus pandemic – appealed to the people of Sedgefield. 'That to me is one of the reasons why the Conservatives have done well this time, because for too long politicians in this part of the world have talked the area down, so the fact that we talk it up is a different tone,' he said. 'If you look back at Blair, Blair always talked about coming through, representing this mining village in the north-east, that sort of thing. He never mentioned this beautiful constituency and all that it has.'

Talking up the area's natural beauty may work during the insurgent anti-establishment campaigns of 2016 and 2019, but it is likely to fare less well in a re-election effort. The Johnson government's plan is to focus on delivering tangible investment people can feel and see – micro-scale economic improvements in contrast to the Blair era's more macro approach to the whole country. Howell was focused on reopening Ferryhill Station, a disused railway stop closed during the Beeching cuts (nearly all red wall seats had a train station closed in the infamous programme). 'Hopefully we're making good progress on that agenda,' he said, noting that arguments about the station's renewal have been running for years.

'I got comments from some of the Labour group [of councillors] along the lines of, well, we tried to do that before but [Margaret] Thatcher stopped us. Hang on a minute, Thatcher stopped you? Right, but the following twenty-four years, you had Tony Blair as your MP. Initially an MP and then the prime minister. And nothing happened. Nothing happened in terms of local investment for this part of the world. That's the message I got back on the doorsteps: yeah we had a Labour Cabinet up here, and what did they do for us?'

It is a sentiment I have heard over and over across Sedgefield and it is one the Johnsonite Conservatives are aware of – no doubt voters will soon be asking, 'We've had a Conservative MP for five years, what did they ever do for us?'

Although Phil Wilson vigorously disputed the notion that New Labour took the heartlands for granted, Howell thought much of his election was based on a 'complacency that they were always going to get elected' and 'the effort on the streets wasn't as good as it could have been.' Although coronavirus has 'inhibited' Howell's efforts to be ingrained in the community, the new Tories will be 'all over' their constituencies.

Levelling up, as the prime minister calls it, is how the Tories hope to fulfil what was promised their new voters. Offering a physical embodiment to those first-time Tory voters that their faith was not ill-founded is key to Howell's hopes of holding onto Sedgefield. 'I need to be in a position where I can say, this is what me and my government have done, this is what me and my government are promising . . . we have to find a way, to use Ben Houchen's term, to show a "record of delivery, a promise of more."'

What that looks like is not too dissimilar to what Blair attempted during his tenure as Sedgefield's MP. 'It's training, apprenticeships, all that sort of thing . . . the infrastructure's about getting people to and from jobs.' Like many of the red wallers, and unlike many traditional Tories who think of fiscal conservatism and reducing the national debt pile, he wants the government to do a lot of spending. 'In terms of getting a community infrastructure in place, making sure that we do some-thing to try and get communities helping themselves through better resourcing of things like community centres, youth clubs, these sort of things, that have come under extreme pressure through the austerity years, but now we need to make sure that those facilities are back in, so you can actually build a heart of a community.'

To the question of whether what happened in 2019 is a trans-formation or a fluke, Howell naturally argued it is a longer-term change. 'I firmly believe that the Conservative Party has been moving more in the direction that would attract these sort of people, that the Labour Party's been moving against it. Brexit focused the mind and got us the eighty majority that we have now.' Even without Brexit and Jeremy Corbyn, he believes the

Tories would have won a majority in 2019. 'Might not have been as big, might not have been as strong, might not have included my seat', but Labour was on course for defeat.

One of the curious things about speaking to Howell is how uncontroversial his prescriptions sound. The red wall Tories are a diverse lot when it comes to finances: some are ardent free marketeers, others are big state interventionists who are devoting their first term in Parliament to demanding money from the Treasury. Howell's political hinterland is typical for a sixty-year-old, his youth dominated by trade union disruption and the 1970s winter of discontent. 'I believe in personal responsibility . . . it's the handout vs hand up argument.' Recalling his school days, when much of County Durham spent the working week on strike, his conversion to the Tory cause came through militant labour movements. 'It never felt right to me that the Labour Party wanted the union officials in Number 10. The union officials are there to look after their employees in factories or businesses.'

Howell's schtick of being a local businessman done good speaks to a desire for aspiration – no matter what improvements he secures on the ground. 'It then comes down to, who is your local guy or girl, and do you think they'll represent you? So I think that, on this particular occasion, the way that the election went, an implant from the south could possibly have taken Sedgefield, but they wouldn't have got the majority I got.'

The artefacts of Blair's time in Sedgefield have worn away. A decade after his election as prime minister, Blair made his last trip to the Trimdon Labour Club to announce his exit from front-line politics. The club closed soon after, going the way of many working-class clubs, and has become a carpet showroom.[8] Instead of spending an evening in a working men's club with live entertainment, social changes mean Trimdon's residents now prefer to drink at home or in one of the local pubs. The closure of this club – and many others like it – is another example of how Labour's connection with the community has broken. The social club is not the only bit of the Blair era that has changed. Myrobella House was listed for sale in 2020 as a 'unique period property' for £299,950, with no reference to being owned by the former prime minister. Blair said he returned to Sedgefield in 2019, before the election, and vigorously disputes any notion that he did not deliver for the place during his time as an MP.

'So what did they get in Sedgefield? They got all their schools renewed, and the results went massively up. They got a new community hospital, a new general hospital just outside the constituency. We have the lowest unemployment we've ever had. And they had massive improvements in pensioner poverty and child poverty. If you were to talk to those people in 2005, that's why they voted for us. We got major factories as well.'

While he blamed 'the distance of time' and 'ten years of austerity' for voters changing their mind on New Labour's record, there is a broader political point. While in power, the party delivered nationwide change to the UK that benefited Sedgefield and the other red wall areas. Schools and hospitals were improved. Child and pensioner poverty was slashed. The National Minimum Wage tackled in-work poverty. Where the party struggled was in singing its own praises. Even the most casual glance at Twitter at any given hour will see Conservative MPs talking up their electoral achievements. Instead, Labour has spent much of the last decade attacking its own record. As Blair puts it, 'The Labour Party itself was saying to those people, "We agree that was just sort of a Thatcher-lite government, never really did anything for you" and the Tories say the same thing.'

'I know again this is what people want to say because they're searching for some deep meaning in what's happened. We put in disproportionately large amounts of investment, you just take one issue. Miners' compensation. Nobody even remembers that now. We put several billion pounds into mining communities and miners' compensation. Most of the people that benefited as pensioners from the improvements we gave to pensioner poverty were in Labour areas.'

Not that this is a new debate. Harold Wilson's Labour governments of the 1960s and 1970s are still maligned by activists for their lack of ambition, despite their advancement in liberalizing society. Blair recalled this attitude from his first election success in 1983. 'Regional policy and anxiety over the loss of traditional industry, that is a debate that goes back seventy years. It was a dominant debate in the 1960s. That's why you have Peterlee [built in County Durham under the New Towns Act] and all these places set up. Our strategy was we invested heavily in the university sector and technology spun off from it in Durham, in Newcastle, in Teesside, we made a real thing of that.'

For Blair, it is about perception. 'If they feel that your party is completely out of tune with them, it changes their perception of what the party's done in the past – and if the party isn't standing up for what it's done in the past, then of course they're left without any leadership. That's why I have no doubt at all if you'd had a serious Labour leader in the 2016 referendum campaign, they would have persuaded a lot of those Labour voters that this Brexit thing was a right-wing Tory plot that was going to do enormous damage to their constituency.'

New Labour was also successful with its cultural attitudes. From its inception, the party was built on a Hampstead-to-Humberside electoral alliance: bridging metropolitan liberal voters, typified in the north London enclave, to the working-class voters in England's working-class towns. Brexit annihilated this alliance, but Labour's shift on other matters set the stage for the demise, according to Blair. 'The problem came afterwards when we broke up the New Labour coalition, and a vital part of that New Labour coalition is that we were strong on law and order, strong on defence. And actually, contrary to how history is being rewritten, we were pretty strong on immigration.' Ed Miliband meekly attempted to continue this stance, memorably with mugs promoting 'Controls on Immigration'. Whereas voters did not believe Miliband was serious about the issue, Blair argued his own credentials were strong. 'No one ever thought I was out of touch with the issue of immigration.

'The first thing we did was try and cut asylum claims, that was a great big battle. Then we had various immigration bills, all of which the Tories opposed, by the way. And then we had the identity card thing, because I said, rightly, the only way ultimately you can deal with immigration is to decide who's got a right to be here and who hasn't.'

But there was one moment where Blair was out of touch with Labour's heartlands on immigration. On 1 May 2004, eight Eastern European countries joined the European Union as part of an enlargement programme eagerly advocated by the Blair government. The UK was one of only three countries that did not implement transition controls, meaning its job market was open to millions of citizens from the new member states, known as the 'A8' countries. Despite the prospect of better paid jobs and a better life in the UK, the government estimated net migration would be 'relatively small', no more than 13,000 a year (with the critical qualification that the figure would rise if additional countries introduced transition controls).[9] In 2004, the year of A8 accession, 53,000 people migrated to the UK from the A8 countries.[10] In 2005 the figure rose to 79,000 and by 2007 it had reached 112,000. It was a serious policy failure: Labour had disastrously underestimated the appeal of the UK to these Eastern European citizens and poured the political equivalent of several drums of petrol onto the immigration debate. The rise of UKIP, Nigel Farage and the events of 2016 can be traced back to this moment when traditional Labour voters felt trust was broken. There was a clear sense they had not voted for this influx of migration, nor had they voted to change the make-up of their communities. It lacked democratic consent: it may have been part of the New Labour modernization agenda to improve the jobs market, but there was no specific commitment to welcoming further migration. It also created a new class of employment, which traditional working-class voters may have felt locked out of.

Blair admitted his government could and should have done more to tackle this issue. 'Now, I agree that after 2004 this Eastern European immigration became a much bigger thing, but we could have dealt with it within existing European rules. We could have done what the Belgians did and said, "Look, you have two months, if you haven't got a job, you go back." We could have made sure the seasonal workers were genuine seasonal workers. We could have done huge numbers of things to take care of that problem. But when we were in power, no one ever could say I didn't take the issue of immigration seriously.' That use of 'we' and 'I' could be a gentle dig at his immediate successor Gordon Brown, who attempted to tackle the immigration issue with his inept 'British jobs for British workers' campaign, which went nowhere. Or Blair could be projecting further, and be speaking about those who ended the New Labour project.

New Labour's economic message of the early noughties is ill-fitted for the post-coronavirus, post-austerity world of the

2020s. While Blair gave no credit to Corbyn for the surprise surge in Labour's vote – 'the 2017 election was a complete freak result for all the reasons we know' – he acknowledged that his erstwhile colleague stumbled on the need for a fresh economic message. Corbyn rallied Labour voters with his radical economic message, which is precisely what Blair believes Keir Starmer has to do. 'The trouble is, post the financial crisis we had ten years of austerity.' With a typical Blair soundbite, he sums up the debate. 'The problem of economic policy is very simple: the radical people aren't sensible and the sensible people aren't radical, that's the problem for progressive politics. So that's why, in my view, you've got to take the fact, the big fact of modern life is this technology revolution, and you've got to turn that into a narrative of optimism about the future.'

The things Blair would do, were he in power today, are similar to Boris Johnson: improving transport links, beefing up the UK's broadband network and adapting to remote working to 'create much more attractive places for people to come to and locate'. Not that this problem is exclusively an issue for Labour. Blair closely followed the 2020 presidential contest in the United States and believed the Democrats are facing the same issue as Labour. 'The problem is they don't have a modernizing economic message, their economic message is basically a bigger state, and more tax and more spending. The problem with that is the only part of that that's popular is the spending and the right wing is prepared to do that in any event.

'If Labour wants to get back, it's got to say this technology revolution is going to intensify and accelerate, there's no way out of it. We are going to manage it and harness it in your best interests, and here are the things we're going to do for that. And ultimately the Tory Brexit vote is a cultural vote that you can defeat. Because in the end, people will realize it's all very well but actually the economy has not got better.'

He was particularly animated during our conversation about the Labour Party's cultural divide with its heartlands, which became most obvious during Jeremy Corbyn's leadership, which was geographically and intellectually wholly rooted in the northern suburbs of London. Blair contrasts how the Conservatives deal with public perceptions about its stance on the NHS to how Labour slants increasingly leftward with its cultural issues.

'The Tory Party understand they've got a huge problem with the National Health Service, so they fall over themselves in professing their love for it. There's no end to the love that they have for the National Health Service, they realize they are weak on it. They constantly, constantly, constantly go on about how much they care about it but the Tory protestations of love for the NHS are hollow.'

The weakness for Labour, and an acute danger for Keir Starmer, is the party's left-wing activist base, which Blair warned could drag them further away from their traditional voters, particularly with political correctness. 'I cannot tell you how much they hate this tearing down the statues, sacking people if they made an off-colour remark. It's death to the left and that is what will keep the right in power, unless you deal with it.'

Blair does not think the red wall has gone for good, but urged Starmer not to be defensive on cultural matters. 'Keir will be smart enough not to engage in the culture war, but I don't think that's going to be enough for that vote, they're going to want him to engage on the right side of it. And that is not, by the way, "We don't care about black lives", it's "We can support the sentiment of these movements, but we're not subcontracting policy to them". So, whether it's Black Lives Matter, Extinction Rebellion, MeToo, trans rights, if you look as if you're in a negotiation with those groups over policy, you're not going to get those people back.'

Brian Lowes, having dispatched the last of his red wine outside the Dun Cow pub, concluded the next election will not be easy for the Tories in Sedgefield – despite whatever new projects their MP brings to the area. 'I'd be very surprised if we get the same result in four years. Boris is doing his best to lose the red wall with how they've dealt with [coronavirus]. It will have a big impact whenever the next election is.' Although Brian is unlikely to back the Tories again, his wife Janine felt otherwise, although was undecided about how she would cast her ballot. 'This is too posh of an area to go back. People might forgive the fact that Conservatives are trying their best – people seem to like a lot of what Rishi Sunak is doing. They might just say, "They can't deliver, we will forgive that."'

But she added a note of caution about her own vote. 'I kind of like Keir Starmer, he's kind of appealing at the moment . . . untested, he's a bit of a non-personality but there's something about him that's steady, he's handled things quite calmly.' Brian agrees. 'The main thing about Keir is that he's not Jeremy.' Or as Blair himself put it, 'With Corbyn, the doors shut in your face. You weren't even having a conversation – he was completely unacceptable and you're insulting us, they felt. With Keir, they'll open the door and have the conversation, and that's a big step forward.' Never mind their front door, Brian and Janine have already emotionally welcomed the Labour leader into their living room. Whether he stays there, or whether Boris Johnson barges back in, is the test of the next four years.

After spending time in the constituency, it is tough to see an electoral path back here for Labour. Sedgefield may prove to be one of the tougher red wall seats to win back. Once voters of Trimdon, Ferryhill and Newton Aycliffe went against the wishes of their grandfathers in 2016, 2017, and in overwhelming numbers in 2019, the historic bond with the labour movement was broken. It can be rebuilt, but it can no longer be taken for granted. Had this seat been in, say, Kent, or another part of the south that had a legacy of voting Conservative, its demographic profile would have made it a safe seat some time ago. With boundary changes set to take in more rural parts of County Durham, it could become even more Tory by the next polling day. In many ways, it is England's new bellwether: Keir Starmer cannot make it to Downing Street without winning it, Boris Johnson cannot remain there without holding it.

Labour's macro record for places like Sedgefield is strong, as the list of achievements Blair and Wilson rattled off showed. It is stronger here on a micro level than in many other red wall seats: the Hitachi factory, NETPark and copious amounts of new private housing are proof of how a Labour MP and a Labour government improved the seat. But the number of people I casually encountered who said, 'Labour did nothing for us', suggested the party did a bad job of selling itself, or it was simply not enough – the level of dissatisfaction I found in the area should not result from having Tony Blair as your local MP. Or maybe Labour was too successful: it made the seats richer and therefore more Conservative. Without a decent narrative for these aspirational voters, the party simply fell out of step.

Next, it was back onto the M1 for an hour and a half's drive south into Yorkshire – past the traditional blue patches in the North York Moors and the Dales, the cathedral city of York and market towns of Harrogate and Wetherby, into the urban core of what its residents insist is God's Own Country.

4. Wakefield

'All my early memories are of forms and shapes
and textures. Moving through and over the West
Riding landscape with my father in his car,
the hills were sculptures, the roads defined the
form.'

BARBARA HEPWORTH,
ON HER YORKSHIRE UPBRINGING

Simon Wallis was fired-up to show off his new wares as he greeted me at the front of the Hepworth Gallery, a low-slung, brooding structure on the banks of the River Calder in Wakefield. The gallery's car park, shared with a National Rail construction site, was deserted except for workmen in high-vis orange jackets and matching facemasks. The dark grey asymmetrical blocks fit neatly into the gritty landscape: rusting barges, decaying small factories, the grinding hum of afternoon traffic. Wallis founded the gallery in 2008, when the site was a muddy riverbank, and has been its director since opening to the public three years later. Before enticing me inside, he took me on a brisk turn around the well-pruned gardens. The plants were carefully allocated into themes, mixed with tasteful sculptures. A photographer from the *Guardian* was present, ducking in and out of bushes to capture the autumnal hues. My horticultural knowledge is next to zero, so I won't try to explain what was there. Wallis, it turned out, also knew little beyond the fact it looked pretty and was commissioned by architect Tom Stuart-Smith. He was more enthused about the building work.

Behind the gallery and gardens, red-bricked Victorian warehouses have stood abandoned for decades. They have been renovated as rehearsal and recording studios during the first Covid lockdown and, during my visit, were on the eve of completion. 'We have artists booked in to come practise and rehearse from London once they're open,' Wallis said, pointing at the blue tarpaulin. The call for such spaces was reduced during a year without concerts, but he was delighted to add another destination to Wakefield's cultural offering – first the Yorkshire Sculpture Park on the outskirts of the city, then the gallery, now the rehearsal space. Art may not be the first thought that occurs when thinking of the small west Yorkshire city – actually a large town with a cathedral – but Wallis reminded me the area boasts two renowned artists: Henry Moore and Barbara Hepworth. 'Any other continental European place would have celebrated that fact decades ago. But in typical fashion for this country, we're just waking up to celebrating our own homegrown talent'.

The airy gallery was designed by David Chipperfield – one of the world's most prestigious architects, meaning Wallis had the onerous task of making good on the £35 million investment.[1] When the Hepworth opened he hoped for 80,000 visitors a year. The first year saw 700,000 people pass through its doors and, before the pandemic, it was drawing in a quarter of a million annually. 'The substance of having a great architect, celebrating a great artist, already having an art collection, and working with some of the best contemporary artists has turned into a formula that's really great,' he said, as we arrived at a glass-walled conference room at the heart of the gallery. He launched into his case for why the gallery has been 'absolutely fantastic' for the area.

'Wakefield doesn't have an awful lot to draw people down here . . . the actual city centre isn't packed with destinations so it's helped build that profile. The fact it's called the "Hepworth Wakefield" and we get such a regular media presence means there is a brand.' The gallery has endeavoured to integrate with the local community, especially through education. Wallis has partnered with Burberry, which has its clothing factory in the nearby town of Castleford, to put an artist in every local school. 'Using creative and cultural education to boost the performance of kids has been really heartening and Burberry are delighted. They've now rolled out the programme to New York – Castleford and New York are collaborating, together at last!' he beamed.

Since its inception, Wallis has strived to ensure all residents feel welcome at the gallery. 'It's a hugely important part of how you get people feeling that these kinds of institutions are resources for them to use throughout their life and are not just for the privileged broadsheet-reading middle-class people.' It appears to have worked: around a third of the Hepworth's visitors come from the Wakefield district, two thirds from within an hour's drive and the other third from the rest of the UK. Two summers ago, Wakefield hosted the Yorkshire Sculpture International, which promoted the area's culture abroad.[2] 'I began to get people realizing that when they come to the UK, it's not just about London and the south-east. Yorkshire is not just about the Dales, or the Moors. You can come here and have an extremely fruitful cultural time.'

Cultural regeneration projects such as the Hepworth are much disputed in England's towns. Their detractors argue they create elite institutions that are out of touch, irrelevant to the daily grind, and create further alienation between different communities. Advocates argue they bring in money, tourism, jobs and help forge a new identity. As I mentioned in the Gateshead chapter, the Baltic Centre for Contemporary Art opened there in 2002, in a deserted flour mill on the banks of the River Tyne.[3] I adore the Baltic building and its aspirations, especially after a teenage summer studying photography, yet my opinion veered towards scepticism given the lamentable state of Gateshead town centre. Why spend millions on an art gallery when there are no decent shops? Why have a beautiful rooftop restaurant when almost every cafe in the town centre is deserted and struggling for survival?

While listening to Simon Wallis's explanation of how the Hepworth had helped Wakefield, however, my scepticism fell away. 'It changes the spirit of a place. You can start to feel civic pride growing. The palpable difference when I came here nearly thirteen years ago and now, it's night and day,' he argued. 'It is about making people proud of having a world-class institution that is accessible to everybody on the doorstep. It's not an elitist organization, it's one that definitely really does make an effort to ground itself in the lived reality of the communities that surround us.' According to the local council, the gallery has contributed £23 million to the city's economy since it first opened, laudable but still less than the original investment.[4] After our chat, I toured the deserted gallery – it was a weekday during the pandemic – taking in the Henry Moore sculptures, Bill Brandt's photography and the permanent exhibition of Barbara Hepworth's work. To have this space filled with such works of art lifted my spirits; I fully appreciated how it could do the same for those who live nearby.

Wallis does not, however, think the UK has perfected the cultural formula for regenerating post-industrial towns and cities. 'Too many politicians are not sophisticated enough to actually understand how to exploit culture-led regeneration properly, they don't involve themselves. They rarely come along to see what happens at openings. They still treat them as either elitist or irrelevant and they're neither of those things. I think a better understanding needs to develop, so we exploit the true potential of the institutions that we've created.'

Wakefield is both lucky and unfortunate in its proximity to the great Yorkshire city of Leeds. The larger conurbation has a stronger jobs base, better shops, more restaurants, so Wakefield has had to find something else. 'We more than match it for what's happened in the visual culture here, there's no question about it.' Wallis, ironically, lives in Leeds and commutes into Wakefield. 'I will be honest, when we first came up here, and we looked at Wakefield, we just thought we couldn't do it. We moved up from London and it was a shock seeing the level of challenge here.' Simon and his wife were initially taken aback by the cultural and ethnic homogeneity that was 'too alienated' from their past lives.

Since moving to West Yorkshire, Wallis has appreciated the need to better distribute opportunities across the UK. 'The centralization of power in this country is obviously preposterous. Centring everything in Westminster no longer works.' He agreed with my take that much of the 2016 Brexit vote was a revolt against that sense of dislocation. 'The push towards such a large Brexit vote in somewhere like Wakefield was that people were fed up to the back teeth of being dictated to by people that have no idea of the reality of what it's like to live here – no idea what the true needs of communities are. I think it was a cry of desperation.' He was harshly critical of recent governments for failing to present an alternative to heavy industry. 'We've not had a strategy for how these former industrial areas are meant to fully reinvent themselves . . . look at the stubborn levels of unemployment in some areas of Wakefield. It is industrious and successful in other areas too. So it's not a sob story of a place that doesn't know how to make anything happen.'

Throughout our conversation, Wallis gushed about the nearby Yorkshire Sculpture Park. 'It's no accident that Hepworth and Moore came from here, they come from engineering and mining backgrounds in their families.' Before delving into politics again, I went back to the car to head into the Yorkshire countryside to continue this mini cultural odyssey. In the heavy morning mist, the Mini's fog lights struggled to cut through, but the roads were glorious to drive along.

In William the Conqueror's Domesday Book, the 500 acres of greenery to the west of the M1 motorway was labelled merely as 'waste'. Over several centuries it developed into the Bretton Hall estate, occupied by the Wentworth family, who built an ornate bed in case Henry VIII decided to drop by – he never did – and hosted bacchanal celebrations with mock naval battles.[5] The family sold Bretton Hall and the estate to the local council after the Second World War, with the imposing manor becoming the Bretton Hall College of Education, training art teachers. In 1977, one lecturer, Peter Murray, had an idea to use the former parkland for sculptures, to inspire both students and those who lived nearby. The Yorkshire Sculpture Park was born. Bretton Hall College was closed in 2007, subsumed into Leeds University, and the hall is being renovated into a luxury hotel, but the YSP remains.[6]

Half a million visitors visit the YSP each year, including 45,000 school children. One of the children who came in its early days was Helen Pheby. She admitted there was 'very little appetite' for contemporary art during her childhood, when the West Yorkshire coalfields were in decline. But that visit 'triggered' something in her. 'Coming here as a child showed me there was another life, there was a window into something else.' After moving to Liverpool for under- and postgraduate studies in art, she returned to the sculpture park, first as a volunteer, and is now head of its curatorial programme, working with local schools. In her cramped but cosy office, packed with paperwork, posters and art history tomes, she explained the park's mission: 'What we want to do is improve the quality of life for people here and create opportunities.'

A decade ago, Wakefield Council's research concluded the biggest barrier for locals visiting was 'not knowing what to wear, not knowing how to behave, not having anyone to come with. But the biggest one was not being able to imagine a life where you enjoy art, so if it's not something you do as a child it's not something you do through school. It's not on your radar.' Pheby explained some locals are put off by the idea that sculptures and contemporary art are the property of 'an urban elite', but her answer is to first let them enjoy the open space. 'People will come for a walk. And then they gradually become more interested in Henry Moore, and then they might come into the gallery – it's definitely a place where people come as families, a place that people want to show off when their friends come and visit.' The park has grown from a hut and six tables to a long wooden and glass visitor centre, contributing £10 million a year to the local economy and employing 180 staff.[7] Along with the YSP and the Hepworth Wakefield, the area boasts the Henry Moore Institute and the Leeds Art Gallery. A whole culture scene appears to have arrived. 'It's a tourism-driven economic agenda around establishing this particular region as the cradle of contemporary sculpture.'

Having lived most of her life in Wakefield, Pheby is aware of the city's awkward standing with its nearest neighbour. 'We used to have a saying at school,' she said. '"Don't talk to me about sophistication – I've been to Leeds."' Tongue in cheek, but it spoke to deeper feelings about aspiration. 'I remember, growing up, Leeds being seen as a very dirty, down-at-heel city, and it's pulled itself up in a way that Bradford hasn't. Parts of Wakefield town centre are grim. Where I live is very nice but to judge Wakefield's identity just by its city centre would be a mistake. Leeds city centre is really thriving, and you can tell it's palpable – like when [department store] Harvey Nichols opened fifteen years ago, that was a really big moment.'

Further back in its history, Wakefield was known for being the 'merry city': Westgate, the main shopping and leisure thorough-fare, has a reputation for debauchery dating back to the sixteenth century. 'Wakefield used to be known as a really good night out – that was a big part of its identity – people came from the north-east and wherever. But that night-time economy is really diminished. It was always a bit rough but it was always fun, and there was an energy.' During the 1990s, Pheby said the culture shifted from partying locally to going out in Leeds. And much like Simon Wallis, she believes that one of the north's biggest problems is being too backward looking. 'We need to let go of a lot of nostalgia. We also need to be much more forward-thinking about what future could be possible for everybody.'

Pheby's view on Wakefield's 62 per cent vote to leave the EU was less about Europe, and more about 'an invisible demographic being given a voice'. Having spent much of her life in Wakefield, her perception is that for many of the city's residents, 'it couldn't get worse, really', and that there was 'a general lack of oppor-tunity and aspiration that has become generationally ingrained. It was being given a voice, it was wanting change, not necessarily leaving Europe, it was just about wanting something different.'

*

After enjoying the countryside it was time to explore Wakefield's maligned town centre. One problem was obvious immediately: parking was impossible. One-way systems and tight streets are unhelpful for an area where motoring is the main transport. Thankfully the Holiday Inn Express where I was based – overlooking a down-at-heel council estate – had one snug space left. The city centre has undergone several regeneration efforts: the Ridings shopping mall was one of the first in England to open in 1983. Other parts contrast each other: the Edwardian civic quarter has maintained some of the grandeur from the days it was West Yorkshire's administrative centre, while around the mainline train station a new complex of restaurants opened to coincide with the modernization of the station itself – I heartily recommend the generous steaks at Estábulo grill – but most of the centre is tired mid-twentieth-century shops. Near the bus station, every other shop is empty. One building imposes itself over the whole city. The first Wakefield Cathedral was built during the Norman age and the structure has been rebuilt and enlarged several times over the centuries. The current edifice is the work of famed architect George Gilbert Scott, who oversaw a restoration in the late nineteenth century. Wakefield's identity as a city is thanks to this magnificent building.

Simon Cowling was ordained as a priest thirty years ago and has served as the cathedral's dean for the last two. He met me outside the refectory dressed in black suit, shirt and jumper, only broken by his white clerical collar. Over fruit scones, he discussed Wakefield's identity. 'It's a former county town, which is why you've got this array of civic buildings.' But those functions have drained away, due to abolition of metropolitan councils in the 1970s. The typical residents today, he said, are more likely to travel to work around Leeds while those living in the five council estates around the city lament 'a lot of what's lost', particularly in the city centre. 'It's also about an awareness that Wakefield once had lots of independent shops that people took pride in. If you go out onto Westgate [the main shopping street], there are probably twenty empty retail units. They were no longer able to be supported because of the state of the economy.' After our meeting, I duly went up and down Westgate; his calculation was sadly correct.

Cowling has devoted much of his time as dean to visiting communities across the Wakefield district to examine social issues. Speaking softly but forcefully, he outlined his concerns about the lack of aspiration. 'A question mark about whether things are going to get better, and that leads to a kind of corrosive loss of pride in the place, and self-esteem. Part of my role here is to help people feel a sense of pride in the place, and understand that things can only get better, to coin a phrase, if we all work at it.' He praised the 'world class' cultural assets and lively arts scene emerging in the city, adding the area was 'less parochial' than some might assume. 'Wakefield has a lot of interesting folk who have come in from outside, who offer that kind of texture and colour to the local scene . . . it is by no means as inward-looking a place as it might be assumed from outside.' He said there is a sense among some that the city is 'a place either for people who are older and retired or a place from which people commute into Leeds, and where they therefore do most of their shopping, and where they know where the entertainment spots are.' A better range of employment opportunities would help that. He welcomed the Johnson government's towns fund, which offers small pots of money to towns that are struggling.

It is not hard to sense from our conversation that the dean veers leftward in his world view, although he is eager to work with all politicians and did not make any overly partisan state-ments. Reflecting on the New Labour years, he said that Tony

Blair did not speak up enough about the party's achievements in places such as Wakefield. 'They were desperate not to appear too left wing, frankly, not wanting to frighten the horses, they actually hid quite a lot of the redistribution that they were able to do, a lot of the initiatives they were able to begin, the family centres and so on, many of which have now closed, and which places like Wakefield benefited from.'

With our tea pots drained, the last crumbs scoffed and the sounds of the afternoon service beginning, Cowling concluded he expects the district to continue electing Labour councillors but remained uncertain about whether the party could take the seat back at the next election. 'People probably distinguish between local culture and national culture, and I think that shows a level of sophistication among the electorate which I find quite heartening,' he smiled.

Wakefield has all the key attributes of a red wall constituency: a solid set of Labour MPs since 1931, including Walter Harrison, the party's legendary whip who featured in James Graham's play *This House* with his noble efforts to keep the Callaghan government in office. In 1997, its then MP David Hinchliffe was elected on a secure 14,604 majority. The Conservatives came within 360 votes of taking it in 1983, thanks to the emergence of the SDP. But the city and the seat are palpably different to the first four stops on the road trip. While Blyth Valley, North West Durham and Sedgefield consist of smaller towns, Wakefield is one major settlement which forms part of a larger urban area. The city has a population of just under 100,000, but the district population, including the towns of Castleford and Pontefract, is three times that. Before Leeds became the dominant city of West Yorkshire, Wakefield was the administrative centre of the county, thanks to its prosperous industries. The inner city was once filled with mills and glassworks. Few of them are left today: I was only able to track down one still going, Castlebank Mill, on the river just south of the Hepworth Gallery, which employs 177 people producing 'non-woven industrial textiles', otherwise known as materials for items such as rugs.[8] The list of closed mills that once dominated the area's employment base is long. Since the 1980s, 45 per cent of local mills have become derelict or unused.[9] David Hinchliffe, who served as Wakefield's Labour MP from 1987 to 2005, pinned the blame on the policies of Margaret Thatcher. He told the House of Commons in 1990 that since she had come to power in 1979 his 'backbone industry' had lost 5,000 jobs.[10]

Textiles were a major part of Wakefield's identity, but as in Blyth Valley, mining was also a dominant part of its twentieth-century employment base. Hinchliffe told Parliament there were 4,395 mining jobs at eight pits in his constituency in 1979. By 1988, it was down to 565 jobs in one pit. In the wider Wakefield district, he stated that 17,000 jobs had been whittled down to just 5,000. When the Wakefield pits of Lofthouse, Manor, Newmarket, Newmillerdam, Parkhill and Walton all went under during the eighties – as much to do with exhausted coal seams as government policy – many miners were lucky enough to have the opportunity to transfer to the new Selby Coalfield that opened in 1983.[11] Several new 'superpits' were built, with large car parks to facilitate commuting. After the interruption of the 1984–85 miners' strike, Selby hit peak production in 1994, with 12 million tons of coal produced that year. But these new mines became unprofitable after the loss of government subsidies and concerns about the stability of the geography. All were closed in 2004, with the loss of 5,000 jobs.[12]

More poignantly, it was Kellingley Colliery, also in Selby, that brought an end to deep coal mining in the UK. In 2015, the last major pit in the land closed, with 450 jobs gone, down from 2,000 at its peak.[13] Kellingley marked the final end of centuries of deep mining. Today, Wakefield's biggest employers are wholesale and retail trade, but manufacturing in other sectors continues – particularly beverages. Coca-Cola employs 450 people at a major factory beside the motorway. Ossett Brewery, home to the delicious Yorkshire Blonde pale ale, has a similarly sized workforce in its brewing and warehouse facilities on the outskirts of town. Microbreweries such as Five Towns and Tiger Tops have emerged in recent years.

Wakefield's population is also more diverse than other Labour heartland seats, due to its urban nature. In the 1950s, large-scale migration from Pakistan began to buttress those British industries struggling to fill positions after the war, and Wakefield was in dire need of workers.[14] Men, typically from Mirpuri and Kashmir, settled in the Agbrigg area of the city, according to a local history project that charted their story. Arshad Mahmood told the project about his father Fazal, who left his family in Pakistan to live in a shared house with sixteen others.[15] Najeeda Asghar recalled the hard work of these early settlers:

> There was a lot of them in one property and they had to share everything . . . they worked long shifts, fifteen-, sixteen-hour shifts. Some would do days, some would do nights, so while some were on nights at Rawson's Mill, those at home would have their sleep and do their cooking. I think they found it very hard, being away from their families. That was the thing that kept them going. They had family in Pakistan, they knew why they were here, it was to support their families financially.

The migrants who came to Wakefield had little intention of staying permanently: they intended to work five or six years to earn money and return home. In 1968, immigration rules were changed so children could no longer travel alone to visit, which marked the start of more families moving to Wakefield. Abdul Aziz, whose father was one of those earlier settlers, said, 'When mothers arrived with their children it tipped settlement more to here. The idea of going back lessened once the family was here.' In the Wakefield district, the ethnic minority community is now 5 to 7 per cent of the 345,000 strong population. The political picture emerging from white working-class communities in red wall areas is clear, but I am eager to know whether ethnic minorities have undergone much of a change, particularly on the issue of Brexit. To find out, I crossed the marketplace from the cathedral to the shopping precinct to meet one of the local Pakistani community's most prominent members.

Forty-something Nadeem Ahmed is leader of the Conservative group on the Labour-dominated Wakefield Council. He has a background in education and now works as a freelance public relations consultant alongside part-time politics. Over an outdoor coffee and flapjack at Costa in the town centre – it was raining heavily and the awnings were near to collapse, buffeted by wind and groaning under the weight of water – he told me his family history. He explained how his father came to Wakefield from the Punjab in the 1950s to work in the mills. The majority of the ethnic minority community was and is based around the inner city, and prides itself on close family values, he explained.

'We believe the family unit has got a responsibility to look after its elderly, vulnerable family members. That stems from the Punjab, where we came from, and the Kashmiri, the idea that we have a responsibility for our family members whether they're elderly, ill or sick and we hope our children will carry that responsibility out as well. It's old, traditional working values: if I go to Barnsley, people believe that as well, they will always look after their grandma, or their aunts and uncles, when they got older.' He said there is some jealousy between generations about Wakefield's post-industrial fortunes. 'Leeds has a market, we don't have a proper indoor market, and they feel that we've lost out because of Leeds.' He exclaimed, 'We wish we were Leeds! The prosperity, the shops, the business. But it's tough for us in that sense. The city itself had a considerable amount of money from mines, textile mills, and it's declining.'

Ahmed studied at the University of Huddersfield, also in West Yorkshire, and remembered his time there fondly. He would like to see a similar institution in Wakefield, and hopes it would encourage Wakefield's younger residents to stay instead of moving away for their studies and not returning. 'Our youth are often getting jobs outside of Wakefield and moving out.' Some of his fellow councillors have argued that the town should be focused on apprenticeships to improve the city's jobs prospects, but Ahmed thinks higher education and small-scale manufacturing are both crucial. 'I feel the problem Wakefield has is creating jobs. There are a few big employers here, but it's trying to get more in because we've got Leeds on our doorstep and they'll favour Leeds over us.'

Wakefield's changing economic make-up has influenced the changing political ties of predominantly white communities, but Ahmed said the same is true across the whole city. His father was a strong Labour supporter, a loyalty founded on his time in the textile industry. 'It was automatic that they joined a union, the foreman would often be a unionist and encourage others to become union members. And from there, they affiliated with Labour. They weren't *thinking* Labour voters, if I can say that!' But now, he says, the older generation are mostly Conservative supporters, while the younger generation are Labour supporters.

Given the economic impact of the Thatcher years on Wakefield, it is still remarkable it voted Conservative in 2019. 'There was an anti-Thatcher element in there that Boris was able to detach himself from,' he said. The closure of the mills and Thatcher's racial attitudes may have made her unpopular in Wakefield's ethnic-minority communities, but Ahmed said the passing of time has dimmed those memories. Plus, the Tory party itself has changed, with several prominent non-white ministers acting as trailblazers. 'Sayeeda Warsi, Sajid Javid and other prominent Pakistani-origin MPs were able to forge and show that you can vote Conservative, you can be a Conservative and be a Pakistani and a Muslim as well. Sajid Javid was quite a force . . . People started rethinking their allegiance.' This shift is perhaps personified by someone I spoke to on a mercifully drier day – Wakefield's first ever Conservative MP.

The Robatary restaurant is in the undistinguished Bullring House building. Above is an employment agency, opposite is an empty shop that once sold mobility scooters. During this particular phase of the pandemic, restaurants were open for outdoor dining, so Robatary had installed outdoor heaters. Even with my suit, overcoat and wool scarf, it was utterly freezing. Imran Ahmad Khan, forty-seven, could see I was struggling with the temperature, so we launched straight into ordering and chat. He arrived with his parliamentary aide, and was dressed in a turquoise velvet suit and yellow knitted tie. Within minutes, I concluded I'd never encountered a newly elected MP so enthusiastic and eager to impart their life story.

Khan grew up in Wakefield. His father was a consultant doctor from Pakistan and his mother an English nurse, and he said he never felt fully at home within one community. 'I've always been slightly othered – growing up in Yorkshire in the seventies and eighties being half. Half the family being Methodists and me being a Muslim,' he said as our Diet Cokes arrived, thankfully without ice. His political memories were potent from a young age: first of the industrial action in 1979, when he was five years old. 'The whole way down Wentworth Street there were rubbish bags, because the rubbish wasn't being collected. All the noise! People were heating dustbins, and the dustbins were full of flames and so on. I was in the back of my father's Rover, and I remember being rather concerned. I asked him "Well, what is all of this?", and he said, "Oh, it's unions, they're worried about pay and fees."'

With hindsight, he said the city was a theatre for the political debates of the Thatcher era. 'In 1982, three or four of our pits in Wakefield were being closed. You're in the crucible of those whole arguments about contracting out, efficiency, state, individual labour.' Khan joined the Conservative party as a boy, and his first campaign was helping Elizabeth Peacock in her successful 1983 bid to become the MP for the West Yorkshire Batley and Spen seat. 'I remember she took me, hand in hand, when I was about ten – that was my first political outing.' Five years later, he became vice chair of the Batley and Spen Conservative association and continued his political activism when studying at King's College London. His career before Parliament is impressively packed with colourful globetrotting: studies at the Pushkin Institute in Moscow, a consultant for M&C Saatchi in London, UN assistant in Mogadishu, advisor on counterterrorism in Somalia and Afghanistan. When I asked what drives his politics, he launched into a mini soliloquy about how all of his experience feeds into a single word:

'If I were a stick of Blackpool rock, what would be written throughout the middle of me is freedom. The freedom to live, work, and worship as one wishes. There is no movement, no political party that champions the rights of the individual like the Conservative Party. That's at our core. If you look at the world – and I spent most of my career overseas in distant places – there is nowhere where you can live, work, and worship freely, that is not also an admirable, free society where business is safe, where corruption is low, where aspiration is built, and achievements are created. Pluralism, tolerance, and the freedom to live, work and worship are fundamental, and we take them for granted a little too often. But when you have lived and you've seen what happens when there's poverty of them, they become central to one's beliefs, as do free markets, free trade, and the invisible hand.

'I have seen such great poverty, whether it's in eastern Africa or Afghanistan or in war zones like Somalia. Nothing has lifted greater numbers out of the pernicious state of poverty than free trade, and for free trade we also require free markets, and also for free markets to really operate, for the invisible hand to roam freely, you need to have an educated population, people often forget that bit. This is why I have no time for those who are anti-capitalist, who beat upon capitalists, their mistakes. Capitalism is all about choice. It's all about freedom. And they mistake capitalism for mercantilism, which is about compulsion, which is about a lack of choice. Or, worse still, socialism and Marxism, which is about taking away control and allowing the state to choose for you. So, if, like me, the most important thing in life is freedom, the freedom to live, work and worship, the freedom to conduct your own business and make your own choices, not to have the state telling you what to do, but only for the state to be there to ensure that you can live life without threat or fear, let or hindrance, then the Conservative Party is your answer.'

It was probably the most passionately I have ever heard a Conservative speak about their political beliefs or party. His enthusiastic spirit for public service is strong across his whole family: Imran's brother Karim is one of the world's most renowned lawyers, elected to be the chief prosecutor on the International Criminal Court in February 2021 after serving as the UN's assistant secretary general.[16] Imran had spoken to his brother, who was in Baghdad, the night before our lunch and the conversation returned as usual to Wakefield. 'Whenever he thinks of home he thinks of here, we were talking about his favourite fish and chip shop, Barracuda, over in my constituency. This is home. What draws you home? That sense of belonging.'

With a first-time Tory majority of 3,358 votes, Khan's is one of the more comfortable red wall seats – benefiting from a ten-point drop in the Labour vote in the 2019 election. His vision for re-election is based on Wakefield as 'the crossroads of the kingdom', pointing out that its transport links are superb. Manchester is forty minutes away, Leeds ten. It has the M1, the M62 and the A1 and London is only two hours away on the train. He is full of praise for the cultural sector. At the time of our lunch, he was producing a manifesto for the city that would achieve the sort of joined-up thinking the Hepworth Wakefield has been promoting. The relatively small size of the city is something he's hopeful of capitalizing on. 'Wakefield, of course, it's a real city, but it's the most perfect size because it's got all the problems of a big, big city, but it's a wonderful place to test concepts, because you can really measure effect, and show that things are working and so on, and what isn't. Then it can be an exemplar we use for other cities and towns, not only across the north, but similar countries too.'

As well as being one of the most ebullient Tories I have come across, Khan is also one of the most enthusiastic Brexit supporters. Much of his victory in 2019 was down to his predecessor Mary Creagh, who took the opposite stance on the EU question and who he disparages as one of the 'Labour politicians from

Islington' in the vein of Keir Starmer. Khan said Creagh reneged on her promise to deliver on the referendum vote. 'In that cathedral there, we're still in the shadow of the sacred spire, she swore in the debate, in the hustings with the Conservative candidate at the time, in 2017 she said she would respect fully the results of the referendum, and would not do anything to frustrate Brexit.' Coming to his climax, Khan concluded, 'I think it is questionable because if you can't keep your promise to the people, I don't think one has a place in public life, frankly. Disagree, lose the argument, and still continue, because we're representatives, not delegates, quite right. But, don't say you're going to do something and not deliver and then do the opposite.' It is quite an accusation, so following our lunch, I sought out Creagh to see if she agreed that Brexit cost her seat.

While I was in Wakefield, Mary Creagh was in London. After losing her seat in 2019, she has moved back to the capital full time. We spoke during one of the full-lockdown phases, when she was out for her daily constitutional. My encounters with her prior to this were mainly during the 2015 Labour leadership contest, when she came in a distant fourth behind the other candidates. Her performances then and serving in Ed Miliband's shadow cabinet as shadow transport and shadow international development secretary were polished, the sort of spokesperson Labour was happy to put on *Newsnight*. We began with her early career, a curious reflection of Imran Ahmad Khan's. She too has looked beyond the British Isles, but Europe runs in her blood. The fifty-three-year-old was born in Coventry in the Midlands and spent four years working in Brussels. She took a European Studies degree at the London School of Economics before entering local Labour politics in north London. She was elected as a councillor for Islington in 1998, working closely with a certain Jeremy Corbyn.

Her marriage and first child delayed her ambitions for a few years – something men in politics do not have to juggle to the same extent – but she continued to harbour ambitions to go into Parliament. When David Hinchliffe retired as Wakefield's MP in the run-up to the 2005 election, she jumped at the chance to be selected – taking the train northwards from King's Cross every Friday, while continuing her day job – working on Islington council and looking after a two-year-old. After she beat off a left-wing challenger, she recalled life was hectic. 'We rented a house, it was a kind of home family project. My mum and dad came up on the train from Coventry at the weekend and looked after my son so that my husband and I could go out campaigning.' Those first few years were 'an absolute whirlwind', but she has fond memories of working with her neighbouring MPs: Ed Balls, who went on to become shadow chancellor, future leadership contender Yvette Cooper and shadow cabinet minister Jon Trickett.

'I had some really interesting times and some very positive experiences. People loved David Hinchliffe and there was a bit of "oh she's not from round here". But, you know, Ed [Balls] wasn't either and nor was Yvette [Cooper] and those kinds of mutterings disappeared fairly quickly.' Her first years as an MP were focused on campaigning: legislation to get Turkey Twizzlers off school lunch menus; justice for two small children who died of carbon monoxide poisoning on Corfu. In 2007, she was pregnant again and had to balance an prospective election – Gordon Brown's honeymoon 'election that never was' – with her pregnancy. She recalled her first trip back to Wakefield with her new daughter and son, and how she felt a deeper connection with her adopted home.

Wakefield, according to Creagh, mixes a lot of public-sector employment – which leans towards the Labour Party – with a 'very rich set of small businesses' and respected private schools. 'It's always had a kind of cultural life, a sense of its own self and a small, but very committed group of middle-class people and people with conservative values.' During her time as the MP, her successes included a multi-million pound redevelopment of the main Kirkgate train station, a new performing arts sixth form college that was at risk of moving to Leeds, a brand new hospital and, of course, the Hepworth gallery. She worked with Arts Council England to bring £8 million of funding for the arts to Wakefield to create jobs in the city. Boundary changes in 2010 made the seat more marginal, but it was Brexit that caused Creagh the biggest headache, which is not a surprise given her studies and career.

'I was always clear, as a daughter of an immigrant, that Brexit was a nationalist project. I think in the twenty-first century nation states that go it alone are weaker, more isolated,' she argued. 'Having been in Brussels and having literally got a master's degree in government, law and policy, I kind of knew what the treaties meant because I studied them.' She vigorously campaigned for Remain in the 2016 referendum and, unlike many Labour MPs, did not vote to trigger the Article 50 exit proceedings in 2017. 'I didn't vote to trigger the referendum right the way through. I just thought I'm not doing this, I'm not being part of this.' A strong majority of her constituency felt the other way, although Creagh said, 'People respected me for it'. In Theresa May's snap election in 2017, she was re-elected with a 2,176 majority thanks to a nine-point surge in the Labour vote, but there was also a ten-point boost for the Conservatives.

The following two years of Brexit warfare only increased her scepticism about Brexit and the government's ability to deliver it. 'Those of us who were following the process very closely, it was like the government doesn't really know what it's doing.' She felt May's withdrawal agreement was 'obviously bad' for jobs, livelihoods and incomes in Wakefield. Yet in her home patch, hostility grew as the parliamentary stalemate continued. 'It became nastier and nastier . . . there was one moment in the city centre, I think around the May elections in 2019, where we have ten sergeants, a riot van and six officers around us. That's not normal, it's not right you can't have conversations with people.' When the 2019 election arrived, when Creagh had fully embraced a second referendum and remaining in the EU, the mood in traditional Labour areas had turned against her and Jeremy Corbyn. 'One bloke just opened the door, saw my Labour rosette and just shouted "fuck off" in our faces. It was like, wow, you know, this is really bad . . . a feeling that the Labour Party was a middle-class elite that was out of touch. We weren't focusing relentlessly on the economy and working people's lives, on making things better for them. And that we didn't have the answers for what was going on.'

The election result was decisive, with a six-point swing away from Labour. Yet Creagh does not harbour regrets over how she acted. 'I approach that with a degree of humility. I approached it as a matter of conscience, because for me I can't bring myself to do something that I know will cause further hardship to people who are already struggling. I can't pretend that something bad is somehow going to be good.' In one of her Brexit speeches to Parliament, she told MPs, 'It'll be like voting against my DNA.' She puts the strong Leave support in Wakefield down to a proxy vote over economic hardship following the financial crash: 'A huge amount of unemployment and recession that carried on for seven or eight years, gradually tearing away public services. And because they [her former constituents] are so dependent on the public sector for employment, these cuts to the police, to the NHS. A lot of people, you know, Tory voters in 2010, came over to me in 2015. It's a very sort of fluid picture.'

Creagh also blamed much of what happened in 2019 and Brexit on her former Islington comrade Jeremy Corbyn. The day after the election, she confronted Corbyn in Portcullis House in the Palace of Westminster, enraged to see him taking selfies with young supporters after she and dozens of other Labour MPs had lost their seats. 'I don't think Jeremy did the cause any favours, he went to EU rallies without mentioning the European Union. He was lost in his own self-righteousness. The whole kind of movement and the momentum around his own personal political project, which I think, in retrospect, is probably not the same political project of the Labour Party's historic mission, which is to get people elected to Parliament. I think Jeremy kind of lost sight of that.'

Creagh has left party politics for good: after the election, she has pursued a career as a communications consultant and is a visiting professor at Cranfield School of Management. Her lifelong passion for Labour and European politics, however, has not waned, and she is impressed so far with Keir Starmer's leadership but warned there is no quick fix for seats like Wakefield: 'The task of putting it back together is very laborious, very time consuming, and hugely emotionally draining. There have been some big wins, he has detoxified our party, he is clearly a person of the very highest integrity, with a complete and utter commitment to public service. But I'd say that Labour has yet to develop a compelling narrative on the economy, and, in particular, the post-Brexit economy and a narrative on Britain's place in the world. And both are very, very deep, enormous tasks and it will require a huge amount of skill and political savvy to do those redefinitions.'

*

For some of my explorations of Wakefield, I was joined by an SW1 special guest. Matthew Elliott may not be well known outside of the Westminster bubble, but he is one of the country's most influential right-leaning campaigners. Through the low-tax campaigning outfit the Taxpayers' Alliance and the civil liberties pressure group Big Brother Watch, his influence on political debate over the last two decades is unquestionably high. But his most consequential legacy is in laying the groundwork for and delivering Brexit. In 2013, he founded Business for Britain, a Eurosceptic pressure group that made the case for reforming the UK's relationship with the EU. In 2015, Elliott launched Vote Leave, which was eventually designated the official Brexit campaign. He served as its chief executive, along with his long-time friend Dominic Cummings.

Elliott grew up in Leeds and was keen to hear more for himself about what happened in the 2019 election and how much Brexit played into it. The bespectacled forty-three-year-old arrived at the train station in Barbour jacket and flat cap and quietly observed my conversations with Simon Wallis, Helen Pheby and Simon Cowling (who it turned out he knew from his childhood days as a budding organist). His childhood memories of Wakefield were of a place with a more 'conservative tradition' than the 'emerging metropolis' of his home city. The cultural renewal at the Hepworth Wakefield and Yorkshire Sculpture Park impressed him and he was especially taken with the idea of how devolution can empower these places. The plight of towns was 'definitely a conscious part' of Vote Leave's pitch to the electorate, he said, pointing out that their infamous slogan of 'take back control' was as much about Westminster and the UK's political elite as Brussels.

Returning to his childhood, he recalled the debates of the Maastricht Treaty and the 'crucial turning point' when the EU morphed into the institutions of today. 'I actually remember choir practices around the early 1990s people talking about this. They were pretty outraged about political power shifting from the UK to the EU. So I could see from that, that there were a set of attitudes in the country, especially in West Yorkshire, and a certain pride in the UK that we could stand on our own two feet.'

As Elliott returned to visit his family and friends over the years, he said those feelings of disconnection festered and grew. 'Politicians who weren't actually standing up for their local people, who were more comfortable with being on the international global circuit, and were increasingly detached. The whole idea of taking back control and bringing back power to Westminster, into the UK, it was fairly obvious that would play well. It was done on the basis of lots of message testing and polling and focus groups – largely done, actually, around the time of the 2014 European elections when I got Dom [Cummings] to come and do a big project for Business of Britain. It was clear at that point that there was that constituency of people removed from the metropolitan area who felt left behind, let down and wanted to regain control.'

Although Brexit was primarily, for him, about sovereignty, he agreed with the common view that there was a strong anti-establishment feeling that grew from 2008 to 2010. 'I feel really strongly that the roots were forged in the period around the financial crisis and the aftermath. You had the country bailing out the banks at great expense to taxpayers and the injustice that people felt at that but going along with it to stabilize the economy. Then, of course, in the aftermath, you have the years of austerity when the country is paying the price and at the same time you had the MPs' expenses scandal. So it was the idea of not only the bankers, but also the politicians.'

On top of these grievances, Elliott believed there was a feeling among voters in places like Wakefield that they were 'being lied to about the effects of the expansion of the EU', which stirred passions. 'By time you've got to the referendum, people hadn't really seen their living standards rise. So not only had their wages not gone up in real terms since the financial crisis but with the austerity in the aftermath, people hadn't really seen public services improve at all, so people were feeling very let down by the government. And I think this was sort of a wake-up call to the government to remember us, we're here, and stop being diverted to the international stage when things go wrong.'

The folks I have met in Wakefield all cited confidence in their local image as the key challenge to overcome. As with the previous red wall stops on the road trip, Wakefield's existence is defined by its industrial past. Its local culture and community was once strong; now it feels uncertain. Is the city destined to be part of Leeds's commuter belt? Can the whole area be structured as a vibrant cultural destination? Or does it face further gradual decline, as the coronavirus-induced turmoil further destroys its town centre? The area has a Russian-doll structure of resentment: in the shadow of Leeds, Leeds in the shadow of London, and England in the shadow of Brussels. All that creates a sense of being far away from power and self-determination, which was spoken to in Vote Leave's all-purpose referendum slogan of 'Take Back Control'.

Local identity should not be underestimated. When Tory chancellor George Osborne began promoting the concept of the Northern Powerhouse in 2014 – linking together the great cities of Manchester, Liverpool and Leeds to take on the might of London – he argued cities were the future. We'll hear more from Osborne later, but one of his comments about this place struck me: 'the Boltons, the Rochdales of this world, the Wakefields of this world, they're not going to succeed if Manchester isn't doing well, if Leeds isn't doing well. But you've got to create two-way traffic between those towns and those cities.' The feeling I got is that the traffic is too much in one direction.

West Yorkshire's regional identity will be boosted by the instalment of its first directly elected mayor. The conurbation of Leeds, Wakefield, Bradford, Calderdale and Kirklees will cover 2.5 million residents, the largest economic area outside of London and the largest economic area in Europe without an urban transport system. Tracy Brabin, the former Labour MP for Batley and Spen who won the mayoralty in May 2021, says she quit Westminster out of a desire for palpable change. 'We've seen around the country what being a mayor can actually achieve and how you can change people's lives in a really profound, tangible way.' These so-called 'metro mayors', championed by Osborne, have sharpened the identity of some parts of the north, such as Manchester and Liverpool, but sometimes at the cost of subsuming the smaller towns around them. The local Tories in Wakefield are concerned that their new mayoralty will put Leeds first, and leave the other parts of the conurbation stuck in its orbit.

Wakefield's cultural institutions are undeniably positive and help the city stand apart from its neighbours. Their contribution to the local economy is clear, the tourism they encourage is welcome, their addition to the physical environment is a relief from the urban sprawl. I was sceptical of their power, citing my home-town experience, but as a visitor to Wakefield I have changed my mind. The cultural identity is something fresh that does not rely on nostalgia for a bygone era. When pondering how to level up the economies in the red wall, Wakefield offers valuable lessons of success. But these new identities develop gradually and do not offer all the solutions: the sculpture park has been around for forty years, the Hepworth for a decade, and the dominant talk in the town was still all about jobs, skills and infrastructure.

Wakefield's resentment about its standing in Yorkshire and the UK was heightened by the Brexit wars of 2016 to 2019. The trauma of the parliamentary stalemate following the 2017 election goes beyond one MP: even those who voted the opposite way to Mary Creagh – by backing Article 50 and a withdrawal deal – were wiped out by the Johnson and Brexit tide. Her personal situation was emblematic of Labour's emotional connection issues: her north-London political background, rooted in a European mindset, was so out of kilter with her constituents. Despite her best intentions, reconciling her personal convictions with those of the majority of her constituents may have always been impossible. In South Yorkshire, the story of one constituency and one MP in particular underlines how disastrous Labour's miscalculation on the Leave question was, and raises the question about whether the fissure can be repaired. It was time to drive another forty miles south, veering around the city of Sheffield, to Don Valley. Four seats into the journey, having skimmed around the big question, the next stop was the moment to tackle the main red wall issue head on: Brexit.

5. Don Valley

'If this is the idea, the end of Britain as an independent European state . . . it means the end of a
thousand years of history'

LABOUR LEADER HUGH GAITSKELL REJECTING
THE COMMON MARKET IN 1962

The Great Yorkshire Way sweeps in and out of Doncaster like
an erratic Picasso brush stroke. The road has the mundane title
of the A6182 dual carriageway, with the formal purpose of
connecting the large South Yorkshire town to the M18 motorway
and the new-ish Doncaster Sheffield Airport (voted the UK's
best airport three years in a row, apparently).[1] The Great
Yorkshire Way helps make sense of the Don Valley constituency:
the seat wraps around Doncaster like a smile, consisting of several
smaller market towns and former mining villages. Travelling
from the market town of Hatfield on the north-east edge to
Conisbrough on the south-west was a chore before the Great
Yorkshire Way.

Through connecting several of the nearby motorways, this
road was responsible for a major new development that has
brought thousands of jobs to the Doncaster area. Bordered by
the slag heaps from Rossington pit, the last mine in the area
to close in 2005, is the iPort: the 'i' represents international,

interconnected or, more accurately, intermodal. Unlike many of the UK's logistics parks, the iPort can take haulage from road and railway. From the front entrance, the park consumes your line of sight: six million feet of warehousing and logistics, the equivalent of fifteen football pitches. iPort was built in partnership with the local council in the early 2010s to capitalize on the area's transport links to the rest of Britain. Donny may be firmly in the north, but thanks to the phalanx of motorways and railways, in terms of infrastructure, it is essentially the middle of the UK.

After looping around the Great Yorkshire Way several times while avoiding the HGVs dwarfing the Mini, I found the off-ramp to the marketing suite – a stack of white cabins. I met Steve Freeman, who oversees the railway terminal, and Michael Hughes, a real-estate investor and chief executive of Verdion, who founded the iPort. Freeman stepped out of his maroon Mercedes convertible in a sharp suit – not exuding the demeanour of a former British Rail executive. Hughes enticed him to build the iPort in order to boost the project's green credentials. For long distances, 'one train can take up to seventy lorries off the road.'

Hughes, in a black turtleneck with professional grey glasses, first visited South Yorkshire in 1990 when he worked for a logistics company on the River Humber. He arrived at a time when heavy manufacturing and mining were dominant but in decline; he concluded the area urgently needed something new. 'Doncaster had a clear sense from the early nineties that it wanted to go to a different place. It wanted to be successful, and do good things,' he recalled. 'And just really good people. A really nice town.'

The project was the fruition of Hughes's long-held passion to integrate road and rail to 'move goods more efficiently'.

Doncaster was the perfect canvas. 'You have [River] Humber ports, you have the East Coast Mainline, you have long-standing great working communities,' he said as we drove slowly around the gigantic warehouses. The conversion of the former RAF Finningley base into the new regional airport and 'poor quality farming land' made this swampy motorway verge perfect. 'iPort as an idea was a hub that would appeal to modern industry and logistics businesses as part of a network, and where we could create a very high quality – in fact one of the first and best – intermodal facilities built in the last ten years.' Freeman said the project began almost entirely speculatively: 'I don't think they'd actually finished building it before Amazon signed up,' he said, in reference to the site's biggest employer.

When iPort opened in 2017, it aimed to bring 5,000 jobs to an area of England that has suffered from higher than average unemployment rates. Amazon employs over a thousand workers on the vast site.[2] Freeman said that from the beginning of 2021, warehouses rapidly filled up: 'We just can't cope. We can't build enough warehouses at the moment.' Hughes added, 'There's not only the number of jobs within the park, it's important to remember that it's a piece of a jigsaw that drives jobs by bringing other companies to the region.'

The drawback of iPort – and hundreds of similar sites dotted up and down Britain's motorways – is the nature of the work. Employment is often based on zero-hours contracts, long shifts and strict conditions. Out here, with the only visual stimulation being the traffic zipping up and down the road, you can sense the loss of the camaraderie from the old industries. As we continued to go around the site – the third phase is under construction – and past the freight containers being unloaded from the railway tracks, the stream of lorries arriving and leaving, it is hard to conjure up an ethos for the place.

Freeman shared some of these concerns: 'Despite the perception that some people may have, the jobs being created at iPort are real jobs. They're not just zero-hours contract types.' Logistics work is easy to attack, but Hughes staunchly argued these attacks are wrong: 'The community spirit is simply shifting into different industries. There's a patronizing tendency to somehow think that logistics is an empty warehouse with a light switch and empty boxes. It's not. We're talking about temperature-controlled buildings, we're talking about medicines, we're talking about Big Pharma and not just e-commerce. All of that complexity demands a lot of people and creates great career opportunities.'

Yet the vision of iPort is reminiscent of a different era for Britain, a pre-Brexit time when reducing waiting times for goods and trading barriers was the chief aim of policymakers. Whatever one thinks of the decision to leave the EU, there is no question that barriers have been raised in the short term. Speaking a couple of months after the UK fully exited the EU's single market and customs union, Hughes said the picture was still positive. 'From the point of view of trade, I think we're all reading there are some regulatory hurdles,' he carefully noted, adding that more goods are moving through the hub than pre-Brexit. 'From the point of view of volumes that are being generated for iPort, they're on the rise. And I think it's pretty common parlance now that the freight industry is actually seeing strength and growth. It's not because of Brexit, it's just not been interrupted by Brexit. Trade continues with the world.'

Hughes acknowledged there were 'clearly negatives' from a trading viewpoint but said they were mostly short-term or 'at worst, medium-term'. He argued the UK's freight industry is 'very, very good' and the UK is fantastic at managing complex supply chains – confirmed during the Brexit period and coronavirus pandemic, when supply chains remained mostly intact and fears of mass shortages proved unfounded. 'We can walk into a garage and pick up a sandwich but to get the product there it has involved tens of thousands of people. The industry is very sophisticated.'

In the run-up to Brexit, Freeman said there was a 'big rush of people bringing stuff into the UK', which iPort managed to cope with. While the site's volumes collapsed in 2020 due to Covid, it has now mostly recovered. There have been some opportunities too: iPort has been granted customs clearing status. 'We can now accept a train from wherever it might be from in Europe, through the Channel Tunnel, right the way up to Doncaster iPort. And we will clear it for customs so it doesn't have to be done at Dover or anywhere like that. And similarly for export it can be loaded here.' Based on conversations he's had with workers in the rail terminal, he said they mostly backed Leave due to being 'so disgruntled and so disillusioned with politics, generally; with the way the country was apparently going.'

Brexit was why I went to Don Valley: 68 per cent of the constituency voted to leave the EU – well above the national average – putting it in the top fifty of the most Brexit-supporting parts of the UK. For Labour, which officially had a Remain stance in 2016, the problem was clear. According to number-cruncher Chris Hanretty, 70 per cent of Labour constituencies voted for Brexit yet just 5 per cent of Labour MPs supported leaving at the time of the referendum.[3] The cracks emerged in 2016 but did not fully break open until three years later.

The story of why this corner of South Yorkshire so heavily decided to quit the bloc is essential for understanding what happened to Labour, given that the Tories never came close to taking the seat until 2019. After bidding farewell to Hughes and Freeman, I braved the M18 again for a twenty-minute drive to Hatfield.

*

The Brexit chaos between 2016 and 2019 was not only painful for all political parties, but the whole country too. David Cameron's abrupt departure from Number 10, the arrival of Theresa May, her botched effort to gain an electoral mandate to deliver Brexit, the gradual collapse of her government and the ultimate failure of Parliament to pass her withdrawal agreement, were all symptomatic of how the referendum came close to breaking parliamentary democracy. When Westminster collapsed into its own nervous breakdown in early 2019, even the Church tried to intervene. Justin Welby, the Archbishop of Canterbury, called for five days of prayer and urged MPs to avoid a no-deal Brexit.

With those higher thoughts in mind, and keen to learn more about the communities of Don Valley, my next stop was the pleasant town of Hatfield and the St Lawrence Church. The grade-one listed building was known to the Venerable Bede and has its origins in Norman times.[4] I met two of its church wardens in their parish office, which was consumed by bulky photocopiers for newsletters. Vivian Stubbs and Vera Owen became involved with St Lawrence six years ago, elected when the last church warden was disgruntled with the arrival of a female vicar (see *The Vicar of Dibley* for more details).

The pair had baked banana bread and small cupcakes, incredibly welcome after time spent on the South Yorkshire motorways. They both agreed with the impression I gained from walking around the village that Hatfield was mostly comfortable and middle-class – tidy shops, a mixture of housing, well-kept countryside. The opposite of what most people will think of as Labour's heartlands. Stubbs felt 'blessed to be living here'. Owen agreed: 'I don't think we do as badly as lots of other places do.'

The community spirit centred on their church came to the fore during the coronavirus lockdowns. The volunteers of St

Lawrence made over a million phone calls to stave off loneliness. 'We've got some people who've gone into isolation and are terrified of coming out, which is not good,' Stubbs said. The pair have also worked at the food bank – a partnership between the church and the local council. The typical food bank users in 2020 were those who had lost their jobs.

Owen said those in poverty in this western corner of Don Valley are overwhelmingly unskilled labourers reliant on zero-hours contracts. When the pandemic hit, much of their employment disappeared. 'I think it's a big problem here.' Stubbs noted that the £20-a-week uplift to benefits through the universal credit system had made an 'enormous difference' to the poorest. 'If you're poor you learn how to manage. Then somebody gives you an extra twenty pounds a week, that makes you rich. It has made the difference between us no longer having people coming in saying "I have no money because I've been feeding the gas meter as it got so cold."' Owen agreed with her that the pandemic, for many in the area, was 'incredibly difficult'.

The ladies felt the biggest challenge for South Yorkshire is aspiration. Stubbs's main grievance was 'trying to convince people that they're worth more than they think they are and that the way out of poverty is through education.' Owen said, 'I was brought up with education, education, education – you must be educated. That was your way out. But they don't seem to have that message in the same way.' Both said the biggest improvement that could be made locally – alongside maintaining that universal credit uptick – would be youth clubs and activities to help teenagers.

Did the pair feel there is nostalgia for the days of heavy industry? Stubbs thinks there was some pining for steady work, but not the kind of jobs. Owen added that the feelings were potent about 'the stable line of work, but I don't think people miss working down pits.' Although neither confessed to being political, they appreciated that Hatfield was a 'very Brexit area'. Neither backed leaving the EU, yet both voted Tory in 2019 – Vivian Stubbs for the first time, for reasons she could not quite articulate. Could the pair imagine going back to Labour in the future? Stubbs felt guilty about rejecting politicians they personally knew. 'In local elections, I might be inclined to vote Labour.' But for the next general, both demurred.

With the banana bread gobbled up, I headed westward out of the upper corner of Don Valley's smile to meet the Labour MP who was popular in the community – Owen and Stubbs praised Caroline Flint several times, as did Michael Hughes and Steve Freeman at iPort – but found herself at the heart of this schism between Labour's long-time supporters and Brexit.

Conisbrough may look like any other small town on the suburbs of a bigger conurbation, but it has an illustrious history. The romantic keep of Conisbrough Castle feels a little out of kilter in such an ordinary suburb. English Heritage reports it dates back to the 1170s, when William the Conqueror made it home to a Norman lordship.[5] During the eighteenth century it inspired Sir Walter Scott's novel *Ivanhoe*, set in England's Middle Ages and charting one of the last remaining Anglo-Saxon nobilities. In the twenty-first century, Scott's work has inspired all manner of buildings in Conisbrough, including a deserted pub overlooking Sprotbrough Cricket Club.

Sam Smith pubs are one of the delights of travelling in England. Inspired by George Orwell's definition of a perfect pub in 'The Moon Under Water', they serve cheap drinks brewed in Yorkshire – never ask for a pint of Coke or Carling – in dark wooden surroundings, with open fires most of the year.[6] Dripping in nostalgia, they are patronized by those who moan about the decline of old boozers. And students, who imbibe their cheap drink. Mobile phones are supposedly banned, along with music and TVs showing sports. Most of Samuel Smith's 200-odd pubs are in England's former industrial heartlands, and the brewery has done a fine job in rescuing buildings and providing a comforting destination for those who live in these towns. The Ivanhoe is a typical Sam Smith's establishment – and was deserted on the Thursday afternoon I arrived to meet Caroline Flint. It was just the two of us and an elderly waitress, just days before all entertainment venues were closed again for another round of lockdown.

Flint was one of the best-known MPs of the New Labour era and also one of the most idiosyncratic. She arrived in Westminster in 1997 as part of the 101 female MPs disparagingly known as 'Blair's Babes'.[7] Although she never rose to be a full Cabinet member, she was a prominent junior minister at the Home Office, the departments of Health and Housing, and the Foreign Office. A household name, if your household was in north London. Her final public perch was serving in the shadow cabinet, where she looked after energy and climate change under Ed Miliband. Now fifty-nine, with dark glasses and a bob of grey hair, she explained why her family settled in the area. 'I've always been a hands-on practical person who felt that you need to keep close to the people you represent, which is why I made the decision that if I was going to be selected in somewhere like Don Valley, it would be my home.'

The Don Valley constituency had returned Labour MPs stretching back to 1922, mostly with large five-figure majorities. Her back story shone through to activists. 'I come from a very ordinary working-class background myself. Not coal, but I'm the first in my family to go to university. I've been through quite a lot in my own life. My family lived on benefits, we never owned our own home. My sister and brother both left school at sixteen and went to work. I can understand that working-class culture, but also not being someone who had all the best chances in life.' She felt that the Don Valley Labour Party wanted an MP who could 'talk about something more than coal mining.'

After she was selected and elected for the first time in 1997, Flint said there were a 'huge stack of problems' that tempered New Labour's ambitions. In Don Valley, schools still had outside toilets. Half of the hospitals in the area pre-dated the foundation of the NHS in 1948. Much of the council-housing stock was in need of refurbishment. But the first Blair term helped her patch. 'The unemployment rate was twice the national average in Doncaster back in 1997. We had to put money into retraining, the New Deal programme for jobs . . . you can look back and there'll always be somewhere to say "Well, we should have done this."' Does she think more should have been done? 'Of course! Look at what happened here compared to what other countries like France and Germany did to support their industrial base, and still do.'

Given that she was an MP for two decades and Labour was in power for thirteen years, the obvious question I put to her was, why did her party not do more? She retorted that if the 2019 result was about economic decline, then how did Labour win in 2005, which came soon after Don Valley's last pit in Rossington closed? It was a good challenge. 'In 2010, with expenses and the financial crash – and this is before people knew about what was going to happen under the coalition government – we didn't win the election, sure, but we held on . . . why we lost Labour voters to both Tories, UKIP and the Brexit Party comes back to the straw that broke the camel's back: Brexit. And it is about immigration.' Such was the latent feeling about the issue that Labour voters gradually fled the party. 'We failed to understand people's concerns about Europe and about immigration,' she bluntly said.

'They voiced their concerns in the 2014 European elections, where UKIP won. They voiced it again in the 2016 referendum. They actually voiced it again in 2017. And then, when they still weren't being heard, they made it loud and clear in 2019.'

Immigration and jobs dominated our empty-pub conversation through a second round of coffee. When Flint was first elected, Don Valley was 'ninety-nine per cent white British', which has fallen to approximately 90 per cent – not a massive change, but enough to create feelings of dislocation. 'You can suddenly find in a village, overnight, the workforce is 50 per cent from Eastern Europe. Now, it's not that people have got a thing against Polish people. But they're saying, "Hang on, what's going on?"' Flint said those out of work in Don Valley found themselves applying to employers who could find EU nationals willing to work for rates locals could not compete with.

Flint was scathing about her Labour colleagues who were unwilling to debate the impact of immigration on England's towns. 'There was a London-centric point of view about this. They didn't understand what was going on in these areas and almost didn't want to hear it, it's too uncomfortable. It's almost like, "Let's just talk about the benefits of migration, the net benefits of migration". And yes, if you put all the pounds and pence together, it makes sense, they're paying tax, but that doesn't deal with community dislocation.' When she raised those concerns with fellow MPs, accusations of xenophobia flew. 'Whenever they started a speech about immigration, it would always start with, "Let me tell you about how great it is". I thought, *Well, that's fine for Camden*, but sometimes, you should just say change is difficult sometimes and start with, "Actually, we've got to make sure that immigration is fair."'

In the Brexit referendum, she dutifully campaigned for Remain but became one of the party's most ardent voices for delivering on the result. Unlike many of her colleagues who told the media and constituents they would back a Brexit agreement, Flint actually did. Flint recalled one strain of thought among Labour MPs that 'actually maybe losing seats in Doncaster and Grimsby was a price worth paying [to stay in the EU].' Flint backed Boris Johnson's revised withdrawal agreement in the autumn of 2019, stating at the time that 'the voices in our mining villages remain unheard, despite their support for Labour over many decades'.[8] But the eight-point national swing at the 2019 election from Labour to the Tories is proof that no matter how good a local candidate is, nor how in tune with their local electorate, their party's national standing matters. Between 2017 and 2019, the Labour vote in Don Valley dropped by eighteen points.

Despite regrets about the past, Flint holds some optimism for the future. She thought Keir Starmer had done well to neutralize Brexit as a subject, but warned the Conservatives' leftward policy shift poses a challenge. 'The Tory Party is not the same Tory Party that faced me when we were in government, the economics of the Tory Party has changed, it's a massive change. They're doing the sort of things you'd expect from Labour.' As we exited through the empty car park, Flint agreed that the red wall seats did not suddenly go in one heave in 2019, and pointed to two older examples of Labour's decline – Ed Balls' old constituency in West Yorkshire going Tory in 2015, and Mansfield in Derbyshire flipping in 2017. She also noted the 'astounding' majorities that Conservatives returned in 2019. Once again, she sighed at the attitude of her Labour colleagues: 'If you think it's going to be a flip back, then you are being as complacent as you ever were.'

Flint's successor, ironically, held the same position on Brexit. After a quick journey down the M18 to Bawtry – one of Don Valley's more affluent market towns – I met Nick Fletcher outside the Town House, overlooking the market place. The pub was not allowing punters inside, so we huddled beneath tall gas heaters. The sun had disappeared, it was utterly freezing. Fletcher was wrapped up with a bulky woollen scarf, I was shivering over yet another cup of coffee. Unlike his parliamentary predecessor, his demeanour was low-key. He has lived in the Doncaster area all his life, leaving school at sixteen and moving straight into an electrical apprenticeship at Doncaster's railway works. One of his first tasks was rewiring London Underground trains after the King's Cross fire in 1987. But as work declined, he was made redundant with sixty other electricians in 1994. 'I couldn't get a job, it was a tough time, I had no real experience,' he said. His story from there is a classic Conservative tale of entrepreneurship: on top of the weekly dole money, he was given additional funding to attend a course to form a business plan. After beginning with a £40 a week grant for the first year of his business, his electrical company has celebrated twenty-six years of business.

At the age of forty-eight, he employs thirty-eight staff. During his eighteen years in Don Valley, Fletcher could see the area needed investment. 'When you get into Westminster and you start hearing about the formulas that they use for infrastructure projects, you start realizing how badly we've been treated over the years.' His first year of commuting between London and Don Valley has further highlighted the gap with the capital. 'You realize the opportunities that have just not been up here, and there's jobs down there that people don't know existed.' His interest in politics is recent. He joined the Conservative Party when his youngest child reached the age of sixteen, when his business and family life were settled. Whereas Flint's politics came from the trade union movement, Fletcher's came from enterprise – similar to Mark Brown in Gateshead.

'When you're in business, especially when it starts getting

bigger, you start realizing how much you actually contribute as a business in tax, but also in people's lives. The more people you employ, the more issues you find out about in people's lives and you realize how complicated it can be, and how the government has such a massive effect on them.' His philosophy is for the state to 'interfere as little as we can', but to encourage aspiration. Fletcher added, 'I never had any dreams of being self-employed, but there was a need. I thought I could do it, and once you start, it gets a hold of you.' In a nutshell, as Fletcher put it, that is his story. He did not spend two decades on the stump, wearing down Labour's majority.

His five weeks on the campaign trail chimed with Flint's view that, for the people of Don Valley, it was all about one topic. 'For the people that wanted Brexit, we were the only party that was going to do that.' His background informed his Remain vote in the 2016 referendum. 'I did it from a business point of view more than anything else. We'd come out of a massive recession, and my business had pretty much done well up until 2008.' His enterprises turned a corner in 2014 but he was aware that Brexit would 'rock the boat'.

By the time he reached the doorsteps of Don Valley in 2019, he was strongly against a second referendum. Even though both candidates held the same positions on Brexit, he said there was a realization that 'the ones that did like her, of which there were many, realized that a vote for her was a vote for more of the same with Brexit, and also, a vote for Jeremy Corbyn, so they couldn't bring themselves to do it.' Voters he encountered were disillusioned with all politicians. 'People were just saying, "We've had enough, you're not listening to us."' He also concurred that immigration was a key issue. 'There was an awful lot of the Brexit vote based on immigration,' he said. He does not think those with concerns wanted all migration to cease, but that it needs more control. 'That's what's so significant about the illegal boat crossings that we're seeing [in the English Channel] – that's not controlled. We just need it cooling off a bit, bring it down . . . and until that happens, it's always going to be one of the top items on the agenda.' Fletcher said he took no pleasure at Flint's predicament and agreed he would be 'very upset, devastated' if he had lost the seat in similar circumstances.

His plan for holding onto Don Valley ties closely to the Johnson government's levelling-up agenda, starting with a new hospital. The Doncaster Royal Infirmary is in urgent need of replacement: the *Doncaster Free Press* reported it has a backlog of £11 million worth of maintenance and is landlocked by housing on all sides, so can't be further extended.[9] Fletcher's hope is for a new hospital on an out-of-town campus. He also hopes to gain freeport status for Doncaster Sheffield Airport and the iPort to incentivize further investment. But his efforts, at the time of writing, have yet to bear fruit. Doncaster was not included in Boris Johnson's first batch of forty new hospitals, unlike the new Shotley Bridge project in North West Durham. In March 2021, the prime minister told Fletcher in Parliament that his NHS trust was 'very much in the running' for the next eight buildings to be commissioned. South Yorkshire was also not included in the first eight freeports announced by Chancellor Rishi Sunak.

Fletcher was also eager to inspire confidence for jobs. 'I'll go into schools and give assemblies. I'm going to fill all these kids with aspiration, to try and cheer them, I'll do a lot of work on it, we need something at the end of it for them.' He thought the Tories have a 'very good chance' of turning around Doncaster's fortunes and making it a 'wonderful' place to live. He did, however, acknowledge that Keir Starmer is a 'completely different' opposition leader and poses a different challenge for his re-election efforts, even if Boris Johnson remains personally popular on the doorstep. 'They do like the prime minister round here. He's just got something about him, he's obviously a very intelligent person, but I mean, the people in Don Valley voting for somebody that went to Eton? It's just . . .' Fletcher trailed off. 'They just love him . . . I think if we can get through Covid, they'll vote for him again.'

Fletcher was preoccupied with thoughts of how the coronavirus lockdowns would impact his patch. Again reflecting on his time as a businessman, he concluded that ensuring businesses survive the pandemic is key to re-election. He predicted the Tories will win Don Valley again 'if we keep to the manifesto and come out of Covid as well as what can be expected', and could take more seats. 'You've got an awful lot of hardworking MPs. Everybody I know that won one of these [red wall] type of seats works really hard, and there's no reason why we shouldn't [win again].'

The journey of traditional Labour voters to the Conservatives cannot be explained without looking at the role of the UK Independence Party. The Liberal Democrats had been the natural protest against Labour in northern England, but UKIP usurped them. In 2014, the peak year of its influence, two Conservative MPs – Douglas Carswell and Mark Reckless – defected to the party from the Tories and won by-elections in Essex and Kent. It was the direct influence of UKIP that forced David Cameron to write a referendum into his party's 2015 manifesto. The 2014 European election campaign was the first time formerly staunch Labour voters of Don Valley found an affinity with UKIP. In the general election the following year, the party came third here with 24 per cent of the vote.

UKIP's campaigning success was almost entirely down to Nigel Farage, probably the most influential British politician in recent history aside from Tony Blair. As an MEP from 1999 to 2020 and leader of the party on and off for a decade, he did more than any other person to take Britain out of the EU and prompt Labour's electoral headaches. His litany of provocative statements on culture and immigration made him a *bête noire* for Labour and metropolitan-minded people. Yet over and over in my travels around England, he is praised in working-class communities. His cultivated image of the ordinary bloke in the pub – adorned with a pint of bitter and cigarette – put him instantly at home in Labour's former heartlands.

Speaking from his home on Kent's North Downs, the fifty-seven-year-old said the foundations of UKIP in 1993 were ideologically diverse. When he became chairman in 1997, Farage shifted the party towards people like himself: disgruntled Tories. 'I used to joke in the mid- to late-nineties that I knew it was a UKIP meeting by the number of Bomber Command ties in the front row. These blokes who were about seventy, seventy-five, would have their RAF blazers on and their wives would put their best dresses on. The voter base was very much the World War Two generation in those days, very much conservative. They saw Maastricht [the treaty, which formed the EU institutions as they are today] and all that had come since as a total betrayal.'

In 1999, Farage was elected along with two other UKIP candidates to the European Parliament, which he called his 'greatest day in politics' – the first time he kicked Britain's political establishment in the teeth. That first election was focused on courts, cost and sovereignty – 'all the things that Tony Benn and Enoch Powell were talking about twenty to twenty-five years earlier' – but the word immigration did not appear once. However, Farage soon realized that the EU's impending expansion eastwards presented an opportunity. 'It was going to bring in a whole load of former communist countries, some of which were quite poor . . . that was likely to be a very, very big watershed moment in British politics.' In the 2004 vote in the European Parliament on expanding the bloc, Farage and the other two UKIP MEPs were the only three from Britain to vote against. 'That was when I began the big crusade about opening the doors to uncontrolled immigration, that huge numbers will come.'

The party's brief flirtation with TV presenter and former Labour MP Robert Kilroy-Silk in 2004 – described by Patrick Maguire in the *New Statesman* as 'the godfather of Brexit' – expanded its profile.[10] 'He did a lot of good. He got the UKIP name out there,' Farage said. Prior to Kilroy-Silk, the party was strongest in the West Country, East Anglia and the south-east. In the 2004 European elections, UKIP won ten extra seats in the European Parliament, with the gains coming from the Midlands and the north. Farage also thought Blair's devolution agenda in Scotland and Wales stoked resentment in England: 'The difference it made to the psyche of the English working-class voter was remarkable. Suddenly, when England were playing football, on the housing estates of Newcastle, the crosses of St George were hanging out of bedroom windows.' With devolution, Farage argued Blair had fostered a sense that 'we should almost be ashamed to be English'.

Farage has made seven attempts in six seats to be elected to the House of Commons and failed in all of them – the last, in South Thanet in Kent, was the closest he came. On his fifth effort in Bromley and Chislehurst, he came in third place and pushed Labour into fourth. His campaigning highlighted an opening for UKIP. 'I was being treated like a bloody hero. Walking up the streets, people coming out of their doors and wanting to come out and talk. They felt a deep sense of injustice. They felt the Labour Party just wasn't for them anymore. The Labour Party was actually for the rich people, central London people now.' In 2014, UKIP won the European elections thanks to 'turnout in the Labour areas'. And by the 2015 general election, Farage said he was being vilified by the media and political establishment. He said, 'Nigel Farage has been made this national monster. I mean, far worse than [fascist] Oswald Mosley ever was . . . how I stayed sane I don't know.'

Farage reckoned the four million votes UKIP won in 2015 were very different to the four million in the European elections before. In the European elections, Farage said he attracted disaffected Tories, but it was traditional Labour supporters defecting to UKIP that helped the Conservatives return their slender parliamentary majority of thirteen. 'I could say this on the television till I was blue in the face. Nobody understood it. Nobody got it. The London-based press corps didn't understand it. And remarkably, the Labour Party didn't understand it . . . we were actually hurting Labour far more than we were hurting Cameron.'

The relationship between Farage and Johnson is frosty, but there is mutual respect. In his *Daily Telegraph* column in 2013, Johnson described the then UKIP leader as 'a rather engaging geezer' who shares many of the same attributes as Tories.[11] Johnson wrote: 'We Tories look at him . . . and we instinctively recognise someone who is fundamentally indistinguishable from us. He's a blooming Conservative, for heaven's sake; and yet he's in our constituencies, wooing our audiences, nicking our votes.' The pair may be too similar to truly get along.

Farage readily argued he was 'the gateway drug' for the red wall flipping Conservative, especially by standing UKIP candidates on a local level in places such as Doncaster. 'We really weaned people away from the Labour Party. And the more they saw the Labour Party write us off as being racist and extreme, the more they said, "But that's me they're talking about!" Until the tribe abuses you, it's difficult to recognize that it's not your tribe.' Had Labour not written off UKIP, Farage argued, these voters would never have made the full journey to voting Tory through him. 'The real problem for the Labour Party now is how do you get these people back?' Does he hold the answer? 'No,' was the firm reply.

Farage recalled an incident in South Yorkshire that demonstrates why he thinks the current crop of Labour figures won't win these places back. 'They just don't speak their language. I went into a working men's club in Doncaster in 2015. I was invited. I walked in and there were a lot of ex-miners: some pleased to see me, some not at all pleased to see me. I had a couple of beers, sat down and Channel 4 racing was on. We had a bit of fun. Ed Miliband's office was four hundred yards down the road, so I said to the governor, "How often does Ed Miliband come in?" Do you know what he said? "He's never been!" Because what would Ed say to a group of miners?' Despite being a privately educated stockbroker, Farage's everyman image found the same appeal as Johnson's.

Now that these disillusioned Labour voters have made the journey from Labour to the Tories, Farage does not see them returning. 'Once you've crossed the Rubicon, it's quite tough to go back. If Boris is sensible, if there is some belief that the levelling-up agenda is really happening – whether it is or not, it's a separate issue – whether people believe it is is what matters.' Unsurprisingly, he was scathing of Starmer for his cultural views, which reminded me of an encounter I had one night in a pub in Hatfield outside of Doncaster. Chatting to a couple of local men, I asked them about the new Labour leader. One bloke whipped out his smartphone and opened up a Facebook group of his mates and showed me a picture of Starmer and Angela Rayner, Labour's deputy leader, down on one knee – the symbol of the Black Lives Matter movement. 'There's no way I'm voting for him. Starmer, he hates white people,' the guy said. No matter how much I explained this was not what the BLM protests were about, they would not listen. 'If I was a Conservative candidate, standing in any election in the Midlands and the north, that's the picture of Starmer that would go on every one of my leaflets,' Farage said. 'Starmer's done with that picture. I don't see a way back for them, barring a catastrophic economic downturn.'

His final thought was on class and why it will be hard, if not impossible, for Labour to win its supporters back. 'There is a realignment going on in British politics and in American politics. We're seeing politics of the centre-right attracting working-class votes, but in danger of losing suburban middle-class votes. And it's the same in America, those Washington DC suburbs can't vote for Trump. But there are bits of the Midwest that voted for Trump that had never voted Republican in their lives. There is a big class change in politics. That, for me, is overwhelming. The middle-class/working-class divide that I grew up with in the 1960s and 70s has gone.'

Before returning to the people of Don Valley, I put these accusations about Labour's disconnect over Brexit to someone at the heart of the debate. Peter Mandelson has been in Labour politics for four decades: first as Neil Kinnock's communications director in the 1980s, then as a key force behind the creation of New Labour. Although his positions in the Cabinet as Northern Ireland and Business Secretary ended with controversy, his sustained reputation as the 'prince of darkness' speaks to his backroom role as the most important strategist and fixer of his generation. Mandelson has unashamedly kept the New Labour flame alive and spoken highly critically of Ed Miliband and

Jeremy Corbyn's leadership of the party. He is also one of Labour's most diehard Europeans, serving as the bloc's trade commissioner from 2004 to 2008, and crucially for the question of Labour and Brexit, as a director of the unsuccessful People's Vote campaign for a second referendum.

Speaking over Zoom from his rented farm, with a newly planted lockdown garden in the background, he sighed that for him Brexit was a 'difficult and raw subject'. During the first year after Theresa May failed to win a majority in the 2017 election, he explained that Tony Blair gathered a group of like-minded Labour figures to convince them that the British people could be persuaded to think again about leaving the bloc. According to Mandelson, Blair's argument at that time was: 'When people see the facts and what sort of deal is available; when they see through all the lies of the Leave campaign, we have a real opportunity.'

Mandelson said the pitch was 'very persuasive'. Even if the campaign was unsuccessful, he thought it could galvanize the pro-EU section of the UK electorate that could in turn exert pressure on the Brexiters in Parliament. But after a long tough year of campaigning, Mandelson realized the campaign was failing. 'As time went on, we managed to mobilize the Remain side very well but we were not gaining traction amongst Leave voters. We weren't converting people. We weren't winning the argument in favour of a second look.' He recalled, 'I said to Tony, "We're not gaining traction here", and he was put out by this. I said it again to him towards the end of this and he said, "I just don't agree with you." You have to understand that Tony never doubts his ability to persuade people, he is a great communicator and he wanted to offer national leadership at a time of crisis for the country.'

Mandelson was unhappy at People's Vote's inability to frame

the question: 'All the way through, I kept trying to focus people on what would be on the ballot paper of a second referendum, but it was insoluble. And they just wanted a referendum. Basically, they wanted a re-run, come what may, of David Cameron and George Osborne's original disastrous campaign.' The greatest 'what if' of this period is what Brexit would have looked like if the likes of Mandelson, Blair and the People's Vote campaign had focused on a softer exit instead of trying to overturn the result entirely. Mandelson explained that ideological purity took ahold for him and the former prime minister:

'Tony always had doubts about a soft Brexit because he believed Britain cannot become a regulatory satellite of the European Union and you have to see his point. I didn't want to become a regulatory satellite of the EU either, that's why I wanted to stay in the EU with full voting rights, because I know that you can't enjoy or exercise the sovereignty outside the European Union that the Brexiters were promising. The "satellite" argument led some to the conclusion that it was better to sever ourselves completely than settle for May's deal, which I accept now was an error. We should have supported May's deal as the least harmful option.'

One target of the People's Vote campaign was Keir Starmer, who was then Labour's chief Brexit spokesperson. Starmer is still targeted by Conservatives and hardcore Corbynistas alike for his backroom advocacy for another referendum – culminating in the party's 2018 conference in Liverpool when he told agitated activists that 'nobody is ruling out remain as an option'.[12] I was in the room for that speech and it was rapturously received. Few of the party's grassroots realized at that moment it would turn off millions of voters in the party's heartlands. Mandelson said Starmer was being 'kicked around like a political football' over the second referendum debate. 'Keir had massive pressure exerted on him by the People's Vote campaign but he was able to see that the campaign was not prevailing and achieving the traction it wanted.' Left to his own devices, Mandelson reckoned Starmer would have gone for a softer Brexit. 'He would have said, "No, we can't reverse this, we have got to go for a version of Norway."' Instead, the now opposition leader was 'caught very painfully in the middle of a pincer movement between People's Vote on one side and Corbyn on the other and that's why when it came to Johnson's final deal he decided he was going to follow his own judgement. He decided to trust his own instincts and put Brexit behind us once and for all.'

The *Sunday Times* reported in February 2021 that Starmer had called in Mandelson for advice on regaining New Labour's winning spirit.[13] So how did he think the leader is doing, one year in to the plan to win back seats like Don Valley? Mandelson carefully said, 'He's doing everything correctly, but not strongly enough and not fast enough.' His main advice was to find a forward-looking narrative. 'Keir has got a fascinating and empathetic family backstory but he needs to offer an account of the country's future as much as his own past.'

Mandelson was still sore at how the legacy of New Labour was trashed by subsequent leaders after Tony Blair and Gordon Brown. 'The Labour Party has just seemed unable, since we left government in 2010, to come to terms with the world – to understand it and interpret it for others, to respond to the global and technological changes underway with a set of coherent ideas and policies that seem relevant to people. As a result, we have been swept up in the anti-politics backlash that has kicked in across many parts of country. Quite honestly, if you are angry and disappointed because austerity has hit you and your local authority and community disproportionately, you are going to lash out at everyone, including those in charge who are nearest to you. At a time of austerity, where you do not have a vibrant private sector and secure incomes to turn to and you are very dependent on government spending, you are going to feel the pain of austerity a lot more than others.' He lamented that the resentment that was stoked up in the red wall during the austerity years was, in his eyes, mainly down to the collapse in the public sector, which Labour had relied on to regenerate those areas.

It was therefore no surprise people in those areas became angry. 'If you are also a minority not doing fantastically well financially as incomes diverge and a yawning gap grows between the very rich and everyone else, you are bound to become very angry. And frankly, you are likely to turn to anti-elite populists, nationalists, however simple their analysis and ideas. These are not policies, they're essentially ways of sowing division, exploiting people's anger, whipping them up into an anti-elite, anti-London, anti-establishment, anti-this, anti-that temper.' Labour, in his view, was not politically alert enough to see the tide of resentment that spilled over in 2016, 2017 and 2019. 'The centre left and centre right were clobbered by a tidal wave of anger and disappointment and resentment, which was much more skilfully exploited by the divisive tactics of populists than we were able to handle ourselves.'

Mandelson summed up the party's plight over the last decade: 'We just had too little to say, too little strength and skill with which to say it, too few people of any charisma or strength of personality to articulate it. After thirteen years of government, the party passed into the hands of people who were not able to rethink and remake Labour's appeal, and instead, devoted their energies to fighting internal ideological battles and attacking the record of the very Labour government of which many of them had been a part! Why on earth would people vote Labour if what they hear from a new Labour leadership is endless negativism and criticism of what their own party had achieved in government?'

To gauge if Mandelson was right, I went back to Conisbrough to find a group of such disaffiliated people.

The Ivanhoe Community Centre, named after Walter Scott's novel, is located between housing estates and luscious playing fields. On a sunny spring morning, I was invited to a coffee morning with the volunteers who run the centre. Most of the Ivanhoe's activities were paused during the pandemic, as the main function room morphed into a Covid testing centre (I was ushered into a complimentary test on arrival, thankfully negative). The function room upstairs was a hodgepodge of antique cabinets and armchairs, as well as having a small kitchen. Anyone growing up in northern England who has attended a christening or child's birthday party would feel at home. Four formidable characters waited and ushered me into the sole empty red-velvet chair, before handing me a mug of strong tea and gesturing towards a tin of McVitie's biscuits.

Carol Fleming introduced herself as the dominant figure who oversees the Ivanhoe. A retired pharmacy technician, she was the only one of the group not born in the town. Before the Ivanhoe opened in the mid-1990s, she recalled the community coalesced around a wooden shack on the football field that ran bingo nights, baby weigh-ins and dance evenings and hosted weddings. After the Yorkshire Main Colliery in nearby Edlington closed while still profitable and employing 1,400 people, the playing fields were donated to the people of Conisbrough and fundraising began for a more substantial community centre.[14]

Fleming became involved with the Ivanhoe seven years ago, after retiring and taking up keep-fit classes hosted there. When she took over the centre, her priority was to ensure the Ivanhoe was welcoming to all parts of Conisbrough's community. 'A lot of people thought when they were going past on buses that it was an old people's home because of the decor we had at the time. It was chintzy drapes and blue high-back chairs.' Barbara Moore, clutching a mug that revealed her age – 'Chuffin'ell! Tha's Seventy!' – jumped in to reel off all the activities the Ivanhoe hopes to restart when lockdown is over: Slimming World, fitness classes, the Mucky Paws and Dogs Trust groups, Pilates, Zumba, cinema nights, boxing clubs, and 'two Vikings who come in on a Wednesday evening'. To do what, exactly, was not made clear. John Jeffcote, a retired bricklayer who helped build the centre, is eager to restart his dancing classes 'whenever'. Carol Fleming is keen for the cafe to reopen soon and for the toddlers' group to start again.

I asked the group why they did all this? What motivated them to devote their retirement years to the centre and the community? 'Because we're daft,' joked Barbara Moore. But she also had a serious reason for her involvement. 'I do suffer with anxiety. And I find that coming here, and being with these people, has made me a different person. I like meeting people and I like being with people. I retired from my job at the racecourse [serving at the bar] and I would have just been sat at home.' Carol McNichol chimed in for the first time to explain her involvement was to stave off loneliness. 'My husband died six years ago and I came here for company.'

Although there was admirable camaraderie among those who run the Ivanhoe, I was curious as to how far it extended into the community. Carol McNichol spoke of the 'brilliant' spirit at the bingo nights and lunches, but added that there 'had been trouble with youths in the village'. The other Carol thought that family ties in Conisbrough were as strong as ever. 'Conisbrough and Denaby [another nearby village] are ex-mining areas, that binds us together. The men in particular, lots of them are miners. And

I suppose it's like ex-soldiers – they've kind of relied on each other to keep each other safe.' But Fleming agreed with the others that it was not as friendly as in the past.

Carol McNichol was born in Conisbrough in 1950 and has lived there all her life. She adores the place and would 'never ever move', despite her husband professing an eagerness to emigrate to Canada. A lot has changed, but she said several times that it was the same for all the villages and towns in the area. 'It's not just Conisbrough, it's everywhere,' Carol Fleming agreed. Both Carols thought people in each of the towns tend to stick together. McNichol joked, 'I would say we're more friendly here. Where've you come from? Well, we've accepted you this morning. From London.'

With the mugs of tea drained and the table covered in crumbs, we moved onto politics. Both Carols, Barbara and John are engaged with politics – they always vote, but despite their similar backgrounds, their allegiances differ. Carol Fleming comes from a Labour family, but is a long-time Conservative voter. 'I didn't feel Labour represented me . . . and then we got Jeremy Corbyn. I thought, *Well, I'm definitely glad that I never did before.*' Her politics were driven by life aspirations. 'I wanted a good job. And a nice house. And to have money to do what I want with it. Go on holiday, buy a car, and so I thought, well, probably they're [the Tories] going to help me more than the others.'

The other Carol was surprised at this. 'I wanted the same things, the house, but I never looked at it like that.' McNichol also came from a family of staunch Labour supporters. 'I voted Labour because I live in Conisbrough and it was the done thing. I've never ever questioned it.' McNichol admitted that she was still scared to vote Tory. 'You know, I've never put it into words before. I think I was frightened for voting Conservative, for going against it, like a religion. But with Jeremy Corbyn, I do think the same as Carol.' Barbara Moore concurred: 'It's always been a Labour area. So like my mum and dad, I voted Labour automatically.'

Throughout his fifty years as a bricky, John Jeffcote was a trade unionist. But his disillusionment dawned with New Labour. Blair turned him off the party. 'I just couldn't take it. I mean, look what he did with Iraq and Afghanistan, I don't think he should have gone into there at all. And ever since then I've thought, *Labour? No.* Then when Jeremy Corbyn came in that really put me off.' For only the second time in his life, Jeffcote voted Conservative in 2019.

Casting their thoughts to the next election, two of the Ivanhoe gang said they would 'vote for Boris' – person first, not party – one said the Tories and only Carol McNichol said she might go back to Labour. And what about Brexit? Four resounding votes for leaving the EU. Any regrets? Four more resounding nos.

Before my road trip, it was obvious that Brexit was a key issue that knocked down the red wall. But until speaking to the people of Don Valley, I had not appreciated the depth of the breach of trust between Labour and its traditional voters. The bond between them had been waning for some time, but Brexit has acted like a bleach for voters' past prejudices against the Conservatives. Voters who might have otherwise backed the Tories, but harboured a grudge for the party's role in deindustrialization, were given a license to support them. It is remarkable that in these former mining areas, those who loathed Margaret Thatcher now love Boris Johnson.

The breach is not a one-off either: in the 2017 election, UKIP's coalition of left- and right-wing working-class voters abandoned the party in large numbers. They overwhelmingly backed the Tories, although some went back to Labour. And again in 2019, the traditional Labour voters went against their tribe. There may be arguments and characters who can win them back, but there should be no illusions it will happen automatically.

When the dust settles and the debate moves on from the 2016 plebiscite, Brexit will prove more problematic for Labour than the Conservatives. The latter initially appeared to publicly suffer the most – as seen when twenty-one of the party's most prominent MPs were kicked out by Boris Johnson. But the party has not lost an election over it. The Tories did what the party does every couple of decades: it shed its past ideology and reinvented itself. The Corn Laws in the mid-nineteenth century saw it turn into the party of free trade. After the Second World War, it accepted the welfare state. In the 1980s, it became the party of free markets. And in 2019, it is now *the* Brexit Party. The make-up of its MPs, membership and voting base is now pro-Leave. For Labour and others, it is frustrating to fathom how the party can shift its beliefs so rapidly.

Yet the alternative is what has befallen Labour. The party is still attempting to straddle its old Remain and Leave coalition, that Hampstead-to-Humberside alliance that came into being when the party was formed. The specific issues around Brexit and the EU will fade away, but the identity question will not and it will take generations for voters to forget what happened in 2016. Nor is the divide in Labour's coalition new. Herbert Morrison, Labour's deputy prime minister in the early 1950s and Peter Mandelson's grandfather, remarked 'the Durham miners will never wear it' when France invited the UK to join the nascent European Coal and Steel Community, which morphed into the EU. Labour eventually embraced the European project, but it did not sign up all of its voters for the journey.

Now it faces the challenge of making those Leave voters feel as if the party is on its side. Gisela Stuart, chair of the Vote

Leave campaign, former minister and probably the sole Blairite Brexiter, recalled telling Boris Johnson during a campaign event in Sunderland, 'Remember, they just want someone to show them respect.' She correctly deduced that Brexit was about 'identity and belonging' and 'recognizing some of the legitimate concerns' about how society had changed. Labour's failure to do that, before, during and after the referendum, cost it seats like Don Valley. It may find a new formula to meet that challenge, but repairing that trust will take quite some effort.

Ian Austin, an apparatchik to Gordon Brown and later the Labour MP for Dudley North – another red wall seat that went Tory for the first time in 2019 – believed that Brexit 'turbocharged' the party's disconnect. He told me, 'It's a bit like a wife who's been telling her husband for years *you're not listening to me.* We didn't listen in 2010, we didn't listen in 2015. We lectured them in 2017 and 2019. So after years and years of being ignored, being lectured by this husband who's not remotely interested in what their wife thinks, the wife gradually is worn down. And in 2019 decides to divorce their husband. You can't just turn up with a bunch of flowers and a box of chocolates and say *I'm really sorry.'*

The UK's forty-year ties with the European project provided the nation with economic and trading benefits. But even its supporters know it created dislocation for certain industries. That is particularly true for coastal communities, dependent on fishing, which saw their livelihoods fritter away. My next stop was closer to the east coast, once home to Europe's biggest fishing port and felt the pain more than anywhere else. No one passes through Great Grimsby – it is at the end of the eastward road from Doncaster. Geography is too often underestimated in politics. Don Valley is closely tied to Doncaster, whereas Grimsby only has itself.

6. Great Grimsby

'Swallow the lot and swallow it now.'

CON O'NEILL, BRITISH DIPLOMAT, ON HIS
ORDERS FROM TED HEATH TO JOIN THE
EUROPEAN ECONOMIC COMMUNITY

The mist lay so heavily over the Port of Grimsby that the road was invisible. As the sun rose on a still spring morning, a blanket of faint heat and sunshine covered the remote seaside town on England's east coast, which was once home to the world's largest fishing fleet. The docks, which have welcomed cargo since the Danes conquered the region, are dotted with signs of its illustrious past. Many of the sloping warehouses and decaying offices from the fishing era are listed and cannot be put out of their misery. For the first-time visitor, these abandoned structures cast an inexorable shadow of decline over the town.

The days where a visitor could walk across the whole harbour boat to boat, without touching the water, are gone. The 900 trawlers from the fleet's 1930s peak have dwindled to just twenty, with the same rate of decline befalling the workforce, which once numbered tens of thousands.[1] The fishing industry is still at the core of Grimsby's identity: 'We sing when we're fishing' is the chant at Grimsby Town Football Club, nicknamed the Mariners. The town's decline can be attributed to a series of events: the

1970s Cod Wars between the UK and Iceland, the industry-wide push to end overfishing, and the UK's accession to the European Communities. The town's perception of the EU Common Fisheries Policy explains why 71 per cent backed Brexit.

Grimsby Fish Market, found at the far end of dock number one, opened in 1996 to primarily process catches from elsewhere. As soon as I stepped into the car park, the aroma of fish was overwhelming. A little too much for such an early start. Four refrigerated lorries were backed into the market and slowly being filled with boxes – the market processes 20,000 tons of fish a year – with smaller vans taking deliveries to the town's shops. Martin Boyers, its chief executive, occupied a glass-walled second-floor office overlooking the sea. He expressed disappointment that the fog curtailed the vista: only two boats were visible from his desk and only the occasional sounds of forklift trucks hinted at the industry below us.

Boyers comes from a fishing family: his father and grandfather were fish merchants. 'I've always been on the docks since I was a boy,' he said, in a forthright manner shared by all of Great Grimsby's residents. He noted that although catching has declined, the town's reputation for processing was strong. 'This is the major base in the UK, by a mile, for processing – therefore the largest distributor of fish, therefore the largest by volume of fish by an absolute mile.' The processing industry, too, has undergone changes, as the nation's tastes have become more refined. 'Consumers don't want skin and bones. When people go and buy haddock and chips, it'll be a piece of haddock without bone in it.' Having enjoyed Grimsby's fish and chips the night before, including an unwanted stray bone, I accepted he was right.

For Boyers, the decline in Grimsby was all down to the Cod Wars. 'Not Brexit, not Europe, not the Common Fisheries Policy . . . Iceland was a very small, expanding country. The first thing was when they expanded their territorial limit to twenty-five miles. That was a ripple. Then the next Cod War was when they expanded it to fifty miles. That was a bigger ripple. But when it got serious was in the late 1970s, when they extended to a hundred miles, then two hundred miles.' For the ports of Grimsby, Hull, Fleetwood and north-eastern Scotland, the new territorial boundaries – accepted by the UK in the face of Iceland's threat at the height of the Cold War to walk out of NATO – proved disastrous for the trawlers.[2] 'It was the ultimate demise of the deep-water fleet, because they couldn't go anywhere.'

Boyers admitted that nostalgia for the days of heavy fishing is heady: 'People think it was a marvellous time, they go on about the good old days. But nobody says anything about the amount of fish that was wasted, the amount of fish that went to fish meal.' It was also a perilous job: one common maxim at the time was that for every man killed in mining, eight died at sea. 'I wouldn't do it. It's a tough job, it's a dangerous job. And people still get killed and die every year going out fishing because of the nature of it. If you applied health and safety rules to a fishing boat, you wouldn't go on it.'

Still, the EU prompted anger among the fisherman of Grimsby, much of it targeted towards the Prime Minister Edward Heath, who was seen to have 'sold out' the fisherman when the UK joined the European Communities in 1973. 'They still blame Ted Heath for throwing away the fisheries. So it [Brexit] was seen as an opportunity to get it back.' During the 2016 referendum, Boyers thought there was 'a lot of delusion' that leaving the bloc would lead to a fundamental shift away from the Common Fisheries Policy that is widely seen to have disadvantaged Grimsby. Indeed, the fishing deal signed by Boris Johnson as part of the UK–EU's trade deal has failed to make much difference.

Over the last five years, Boyers said there has been a 'marked decline' in Grimsby's fishing. 'Quite a number of fishermen have thought that they should get out of it, take the money. The quotas have become a tradable commodity, the value of quota has outstripped the value of the actual vessel.' When the new fish market opened in 1996, it processed 20,000 boxes a week. Twenty-five years on, it is down to 4,000. The wider industry, however, remains one of Grimsby's biggest employers. 'The biggest seafood company in the UK, Young's, they're based in Grimsby. The second biggest seafood company in the UK is Flatfish, they're based in Grimsby. The third biggest is Seachill, they're based in Grimsby. The only supermarket that has a processing operation is Morrisons, based in Grimsby.'

Boyers took over the market in 2001 and soon saw the need to diversify. 'We were getting less vessels, we then thought, looking at the longer-term, that we needed to diversify, we needed to look at other opportunities.' Grimsby is now predominantly a renewables port. 'For the older generation, Grimsby is synonymous with fish. But the younger generation have been brought up where Grimsby is a renewable hub. It's a wind-farm base and that's a completely different perception.'

Grimsby's image as a deprived fishing town will take time to adapt. 'It's been assumed to be something that it probably isn't, because of its history connected to fish.' Boyers said it was 'quite a nice place', especially the surrounding countryside. Driving along the A180 from Doncaster, I was struck by the unyielding landscape and the isolation of Grimsby. There are no major settlements en route. Or, as Boyers put it, 'It has to be a destination, you cannot pass through it.' This remoteness has forged a particular identity. It has also made the sense of decline more harshly felt in some parts of the town. 'People do think it's just a bloody shit old fish place. No, it's not. If you went round, we've got a shipyard, we've got quays, we've got the renewable centre. It's absolutely spanking clean and tidy.'

With a fifteen-point swing from Labour, Great Grimsby elected its first Conservative MP since the war in 2019. The Tories have plugged away at the seat for several election cycles, coming within 710 votes of taking it in 2010. Boyers had a ringside seat for the town being won over by the Tories. Boris Johnson visited the Grimsby Fish Market in December 2019, posing for the customary early morning photo with a big snapper. 'Boris was very jovial, very impressive. We had a good one-to-one chat,' Boyers recalled. 'He was just sociable, talking to as many people as he could. And I was flabbergasted that he got this support. I thought people were going to have a go at him – that's what's happened in the past. A Conservative MP trying to get a seat – no chance! But Lia Nici stood alongside Boris, and they were treated like king and queen.' From that moment on, Boyers realized 'it was going to be a landslide'.

Not everyone is as accepting as Martin Boyers of the change in the fishing industry – and the disappointment over the new quotas in the UK–EU trade deal. One of the angriest is June Mummery, a fifty-seven-year-old fish auctioneer based in Lowestoft, Suffolk. Mummery was part of the Fishing for Leave campaign, which campaigned for Brexit in 2016 to 'ensure the restoration of the sovereignty of our Parliament and people, and, with that, the restoration of our waters to national control'.[3] Mummery later stood for the Brexit Party in the 2019 European Parliament elections and took a seat in Brussels until the UK formally left the bloc in January 2020.

There is no sole adjective that can capture Mummery's anger at the government and the fishing deal. After the Brexit trade deal was signed at the end of 2020, she turned down all media appearances. 'I couldn't speak for three weeks. I couldn't do any interviews. The BBC and ITV, I just couldn't because I was crying,' she said. 'They sold us out. This government just took away aspirations and our opportunities. By handing over our industry straight back to the EU when our prime minister said that he would take back full control and the 200 miles.' What did she make of Boris Johnson's pledge during the 2019 election to 'take back control' of the fishing waters?[4]

'He's useless. He didn't even secure our territorial waters. I mean, how the hell in your wildest dream could you ever get a deal like that? We have failed the boys and girls at school who want to go into an industry where you don't need a degree.' Given how Brexit has turned out, does Mummery have any regrets about supporting Leave? 'No, no, no.'

Mummery accepted there would be some trade-offs, and that the UK's twelve nautical-mile territorial waters might not be fully secured. But she thinks the UK's situation is now worse than the one Ted Heath negotiated in 1973. 'A hundred and eighty-six MPs representing coastal seats voted for that deal. They all voted for that awful deal. It's worse than what Edward Heath did.' During the referendum, she had a one-to-one meeting with Johnson and feels the betrayal personally. 'This was a golden opportunity to get full control. I don't go around lying for a living. I sat in an office with Boris Johnson. He told me "we will take full control" and I made damn sure I asked that about twenty times . . . I've got all his speeches written somewhere. The bloke is a bloody liar.'

During her brief time as an MEP, Mummery visited Grimsby and professed to being full of sadness after her visit. 'We went to see the processing side, that is great.' She went drinking with the fishermen in one of the town's many pubs and found herself at home but melancholic, and the fact that Grimsby has not seen the renewal promised by Brexit campaigners has made her pessimistic about its future and that of similar towns. 'There were so many jobs in places like Lowestoft, Grimsby, Hull and Hartlepool. They said that the GDP of the industry is not worth enough. Well, it's not worth a lot because we've given away the crown, we've given the emeralds and the diamonds to the EU.' She wanted Grimsby to be self-reliant. 'I want to see Grimsby with boats rather than relying on fish from overland coming. How sad is that! How weak that we have to rely on fish from Iceland. I want to see fishing boats back in that town. I want to see that town vibrant.'

Mummery, who counted herself as a Conservative supporter, is disillusioned with the party and argued the people of Grimsby will be too. 'They've [Tories] used fishing. Well, they've used it for the last time because they can't come back and knock on Mr Smith's door in Grimsby and say, "Oh, Mr Smith, if you vote for us, we'll bring back fish to Grimsby." We've done that and you've made us look like idiots.' She has even joined the RMT trade union, paying monthly £9 subs to further her cause. She has not, however, developed an affinity for the Labour Party, who, in her words, 'couldn't give a damn' about the industry. Mummery is mulling over starting her own political party to focus on the needs of these towns. 'I think that we need a party that concentrates on our coastal communities. I really do, because they're precious.'

Putting aside her own disillusionment with the Tories, does she think the Conservatives can hold onto Great Grimsby, given how the fishing pledges have frittered away? Before stating she never wishes to be rude, she argued that Lia Nici, the Tories' first representative for Grimsby, has 'done nothing' and she will debate her anytime. After a short drive from the docks to Grimsby's town centre, Nici was conveniently the next person I met.

*

The town hall is one of Grimsby's grandest buildings, a testament to its past wealth. Lia Nici greeted me outside for a wander through the town she was elected to represent in 2019. Fifty-one, with short blonde hair, Nici was cheerful and engaging, as you would expect from a former teacher. Aside from a couple of years studying in Newcastle, she has lived in Grimsby her whole life. 'Grimsby has a pull and a feel to it that I've never felt anywhere else,' she said as we crossed the road toward Freshney Place, the mid-twentieth-century shopping precinct. The open town square around the shopping area was filled with construction works for another redevelopment.

Before entering politics, Nici taught at the further education college, the Grimsby Institute, while concurrently working in the local media (she helped set up the town's own television station). She served as a parish councillor for several years and entered party politics in 2017. It was Nici's love of the area that took her into the Tory Party: 'Working in the local area, I started thinking about wanting to do something for the town I'm passionate about. I think Grimsby is a great place, great history, good-hearted people, and I didn't feel that we'd been particularly well represented.' She stood in the constituency of Hull North in 2017, across the River Humber, and decided she enjoyed political life enough to do it again.

As with Martin Boyers, Nici cited the biggest misconception about the town was that it was all about fish, but acknowledged the significant social challenges. 'We've been fishing for over a thousand years, the coast is very important to us. But with the loss of the fishing industry we have become very down at heel.' The end of the catching industry was 'catastrophic' because the town 'didn't have anything else to hang our hats on'. So her drive, and why she is a Conservative, is to reshape those perceptions. 'Grimsby needs people to speak for it in a positive way. If we were writing a brochure for Grimsby, you wouldn't put on there, "It used to be great but now we've got no fishing here", you would say we have everything we need. We have coastline, great spaces to live, countryside, we have great engineering skills, pharmaceutical skills.'

The town's name has long been a subject of perceived negativity. Sacha Baron Cohen's 2016 film *Grimsby* is an example of how the town can be held up as the archetypical left-behind community. 'People think, *Grimsby, grim, grim up north.*' The name, to my surprise, comes from an ancient legend. A Danish fisherman, Grimm, was awarded the area for allegedly saving the life of Havelock, the Prince of Denmark. 'Maybe Grimm doesn't exist – I'm sure it's a piece of propaganda,' she smiled. 'But the fact that Grimsby has that legend shows how powerful and well known it was across continental Europe.'

When asked to rank the factors that swung Great Grimsby for the Conservatives in 2019, she listed them in order: 'Brexit, Boris Johnson, and the dislike of Jeremy Corbyn.' Nici did not vote to leave the EU over fears about the economy, but her Remain stance did not hinder her campaign. On the doorstep, the support for Leave was due to a sense of abandonment. 'When there was a New Labour government, people felt there would be a change and there wasn't.' How does she feel about the fresh anger from the likes of June Mummery and the fishermen who backed Brexit and bought into promises of change? As we paused outside the permanently closed House of Fraser department store, Nici spoke carefully. 'There are things we still need to settle, obviously, because coming out of the EU and becoming an independent coastal state, we've got negotiations now ongoing and those negotiations are taking time. I think it'll probably take over a year to properly settle down.' She admitted exports had been 'challenging' due to 'having virtually no market in Europe at the moment'.

As we continued through the indoor market – also soon set for redevelopment – Nici said the most significant campaign factor was Johnson's boosterism. 'He's infectious. When you meet him, you get a feeling that he's got a good heart and wants to do good and make changes.' On the stump, she found his reputation was strong even in the poorest parts of the town. 'People were coming up to me and saying, "When's Boris coming? He's going to get us what we need. He's going to get us Brexit, a breath of fresh air."' Despite his privileged background, he passed the Nigel Farage test of someone voters would like to share a pint with. 'People didn't feel that Jeremy Corbyn was going to do anything for them other than give them a state-owned country where they would have to pay many more taxes, and lose their freedoms.'

Given her background in the sector, Nici's focus is on skills and education, particularly education after secondary school. Nici is a further education ambassador for the Johnson government and hopes to improve non-university education provision across the country. 'We've got to get people to understand that there are lots of very good jobs out there. Businesses are telling me they've got skilled jobs . . . I'm working with colleges and businesses now to talk about what we can do to have some joined-up thinking – talking to young people about how they can change things rather than thinking that somebody else will change things for them.'

As we walked past the 1960s library, with four tasteful naked concrete sculptures amid the pebbledash, Nici lambasted New Labour's education policies and how they changed perceptions in her old college. When Tony Blair set out his aspiration in 1999 to send 50 per cent of the population to university, the excitement was not shared in Grimsby:[5]

'It killed what we were doing locally. When I was working for the [Grimsby] Institute in the media department, we had a very good reputation. We were teaching university courses from Hull, Lincoln and Lancaster. As soon as the fifty per cent to go to university policy decision was made, all of that stopped. The entry level for getting into university dropped . . . we had people saying, "Well, I can go to university now with two Es, and your HND [a technical qualification] course is asking for two Cs." So a degree became a commodity, to go and study and have a lifestyle in a city university, rather than thinking about what would have been a more technical higher-education qualification.' Instead of people coming to Grimsby to study at its college, the focus on universities created a brain drain. 'They can't get what they want here in Grimsby, so they go elsewhere and then we maybe never see them again. Or they may come back when they're in their forties, when they want to have an affordable house that gives them half an acre of garden.'

Nici's 7,331 majority is one of the largest in the first-time Tory seats, yet she is aware Labour will be targeting her aggressively at the next election. 'They've had every opportunity in the last seventy-four years to actually do something and they haven't.' The coronavirus lockdowns have challenged Nici's ability to establish herself in the community. As we circled back to the town hall and Grimsby's ornate buildings, she accepted the pandemic had hindered her chances. 'I am quite aware that I have a very short window of time to try and make some change, to prove my worth to people, because I know that a lot of people voted Conservative for the first time ever and were incredibly nervous about doing that, so I have that weight of responsibility on me, and I will do my darndest.'

Could she envisage herself being a one-term MP, if the town turns on the Tories over fishing? Or if the people decide she has not done much better than her Labour predecessors? 'I will rise or fall at the next election depending on what people think of me, that's the beauty of democracy. But I will do everything in my power over the next three and a half years to stand at a hustings and say, "This is what I've been able to do, and this is what I've started to do."'

Before I met with the Labour candidate who lost Grimsby in 2019, I wanted to explore the fabric of Great Grimsby's community. The town centre is not as dilapidated as some of the other red wall seats I visited. Venture a couple of streets away from the shopping precinct, however, and the vast council-housing estates begin – not all of them well-kept and many showing signs of deprivation. North of the docks was my next step, West Marsh, one of Grimsby's core working-class communities, where the average house price is £65,150, according to Rightmove, compared to £327,797 for the rest of the UK.[6] At the centre is the West Marsh Community Centre, based out of an old primary school overlooking caged-in football fields. For two decades, the centre has provided activities for all ages in West Marsh. Chiefly staffed by sixty volunteers, it has recently hired its first, and only, paid member of staff. Alan Burley organizes activities and runs the centre. His aim is to link the needs of the residents with the centre's offering.

As with many of Grimsby's residents, he has lived in the town all his life and, at sixty-four, has witnessed the end of fishing and the struggle for jobs that followed. He has trouble with his leg and, with a black walking stick in hand, he moved stiffly to greet me. Outside of the main hall, beside a Coca-Cola vending machine and a noticeboard promoting the activities of the local police, he explained the centre's main focus was aiding the oldest and youngest. 'We've always done things like older people's groups, arts and crafts groups, and whole community bingo sessions. Since I came on board, we do tea dancing, we've introduced cricket for young people, and we've focused on the history of the West Marsh because people want to hear the stories. We're trying to start a book club.'

West Marsh's residents are mostly families and single parents. 'It's a solid, traditional community, a lot of older people who have lived in the community all their lives.' Most of the residents are white working-class men and women retired from the fishing community, although Burley said there was a growing Eastern European community in the last five years. The centre has started producing its literature in Polish and Russian to forge links. 'As you come in the centre,' he said, pointing at the creaking door, 'you'll see "*welcome*", but it will be in all different languages. We do get Eastern European people coming in and, ultimately, we want to engage with them.'

Burley reckoned many of the challenges the community centre encounters are down to the consequences of industrial decline. '[Grimsby's] on a par with Yorkshire when the pits closed, all those Yorkshire towns had to reinvent themselves. Jobs have been scarce – it's not unusual to see two jobs advertised and four or five hundred people going for them. But the community has a habit of just looking after itself.' He praised the togetherness in West Marsh. 'They'll stand by each other and when people are in times of difficulty, they're there for each other. The bad thing about the community is, like everywhere, we do suffer from antisocial behaviour.'

His main concern is that the area still suffers from unstable families and food poverty. 'If somebody said to me when I first started a year ago, "Do you think that there's a big issue with single-parent families in West Marsh?" The answer at that time would have been, "*No more than anywhere else.*" But now from talking to people, we know there is.' He cited a case of giving

£50 from the centre's funds to pay for shopping for a family where the main earner was on a zero-hours contract and lost their work during the pandemic. 'We found people crying, saying, "You just don't realize what good you're doing here."'

After discovering the number of families struggling with food poverty, Burley started a weekly larder at the centre. Ninety people in the community are registered to use it, half adults and half children. 'We give them enough food that will actually support them and their children so they can eat better for that week.' He lambasted the lack of attention to poverty as disgraceful. 'It's absolutely criminal that probably the biggest growing businesses in the country are food banks. In this day and age there shouldn't be need for food banks.'

While the centre caters daily for the retirees, who often visit for their only daily or weekly activity, it is the younger residents and those who are engaged in gangs that cause Burley more concern. Sometimes teenagers get involved because they are bored. 'That's not an excuse for it, but it's a reason,' he hastily said. 'That's why, in terms of centres like this, it's important that we look at how we run youth activities.' Centres like West Marsh are also important for dealing with problems that might otherwise be unnoticed. 'It's simple things, like if somebody is down . . . they haven't got the confidence to talk to somebody about an issue. Whereas in a place like this, it may well be that we're having a cup of tea and people come and talk to us.'

I asked Burley whether the town suffers from a 'poverty of aspiration', a phrase often used by Conservative MPs, and whether its residents struggle to see a world of steady work. 'Yeah, without a doubt,' he said. 'I think if you look at somebody who lost his job in the fishing industry and reinvented himself and found work in the food industry, but then lost his job, he hasn't got the relevant training or skills to move into renewable energy.' The problem can ripple through the generations as well as through an individual working life. 'You've got the grandfather who's a fishermen, you've got the father who's worked in the factories, and then you've got the young person who hasn't got the skills.'

And about outside perceptions of the town? Has Burley witnessed much change throughout his life? 'It's as happy today as I remember it. It was a different time. I never wanted to work with the fishing industry. Grimsby, everybody says it's a dark place, it's always raining and some portray it that way.' But he is convinced the town's location on the eastern coast has created extra resilience, echoing Martin Boyers almost word for word: 'You don't pass through here, you come here. And when you are here, you make the most of what it is. Yes, life's shit, too much crap at times. But you get by and think, *Life's not going to drag me down.*'

Tucked away behind Grimsby Town train station, which will have direct services again to London from May 2022, is Abbys Bistro – a smart restaurant down a little alleyway of boutiques and small shops. Waiting at a table was Melanie Onn, Grimsby's Labour MP from 2015 to 2019 (also its first female MP). The forty-one-year-old grew up in the town's housing estates and had a reputation in Westminster as one of Labour's more cheerful personalities, greeting me with socially distanced elbows.[7] As we tucked into fish – what else? – and wine, she began with how her upbringing took her into politics.

'There's lots of things that I'm interested in: animal rights, women's rights, and I think I had quite a strong sense of morally what was right and wrong.' Her teenage years were dominated by instability and poverty. 'There had been a breakdown in the family. I was a stroppy teenager, so I ended up living alone at quite a young age, seventeen. Then you get a sharp shock of the real world. I was living in a shared house with other similar-aged girls, who also weren't living at home, on benefits and still going to college.' After university, she worked at Labour Party HQ in London as a compliance officer before returning home to become a trade unionist. 'When I went to work for Unison and moved back up to Grimsby, it was great. I really loved doing that. I was regional organizer, batting for people to save their jobs, trying to organize bigger campaigns.'

Standing in the 2015 election, she boosted Labour's majority by eleven points before it slumped again in the post-Brexit election of 2017. The Tories surged in that campaign as the UKIP votes slid away. Two years on and the Tory vote rose again. Onn's share dropped by seventeen percentage points. The memories of that election campaign were raw. 'It was awful. From start to finish it was really soul destroying. The places that you would go and think, *This street is always absolutely supportive*, suddenly people would not answer the door, they couldn't look you in the eye, they'd be angry.' Grimsby's coastal climate did not lift spirits either: she recalled it was 'absolutely freezing and soaking', requiring a steady stream of hot food and drinks for sodden campaigners. 'All the volunteers were heartbroken on the night. And I knew it was coming.'

She places the blame on a long-standing trust breakdown between Labour and its traditional supporters. 'I know there are lots of people who don't like that, they don't want to say that Brexit was a massive factor, but it was. We can blame the party's position on it, which was ultimately a leadership issue, but there was an awful lot of deep-rooted cultural response where people just didn't trust the brand.' No matter how much Onn spoke on housing and leadership, the audience had tuned out. 'People felt everything we were talking about wasn't reflective of their lives.

Ultimately, they wanted somebody who was upbeat, they felt Boris was so sure of himself, he obviously knew what was right for the country. Labour's message in 2019 did not present its own version of that optimism.' The anger of Grimsby's voters about Labour was especially potent. 'We were suddenly all communists, Marxists. People hurling these labels, perhaps not even thinking about what that really meant . . . it was a bolt out of the blue.'

Like Lia Nici, Onn was a Remainer standing in a Leave seat. Although she ultimately voted for Boris Johnson's revised withdrawal agreement in October 2019, she did not back Theresa May's softer withdrawal deal earlier that year – something she now deeply regrets. 'Hindsight is marvellous,' she said. 'I should have voted for Theresa's deal, and I didn't. I was convinced by the party at the time not to and I stuck with my party. I look at everything it's led to now and I think if Labour had supported that, or even not opposed it, things would have been very different.' Even if she had backed May's deal, however, she was sceptical about whether it would have improved her electoral prospects – citing the example of Caroline Flint in Don Valley, who took a much more pro-deal stance in Parliament and was still wiped out in 2019. 'People felt it was self-serving and didn't believe it, because there was already such a lack of trust in the party. They were like, "Actually, you're doing this to save your own skin", whereas the fact was I spent many nights not sleeping.' The pain of that period was palpable. 'I found myself incredibly stressed and upset about these series of votes and trying to really go against my own conscience to deliver for a constituency that was so opposed to my own personal views. That was really difficult. I was in a real sense of turmoil.'

Labour has an illustrious heritage in Grimsby. From 1950 to 1977, the town was represented by Anthony Crosland, the great theoretician of post-war social democracy, who served as foreign secretary (Crossland's time at the Foreign Office was dominated by the Cod Wars, he joked that 'fish' would be engraved on his heart). Reflecting on her four years as Grimsby's MP, and the ninety-five years since the town last returned a Conservative, she felt Labour's priorities were out of kilter. 'In 2015, I was talking about a sense of fairness for people. If people wanted to talk about immigration as a concern, we could have good conversations.' Labour's stance on unfair energy bills and the cost of living during the Ed Miliband era did connect, she felt, but she said there was a disconnect under Corbyn. 'In the intervening five years, there has definitely been a drift from those things people feel are important.'

Onn has moved on from politics, for now, working as deputy chief executive of RenewableUK – a lobbying group for the renewable energy sector. From this perch, she is innately involved in Grimsby's efforts to regenerate into a green hub. The sector, she argued, is crucial for improving the quality of jobs. Fish-processing, for example, does not offer an easy life. 'It tends to be long hours on minimum wage. I don't know how people do twelve hours on a factory processing line, it's absolutely back-breaking, and it's cold.' The public sector, pharmaceutical and petrochemical employers provide jobs for the town, but she remained worried that prosperity is not widely spread. 'For some reason, there is still a sense that wealth hasn't fed through to the town, which I think is about the fact that not enough people who work in those places actually live in the town, spend in the town, invest in the town.'

As in my other encounters, Onn emphasized the uniqueness of Grimsby. 'It is misrepresented as having very little going for it. Sometimes even locally people will talk it down, but in actual fact, it's got a huge heart, and communities you don't find anywhere else.' Due to its geographical remoteness, the strong feel of neighbourhoods, which has been lost elsewhere in England's towns, remains here. 'Even when things are tough, people have still got the comfort of neighbours and family living close by. Bringing up your family here, it's brilliant, it's not ridiculously expensive, people can live a nice life on a modest salary.' She agreed there was deprivation, but it mostly has an upbeat outlook. 'People work hard and then want to have a lot of fun, that's an uplifting side of it. People with practically nothing, compared to the fortunate position I've found myself in, would give me bags of crisps and bottles of pop for my kids and dig in their pockets to give them pocket money.'

Onn maintains her passion for Grimsby. 'We probably don't talk about it enough, don't celebrate it enough, and there's a lot of desire to make things better for more people, so there's a lot of people who are really committed to that notion of community, and trying to make things better for more people.' But does she think Great Grimsby will go back to Labour at some point? 'Yeah, I don't know when, but yes.' The numbers are tough for the party. The challenge of overturning a 7,331-vote majority will be 'significant and shouldn't be underestimated', in her view – especially if the Conservatives continue to ride high nationally. Onn had not yet made up her mind as to whether she would try to win the seat back. Her love for Grimsby is great, but the bruising experience of losing her seat has not been easy to overcome.

Every person I encountered in Grimsby referenced the uniqueness of its community, which weathered the collapse of its fishing industry. Whether it was mining in Northumberland, steel in County Durham or fishing in Lincolnshire, there was a collectivized lifestyle in the red wall that bound people together. In seats closer to urban centres, with better connectivity to the rest of England, this community ethos has more rapidly withered away, but has continued to thrive in more isolated places. Much of the decline in this collectivization occurred during the 1980s, when Margaret Thatcher shed the UK's economy of its less productive sectors. Opposing her at the House of Commons Dispatch Box for seven of her eleven years in Downing Street was Neil Kinnock. A son of the Welsh mining valleys, he took over the party following its disastrous 1983 general election result (only worsened in modern times by its result in 2019). Through two general elections, he eased Labour away from its more left-wing elements, ejected radical entryists and paved the way for the New Labour modernization project. Lord Kinnock, still an active member of the House of Lords at seventy-nine, sees many parallels between the party's challenges in the early 1980s and those it faces in 2021.

Speaking from North London, Kinnock expressed surprise that Labour did not do even worse in 2019. 'You only had to knock on any ten doors, especially in Labour seats, to know the breadth and depth of the antagonism towards what people thought Labour had become.' He placed much blame on the leadership, seeing the election outcome more as 'an active rejection of Corbyn's Labour' than any active support for Johnson's Tories. He harked back to the February 1974 election in his old constituency of Islwyn in South Wales to explain why the red wall collapsed so dramatically:

'My dearest comrade and friend Barry Moore and I, together with a couple of other mates, canvassed the one Tory street in my constituency. It had been Tory since 1930 . . . we usually went there just so the bastards couldn't say, "We never see you." We were walking away after getting the usual redneck rubbish and going up to the pub. And I said to Barry and my agent,

"What a bunch of bastards." And Barry said, "Yep, but you better hope that those bastards never get organized." And I've remembered that to this day. He should have added, "and financed, assembled and regimented." The working-class Tories are not an isolated crop who are separated from the communities in which they live. They have relatives, they have friends, they have workmates, they have drinking buddies. When an area switches, it switches rapidly and suddenly.'

I put to Kinnock the view that the red wall's collectivized constituencies have become richer in the years since his time in frontline politics, which has in turn made them more economically and culturally Conservative-leaning. He shot back that they may have become 'more capable of consuming' but the richness has been harmed in other ways. 'I'm not being misty-eyed when I say I am not sure they are richer, because a lot of the dependable social fabric of enrichment is not monetary,' he said. 'It isn't that they were collectivized, but that they were securitized in the world. Going way back, there was widespread poverty. The universality of poverty was in itself cohering. Solidarity flourished as a great defence mechanism, but also as a platform for advancement. What's gone is that commonality.' Shared poverty, however, is still poverty, but Kinnock continued to decry how British society has changed. 'The individualism that's fostered is a source of choice, but it's also a source of weakness and insecurity. You're on your own. In the previous decades, the one thing you weren't, in richness and then poverty, was on your own.'

Kinnock did not serve in the New Labour governments – he was a European Commissioner from 1995 to 2004 before rising to the House of Lords – but acted as a mentor and (sometimes critical) friend to the Blair government. Does he think the voters of Grimsby were taken for granted? 'The important thing is people felt they were being taken for granted,' he replied. He blamed the attitude of New Labour, with its electoral sights focused on the wealthier marginal seats in the south of England, for creating such an impression – and for not speaking up about socialist ideals. 'People did vote to reject the Tories, but they also voted to have a new start. Labour had a real mandate, but they never convinced themselves that, to use that horrible phrase, they were the natural party of government.' Kinnock strongly felt that the failure to speak of Labour's universal ideals, and show the fruits of its reforms to the public sector, meant there was no national sense of renewal. 'Tony didn't fully comprehend the idea that the source of individual liberty is collective provision, never got hold of that really. It just wasn't part of him. Gordon fully comprehended it but didn't speak about it.'

The feelings that Labour did not care – nor the Conservatives – fostered the Brexit vote. 'What do we do when nobody cares about us? We kick them up the arse,' Kinnock laughed, deeply and despairingly. 'That's why it was fifty-two per cent for Brexit and not fifty-two per cent for Remain. That isn't the only reason, but it certainly crystallized and reinforced that idea of nobody gives a damn, we're abandoned. We're ignored. We're left behind.' The collapse of civic pride in the nation's towns fed into that notion. After fire stations and libraries were closed during the austerity years, replaced with charity outlets and vape shops, many places felt ignored by Westminster. Kinnock agreed: 'All of that sense of abandonment, which I understand and bloody hell I share it, is massively reinforced. Public institutions give meaning to a community. When you take those things out, nobody's saying where or who you are.'

One critique of Kinnock's years leading Labour was that he was too backward-looking. While Margaret Thatcher presented a buccaneering free market vision for the UK's future, he appeared to represent its declining industrial past. Nostalgia is rife in the red wall communities and he thought it has had a distorting effect on how these voters see the world. 'Coal mining is a bloody horrific industry – just in the act of getting in there. The absence on any coal seam in the country of a toilet, just something as bloody basic as that, apart from the danger, just the sheer bloody, vile unpleasantness.' As a young man, he worked part-time in the Welsh blast furnaces and recalled the working environment. 'Sometimes you literally could not breathe because of the dust. Even as a rugby-playing, fit seventeen-year-old, I couldn't breathe. And yet people yearn for those days!'

Kinnock is hopeful that the turn of the red wall from Labour to Conservative is temporary. But he thinks to win the seats back will require 'the politics of reassurance', although the task facing Keir Starmer is 'very, very, very difficult.' Echoing the language of Claire Ainsley, Starmer's chief policy advisor and author of *The New Working Class*, he set out why Labour has to build a narrative around security. 'If Labour can manifest itself as the "security party" in terms of personal security, employment, education, enterprise, national security, all of the many facets of security, then it's capable of getting over the identity demarcations that produced the referendum result.' It is a thesis he has promoted for several decades and tried to sell to Tony Blair, Gordon Brown and Ed Miliband. 'I wish I'd thought of it when I was leader! Because it would have been a really solid basis to build all the dimensions of policy.' Ironically, the leader who spent almost a decade trying to offer an alternative to Thatcherism has touched upon what might be the response to its long-tail effects. It was the first convincing thought I'd heard about how Labour can reconnect to its lost voters.

Kinnock echoed the warnings of Jeremy Corbyn and Ed Miliband about the growth of the 'shadow economy of zero-hours contracts' and said Labour's pitch should be for 'a common need for high-quality, easily accessible, dependable services in communities.' By making itself the party of security, Labour has the opportunity to 'pierce those invisible walls in people's consciousness'. Kinnock agreed with me that the 2016 referendum created a new Remain–Leave identity divide that smashed Labour's old voting coalition: 'For lots of Labour voters, it was the first time they rebelled against their historic family view. You know, "I voted Labour, my granddad voted Labour, he would be turning in his grave." But come the referendum more people went against Labour. Once they've done that once, it's easier to do it again – that's what we saw in 2017 and 2019.' Convincing those people to look at the party again will require something new. 'You can't go back to those old bonds, because Brexit broke them.'

Kinnock's ideological successor was Ed Miliband, who he enthusiastically supported for the leadership in 2010. 'He had a degree of natural humanity, as well as high intelligence, that marked him out from [his brother] David. Ed has an ease and natural politeness and concern that could communicate itself much better.' But after he won the leadership in 2010, those qualities 'reduced and reduced, almost as if they'd been shaved off the block.' Kinnock remained mournful that this 'man of great capability' lost his way. Keir Starmer's politics are still somewhat unfathomable, and he is often described as the Kinnock of his generation: a connecting figure who can bring the party back from electoral oblivion, but may lack the star power to win. What does Kinnock make of the comparison? 'I think it is more Attlee than Kinnock,' he said, again with a hearty laugh. 'The big difference is that Attlee had three or four years in which to demonstrate his trustworthiness as a leader in government. Keir is going to have to do it without getting that.' But he does think Starmer passes the taste test of being prime minister, 'which I didn't'.

As well as securitization, Kinnock was ebullient about the possibilities of green energy to revitalize places like Grimsby. 'The potential there for the restoration of very forward-looking, cutting-edge engineering, design, manufacturing, as well as the actual operation of the energy-generating facilities, is bloody gigantic.' The windy and wet climate of the UK is, on this occasion, a natural benefit. 'You've got a much better load factor [capacity to generate electricity] from offshore wind, which can be made invisible with modern techniques of construction. You can ensure there's hardly a bloody wind farm that anybody can see.' He is, however, surprised that the Conservatives have so readily embraced this technology. 'Getting from that mentality, ideology, philosophy, practice, to one in which a Tory government is willing to spend judiciously, with enough foresight to generate a sustainable recovery? It's a bloody big leap for them.'

Opposite Grimsby's fish market, where my visit started, a low orange building connected to a series of warehouses symbolizes its future. Ørsted, a Danish energy company and the world's largest wind-farm operator, was one of the first to set up shop in Grimsby. The company has four farms off the coast of Grimsby: 375 turbines providing energy to power three million homes. Hornsea One, which alone provides enough power for a million homes, is the world's largest wind farm and Ørsted is plotting to beat its own record with two additions to the Hornsea project in the coming decade that will plant another 400 turbines offshore.

At its operations centre in Port of Grimsby, I met Emma Toulson, who oversees Ørsted's engagement with British stakeholders. As well as activities in the Humber, the company has twelve wind farms around the British Isles – including in the Irish Sea, off Birkenhead and Barrow-in-Furness – producing electricity for four million homes. Across the country it employs 2,800 people. Grimsby was selected as its east-coast hub due to its location: it is always windy, as any visitor attests, has a deep-water estuary and strong support from central and local government. It also benefited from the Siemens blade factory across in Hull, kickstarted by Gordon Brown and Peter Mandelson at the very end of Labour's time in office.

As we circled the warehouses and buildings, built on an old timber yard, Toulson enthusiastically made the case for how her industry is giving Grimsby a new lease of life. 'I'm quite excited and passionate about the growth that it can bring, particularly in places that have had a history of declining traditional industries.' Ørsted arrived in 2014 with a few Portakabins, before constructing its operations centre. Four hundred people work at this hub on the quay, of whom 45 per cent come from Grimsby. 'We are really pleased that we've got a very good local workforce. And we've got an apprenticeship programme to feed in new talent.'

Further along from the main centre, two types of boats are docked that provide many of the new jobs. The smaller vessels are used to zip out to the wind farm to carry out daily maintenance on turbines closer to shore. The dock also houses two large tomato-red service operational vessels. Handily, one of them was docking as we arrived (Toulson admitted it was not put on especially for my visit). Crews on these ships go out to sea for two-week shifts to maintain the hundreds of turbines further away from the land. To my unknowledgeable eye, the docking vehicle appeared sophisticated: a helipad on top, a steel gangway curled up like biceps. The accommodation on board is 'posh student accommodation', Toulson joked. The crew coming into dock, waving at their colleagues on shore, appeared pleased to be returning to terra firma.

The Johnson government has set very ambitious targets for reducing carbon emissions and increasing renewable energy, which is likely to benefit Grimsby (along with Blyth, Hull and many other eastern red wall coastal towns that were once fishing hubs). The UK presently has ten gigawatts of offshore wind capacity, yet the government wants that to quadruple by 2030. Combined with legally binding targets for net-zero carbon emissions by 2050 – and a 78 per cent cut in emissions by 2035 – Toulson is confident there are many more opportunities ahead for Grimsby.[8] 'There'll be a requirement for even more offshore wind in the future. The Committee on Climate Change talked about seventy-five gigawatts, but possibly even more. We are still on the journey.'

The jobs at Ørsted may not be as plentiful as in the fishing days, but they are skilled and stable. 'When the turbines go in, they need to be serviced to keep them running smoothly. The life cycle of the turbine is twenty-five years or more. You've got longevity for those good-quality jobs.' RenewableUK has predicted there will be 69,000 jobs in offshore wind by 2026, up from around 20,000 in 2020.[9] As we looped back towards the main building, with the crew changing over, Toulson spoke of her delight at the collaboration with local colleges to improve skills and jobs. 'Seeing young people from the area, they're super passionate. It's not just that they want a good job but to do something with a purpose. You think, *This is a really exciting opportunity for young people or older people wanting to transition*. I think there's momentum now.'

Much of Toulson's job has been working with the community. Ørsted has donated £460,000 to community projects, sponsored the town's 10k run, cleaned up the beach and tried to integrate itself into Grimsby life A sense of renaissance with a 'green future' is there, she thought, along with a renewed reason for putting the town on the map. Toulson is pleased that the message of the town's renewal is spreading. 'If you asked somebody outside of the area, "What do you know about Grimsby?", they would probably still say fish. In Grimsby, we've had visitors from Taiwan, Japan, North America and South Korea. Someone has got on a plane in Japan to come to Grimsby to see what offshore wind is.' What was possibly once the world's largest fishing port is forging a new identity. 'That recognition, in that global sense, of our industry is there. We're on a journey to grow.'

Prior to my visits to Grimsby, my knowledge of the town was limited to the stereotypes its residents decry. The people I met were hardy but welcoming. Few were consumed with nostalgia or pessimistic about the future. On my last night in the town, I spent an evening at the Barge pub, a local institution in the centre of town. The temperature was bitterly cold, yet every picnic table beside the old boat was packed with drinkers supping pint after pint, bottle after bottle of Prosecco. It is not the party town – Cleethorpes, just down the coast, takes that mantle for Lincolnshire – but Melanie Onn was right; once you dig beneath the grit, there is a warm atmosphere, a proudness and deep loyalty to Grimsby. Those intense feelings make the travails it has suffered during the twentieth century all the sadder.

The green renewal is what the town has been yearning for, but it should not be Panglossian about it. The UK's journey towards net-zero carbon will be painful, far more so than Boris Johnson admitted when he confidently set out some of the most ambitious climate-change targets in the world. There will be difficult economic choices ahead that will clash with the political priorities for towns like Grimsby. The decision to kibosh the West Cumbria Coal Mine project highlighted how the green agenda and Johnson's pledge to 'Build Back Better' after the coronavirus pandemic will not always fit with levelling-up.[10] The mine would have created 3,500 jobs in a remote corner of north-west England. The overarching desire to hit net zero, however, along with the timing of the UK hosting the COP26 climate conference, meant the scheme was doomed.

I left Grimsby with a sense of optimism about its future and its people. The frustration among the residents about their fishing and Brexit has not abated and the Tories should be careful not to underestimate that sentiment. Bold promises were made on fishing that could never be fulfilled and some political backlash may emerge. But improving the town's education and skills offerings can chime with the renewables sector. It is no coincidence that Johnson emphasized his 'vote blue, go green' credentials when the country was casting around for an explanation of what 'levelling-up' means.

Whether you abhor Britain's decision to leave the EU or not, one benefit of the upheaval is the focus on places like Grimsby. Politically and economically, they were overlooked as successive governments took easier routes to create wealth in the south-east and big cities. During a long chat I had with Austin Mitchell, an avowed Eurosceptic who served as Grimsby MP from 1977 to 2015, he referenced how Brexit and the political disruption of the last five years had made Westminster focus on towns like his: 'Attention has shifted back to the small towns like Grimsby and especially the north. After we've been badly treated, change moves very slowly. It's like a glacial process. You don't get overnight changes. Things do improve and gradually, people see sense. It just takes a long time.'

Mitchell, who once changed his surname to Haddock to promote fish, described his old constituency as 'tough' and 'difficult to love'.[11] His own brusque manner reflected the character of the town. At eighty-six, he still had 'great faith in Labour' and thinks his party is best placed to make the changes Grimsby needs, although he did not think he would be around to 'see the end of it'. For Lia Nici, there is little time to do what successive generations of Labour politicians failed to: make Grimsby feel loved and prosperous once again. Having gone as far eastward as the journey took me, the next stop was just over an hour westwards through Lincolnshire and into the natural beauty spot of the Derbyshire Dales.

7. North East Derbyshire

'Around 80 per cent of British families would like to own their own homes. Only 56 per cent actually do so. Barratt are doing more than any other company in the country to meet [that demand].'[1]

BARRATT HOMES IN 1980, THEN LED
BY SIR LAWRIE BARRATT, THATCHER'S
FAVOURITE HOUSEBUILDER

Sixty-six miles inland from Great Grimsby, the village of Killamarsh is wedged between the suburbs of Sheffield and the green expanses of the Derbyshire countryside. The village has an agrarian and industrial history harking back to the Middle Ages and, until the 1980s, the main source of employment was Westthorpe Colliery. Most of the residents lived in small houses and bungalows built for the miners. On the corner of Upperthorpe and Manor Road, high up overlooking the old pit, now consumed by an industrial estate, I met Pat Bone, who runs the Killamarsh Heritage Society. On her extensive website, she has collated hundreds of photos and memories from the area.[2] Many feature steam trains puffing into the town's three train stations (the last, Killamarsh Central, closed during the 1960s Beeching cuts).

As we set off for a stroll to look at the variety of housing, she explained how the village has changed during her lifetime. Bone's father worked in the pit, doling out wages each week in little brown-paper envelopes. As with young men like Ronnie Campbell in Blyth Valley, going down the mine was the obvious, and sometimes only, route when they left the village school. Since Westthorpe closed in 1984, the local jobs market has become more diverse but opportunities remain scarce. 'There's not a lot of employment. There's a variety of things on the industrial estate [built on the site of the old colliery]. One of the bigger ones is Macdonald Joinery, they do shopfitting all over the country.' Bone has never felt Killamarsh was a poor village, either during its industrial prime or more recent dislocation. 'There were four of us, one sister and two brothers. I never felt like we didn't have any money. We never went without things.'

As we walked past the tiny village school and the Nag's Head pub – typically closed due to the pandemic – she recalled the village's most troubling episodes in recent history: the 'horrendous' miners' strike. Some families struggled to eat. 'At the time, these families had young children,' she said, gesturing at the small terraced houses. 'It was so bad that during the miners' strike, it got to the point where some of them had to sell their cars or TVs. They hadn't got any money.' Distrust still flows between those who took to the picket lines and those who continued to work during the strike. 'They've pretty much got over it, but most will never forget what they went through,' she added.

The Heritage Society, to which Bone has devoted much of her retirement, encourages nostalgia. She thinks it is especially strong in this village. 'They love it. We've got a charity site, a Facebook page and I put photographs on of the pits but also old ones of the village. Views of the village, and they love that.' She's posted pictures of Killamarsh's demolished buildings, forgotten social venues and lost green spaces. What drew her to find all this material and share it? 'It's really good to keep a record. We go to exhibitions, any local events. We put up our stall and our photo boards, it really attracts attention.'

We next reached a housing development Bone called 'White City': street upon street of thousands of prefabricated houses built in the 1940s and 1950s to accommodate the booming post-war population. The properties did not appear to be in good shape. Damp was rising up many of the walls, the white paint stained by years of neglect, pavements littered with empty cider cans and used NOS canisters (nitrous oxide, inhaled through balloons to give a quick sensation of euphoria). Most of the houses have cars, but these streets are the grittiest I've visited. Roughly half of Killamarsh's stock is council houses, the other half privately owned. Bone was brought up in one of the small miners' cottages once owned by the Coal Board. And as with millions of England's working class, she took advantage of the Thatcher government's Right to Buy scheme to purchase the council house she had lived in for fifteen years at a discounted rate. She then sold it on and purchased a larger home for her family.

Many of the children Bone went to school with still live in Killamarsh, but they have been joined by thousands who have moved into the village to make the brisk twenty-minute commute into Sheffield. Commuters were initially drawn to Killamarsh by the sprawling Wimpey housing estate; built in the 1970s it occupies a third of the village. As far as the eye could see from Delves Road, where we had stopped, the streets of council houses morphed into semi-detached suburbia – triangular roofs, sloping driveways with space for two cars, well-kept lawns. Houses that were built for the aspirational middle-class lifestyle Mike Leigh satirized in 1977 with *Abigail's Party*. Initially, Bone said the appeal of such housing was its affordability. 'Would you believe you could buy a new three-bed semi for £2,500? That was cheaper than buying in Sheffield, so people came out here. At the time, they all sold like hotcakes,' she said. 'That was basically the start of people coming in from Sheffield and it's continued.'

As Killamarsh's private housing expanded, its bus services declined. Bone guided me back towards the council estates and a small row of shops; she noted one of the few bus stops. 'A village of this size, just over 11,000 people including children, we get just one bus an hour. It's a really big issue because everyone wants to go to Sheffield for shopping and work.' Her sister, who has worked in the Royal Hallamshire Hospital for forty years, spends hours waiting for buses to head to and from her job. Bone has started an action group to improve the services that have been gradually cut as buses were privatized, again by Margaret Thatcher, in 1986. 'I formed a group because people wanted to come together to solve this,' she added. Killamarsh's older residents, especially those ex-miners who did not need cars, have increasingly found themselves stranded. 'People didn't have cars. All my dad did every day was walk across the field. All the miners on our estate walked to work. It must have been very pleasant,' she smiled, thinking of the past.

Today thirty-eight per cent of the North East Derbyshire constituency is classified as green belt, which makes planning permission and construction extremely difficult. Much of the northern parts of the seat, especially touching on Sheffield, are restricted to avoid further urban sprawl. Yet in Killamarsh, plans are afoot to build 400–500 homes on parts of the old Westthorpe pit. Bone wants to keep the green belt, despite the ever-rising demand for houses.

As we hiked back to the top of Killamarsh, I asked Bone how the gradual influx of commuters had changed the character of the village and whether the new commuting arrivals were as keen on her historical work. 'I find that if you talk to people, they're friendly and do want to chat to you,' she said. 'But you have got that small element of people who come here, buy a house, go to work in Sheffield and don't really mingle very well.'

In every red wall seat I visited, new housing estates have emerged outside the traditional town centres. Most were from the 1980s and 1990s, judging by the styles of brickwork, while others were still under construction. On the outskirts of Sedgefield, Wakefield and Consett, new detached houses were appearing in every spare corner. The psephological term used to describe the voters who reside in these developments was 'Motorway Man'. As the *Financial Times* reported in the run-up to the 2010 election, this person was a 'materialistic and car-dependent middle manager' who lived on newish housing estate along the M6 or M1 motorways.[3] Nearly all of the constituencies which are the natural habitat of this voter turned blue in 2010 and 2015 – notably Morley and Outwood, near Leeds, where shadow chancellor Ed Balls dramatically lost his seat. Some of them have become the safest Tory seats in the country: Nuneaton in Warwickshire now holds a 13,144 Tory majority.

Motorway Man was markedly different from Mondeo Man, the stereotypical voter Labour aimed to win over in the 1990s. Addressing the party's 1996 conference, Tony Blair recalled campaigning in the Midlands and meeting an electrician who had abandoned the party: 'He used to vote Labour. But he'd bought his own house now. He'd set up his own business. He was doing very nicely. "So I've become a Tory," he said.' Mondeo Man was, himself, a continuation of Essex Man: the traditional Labour voter who switched to supporting Margaret Thatcher in 1979 and formed the bedrock of the party's eighteen years in office. In 2019, the latest incarnation was Workington Man, representing the white middle-aged Brexit supporters residing in post-industrial towns.[4] These pollster labels are not necessarily helpful for understanding the country, as they tend to throw voters of different persuasions into the same bucket without examining the places and circumstances in which they live. They do, however, give an indication of who each party is attempting to win over. What they all have in common is home ownership and aspiration: as voters purchase their own properties and become wealthier, they are more inclined towards the Tories. The only deviation was the New Labour years, when its aspirational message spoke to Mondeo Man.

In the red wall, the voters who live in new out-of-town estates, dependent on their cars for transport, were identified by *The Economist* in 2021 as 'Barratt Britain' (in North East Derbyshire, 'Wimpey World' was more apt).[5] These people do not feel hard up or left behind. According to the magazine, the towns that voted Tory for the first time are 'often surrounded by gleaming new suburbs: a British counterpart to the American dream, where a couple on a modest income can own a home and two cars and raise a family.' The Conservatives returned to power in 2010 thanks to voters living in comfortable circumstances and to understand the red wall is to appreciate that many parts of it are wealthier than ever.

The prominence of these new estates has been growing for decades. The end of building controls in 1954 allowed builders such as Wimpey to enter the private market. By 1972, Wimpey was building 12,500 houses annually – three times as many as its competitors. Barratt, the builder which symbolized the Thatcher era, sold 100,000 new homes in the 1980s. Although inner-city redevelopment became the later focus for the UK's major builders, their initial focus was on new private estates built on cheap land in the old Labour heartlands.

Neal Hudson, an analyst of the UK's housing market, said the shift away from city living began in the 1930s – the 'metro lands' around London championed by poet laureate Sir John Betjeman. The trend continued after the war, as much to do with the nation's health as its prosperity. 'Getting people out of urban areas into suburban markets and knocking down city-centre tenements was about getting them into better-quality housing,' Hudson said. 'For a long time, housing was under the remit of the Department of Health, which shows you where the priorities were. It was very much viewed as the need to have a healthy population, it was up there along with healthcare and nutrition.'

When the Labour Party emerged as a national force at the turn of the last century, the majority of the country did not own their own property. In 1918, when the first reliable stats became available, around two thirds rented. Conservative governments since the war have consistently championed home ownership, as seen in Harold Macmillan's achievement of building 300,000 a year in the 1950s.[6] The party believed homes played a significant role in keeping Labour out of office – and it did so for thirteen years until 1964. As the Conservative Party's 1951 manifesto declared, 'Housing is the first of the social services. It is also one of the keys to increased productivity. Work, family life, health and education are all undermined by crowded houses. Therefore, a Conservative and Unionist Government will give housing a priority second only to national defence.' Margaret Thatcher's Right to Buy scheme went further, shifting a significant portion of the nation from social renting into ownership, including my paternal grandmother and much of her family.

The UK is said to be in the throes of a housing crisis; a lack of supply has pushed up prices and made it nigh impossible for younger people to clamber on the housing ladder. In London and the south-east, this is certainly true: the average 2020 house price was £674,668, compared to £327,797 for the whole UK. According to Rightmove, the average price in Derbyshire was £184,849. But Hudson said that the biggest problem in housing across most of the country is quality, not supply. 'What comes up as actually a far bigger problem in that market is distribution of housing – that's going to be a combination of both the quality but also lots of older people living in bigger housing.' He also cited a weak demand for new housing in some post-industrial towns due to underperformance in the local economy. Killamarsh comes to mind. 'It's the lack of long-term, secure, high-quality, high-wage-paying employment and that's the barrier to people being able to afford housing rather than it being an outright lack of supply.'

Labour continues to do well in parts of England where renting is rife, and the Conservatives do better where home ownership has increased. This divide has created headaches for both parties. For Boris Johnson, his government faces a desperate need to build more homes and forge the same grateful class of voters that worshipped Thatcher in the 1980s. He will encounter a clash between the party's old and new voting base: the Home Counties Tories adhere to nimbyism – not in my back yard – and their passions for protecting a green and pleasant land. All of the red wall Tory MPs I have encountered are eager to wheel out the bulldozers and cannot pour out concrete fast enough.

Labour has to find a way of appealing to the aspirational voters who have purchased their own home, or at least aspire to. During the 2019 campaign, Jeremy Corbyn devoted much of his energies to policies tackling exploitative landlords with a 'property MOT' and a charter of renters' rights. He also made a commitment to building 100,000 council homes each year.[7] The Conservatives, on the other hand, pledged to reform the planning laws to make it easier to build. Corbyn's sentiments were worthy in their goals, with the poorest in society at the front of his mind, but they spoke primarily to Labour's core base. There was little that he or the party said that would appeal to the middle classes who live near motorways, possibly in Workington in a Barratt home, and would have driven a Ford Mondeo. As the results of 2019 confirmed, these voters are increasingly dominating the seats Labour once called its heartlands.

The housing of North East Derbyshire may be similar to other parts of the red wall, but it has one standout political character-istic: it flipped Tory two years earlier. The 2017 snap election was called by Theresa May to gain a mandate to deliver Brexit, after the party was riding high in opinion polls and David Cameron's majority of thirteen was proving problematic. She led an appalling campaign, notably due to a series of ill-considered policies, a dense manifesto and flaws in the manner she came across to voters. The party made a net loss of twenty seats and clung onto power with the assistance of the Democratic Unionist Party. The Tories did win 42 per cent of the national vote, its highest since 1983, which heralded the return of two-party poli-tics after the prominence of the Liberal Democrats and UKIP.

Crucially for what was to come next, the party gained four seats it had never won before: Middlesbrough South and East Cleveland in the north-east, Walsall North in the West Midlands, and Mansfield and North East Derbyshire in the East Midlands. During that election, I toured the country in a maroon Morris Minor to produce a series of videos on whether Labour was really in trouble. The conventional wisdom that Jeremy Corbyn's unpopularity would sink the party was proved badly wrong, as Labour edged closer to power and a wave of youthful optimism surrounded his leadership. But along with the seat of Copeland in Cumbria, this quartet was the first batch of bricks to be chipped out of the red wall.

Lee Rowley was the first Tory MP in North East Derbyshire

since 1931 and is rooted in his constituency. We met outside Staveley Hall, built in 1604 and now home to Staveley's town council. The settlement is typical of North Derbyshire: a former mining village, now dominated by housing and a giant Morrisons supermarket. With no cafes or pubs open, most of the shoppers kept to themselves, heads down, shuffling to their cars. In the afternoon sunshine of the car park, overlooking a surprisingly lush green field, Rowley spoke of his family roots. His father was a milkman, his mother an adult education teacher. He came from a Labour family, who were horrified with his decision to go into politics against the family tradition. 'Because I just didn't like what was happening in my part of the world and my part of the world was run by one group of people,' he said in his homely manner.

After studying at Oxford, he moved to London and entered local politics as a Conservative councillor in the extremely affluent Maida Vale. When his father experienced health issues, he felt a pull to return home. His first attempt at Parliament was in 2010 in nearby Bolsover, held by Dennis Skinner, where he gained 8,000 votes (the socialist firebrand lost his seat in 2019 after forty-nine years in the House of Commons). That campaign was 'strange and brilliant' because the party was out on such a limb. 'It was like a curiosity show, because they didn't know what to do with a Conservative turning up on their doorstep delivering leaflets.' Judging by the number of passers-by that Rowley said hello to, the curiosity has turned into familiarity. In the 2010 election, Huw Merriman – now a Conservative MP in East Sussex – pushed the Tory vote up by seven per cent in North East Derbyshire and laid the foundations for future success.

Brexit, in Rowley's view, convinced North East Derbyshire to look at electoral alternatives. 'People were attracted to the party, but they needed a pathway to get there. And so you had to build it yourself. That took literally a decade or so to build up.' Unlike many of the new Tories in the red wall, he is a true Brexit believer who chimed fully with his constituency. In the 2015 election, his first campaign in North East Derbyshire, he recalled from the doorstep: 'My area had their baseball bats ready for Europe. If they got a referendum they were coming after Europe – primarily for reasons that they didn't like the EU, but secondarily, because they just didn't like where politics was and they wanted to change the establishment.' UKIP was initially the outlet for those feelings, gaining ten points in that election, but their vote soon transferred to the Tories.

What changed between 2015 and 2017 was the working-class vote. In his first campaign, Rowley built up the Conservative vote in suburbs and rural areas but struggled in the mining areas. Two years on, after the referendum, those pit villages swapped their affiliations. 'They've become comfortable with the Conservatives in a way that they weren't ten or fifteen years ago. And they've had enough of the Labour Party,' he said. The shift is wholesale: most of North East Derbyshire's district councillors are Tories and many of the parish councils have left Labour. 'We'd done the whole process of people finding out the Conservative Party didn't eat their babies and all the rest of it.' Plus, he reported an 'immense dislike' of Jeremy Corbyn. By 2019, the seat's Tory majority had risen to near 13,000.

The sprawling landscape of North East Derbyshire raises pertinent questions about what the levelling-up agenda will look like here. Rowley represents forty-one villages and towns, all of which have economic and geographic challenges. He admitted there are structural challenges in reinvigorating parts of the seat. 'Most of the kids I went to school with, about a third to a half have come back, or stayed here, regardless of their economic interest. They come back because they want to raise a family near their parents.' Does he see the future of his seat as a suburb to Sheffield? He cited the town of Dronfield, population 22,000, which has the benefits of being close to the city. 'It's pretty close to Sheffield, it's got a railway station, which is a positive.' But wandering around its town centre, there appeared to be too much commercial property – one of those 1960s civic centres that struggles today to sustain a big butcher and baker. Rowley is optimistic for reviving the parts of his constituency that are well-connected, but acknowledged others will be more chal- lenging. Their best hope may be the connectivity to the M1 and the continued rise of logistics and warehousing.

Despite having won two general elections and now sitting on a healthy majority, Rowley believes he needs to oversee tangible change by the next election to secure his position as its MP. As deputy chairman of the Tory Party, his fortunes are tied to Boris Johnson's. Many parts of his seat will benefit from the government's numerous funds to improve town centres and infrastructure, but he admitted there are deeper problems too. 'You can make a very strong case in 2024 on roads and railways, but you probably can't build them before 2029.' The red wall Tories actually need to show some progress, as well as promising more. As we stretched our legs with a wander around Staveley Hall's gardens, Rowley showed me a print-out of a table of policy topics where North East Derbyshire is struggling, improving, and succeeding compared to the national picture. Unlike the UK's electoral map, it is a sea of maroon. 'A lot of these red marks on this table need to go green, in order for them to feel like it's easier to get on.'

As we bid farewell, Lee Rowley mentioned he had a soft spot for his predecessor and told me the pair had become friends despite his victory and her defeat – a rare thing in politics.

Natascha Engel, North East Derbyshire's Labour MP from 2005 to 2017, was a prominent Westminster figure and her defeat was a shock. As deputy speaker over her last two years in Parliament, she commanded the chamber in some of its most difficult Brexit moments. Unlike Rowley, her connections to North East Derbyshire were looser. Before entering Parliament, Engel was the party's trade-union liaison officer, but was exasperated by the lack of women in Parliament. Deciding to stand for the seat a few weeks after her first baby, she was surprised the constituency Labour Party did not select a local candidate. Engel was born in Berlin and educated privately in Kent. Speaking from her home in London, where she has moved on from political life, she said of her selection, 'There was no bloody way that I could say that I was local,' adding that people were not much interested in what she had to say. 'It was about me listening to them and hearing why it was they were so concerned about it. They weren't bothered about what I thought about it.'

Her memories of her old seat, and the hodgepodge of towns and villages thrown together by electoral planners, were warm. 'When you go from Killamarsh to Dronfield to Clay Cross, there are three different accents,' she said (my ears were ill-tuned to the East Midlands dialect, so I confessed that everyone sounded the same to me). The name 'North East Derbyshire' is not a destination, but a geographical locale. If asked on holiday, Engel said residents would say they'd travelled from Chesterfield, Sheffield or the village where they live, not 'north-east Derbyshire'. Despite this ambiguous sense of place, she reported a 'very strong sense of civic pride', even in the more run-down towns. 'Most people haven't moved very far away – I'm talking working-class voters, the kind who used to vote Labour and have recently voted Conservative in very large numbers.'

She felt much of the constituency has a 'real feeling of isolation', not least as the lack of a redevelopment plan turned closed pits into dumping grounds. 'The pits left voids and those voids were perfect for landfills. The villages were built quite close to the pits. There was a permanent problem.' Similarly to Pat Bone, she decried the transport links that had stoked the sense of isolation in smaller parts of the seat. 'All these villages aren't that far away from each other as the crow flies. But as there were no bus services, people would walk for miles from one village to another.'

During her dozen years as an MP, Engel saw North East Derbyshire change 'quite dramatically' due to the number of new homes. 'They were everywhere on the edges, it was prime territory for all the pit villages. They were all brownfield, so they just built onto them. These little towns became joined up. If you go outside Grassmoor [village], for example, all the areas started to be linked together because they were being filled with new housing.'

In her first election campaign, Engel was returned to Westminster with a 10,065 majority, with the Tories a distant second place. Her majority dropped sharply in 2010 and again in 2015 before she lost in 2017. During the 2015 campaign, she concluded the seat was gone. Engel ran a highly personal campaign, with few Labour markings on the literature, and worked the doorsteps hard for five years. With the snap 2017 election, she realized 'we just didn't have the time' to canvass in the same way. What went wrong? Was it Engel, Labour or the seat? Top of her blame list is Jeremy Corbyn, who found little support in the old pit villages; his messages had 'no relevance to the lives' of people who were focused on finding enough petrol to fill the car.

Engel, who has never declared how she voted in the 2016 referendum, said the referendum motivated the non-voters in

North East Derbyshire back into politics, but she denied that the vote was driven by xenophobia. 'I still get really upset with people saying that the reason why places like North East Derbyshire voted Brexit was because they were all obsessed with immigration and they were racist . . . it was labelling this type of person without trying to understand what it was that they really valued about their culture and their lives.' Corbyn's leadership symbolized a wider disconnect. 'It was cultural, in that the Labour Party didn't seem to represent their kind of people anymore.' During her time as a trade union officer, she travelled frequently around the traditional heartlands and saw the cultural disconnect grow during the years Labour was in government. 'We were very much a middle-class party with working-class voters. The assumption was there was nowhere for this group of voters to go.'

Yet Engel insisted these were not voters who were 'left behind'. Instead, they felt the government had not given them adequate support. 'They thought, *Leave us alone, give us the tools to help ourselves.* "Left behind" implies they were not capable, or there was some way in which people were not properly equipped.' Part of this is the collapse of the monolithic industries that dominated North East Derbyshire. In their place were distribution centres, dotted across the seat, which do not offer a resilient or stable base.

She was very pessimistic about winning these voters back due to the great cultural gulf. Even the way Labour talks about the red wall rankles her. 'There's a slightly operative tone when Labour talks about the red wall, as having to win back those votes if they want to get into government, rather than say these are our people and we love them, we want to represent them.' Although she thought Keir Starmer had done an 'absolutely amazing job in a short space of time', Engel was downbeat over whether the divide between Labour's left and right could be healed to speak to both sides of the Hampstead–Humberside alliance. 'I don't think there is accommodation to be had between the left and the right of the party.'

She concluded that Starmer may have to decide which part of the electorate to address. 'Do you face towards the Remain-voting middle class? Or do you face towards the more Brexit-voting working class, who are culturally very different from one another? How do you combine the two?' On a local level it can be done, as she saw in the 2015 election. But nationally she is sceptical. 'You've got to have a much stronger political narrative to do that.'

The divide between the left and the right within the Labour Party was most acutely seen in the 2017 election. For supporters of Jeremy Corbyn, the party was a mere 2,227 votes and seven seats away from the opportunity to form a rainbow coalition.[8] For the Labour right, particularly embittered Blairites, the party was barely ahead of its total from 2010 and hopelessly far away from winning a parliamentary majority and governing as a stable majority force. The indisputable trend, which both sides agree on, is the coalescing of votes: UKIP collapsed, with its voters flocking mostly to the Tories, and the Liberal Democrats shed votes to Labour in the big cities. The rise in vote share for the two main parties makes assessing the merits of that election very difficult.

David Blunkett was the Labour right's most prominent figure for several decades, who has little time for the narrative that the 2017 election laid the path towards a socialist government. Born into one of the most deprived neighbourhoods of Sheffield, he rose to become the most senior minister in the New Labour era: serving as Education, Work and Pensions and Home

Secretary. Now Lord Blunkett, he spoke of a sense that Labour's support in seats like North East Derbyshire was 'seeping away' based on his doorstep activities. 'I tried to explain to colleagues and friends that 2017 was an aberration – not just because of the poor campaign which Theresa May ran, but because of the local elections four years ago [2016], were dire for the Labour Party. Absolutely dire. We also mopped up virtually all the Green and a great deal of the Lib Dem vote, so the anti-Tory vote coalesced.' Corbyn's manifesto commitments were also more tempered in 2017, although not by New Labour or Ed Miliband's standards, which Blunkett felt helped on the doorstep.

In the 2017 campaign, many Labour MPs I have spoken to stated their primary message to voters was, 'We're not going to win and Jeremy Corbyn won't be prime minister'. In Sedgefield, Labour's Phil Wilson went as far as to write on his leaflets, 'I am not for Corbyn', which others followed.[9] Blunkett said the primary message in his area was, 'Please vote Labour, don't let it be a landslide for Theresa May', which was a credible offer for those who did not have much love for the Tories. In the following two years, opinions in the red wall hardened against Jeremy Corbyn. Blunkett put the party's collapse down to 'people just wanting to get back to some sort of stability, to get Brexit over and done with.' Plus he found a 'complete alienation of the Corbyn Labour leadership' in seats like North East Derbyshire, due to 'the Labour Party having ditched its normal commitments on security, on issues of safety that are really close to the heart of those areas.'

Blunkett agreed with my emerging conclusion that Labour's collapse in the red wall was in part due to structural changes, not purely the immediate consequences of Brexit and Corbyn's leadership. The collapse of heavy industry, followed by the financial crisis and the austerity cuts to public services, resulted in a 'complete change' in people's lived experiences. The old world of apprenticeships that were 'relatively well paid' in shipbuilding, engineering and steel gave people 'dignity in work and the community', he said. 'When that disintegrated, as it did in the eighties and early nineties, it wasn't replaced. It was a mistake we made. It wasn't that we neglected the so called "red wall" seats, we did a fantastic job on transforming the lives and the prospects and the opportunities. It was that we didn't understand that there needed to be a model, a very different prospectus in terms of that security, that feeling of community.'

This change emerged gradually across the East Midlands, Blunkett explained. 'You could see the same type of areas, it creeps in gradually. With North East Derbyshire going in 2017, it was almost inevitable Rother Valley would go in 2019.' The neighbouring seat did indeed go Tory for the first time. 'It's a reflection of the whole change in the social and economic experience people were having.' There was also a crucial age differential: just 17 per cent of over sixty-fives voted Labour in 2019, which reflected how its traditional voting base had gone. 'That reflects very heavily on the way in which, since the collapse of heavy industry, older people who had pensions, who had built up some capital, perhaps able to buy their own house, are now of an age where they don't feel like the younger generation.'

The question of whether these voters were taken for granted is one Blunkett thought had roots going further back. 'It's a myth that the working classes were overwhelmingly Labour. In the industrial areas, the heavily unionized in large plants and mining communities, where political education and solidarity were instilled into people, the Labour Party was very strong.' But he noted that there were voters in the same class and income brackets in other parts of England who voted Conservative. 'That's why the Tories were in from 1951 to 1964, from 1979 to 1997.' His party also tends to be focused on the past rather than the future. 'The Labour Party has been brilliant at fighting the previous election rather than the current one. We've done it historically – you only need to look at the debates in the Labour Party conference in the late fifties, particularly 1959, when we lost that third election then, and the astonishing nostalgia.'

Blunkett was especially angry throughout our chat about the narrative that Labour governments did not do enough for working-class voters – particularly espoused by Jeremy Corbyn's supporters. He recalled an exchange with a voter during the 2005 campaign in his old Sheffield Brightside constituency:

'A man said to me "You've done nothing for us." And I said, "Have you got any children?" He had, and I pointed out the Sure Start centre, the nursery classes around him, the market renewal of his house, and then I said, "You've got a daughter, you said, of sixteen. Where is she going?" and he said, "Oh, she's going to that Longley Park College." I said, "Tony Blair and I opened that £30 million college. Where do you think it came from?" He said, "I don't know." I said, "It came from us. This is our government. This is us, actually repaying you for voting Labour by being able to put that in place." "Well, I didn't think of it like that," he said. When you don't have a clear narrative of what you've done, and you don't sing about it in a way that relates to people's lives, and when you then find your own side trashing the things you've done, it's not surprising that people get the exact opposite message.'

In Blunkett's book, the 'fantastic achievements' of New Labour's time in government were not praised enough by Gordon Brown, Ed Miliband or Jeremy Corbyn, which created dissatisfaction in its traditional heartlands. 'You've got this consistent, repetitious message that the Labour government failed, and failed the working class – despite the national minimum wage, despite a transformation in the education system that led their children to go to university, despite the refurbishment of many of the older housing estates, despite reducing waiting times from eighteen months to eighteen weeks, and then to six weeks.' Without a proper narrative since the party left office in 2010 to build on these transformations, Blunkett said the 'umbilical cord' between the party and its voters was cut.

Agreeing with Neil Kinnock and Tony Blair, Blunkett feels the party needs to find a new message for these voters that reflects the impending economic upheaval due to the rise in automation and the ageing population. The opportunity will be presented by 'automation and the whole issue of AI and robotics, the nature of big social care issues and the way people are treated in jobs which are not traditional working-class, often insecure, part-time and lowly paid.' This is not reinventing the working class or speaking to nostalgia, he added.

Although optimistic about forging a new economic message, Blunkett was concerned about the cultural disconnect between Labour and places such as North East Derbyshire as political affiliations have reshaped around issues of identity. He said, 'They detest the idea of identity politics. Everybody I speak to in my own constituency – I still visit it because I used to go to football matches – they don't know what on earth the liberal intelligentsia are talking about. They just don't relate. They're not on the same wavelength. So what appeals to under forties is anathema to many of the over sixty-fives.' Nor does he think the cultural divides will wholly benefit the Conservatives, particularly with an eye to other parts of the country with more diverse populations. 'The Tories are putting all their eggs in the basket of being able to play off people's fears about the rapid way communities are changing culturally and socially.' What he described as the 'different offer' to win these places back does not rest on memories of old-fashioned work or 'waving of the flag', instead it needs to be rooted in place. 'An understanding of where those people are coming from, and why in 1997 similar people voted Labour for the first time in the south of England and the Midlands.'

Although he sees a route back for Labour in the red wall, he remained concerned that the Rubicon has been crossed and some convincing will be needed. 'Once you start voting Conservative, even through gritted teeth, it's not as hard the next time. That was true in reverse of Tories who voted Labour in 1997 and 2001. In 1992, once people had started to get used to voting Labour, they were very happy to do so in 1997 and stuck with it in 2001. And against all the odds, because of Iraq, they pretty well stuck with it in 2005,' he said. The offer has to be for what he calls the 'reasonably affluent', the asset-rich but sometimes income-poor older people. 'We can't win a general election with the disparity between the eighteen- to thirty-year-olds and over sixty-fives upwards, not least because the older generation vote and young people don't.'

Blunkett was scathing of the Johnson government's levelling-up agenda, which he thought would only make superficial changes to red wall communities and not tackle the underlying issues. 'They're going to do a bit with the cosmetic physical environment. And people will say, "Well, you can see it's a bit better in the town centre." It won't have changed their lives at all,' he said.

Blunkett's vision for Labour's future is of a communitarian party, built from the grassroots upwards and rooted in the communities it lost in 2019. He is concerned that it appears too paternalistic. He advocated a new social contract of 'mutuality and reciprocity' that links the state with personal responsibility. 'If we do this for you, you will do this for yourself, you will play your part and we will play ours.' But above all else, he said his party needs to be relentlessly optimistic about the future. 'The only times we've been able to succeed as a Labour Party as a force for social democracy, is when we've actually reached for the future.'

If the 2017 election was deemed a disaster by the Labour right, it was hopeful for the Labour left. For the long marchers, disciples of the radical socialist Tony Benn who led the fight against Tony Blair's efforts to reshape the party, the gain of thirty seats was proof socialism could find an audience in modern Britain. John McDonnell was central to Jeremy Corbyn's five-year reign. As shadow chancellor and the intellectual ballast behind 'the project', he was by far the most thoughtful and determined mind in the leadership. The resounding defeat in 2019 sent Corbyn and McDonnell to the backbenches and semi-retirement. While the former has been marked in his criticism of Keir Starmer, McDonnell has been careful with his interventions. Speaking from his West London office, he reflected that Labour did not want the 2019 election. I have clear recollections of Labour arguing for another election almost every day after the 2017 poll, when the opportunity of gaining power was obvious. That appetite drained away, funnily enough, when Boris Johnson became prime minister and the Conservatives moved ahead in the opinion polls.

The mistakes of 2019 were twofold, according to McDonnell. One was the lack of time, due to the abrupt manner in which the election was called (given the lack of a stable parliamentary majority, Labour might really have given the prospect some thought in, say, the intervening two years). He said, 'From 2017 to 2019, we never had a clear enough narrative of how all the individual policies welded together to create a new vision. When it came to December 2019, the individual policies might have been popular in themselves but because they weren't part of an overall narrative, they lacked credibility.' Labour's other major error was in communication, which McDonnell admitted 'wasn't good enough'. He was right that the 'incredibly creative' team that emerged from Corbyn's leadership campaigns led the political pack, with creative and punchy messaging, but the Tories caught up.

Reflecting on 2017, he pinned the project's success on policies designed to 'give a bit of zest' to politics. He felt that after six years of a Conservative government, voters were fed up with austerity. 'By the time you have been through the first five years of austerity, people just didn't see any light at the end of the tunnel.' Oddly, however, the political reaction to that anger was not immediate – the Tories won a majority in 2015 – but McDonnell felt the anger was bubbling. 'People get angry and react, not necessarily when you're in the depths of a recession or when it's the hardest. It's when politicians or governments or others are telling you things are improving, and you don't feel you're sharing in the benefits of the improvement.'

McDonnell admitted that the party was expecting 'a bit of a drubbing' in 2019, but pinned its issues on the EU question. 'Brexit was absolutely dominating everything. Even where we were trying to shift the agenda onto other issues like anti-austerity, like jobs, like the NHS in particular, people reach those subjects via Brexit. When you raise the NHS, they'd say, "Oh, yeah, that's great, because we'll get so much more money for the NHS when we leave the European Union", as dictated on the famous bus advert.' On economics, where McDonnell said his leftward anti-austerity push had 'won' the debate on public services, everything came back to the EU issue. 'Here's the irony: where we were convincing people on every policy, we were also reinforcing their antipathy to us because of Brexit.'

When Theresa May's momentum stalled after the 2017

election, he was part of the negotiating team that attempted to piece together a cross-party withdrawal agreement that most, if not all, of the Tory and Labour MPs could support. Whereas senior Labour figures such as Alan Johnson have argued this was the party's great missed opportunity to shore up the red wall, McDonnell said there was no plausible opportunity for a deal. 'We couldn't get a deal that Theresa and our party could both deliver on. But in those negotiations, the Tories were falling out literally in front of us.' He did not think May was acting disingenuously, but the internecine warfare within the Tory Party made a deal impossible. McDonnell was also concerned that a soft deal to satisfy the middle ground of Labour would 'march our people to the top of the hill' by whipping them to back the deal, yet still lose a significant chunk of MPs, particularly those who were 'hooked on having a People's Vote'. He believed there was a real risk that those talks would have produced a deal that would have seen Labour 'falling flat on our face' in Parliament.

The Brexit knot, in McDonnell's view, was impossible. Referencing a maxim of Tony Benn – 'walk down the middle of the road and you get run over' – he felt Labour could not keep both sides of its coalition happy. 'We couldn't offer a better Brexit position than the Brexit Party or the Tories. If we leaned towards the Remain vote we then alienated our Brexit supporters in our own constituencies.' A historical contingency, a nightmare, that McDonnell felt was out of the party's hands.

As one of Jeremy Corbyn's closest political allies for decades, he must have detected the concerns among red wall voters about his leadership. No, it transpired. He felt it was all whipped up by the media. 'Every time when it came down to it, there wasn't "I hate Jeremy Corbyn", it was more about the Brexit issue in particular constituencies. We can overcome any issues around Jeremy and criticisms of him. But people weren't listening to any other message other than the Brexit one.' Corbyn and McDonnell had a testy relationship with the media, which in turn took a hostile stance towards his leadership. As a political journalist through that period, I can confirm the leader's office did almost nothing of substance to engage with the *Financial Times*, and almost all newspapers were ignored by the leadership. McDonnell insisted that 'from 2015 to 2019, we had a four-year campaign in the mainstream media – and increasingly on social media – that was character assassination. It was quite appalling. I don't think we've ever really seen anything like it in British politics.' His response to the Salisbury poisoning, for example, which proved so toxic to traditional Labour voters, was not filtered through any media lens. Giving Russia the benefit of the doubt over the terror attack was done through his words at the dispatch box in the House of Commons.

The Labour left has been vocal in its criticisms of Keir Starmer's leadership, judging him too meek in his scrutiny of the government during the coronavirus crisis. Treading carefully, McDonnell stated Starmer had done the right thing in working with the Johnson government. 'When you're in a national crisis, what you want to do is work together, you don't play petty politics.' But he reflected a criticism of many colleagues in urging Starmer to be bolder. 'We're at that stage now where there needs to be a bit more passion, both in terms of how you critique the government, but also then how you recreate the image of the sort of society that you want to create.'

Reflecting on the Corbyn project, which failed to get Labour elected but shifted the party, McDonnell thought the greatest achievement was forming 'a mass social movement' and expanding the party's grassroots activist base. He was very satisfied at the shift in the political debate, which has seen the Tories and Labour shift leftwards on economic issues. In many ways, the Corbyn project lost the election but won the argument. 'The whole flow of the debate is towards our ideas about how you create a more equal society, how you use the state to do that, and how you look at the fairer distribution of wealth and power.' He was right: prior to the Corbyn project, the economic debate was focused on fiscal prudence. He did not, however, buy the argument that the Tories were doing things in power that would fulfil even his wildest fantasies, such as spending £300 billion during the pandemic.

'I keep getting this: "Sunak is implementing your budget or your policies." That's absolute bollocks,' he laughed. 'They've taken our rhetoric, but not the substance. And so therefore it's the same as a Boris Johnson-type approach that doesn't really tell them whatever they need to be told.' He was also dismissive of the levelling-up agenda and the government's pledges to renew infrastructure in the red wall. 'The Tories will never be able to match Labour and its ambition around how you want to transform people's lives because they don't want to shift the balance of power or wealth.' For the second time, he quoted Tony Benn. '"Labour's role is an irreversible shift in the balance of power and wealth in this country in favour of working people." That will never happen under the Tories.'

His deepest regret is that he never made it into government to use the levers of power to reconfigure how the British state works. 'The state is a set of institutions, but also relationships . . . our role was to go into the state and be against that [status quo]. You go into these institutions, but you change the relationship as you distribute power outwards and empower people to control their own lives.' Despite the failings of the project, McDonnell thought that a radical Labour government can be elected. 'Oh, of course. I think we'll see when objective reality intervenes as well. How people are being dealt with and how they're feeling within society, what their lives are like, and the desires that they have as well as the frustrations that they feel. The issue there is how those feelings are mobilized, and how those emotions are channelled so that they affect the political chain.' Although he sounded increasingly Marxist, implying that the contradictions in capitalism make its collapse inevitable, McDonnell insisted he was not a historical determinist.

Given how Labour's voting coalition fractured due to Brexit, I was curious to hear his take on a commonly held view among Labour MPs that their 2019 manifesto was targeted at an electoral coalition that did not exist, and whether the economic and demographic shifts in the red wall were detrimental to Labour. In response, he quoted another left-wing thinker, Antonio Gramsci, and his concept of hegemony. 'Your ideas can dominate, you can shift the whole paradigm if your ideas resonate with people's lives,' he said. 'If you look at a lot of what we were trying to do, it wasn't that they were quite broad-ranging dramatic changes to people's lives – of course they were – but they had a broad-ranging effect across the classes, in many respects.' He insisted that Labour's policies on wages and public services had a 'majoritarian appeal'.

His biggest instruction for the left was professionalism. 'It comes down to the levels of dedication, commitment, professionalism, lessons learned through past failures and I'm hoping that's the period that we now go into.' McDonnell also thought ground campaigning should not be underestimated. 'We generally reinvented word of mouth as a form of physical communication. People derided all these big rallies. But actually, they're incredibly successful. We have a huge movement, which developed as a result of those rallies all around the country.'

McDonnell concluded by admitting the left made mistakes but they were not always a bad thing. 'It was experience to learn those lessons and move on and also, to a certain extent, don't be ashamed of errors or mistakes as well. Sometimes you just have to fly a few kites. Sometimes they take and sometimes they don't catch the wind. But the worst thing to do is to almost be frightened of taking the next step because you're worried the ice will break.' The issue for Labour, however, is that the left's mistakes resulted in five further years of Conservative government, scores of seats abandoning Labour, and Brexit delivered on terms few on the political left, or even in the centre, are happy with.

Having visited two of North East Derbyshire's working-class suburbs, I finished up by visiting Dronfield, mentioned by Lee Rowley and Natascha Engel as one of the most affluent parts of the area. The centre of the market town has a gritstone tribute to Robert Peel, the Tory prime minister who repealed the Corn Laws and paved the way for the Victorian age of free trade. Opposite the monument was the Peel Community Centre and a small 1960s shopping centre. After visiting on three occasions at different times of the day to find it almost empty, I felt Rowley had a point: this is the particular form of market town that struggles with having a major shopping destination, Sheffield, just twenty minutes' drive away.

Yet below the surface, Dronfield – named after the River Drone – has one of the most tight-knit community spirits I have seen. Several residents told me to seek out Jill and Tony Bethell as examples of pillars of the community. Venturing back into the countryside, after several wrong turns through sleet that rapidly turned into sunshine, I found their grand manor and was ushered in for coffee and cake. Their residence was built on an old mine, which closed in 1890, and has vast grounds for garden parties that they hold to raise money for the community.

Amongst the pots, plants and mustard sofas, they told me

their story. Jill, a general practitioner for forty years, and Tony, who turned to medicine later in life, were married in 1970 and moved to the area soon after. She described Dronfield as 'wonderful' precisely because it is a 'dormitory area'. The residents, she cheerily said, were 'middle class and middle aged'. The town rapidly grew in the 1950s and 1960s, chiefly for teachers and doctors who preferred countryside living. Tony recalled that Dronfield had a manufacturing past, which was present but waning when they first arrived. 'A lot of places in north-east Derbyshire have changed dramatically as they lost the heavy manufacturing.' Beyond the old miners' cottages, council houses are few. The Gosforth Valley housing estate in Dronfield, built in the 1970s, was once Europe's largest private housing estate and its creation sped up change in the town. It is another example of how the collectivized communities have morphed into individualistic lifestyles – as seen in other parts of the red wall. 'That made a change to the demographics and the sort of things that people were looking for, rather than just the local pub,' Tony said.

For such community-spirited people, this change was not wholly welcome. Jill said the arrival of the vast private estate meant that 'neighbours didn't neighbour'. Yet since their retirement, Tony and Jill have done their bit to rebuild that spirit. Starting with their involvement with the church – both are practising Christians – they launched a cardio club for those struggling with chest pain. Tony founded the Dronfield Heritage Trust to celebrate the town's legacy. Jill has worked with a small magazine, the *Dronfield Eye*, to celebrate events and stories of the area. Both were involved in a (successful) campaign group to return better train services into Sheffield. They set up a local day-care centre for the disabled. Both are governors at local schools and involved with St John's Ambulance. Their aim has been to 'turn Dronfield into a community where everybody feels they have a certain degree of ownership along with a certain degree of responsibility. It's that balance of the two that I think makes Dronfield distinctive as a community.' Politically, neither are party-minded but were close friends with Engel and supportive of Rowley. They counted the town lucky to have dedicated local advocates.

Housing has undoubtedly played a key part in the changing character of the red wall. When North East Derbyshire was filled with mines, its ties to the Labour Party were natural. Now that it is filled with private housing estates, like those in Killamarsh and Dronfield, commuting is its main purpose. The inherent lifestyles of those living in these estates are aspirational, even if not in an overt sense. When I asked Jill and Tony about the problems facing Dronfield, they both struggled to name any substantial issues. Many of the places that voted Conservative for the first time are content and the dystopian vision of society painted by Labour in 2019 was sharply out of kilter with the world they know. This suburban lifestyle is where future elections will be fought.

North East Derbyshire also added credence to the notion that the collapse of the red wall in 2019 was not a one-off event. Lee Rowley's increased majority, and Labour's struggle to bounce back – it dropped ten points between 2017 and 2019 – is an indication of the structural change that has taken place. I asked three other Conservatives who won red wall seats in 2017 why their seats had not switched back.

Simon Clarke, representing Middlesbrough South and East Cleveland in the north-east, thought Labour was too negative. 'They're just seen as having offered nothing positive, and this actually is where it runs deeper, once the dam broke it swept the whole thing away, I don't think it was a short-term thing, there was no alternative to Labour for a long time and now there is – that's not going to reverse quickly.'

Eddie Hughes, in Walsall North across in the West Midlands, said the Conservatives had grasped the use of language that connected with those who are not fully engaged in politics. 'The ordinary voters, they only tune in for a limited time every day, so you need to be able to link this kind of theory or concept to something that matters to them on the ground and they've got to be able to see it.'

And Ben Bradley, in nearby Mansfield, thinks that the cultural divide is chiefly to blame. 'We said we were going to do things Labour was fundamentally opposed to. They are wedge issues because Labour will find it very difficult on subjects like immigration and free speech, equality and human rights. When those discussions come around, they find that really challenging because what they're going to say is fundamentally at odds with what the vast majority of my constituents think.'

Combining all those issues together, which Boris Johnson did in 2019, is a potent mix. Some of Labour's challenges lie in policy, but far more of them are about personality and style. Until Labour rediscover that mix, Barratt Britain will continue to stick to its new voting pattern. The next stop, across in the West Midlands, *almost* went with the other red wall seats. The demographics of much of the red wall are favouring the Tories, but there are plenty of others where Johnson's party are facing their own cultural challenges.

8. Coventry North West

'People are rather afraid that this country might
be swamped by people with a different culture'

MARGARET THATCHER IN 1978

The Al-Madinah Institute is tricky to find. Along Queen Mary's
Road, in a northern suburb of Coventry, it is nestled between
car workshops and small warehouses, behind long rows of small
terraced houses. The area is one of Coventry's working-class
neighbourhoods: the streets are lined with Vauxhalls and Kias;
every property has a small Sky satellite dish; the pavements are
clean with no rubbish. The Al-Madinah's building has a varied
history: first it produced steel, then housed spare car parts. Now
it is the centre of the city's Muslim community: a 16,000 square
foot space of prayer rooms, classrooms, libraries, kitchens and a
mortuary. Maulana Nabeel Afzal, who founded Al-Madinah a
decade ago, welcomed me into his institute and apologized for
the lack of sustenance – meeting soon after a lockdown, the
centre was slowly reopening as a hub for the community and
supplies were limited.

Inside his office, lined with white leather sofas and colourful
Islamic textbooks, Afzal explained his role as the Imam, head
teacher and principal of the centre. Al-Madinah is the primary
mosque for the area: as well as the five daily prayers and 350

Islamic Studies students, 1,500 people attend Friday congregations. Every week night, the centre also teaches the Qur'an for pupils from five to eighteen years old. The city's largest Muslim community is in the north-west of the city, but Afzal said the area is especially diverse. 'The majority are from a subcontinental background, from Pakistan, India and Bangladesh. But over the last twenty years or so, we've also had the Somalian community, we've got the Iraqi, Kurdistani and Afghanistan community.'

Afzal spent a decade away from Coventry studying his faith. After boarding school, he travelled to the Al-Azhar University in Cairo and realized 'the whole purpose behind our religion is to help people as much as you can', hence founding the mosque and community centre. Al-Madinah began in a house and moved into this former factory in 2016. As well as religious activities, it has aided the community through other means, such as teaching English and offering advice on driving licences. 'From things as small as completing forms to overseeing funerals, we try to do our best to help people.' Coming from the Sufi school of Islam, Afzal said his beliefs are a major part of why he strives to reach those of other faiths, particularly the Sikh community, which is also long-established in the city. 'Our foundation is serving humanity, that's what we're all about. I'm quite a staunch Sufi in that sense, it's all about love, peace and tranquillity and thinking everyone is God's creation.'

Most of Afzal's community are affiliated to the Labour Party. Councillors for the Foleshill ward, where Al-Madinah is located, worship as part of the congregation. 'My family, being labourers, obviously they've been supporting Labour from day one.' There are Conservative candidates in the area, but he wants to 'keep the mosque free from politics as a whole'. Afzal was a keen supporter of Jeremy Corbyn, 'someone who's been one of the people' in his eyes. Corbyn's stance against the Iraq War and his growing of grassroots politics appealed. 'He had great influence, he was someone people will look up to. Not somebody who only talks the Queen's English and is very posh. This was a politician who can be really bought into. Young people who actually came into politics, for example, and are now standing as councillors by following Jeremy Corbyn's example.'

But by the 2019 election, when Labour's majority in Coventry North West dropped from 8,580 to a mere 208 votes, he reported a 'sour taste' in the community. 'Their views were more favourable towards the Tory policy on Brexit, which was let's get it done and move on.' He felt a significant part of the Muslim community eventually bought into Brexit – in part due to the political chaos, but also due to the influx of migrants from Eastern Europe. Afzal stressed there are 'some hardworking people' but was disparaging about some of the recent arrivals. 'Some of the things that have happened . . . crime, car-parking issues, tenancies, jobs or whatever it may be, some people were thinking, *If we get Brexit done, these problems will go away.* But obviously, that wasn't the case.'

Afzal's family history is typical of Coventry. His grandfather migrated to the UK in 1954 for work. 'When you go back twenty, thirty or forty years, the majority of the community was working in either steel or bakeries. And unfortunately, there's a lot less of them now here in Coventry,' he said. The Foleshill Road, once home to major manufacturers that welcomed migrants to the city, is now full of 'clothes shops, fast food outlets, restaurants and jewellers'. During Afzal's life in the city, the biggest change has been the growth of two highly rated universities, Coventry and Warwick, but also the decline of its factories and the 'hard graft' that came with them. He recalled, 'I remember my dad going to work with the whole street, fifteen or sixteen of them, they used to walk there and back. There was a really tight spirit, sticking together and covering each other's shifts.' As those industries have gone, so has that spirit. 'People are busy now with things which involve less engagement with others, and fewer community ties. That's something I miss. When I was younger, I remember on our street, all the family, all the neighbours, used to get out on hot days to sit around and have a chat. There's none of that anymore.'

As stable employment has dried up, the north-west suburbs of Coventry have suffered from deprivation. Rough sleepers and crime were Afzal's biggest concerns. 'That's something we try to tackle from the mosque, we try to solve it in our regular Friday lectures. Antisocial behaviour and crime is something which is, unfortunately, still on the rise.' Two days before we met, he noted there had been a shooting a few streets away from Al-Madinah. He puts the rise in crime down to tensions between different communities. 'Different nationalities have come here in the last ten years. There are misunderstandings and rifts . . . because there are more impoverished people in the area that leads them to crime.' He was concerned at the education provisions. 'Our religion teaches us that knowledge is to be studied from the cradle to the grave and that's something which is an issue locally.' Afzal said he hopes schools will improve, particularly at the secondary level, and in turn improve life chances. 'I've got people here, my congregation, who have been born and bred in these streets, they are now chemists, doctors, barristers, lawyers. There's a lot of talent.'

Throughout the coronavirus pandemic, Afzal has sought to work with other faiths. 'We have a regular food bank and soup kitchen in the mosque, which is open to the whole community. It's not only for Muslims or for people of Asian background. The majority of the people who use it are non-Muslim.' He is also converting the rear part of his building – a disused warehouse

– into a sports hall. 'It's going to be a full area dedicated to sports activities, close-contact boxing, martial arts, indoor football, cricket, basketball and netball. We are trying to help the community as much as we can.' His parting message was that the community can overcome its challenges. 'Coventry is a city of peace and reconciliation. I hope that's not only words, and it can become a city of peace in terms of tackling crime.' Afzal noted that 'this gap between those who are affluent and this area' is widening. Something he strongly felt must be tackled.

Coventry is the notable exception in my road trip. Here, Labour managed to cling on, despite the election of Tories in the surrounding West Midlands area and a Conservative mayor who runs the conurbation. Coventry is the eleventh-largest city in the UK, the ninth biggest in England and in the West Midlands second only to Birmingham.[1] Its industrial prime came in the 1930s, thanks to a plethora of aircraft and car manufacturers. This made the city a particular target for bombings during the Second World War. Its fourteenth-century cathedral was destroyed in November 1940, along with two thirds of the city's buildings and its critical infrastructure.[2] Seventy-one factories and 41,500 homes were eviscerated, with 568 people losing their lives. The city was rebuilt after the war, with mixed success. A new modernist cathedral was opened in 1962 alongside the war-damaged ruin. The town centre was rebuilt as one of Europe's first pedestrian precincts, but today the brutalist buildings are rather tired and Coventry's city centre is surrounded by interlocking ring roads that are not especially welcoming for pedestrians.

The rapid decline of the British car-manufacturing industry in the 1970s and 1980s was responsible for much of Coventry's economic woes. At its peak, over a hundred car and motorcycle companies operated in the city – from international brands such as Peugeot and Daimler, to domestic icons such as Jaguar, Morris and Triumph. The *Financial Times* profiled Coventry North West in 2017 as a city seeking electoral change, noting that 55,000 jobs were lost between 1975 and 1982.[3] That heritage is still present: Jaguar Land Rover maintains its headquarters in Whitley, south of the city. Combined with the nearby London Taxi Company, owned by China's Geely Auto, the region produces more cars than ever before – albeit with significantly fewer workers. The decline of Coventry's traditional employers is the root of its social issues. According to the council, 20 per cent of Coventry's population live on the breadline, which means no spare money after paying for housing, fuel and food costs.[4] Unemployment, however, was only 0.1 per cent above the national average prior to the pandemic.

Having skulked through a series of underpasses into the town centre, I found a hodgepodge of post-war redevelopment, modern refurbishments with the odd remnant of Coventry's past. The Tudor-style hall is intact. The sun shone through the ruin of the original cathedral, while the light filtering through stained-glass windows of its replacement created an ethereal beauty. The combination adds to the sense that Coventry is a place caught between the old and the new, without its own clear identity. Many of the older buildings still have scars from the wartime shrapnel.

The buildings of Coventry University dominate much of the city centre – one of its clear success stories. The university was ranked as the UK's thirteenth best in 2019 by the *Guardian*, and received a gold rating for teaching excellence. It is also one of the most affordable for students' living costs and has developed a specialism in video gaming courses: the West Midlands is home to the UK's largest regional tech cluster of 130 gaming companies.

The most recent developments gave parts of the city's civic centre a fresh and well-maintained feel. Enormous investments have been made; old offices have been transformed into bars, pubs and restaurants. But the number of hollowed-out shopfronts pointed to the post-Covid challenges. The city centre has too many retail units and with an existing plethora of restaurants offering outdoor service, it is not obvious what can replace them. It's not a challenge unique to Coventry, but it felt particularly acute in a town centre with dour architecture.

Local Conservative politicians I spoke to expressed their surprise that 59 per cent voted to leave the EU. Coventry is one of the most diverse parts of England. According to the 2011 census, two thirds of the population described themselves as 'white British' compared to 78.9 per cent for the whole country.[5] The ethnic minority population increased 22 per cent in the decade running up to the census, with a particular rise in the Asian and black communities. Those identifying as Christian are still the largest religious group in the city, followed by those with no religion, with Muslims the third-largest group. Gary Ridley, a Tory councillor, said a hundred different languages are spoken in the city yet it copes with the challenges of integration well. 'In Coventry, it works really well. We haven't had the sort of tensions that you've seen in other cities, shall we say.'

Coventry North West swapped out Labour MPs in 2019, which had an impact on the party's vote share. Geoffrey Robinson, eighty-two, was its representative for forty-three years. His connection to the seat is lengthy: Robinson was appointed chief executive of Jaguar cars at the tender age of thirty-five and worked in several positions in Britain's ailing car industry. He eventually moved onto more profitable pursuits and became a multimillionaire, and at one time was the owner of the *New*

Statesman magazine. In an exchange of emails, Robinson reflected that during his initial days in Parliament, Coventry was 'a hive of car manufacturing and associated supporting engineering companies'. Jaguar is still present in Coventry, now owned by the Indian giant Tata, and employs over 5,000 workers.[6] The old Browns Lane plant, where Robinson was based, is now an Amazon warehouse and housing estate. He expressed concern that after Brexit, trade barriers would mean the industry 'does not make economic sense' and operations would shift to Europe.

He was not surprised, however, that the seat almost went Tory. Local political leaders apparently informed Robinson that North West would have gone blue before were it not for his personal standing. 'Conservative voters voted for me because of my long supportive history in the community.' Over the last four years, he sensed a volatile mood. 'Many voters in Coventry felt disenfranchised and left behind. Recent Tory cuts to the council budget were savage and brutally impacted on the most needy, the disabled, the less educated and the unemployed. Voting for Brexit was, I believe, a protest vote.'

Robinson was personally close to Tony Blair, loaning his Tuscan villa for one of the prime minister's summer sojourns. He professed to having little time for Jeremy Corbyn. 'Corbyn became mired in the anti-Semitic fights within the Labour Party and did not clamp down on them as he should have. Corbyn also allowed the Labour leadership to be hijacked by Momentum [the left-wing grassroots campaigning group].' He also felt that rising local unemployment and the sluggish pace of wages were to blame for Labour's struggles. Keir Starmer is much more Robinson's sort of politician, who he described as 'solid and admirable' and a 'worthy foe' for Boris Johnson. But he thinks Starmer faces a significant battle to overturn Labour's errors of the past. 'Particularly the lack of investment in the north-east and old Labour strongholds, where defection to the Tories is hard to reverse. New young Labour Party members recruited by Corbyn will be hard to hold in the party too, and perhaps some of those will be lost.' Although Robinson felt the impact of coronavirus on employment would enhance Labour's electoral chances, he was pessimistic overall. 'The drift to the Tories is, I think, irrevocable.'

Taiwo Owatemi was left to deal with Labour's drift, but clung on in 2019 by 208 votes. The twenty-nine-year-old became the Labour candidate for Coventry North West in slightly odd circumstances. She was a London-based pharmacist (with an aunt in Coventry), and LabourList, a website that specializes in internal Labour politics, reported that the constituency Labour Party rebelled at the national party's decision to exclude several local candidates from the process.[7] Owatemi was the surprise choice, but was praised by local activists for being an 'articulate and passionate young woman'. In our conversation from her constituency office, she was careful and more than a little cautious in speaking about the election.

Her politics were informed by her upbringing. Owatemi's grandmother, a great influence on her life, encouraged her feminism and she joined the Oxfam Youth Board. 'I got involved from a very young age, on things such as the Robin Hood Tax, the arms trade treaty. It really empowered me to understand how I can make a difference in communities,' she said. Owatemi attended an ordinary state school while her brother went to a grammar school, making her particularly aware of inequalities caused by circumstance and education. She was also concerned about gang crime. 'The crime that really surrounded us was quite apparent. Some days I remember finishing school and seeing gangs waiting outside and police waiting outside to counter them. That's one of the reasons I decided to be co-chair of the

All-Party Parliamentary Group on knife crime, because I under-stand how much crime can affect one's opportunities in life.'

During her first year and a half in Parliament, most of her campaigning – through her enthusiastic speeches in the Commons shared on social media – was informed by her work in the NHS. 'As a pharmacist, having treated cancer patients and speaking to patients every day, I saw the impact of cuts.' She was angry at funding decisions and became motivated enough to join the Labour Party. 'I just remember constantly being frustrated. One day I walked into the kitchen and I remember my mum turning around saying to me, "Look, you just need to stop. If you're angry about something, you either do something about it or you keep quiet." I was really shocked because I wasn't expecting that kind of tone from her. And so I thought, you know what, I'm going to do something about it. I channelled that anger into activism. And I switched on my laptop, joined the local party and immediately got really involved.'

During the campaign, Owatemi said most constituents wanted to speak to her about public services. The NHS is one of the largest employers in Coventry and despite the service receiving several enormous cash injections from central government in the last five years, she reported that cutbacks were harshly felt. 'On the doorstep, most people really wanted to speak to me about the brutal cuts to NHS services over the past ten years and how that has really impacted their lives. Brexit did come up, of course, it had to. But honestly, the focus of conversations were the hardship that people in Coventry were facing. You have to remember that in the last ten years Coventry City Council has suffered cuts of up to £120 million, and we are living in a situ-ation where nearly 70 per cent of people living in poverty still have jobs. We have children living below the poverty line. So, you know, I'm glad that the Leave and Remain debate is over.'

Policing in the West Midlands is another key issue Owatemi hopes to campaign on. 'The West Midlands authority has experienced one of the largest cuts in police services . . . I speak to my local police teams on a regular basis and understand the pressures they are under, and the fact they need that additional support.' Yet she also believed there is a strong community spirit. 'What you can see in Coventry North West and we can see across Coventry that people are always able to rebuild, stay strong and come back from the devastation and destruction.'

Given that the Tories hope to overturn her slender majority, how does Owatemi hope to hold onto the seat? After all, her party is not in power in Westminster or in the West Midlands, so gaining extra funds and progressing infrastructure projects will not be easy. Since the election, her focus has been on being a passionate advocate for her community: 'I hear people often say to me that they didn't vote for me – and they're very honest about that – but they are glad that I'm standing up for Coventry, and that they will be voting for me in the next election because they see how honest I am, how committed I am to our local area and the fact that I genuinely care about helping people in Coventry.'

Jubilee Crescent is an oval shopping centre in the Radford suburb of Coventry. Facing a small Asda supermarket is an eclectic mix of shops – Acti-Vape, Dixy Chicken and Babylon Euro Mini Market, plus Jubilee Appliances and Electricals, complete with boxed-up fridges on the pavement. Charity shops were scattered throughout, but unlike many of England's smaller shopping streets, there were almost no empty windows. From this hub of a shopping centre, the spokes of streets off the crescent contain 1930s terraces mixed with local-authority housing. Some were well-kept, others were littered with debris.

An encapsulation of an ordinary middle-England area that typically decides elections.

Clare Golby was waiting in her red Fiat 500 for a stroll around Radford. After picking up coffees from Greggs, we wandered through the streets as she explained how she nearly became the first ever Conservative MP for Coventry North West. In manner she was ebullient and chatty. Golby gave her backstory in a broad Salford accent; she is a local councillor in nearby Warwickshire who came from a Labour-supporting background. When she was selected as the North West candidate, it fitted her personality. 'It's got more in common with where I come from.' A grittier sort of place? 'Exactly. I know these sorts of streets, it was easy for me to communicate with people. I'm not what people think a natural Tory is. The amount of times people have said to me, "Why are you a Conservative?" It's the way I talk, the way I present myself, it's my accent,' she beamed.

Whereas the Coventry South seat is mostly student accommodation (despite which, Labour only scraped in there with a 401-vote majority), Golby said the North West seat is predominantly families of all ethnicities. 'There's a lot of diversity in Coventry North West. There's quite a high Asian population of Sikhs and Hindus. We'd go to the Gurdwara quite a few times because it's a big central point for the community.' She found that the Asian community was overwhelmingly hardworking and community spirited – delivering food to the homeless and looking after each other. But the old pull towards the Labour Party remained. 'In the more diverse corners of the community, they seem to be entrenched. It's more about vote for Labour, rather than vote for them because they can do something for you. It's an expectation.'

She did believe that voters were increasingly looking at politics through a pragmatic lens. 'The majority of people stepped away from the identity politics and looked at the policy politics. I think that really helped in the election where policy made a big difference, rather than "Don't vote for them because they're going on a fox hunt." I'm glad that I actually got away from the identity politics because I think that's toxic. Look at me, for example: a northern woman standing as a Tory candidate in a Labour heartland. It's not what people expect.'

The 2019 campaign was arduous for Golby due to the 'terrible' weather. 'I got really ill, I had a bad chest infection.' She took a leave of absence from her work – Golby has since been made redundant during the pandemic – and devoted twelve hours each day to constant leafleting and door knocking. The Tory campaign team was small; a core of five people canvassing an electorate of almost 75,000. Sometimes it would be just Golby and one other volunteer. More support from Conservative Party HQ would have helped her. 'There were not a lot of people. We could have done with quite a few more, actually.' She was disappointed Boris Johnson did not visit her on the trail. 'He would have been absolutely mobbed if he had come up to Coventry.'

Not everyone was receptive: during the campaign, Golby's ethnic-minority staff suffered racial abuse. Generally, however, she was pleased with how the campaign was received. 'There were a lot of people who you would really not expect to be Conservative supporters who were very pleased to support us.'

Unlike her Labour opponent, she said Brexit was the dominant issue, along with Jeremy Corbyn's leadership (possibly a sign of confirmation bias, as how each candidate wanted to frame the debate). 'They'd voted Leave for whatever reason, and they felt they weren't being respected because all the Labour campaigning was about "we might want to ask the question again". The general feeling was, *No you've asked the question, you've got an answer. Get on with it.*' On election night, she felt quite optimistic. Golby, who voted for Brexit because she felt the EU was a 'one size fits all solution', believed she would have won the seat had the Brexit Party not taken almost 2,000 votes.

According to her campaigning efforts, Corbyn's leadership did not connect with many of the retired manual workers in the constituency. 'The car industry is very big in Coventry and very unionized, it certainly was in the 1980s and 1970s. Now, when we were door knocking, we were reaching a lot of people who had worked through that. They've retired, they've got a nice house, they've got a nice pension, and they absolutely did not want that taken away. The view was that some of the crazy things that Corbyn was going to produce, that was a risk for those people. They did not want to jeopardize that at all.'

As we arrived back at her Fiat, Golby said she was uncertain about whether she would stand again here or in a different seat. Come the next election, she thinks Coventry North West could go either way. 'It's difficult with cities because they aren't traditionally Conservative. If it was a town with a two hundred majority, I would say, "Absolutely."'

On the Conservatives' red wall target map for the 2019 election (see p. viii), most of the eleven that did not go blue share a trait that makes them stand out against the others. Whether it's Batley and Spen or Bradford South in Yorkshire, or Coventry North West and Coventry South, those near misses for the Tories have significant ethnic-minority populations. The Tories have long struggled to appeal to non-white Britons, much of which is tied to the legacy of one man: Enoch Powell. In 1968, the MP for Wolverhampton South West and a prominent spokesperson for the party, delivered the most infamous and toxic speech in modern British history.

Although much of Powell's speech was quoting reported

concerns from residents about the changing nature of their communities and the pressures post-war migrants were putting on public services, the incendiary language was laced with hatred. Powell quoted a working-class resident of his seat saying, 'in this country in fifteen or twenty years' time the black man will have the whip hand over the white man'. The speech's name – 'Rivers of Blood' – comes from the best-known passage, where Powell quoted Virgil's *Aeneid*:

As I look ahead, I am filled with foreboding. Like the Roman, I seem to see 'the River Tiber foaming with much blood'. That tragic and intractable phenomenon which we watch with horror on the other side of the Atlantic but which there is interwoven with the history and existence of the States itself, is coming upon us here by our own volition and our own neglect.

Although an opinion poll at the time found three-quarters of the country agreed with what Powell said, he was promptly sacked from Ted Heath's shadow cabinet and became a political pariah for the rest of his career.[8] But his influence over the party and Margaret Thatcher – especially on economics – remained strong. Powell left the Tories in 1974 over their pro-European policy – he was a prominent advocate against European integration for his whole career – but the legacy of that speech and the sense the Tories did not welcome ethnic minorities lasted for decades.

The picture has not been static. David Cameron made widening the party's appeal among non-white voters a key part of his 2010 campaign, which saw the parties' vote share among BAME voters jump to 16 per cent. Five years on, it had increased to 25 per cent.[9] According to the Runnymede Trust, Labour continued to have a strong lead with black voters in 2015, whereas the Tories did especially well with British Asians. Although Labour continues to overwhelmingly win the votes of non-white voters, the Tories are increasingly challenging them. Its efforts, however, were dented by the political realignment after Brexit. As Labour increasingly piled up votes in cities, which tend to have greater levels of diversity, and the Conservatives focused on more homogenous parts of the country, their ethnic minority vote share dropped to twenty per cent.[10] That remained static in 2019, despite the Tories entering the election with two of the great offices of state occupied by persons of colour.

The most striking change has been the rapid rise of black, Asian and ethnic minorities within the parliamentary Conservative Party. While Labour has forty-one ethnic minority MPs as of 2019,[11] a fifth of its parliamentary party, the Tories had twenty-two. But as recently as the 1997 election, every single Tory MP was white. The difference is striking, especially as, in 2021, Boris Johnson's Cabinet is the most diverse in British history.

One of the most prominent of this new generation of Tories is Sajid Javid, a trailblazer for the Conservative Party and the country. As the first person of colour to serve in the Cabinet roles of Culture, Business, and Local Government Secretary, he went on to become the first ethnic-minority Home Secretary and Chancellor. Javid, fifty-one, entered Parliament in 2010 for Bromsgrove in Worcestershire, before rapidly rising through the ministerial ranks. He challenged Boris Johnson for the party leadership in 2019 and was knocked out in the third round of voting.

Speaking to me from his House of Commons office, he acknowledged the 'significant gap' between the party's national performance and within the non-white community: 'Clearly the party has a way to go. There's lots of ways to work on policy prescriptions for issues that are of disproportionate importance to ethnic minorities. Take the tough year the whole country has been through with Covid. The government's decision to order an inquiry into why ethnic minorities have had a higher mortality rate shows that it cares.'

Javid recalled his election as a Conservative MP proved a shock to his family. 'I remember my dad saying to me, soon after, that his friends down in the mosque on Fridays "all think you're a Labour MP". "And why is that, Dad?" He said, "Do you want me to tell you in two words? Enoch Powell."' The memory of Powell was still strong during Javid's childhood. He was born the year after the Rivers of Blood speech, and its legacy made the Conservatives appear 'unwelcoming and racist'. The view of his father's generation was 'they weren't seen as a welcoming party for people of colour.'

Studying at Exeter University in the early 1990s, he also recalled that not all Tories were accommodating. 'There was a very active Conservative Students group and I was appalled by the comments of then Conservative MPs in an organization that was called the Monday Club. Trying to justify apartheid, for example, made my stomach turn. Even sometimes I would think: *Am I actually in the right party?*' He accepted, however, this was a 'tiny minority' and he wanted to be part of the effort to make the party more appealing to ethnic minorities – even if the memories linger among older voters.

Javid said that the passing of time meant that second-generation immigrants were more open to different voting options. 'The old baggage has gone and so people are much more open-minded with their vote,' he said. In seats such as Coventry North West, these generations have fewer memories of the Tories' past, and their lifestyles and types of work mean they are not intrinsically tied to Labour – the same change that has been seen among white working-class voters. 'They don't have the same sort of experience or motivation as their parents and grandparents. I think of my own parents, who came for work. They were inevitably in the semi-skilled and low-skilled jobs that were heavily unionized. Because of their lack of English, and not understanding the culture, those early arrivals relied on others for support. Often that was unions, which made them very supportive of Labour.'

But he does not think they have all become natural Tories. Instead, he thinks Asian voters are 'more neutral and flexible' and willing to shop around their vote. 'This is their home, they have no other home, they want to make the most of it for themselves and their family. So they're looking around to see who is going to offer the best deal for their families.'

Winning over more ethnic-minority voters will depend much on how the party navigates cultural issues and the challenge of improving integration between different communities. The Johnson government faced a torrent of criticism for the Sewell report into racial disparities. While the detailed report contained many fascinating and thoughtful statistics on the gaps between different communities in the UK, it was mostly noted for stating there was no institutional racism in the country.

Javid thought the report 'broadly landed in the right place' and related to many of the policy recommendations based on his work as Communities Secretary when he commissioned a review into integration. 'Louise Casey's excellent report from that time is still the most important review into this ever done. It shows clearly where we still have work to do as a country to better integrate people that have settled in the UK. In the report, we found there were almost 900,000 residents in the UK that do not speak English. That's a problem not just for them, but also for their neighbours. People reasonably will think that if you live in Britain, settle in Britain, you should at least learn the language.'

Soon after the Casey report landed, Javid was moved to become Home Secretary, after his predecessor Amber Rudd was forced to resign over the government's handling of the Windrush scandal – the wrongful detention and attempted deportations of the first wave of post-war migrants who came to the UK. Javid remained disappointed that a lot of momentum was lost on the integration debate due to the 'Brexit shenanigans'. He spoke of a ministerial visit to his home town of Rochdale to illustrate his point:

'I went to a great primary school that was doing really well. Ninety-five per cent of the kids were from ethnic-minority backgrounds. Less than a mile away, literally down the road, there was another primary school where ninety per cent of the kids are white kids. That is not because of any government policy, it was self-segregation. What worries me is that those kids live within the same neighbourhood, but they are split on ethnic lines and that's creating long-term challenges. As a country, we have to get to a point where all these kids grow up together in mixed schools and hang out with each other.'

Casey's report identified 'a lack of integration and too much segregation', Javid said, as well as seeking to improve the teaching of the English language. He thought it was especially important to ensure this happens to avoid giving succour to 'the far right, but also to the far left, who have agendas that thrive on division.' During his tenure as Home Secretary, Javid sparked controversy over two issues surrounding ethnic minorities: one was the child-grooming scandals that have enveloped some of England's towns with prominent non-white communities. His description of a Huddersfield gang as 'Asian paedophiles' drew criticism for being divisive, but he has no regrets.[12] 'You need to say it as it is and confront it. If you don't, all you are doing is playing into the hands of the far right. For the EDL and Tommy Robinsons of the world, you stoke division more easily if people are ignoring the obvious.' Javid said his comments were factual. 'If you look at the convictions of grooming gangs, in the most high-profile cases, a disproportionate number are from Pakistani heritage. It saddens and angers me, especially being someone of that heritage myself. But issues like that have to be confronted, not least by the criminal justice system, because the victims deserve justice.'

The other case was his decision to strip British citizenship from Shamima Begum, a London teenager who fled the country to join ISIS. Some prominent Conservatives criticized his decision, arguing she should have been tried on British soil. He recalled, 'People said "You're only stripping her of nationality because she's an ethnic minority." Obviously, that's complete rubbish. There were other cases that made it clear that you can be white, you can be brown, you can be any colour, but if you are a threat to this country, the government will take action.' He blamed left-wing activists for ignoring that people of all ethnicities have been stripped of their nationality for national security purposes. 'But they pick on the bit that feeds their particular narrative and their racist world view.'

Although such cultural issues continue to dominate Britain's political discourse, along with their propensity to split voters of all backgrounds, Javid is hopeful for the Tory Party's chances to improve its standing among non-white voters. 'Look at the diversity in the Cabinet. I think that does make a significant difference for young Asians, or any ethnic-minority voters, that you look at the Conservatives and you see they are certainly representative of modern Britain. It's much more so today than in any government before, Labour or Conservative.'

With Chancellor Rishi Sunak, Home Secretary Priti Patel and Business Secretary Kwasi Kwarteng, Javid is delighted that the Conservatives are making strides at this high level of politics. 'It's great we've already had one BAME minister in these roles before and it all happened under the Conservatives. This is important, no one can sit there and say this is some kind of one-off thing that the Conservatives just did for political purposes. It's all done on merit.'

Labour's most prominent black politician takes a rather different view on race. David Lammy, who entered Parliament in 2000 for the North London area of Tottenham, is one of the most articulate and passionate figures of his generation. After serving as a junior minister at the end of the New Labour governments, he made a run at being the party's Mayor of London candidate and returned to frontline politics as Keir Starmer's shadow justice secretary. During the Brexit wars, he became particularly well known for his vigorous campaigning in favour of a second referendum, which brought him many detractors. Some Brexiters caricature Lammy as the typical London metropolitan-minded Remainer, who does not understand the parts of Britain Labour lost. But across several conversations I had with Lammy – him dashing between trains as he scooted around the country to campaign for the party – it was clear he appreciated the depth of Labour's challenges in the red wall.

Although Lammy is proudly identified with Tottenham, he also has ties to Peterborough, one of the bellwether constituencies in the east of England the Labour Party must win to form a government. Having lived there for seven years while at school, he explained, 'I've always had one foot in both places and I've always understood that Labour does not form a government unless it's persuading the people of Peterborough.' In 2019, he found Labour's platform was warmly received in his constituency but not in Peterborough. He also said the issues for Labour have been building over years. 'We were piling on votes in cities, particularly cities that were diverse and in university towns among those who had gone to university there and experienced higher education. But with a whole swathe of workers who work beyond the public sector, those who had not been to universities, and those who were not diverse, we were doing extremely badly.'

I quizzed Lammy on the cultural questions, and how Labour can appeal to liberal-minded seats like his and more conservative voters elsewhere in England. His view was that you 'don't take the bait' and seek to make the argument on Labour's terms. 'It's important that people know you genuinely love your country. You've got to be able to maintain this and at the same time be able to critique and improve your country.' The tone of the Corbyn era was often 'bleak and hopeless', he noted, and gave a sense that the party did not like significant parts of the country. The divides were exacerbated by Brexit too. 'There was too strong a sense among Remainers of disdain among some of them for significant chunks of people who voted Brexit. You've got to avoid that and establish yourself as being fond of the place you represent.'

Lammy concluded the Conservatives were taking lessons from the 'Trump playbook' to drive a wedge between his party and its traditional voters. He said the party has to 'box clever' and stick to its main messages. Citing the furore around the Sewell report, which he described as 'horrific', he warned of an 'ugliness in this kind of politics' that is 'mean and narrow'. To combat this, he urged Labour to move itself into a 'position of hope'. 'On the whole, progressive parties win elections when they can define the future. Some of this culture war stuff is very backward looking. Boris tweeted six times in one day about Churchill's statue in London. By the time you get to a general election, if you've not really improved people's lot, they start to see that for what it is. We've got to just be really careful not to speak entirely to voters in the seats that we're likely to hold, like mine.'

When I asked Lammy about the sense in Coventry that increasing numbers of ethnic-minority voters were peeling away from Labour, he acknowledged there was evidence the party wasn't doing well among voters of Indian and Black heritage. Yet he remained convinced that Boris Johnson's electoral pledges will backfire and the voters who trusted him will be let down. 'I don't believe he's waking up every day worrying about how to improve the lot of those voters . . . I don't think the jobs, the public services and the prospects are going to return to those communities under Boris Johnson.'

Whatever Johnson does, Lammy acknowledged there are significant changes ahead for left-wing parties, in Britain and beyond, where unionized jobs have also gradually disappeared. 'When progressive parties spend too much time talking about issues that are not central to them, they have turned away. Labour has experienced that without doubt. We're being outflanked, outspent and definitely politically outmanoeuvred by the right [in England], because we don't appear to be talking about the things that matter to people in their areas.' To achieve this, he thought Labour must follow Joe Biden's recipe for success in 2020 for the US Democrats. 'We don't seem to be talking about the economy in the way that people want to hear.'

Lammy felt that now Jeremy Corbyn had left the political stage, it 'freed up' those parts of the country to vote for Labour again. 'There are some who we will have to do a lot more work to get them back. I don't think this is a binary thing. But it's definitely the case that a year after the election, it's still about being heard. It's the brand. Because Boris Johnson is a brand built over years.' But he also appreciated the mathematical challenges. 'Right-wing and populist governments go down because of sleaze and the populism, they drown in it in the end. This will take some time. The truth is, we lost the last election by a significant amount. It's going to take an almighty swing for us to win the next election. And that should not be underestimated. I hope that we win the next election, but in truth, it may well be a project that's bigger than the cycle that ends in 2024.'

My penultimate stop in Coventry North West was to visit a prominent member of the Sikh community. Balbir Sohal resides in a well-kept semi-detached property – traditional outside with a modern interior. Over cups of Nespresso coffee in her lounge, decorated with pictures of her family, she spoke with articulate passion about the political activism of her youth. Sohal, sixty-five, was born in India and emigrated to the UK with her family at the age of three. Her father came to Coventry via East Africa with £3 and a British passport, and worked initially at a steel foundry in nearby Nuneaton. He lived in the north-west part of the city with ten or twelve people in one house – a typical situation of the time. 'You kept the beds warm so there was a night shift and the day shift. They shared out the duties between them.' She was the first in her family to attend university. 'In those days, it was quite rare for an Asian woman to study. I went to Warwick and I did history and then became a teacher, which is what I always wanted to do.' She purposely decided to live in the area in which she taught and stayed there for her whole life, aside from a period living in America.

As well as teaching, Sohal has been a citizenship advisor for the Department for Education and an education officer for Prevent, the government's anti-radicalism programme. Why did she get involved? 'It was after the London 7/7 attacks. No one else wanted to do it so I thought I would because I believe that in order to make change, you have to make change from within.' Prevent has been criticized by some for unfairly targeting the Muslim community, something she tried to overcome. 'What was interesting in Coventry, we actually chose not to look at our Muslim communities, we called it "building resilience". And we had the Home Office slap our wrists because they wanted us to report back on the Muslim community. But in Coventry it's always been issues of the far right. Although yes, there are elements of Islamists.'

As the coffees cooled, Sohal spoke of how Coventry has changed during her lifetime. 'When I first came to this country, there was nothing like English language classes to support you. The Gurdwara was only established later on. That element has really changed, because now you've got Punjabi classes, and the Gurdwaras are well established.' She said tensions within the community are limited, although she too was concerned about the rise in knife crime. 'Quite a lot of our children have been sent to other cities for their own safety, there's a whole thing around county lines [drug gangs].' She blamed cuts to youth services over the last decade for creating these problems.

The main change in Coventry's Sikh community during Sohal's life has been the rise in prosperity. She described it as a 'very wealthy' community that has undergone significant changes in the types of employment its members have. 'A lot of our young-sters are in white-collar jobs as opposed to my parents' generation, when a lot of them were in skilled manufacturing. We've also seen a growth in terms of the level of skills and education within the Sikh community.' The aspirations of the community are to be doctors, lawyers, pharmacists or teachers, what she described as the 'middle-class dream'. This change has made the Sikh community 'far more affluent'. She explained, 'You've got this nucleus of middle-class Asians . . . all of us might have come into areas like Hillfields or Foleshill, but as soon as you've got the money it's about what's best for your family, as well as the big cars and flash houses, it's a status thing.' All this has made the community more open to voting Tory. 'A lot of their mentality is aligned with what you could call right-wing Conservative thinking.' To her dismay, many supported Brexit – mostly out of a desire to reduce migrants from other countries. 'I just thought, *Oh my god, you're an immigrant yourself and you've come to this country.*'

In the earlier generations of Coventry's Sikh community, she said political interactions were mostly overseen by 'gatekeeper politicians', as many of the migrants who arrived in the UK had little education, spoke poor English and had little sense of how British society worked. There was often one person who 'if you wanted something done, he could do it' as Sohal put it – be that a housing application, dealing with the council or business transactions. These leaders were not necessarily diehard Labour supporters, but they were naturally aligned with the party and would play an electioneering role. 'They would play into the pockets of politicians. For example, "I can assure you that we'll get a hundred votes from this constituency or a thousand from here" you know? People thought *"If it's our community leaders, they're educated, they must know what's best for us,"* and they would follow that lead.' But when that generation died out, the community became more individualistic and the role of gatekeepers declined. 'It's not just two or three people that represent the Sikh community now. You wouldn't ask that of white people, so why do they ask, "Who is representative of your community?" We're all different.'

Sohal, as you may have gathered, is a committed Labour Party supporter for the same reason as Sajid Javid's father. She recalled Enoch Powell's Rivers of Blood speech, listening to it on the radio at the age of twelve, and the impact it had on her community: 'There was so much, almost like, fear and panic within the community about our status here.' Yet she voted Conservative. In the 2017 mayoral election, she supported Andy Street, the former chief executive of retailer John Lewis who became the region's first directly elected mayor. 'He has brought a lot of stuff to the region, he is very forward thinking.' I contacted her after my visit to ask if she voted for him again in the 2021 mayoral election. Sohal demurred, which I took to mean that she might have broken her habit for a second time.

After I left Sohal's house, I drove over to Coventry train station to find the views of Andy Street on whether the Tories can make further gains in the region. The bright and cheery fifty-seven-year-old was on the campaign trail for his (successful) mayoral re-election bid, boosted by the party's progress in the 2019 campaign. He said the Tories' progress in the city's North West and South seats was built on the local base of councillors and mayors, as well as delivering improvements. 'Demonstrating that a combination of a Conservative mayor and a Conservative government can invest and win for Coventry is critical.'

He also pointed out that the party has been gradually winning seats in the West Midlands that share demographics with the red wall. In 2005, the Tories had three seats in the region; by 2019, it was fourteen. 'This trend is deep, and if you look beyond the immediate urban area of the West Midlands, lots of seats that were in Tony Blair's alliance – Tamworth, Redditch and North Warwickshire for example – they are all now strong Conservative seats.' Street won a second term, in part due to his success in ensuring the High Speed 2 railway was built – connecting Birmingham to London in forty-five minutes. He saw delivery as vital for holding the trust of voters. 'That's why the word I keep coming back to is delivery: getting things done, proving that we elected a Conservative set of leaders that actually change things on the ground.'

His re-election in May 2021 for a second term as West Midlands Mayor came after the region suffered particularly badly from the coronavirus pandemic. The successive lockdowns hurt the retail sector in Birmingham – coincidentally closing the John Lewis where Street once had his second office. During the 2019 general election, he sensed a resentment towards Labour, who had been in charge of many of the local councils for some time. The other major factor was resentment towards the capital. 'My business, John Lewis, was based in London – I've got absolutely nothing but goodwill towards London, but you often get a real sort of feeling that the metropolitan elite just don't understand how it is here in Walsall.'

Street has long argued the West Midlands is especially important for the Conservatives as a guiding light of where the rest of the country is demographically heading. Britain is becoming more diverse and the Tories will have little choice but to widen their appeal. 'All of our cities and regions are by national standards diverse, and some of our areas in Birmingham are obviously super-diverse.' But he said there was 'incredible harmony between communities' of which he was intensely proud of. 'It goes right back to why I wanted to be mayor here. Not only is it my home town, but it's actually a place that I think reflects how Britain is going to develop in that tolerant, inclusive way.'

Looking back on 2019, Street said the party 'saw enormous progress in the Hindu and Sikh community. It is a fact that our share of the vote in the Muslim community was not what we hoped it would be and we've got to work hard to demonstrate that we can deliver for those communities. But I see absolutely nothing in terms of the aspirations of the Bengali community, the Pakistani community that tells us that we can't connect with those communities.' He concluded, off to canvass the voters of Coventry that he would have to win over to have a second term as mayor. His victory on 6 May confirmed he did.

Coventry North West was the most urban seat I had visited so far. Although it has suffered from the same deindustrialization as the other red wall constituencies, its high levels of diversity were chiefly the reason that it did not flip Tory in 2019. Similarly to the other seats that did not turn, however, I gathered a sense that a little extra ground work by the Conservative Party, plus the lack of the Brexit Party in future elections, may tip it into the blue column. Labour, on the other hand, may find it easier to use existing footholds to keep the seat and others like it.

Although Coventry's post-industrial economy is more resilient than other parts of the red wall, the tales and statistics of deprivation do require urgent attention from both the mayoralty and national government. Tony Sewell's report on racial integration may have garnered some negative headlines, but its recommendations on tackling the socioeconomic issues within ethnic-minority communities should not be dismissed. The same is true for Dame Louise Casey's report on improving integration. She told me that many of the trends – such as the lack of English language in some communities and the role of women – have yet to be tackled. 'I don't think the government, since the report, has really grasped it. I think we should try and integrate with each other more than we currently are. Some of the money that they handed out to places like Bradford has been used to set up a kind of communities' fund. I think some of that money has been spent well and will have made some difference. I'm also a huge believer in English language courses, I'd make it mandatory.' Dame Louise also felt that coronavirus should provide the government with the impetus to examine the policy challenges highlighted by Brexit. 'The pandemic has gifted the government the ability to look at things fresh and new – particularly around issues to do with poverty and hunger, they've got the gift now to say *let's sort something out*.' During her travels around the country for her integration report, she recalled a surprise that the Leave vote was not higher than fifty-two per cent. 'People were so disaffected. From my review, you could predict it – the divide between the rich and the poor. I'm not a party-political specialist, but I think it was a natural consequence of wanting a different leadership.'

The West Midlands region is the nearest the UK has to a US swing state – a British Pennsylvania. Whenever Labour or the Tories are on the up, so is their seat count in the heart of England. Birmingham is often described as the UK's second city and its politics remain strongly Labour (the Tories gained one suburban seat in 2019). But the rest of the area has plenty of other towns that fit the more typical red wall mould: Dudley North went Conservative for the first time in 2019, as did the pair of West Bromwich constituencies. The West Midlands is often overlooked compared to the north of England, but it is just as central to the story of Labour's collapse.

My most striking conclusion from Coventry, however, is that the same collapse of collective institutions is taking place among ethnic-minority communities as has been seen among white working-class voters elsewhere in England. Although personally neither were inclined to vote Tory in the 2019 election, Maulana Nabeel Afzal and Balbir Sohal noticed a change among their friends and family. As these communities become more individualistic, they will be increasingly open to voting Conservative. In the same way Labour may have taken parts of the red wall for granted, it risks making the same error with BAME communities.

The party can always rely on public sector workers, but it needs to appreciate how non-white communities are no longer homogenous in their political outlook. The other challenge for Labour is whether they will alienate parts of some ethnic-minority communities in their efforts to rebuild the red wall. Particularly on cultural issues, Keir Starmer has a fine line to tread. And for the Tories, the question remains whether their stance on cultural issues will alienate or bring in more supporters from these communities.

Support for the Tories is growing in some of England's most diverse seats. I was struck by Leicester East: a similar constituency to Coventry North West, which last returned a Tory in 1983. Although Labour's Claudia Webbe was elected with a comfortable 6,019 majority in 2019, the Conservatives increased their vote by fourteen percentage points. In the neighbouring Leicester West constituency, the Tory candidate put six points onto their vote and again slashed Labour's majority. And in Bradford South – one of the red wall targets – Labour's majority was reduced to 2,346.

Or, as one Conservative Cabinet minister put it to me, 'splitting the ethnic-minority vote is the next shoe to drop for Labour. If we can revert to our 2015 [election] strategy and win over aspirational people in the black and Asian communities, there are a whole host of seats open to us.' It is wholly possible that by the next election, three of the great offices of state will be held by non-white ministers. That alone may not win these seats for the Tories, but it is a clear sign of where the party hopes to pick up votes in the future.

The Westminster parlour game of 'who will be the next Tory leader' is likely to be some way off, but it is easy to imagine the eventual race to succeed Boris Johnson could be made up of all non-white candidates. Chancellor Rishi Sunak is almost certain to stand, seasoned party activists think Home Secretary Priti Patel and Foreign Office minister James Cleverly are also likely to run. Fifty years after Enoch Powell's speech turned a generation of ethnic-minority voters from the Conservatives, would such a contest complete the party's reinvention as a welcoming institution for all?

Coventry was as far south as my road trip was headed. After bidding farewell to the ring roads and underpasses, I swung back onto the M6 for the two-hour journey to my final two stops, in the north-west. Heywood and Middleton, on the peripheries of the Labour stronghold of Manchester, was where I went next, with thoughts of mayors and devolution in my mind as I went up the motorway.

9. Heywood and Middleton

'Mayors are not so much post-ideological as they are oblivious to ideology, seeing in ideology an obstacle to governance. Because in the city, governance is about solving problems, making things work.'

BENJAMIN BARBER, AUTHOR OF
IF MAYORS RULED THE WORLD

Less than ten minutes after arriving in Manchester, I heard the sounds of The Smiths. Beside the Rochdale Canal running through the city centre, Andy Burnham and I found a metal bench well away from the teenagers enjoying a series of cans on a Wednesday afternoon. Dressed every bit the northern man in a short-sleeved shirt and matching black trousers, he embraced the scene. 'It's the perfect Manchester experience!' The swans and geese circled the city's mayor, threatening to snap at our legs before some gentle gesturing pushed them away. Burnham, fifty-one, was especially cheerful on this sizzling afternoon, having received his first coronavirus vaccine that morning. Yet as soon as we launched into the topic of Labour and the red wall, his spirits dampened as he set out his case for being the John the Baptist of Labour's troubles. During the 2015 Labour leadership contest, when he came a distant second to Jeremy Corbyn, Burnham recalled he was the only candidate arguing the party should be concerned about its traditional heartlands, such as his former seat, the town of Leigh on the outskirts of the city.

'I think it has been a long time coming,' he said in his Scouse accent, softened by his years in Westminster and latterly Manchester. 'People used to laugh at me because I was complaining about Labour being too London-centric. But eventually, the public started to feel the party was way too London-centric.' In 2015, Burnham cited the fact he was booed for discussing immigration controls; a sign that 'the party, internally, was increasingly not picking up the mood of how people felt.' His prophecy came true: Leigh elected its first-ever Conservative MP in 2019 – a seat that returned a Labour majority of 17,272 as recently as 2005. Labour's decline in Burnham's old constituency mirrors another: Heywood and Middleton, a similar seat on the outskirts of the city that now sits in his purview as mayor for the Greater Manchester region.

After (again) edging away the aggressive swans, Burnham explained why the party was in denial about its situation in the north of England. He put the 2019 election outcome down to the party's leadership and Brexit, adding that people 'were emotionally making a break.' The 2016 Brexit referendum was the moment 'the umbilical cord was being a bit broken'. Referendum day was heartbreaking for Burnham because he sensed Leigh had left him. The results proved it had: 63 per cent of its residents voted Leave.

One of the 'what ifs' of recent political history is whether, had Burnham won the 2015 leadership contest and campaigned more forcefully than Corbyn for Remain in the referendum, Brexit could have been avoided. 'I'd like to think I would have pulled some Labour voters back to Remain if I'd won the leadership.' Burnham mentioned he pressed Corbyn on the Brexit issue and whether he would campaign ardently for Remain but 'he wouldn't answer' and 'it was getting late in that Labour leadership contest' to change the minds of the membership.

Burnham professed to 'loads' of regrets about the 2015 leadership race, where he ultimately won just 19 per cent of the vote. He blamed conflicting advice and the pressure of being the frontrunner for suffocating him and 'losing the sense of [him] self'. MPs faced 'massive pressure' on social media to nominate Jeremy Corbyn, he recalled. As soon as he was into the final contest, Burnham claimed that he knew his campaign was in trouble. 'I remember the day when [Liverpool City Region mayor] Steve Rotheram, who was my campaign manager, rang me and said "Jeremy's got in by one." My heart metaphorically hit my boots, I thought, *That's it.*' The safeguards of the past, where MPs had the final say on which candidates made it onto the ballot paper, were 'washed away a little by social media' according to Burnham (also influential was Ed Miliband's decision to allow registered supporters to vote in the contest for £3). He also felt some deeper feelings within the party aided the rise of Corbyn: 'The Labour Party has an inbuilt love for the kind of dreamy radical romantic.'

The decision to walk away from Westminster in 2016 to run for Greater Manchester mayor was not a difficult one for Burnham. Although he served in Corbyn's first shadow cabinet, he was not 'particularly on board with a lot of the policy direction', particularly 'the lack of patriotism'. Although claiming to be 'economically more left wing than New Labour', he insisted, 'I am a patriotic person, pro-police. My great-grandfather died in the First World War, it's a bit inbuilt for a lot of people in the north-west of England.' He also 'struggled' with Ed Miliband's leadership due to the fogginess that clouded his policy agenda (Burnham noted he 'loved' Miliband and the pair remain good friends). 'Why did I leave? If I'm just honest with you, I was falling out of love with the Westminster world pretty much from 2010 onwards, even before the election.'

Burnham has no regrets about leaving the national stage, describing his current role as 'energizing and liberating' and lambasted Westminster for 'making a fraud out of you'. He has also deeply fallen out of love with party politics. 'You end up in a place that you're not sure of yourself anymore, because you're voting in ways that you don't always believe in. You've been told to say things that you're iffy about sometimes, that's the effect of being a front-bench politician in this country.' Ministers are not able to speak personally and passions about issues that concern politicians are stymied in his view due to the need for party unity. 'I guess my character isn't suited to that in the long run.'

His first term as Greater Manchester mayor was hectic, including the Manchester Arena bombing in its first weeks, the 2018 wildfires on the outskirts of the city and the coronavirus pandemic. But Burnham said, 'It's been draining at times but I've loved it, I've genuinely never looked back.' His public profile has never been higher. During the coronavirus pandemic, he was dubbed 'King of the North' for his tough stance in negotiating with Boris Johnson over the terms of further coronavirus restrictions for Manchester. He was very comfortably elected for a second term in May 2021, but could he imagine returning to Westminster? 'I think I've got a lot of work to do. I wouldn't rule it out. I do expect this to be my last job,' he said, adding that his wife would not be entirely happy with the prospect. The left-wing parts of Labour disaffected with Keir Starmer's leadership were particularly eager to talk up his candidacy. Reflecting on his failed leadership bids of 2010 and 2015, he has a single motivation to return to Westminster: 'I'm not going back to just go back [to national politics for the sake of it], if you know what I mean. I'd be going back to try and reconnect Labour to the north if that's what was needed at the time.'

As Labour's most prominent national figure, Burnham was worried that Labour was not taking the Johnson government's economic and devolution agenda seriously. With George Osborne's Northern Powerhouse project, for example, Burnham was worried his party was outflanked (something I put to Osborne himself later on this stop). 'I've been saying to the party they need to get behind what we're trying to do here, that this is the way to reclaim Labour's lost emotional connection with large parts of the north that it needs to get serious about regaining.' Although he would not openly admit it, Burnham was palpably pleased that regional politics are now central to the UK's discourse. 'For good or ill, when the Tories talked about the Northern Powerhouse, they have now opened up regional divides as an issue. The Tories are not fulfilling it now they've started it, but it's still a slogan to people here . . . there is a bloody big hole for the Labour Party to say "we come in and we do this properly".'

His proposals for 'true levelling up' trade off Disraeli's one-nation philosophy. 'What the pandemic has shown us is that a third of people in the UK, possibly closer to half in parts of the north, have lives that are fundamentally insecure because of poor work and poor housing.' The two nations divide was demonstrated during the Brexit debate. 'There's almost people living parallel lives in this country, the lives of some people are unrecognizable from others. And I think levelling up post-pandemic should be about lifting people into much better circumstances, to a position where they have better mental health and wellbeing.' Burnham agreed with Neil Kinnock that economic security is key for any new Labour message. 'A lot of people in this city are living in a very precarious position, unsure about their income, unsure about their housing situation, and that eats away at their mental health all the time. I think the way back is to speak to that reality and be clear about regional identity.'

I was curious about the concept of Greater Manchester. Where I sat with Burnham was like any other major city, yet his conurbation includes dozens of smaller towns that don't feel like that at all. He made the case there was a 'growing feeling of a Greater Manchester identity', with Greater Manchester policies – citing his success in reducing homelessness. He also pointed to the bee, the city's symbol, and lifted up his arm to show it tattooed on his biceps. 'It appears everywhere, even in Leigh, you see the bee everywhere. If you look at the bin there,' he said, pointing to one, now full of empty beer cans, which had the bee logo engraved on it, 'that's a Manchester symbol, but it's now a Greater Manchester symbol.' For anyone under the age of forty-five, Burnham thought the Greater Manchester identity trumps that of the traditional locales of Lancashire or Rochdale that envelop the towns outside of the city. This identity passes the holiday test, he thought. 'People often say that anyone on holiday from anywhere in Greater Manchester when asked, "Where are you from?", they will all say Manchester. That identity has been built.'

Changing employment has also reshaped these identities. When the primary source of employment was the coal mine in a north-west town or village, its residents did not have to think or travel beyond their locale. But as more people in towns such as Heywood and Middleton were employed in the city, they increasingly looked outward. 'I think they see the excitement of cities . . . buying into the Greater Manchester identity.' In Tory towns such as Leigh and Middleton, which Burnham acknowledged are fiercely proud of their independent identity, he said he continues to promote the GM ideal.

One area where that identity has not built up is within the Labour Party. Burnham remarked that 'city Labour' is markedly different from the constituency parties in small locations. 'Labour Manchester is more modern, if you like, in terms of sensibilities. It's more green in terms of placing a higher priority on zero carbon . . . it's not had the same loss of emotional connection that your "town Labour" had.' Mayors, for Burnham, are vital for Labour in rebuilding the party's ties in such areas. 'Speaking through the party, the public don't really connect with that at all . . . when I do this role, people can connect.'

The Heywood and Middleton constituency brought me into contact with the only major city in the red wall journey. The constituency was created from two previous seats that separately represented the two towns, both of which had returned Conservative MPs in the past, but the combined seat has been solidly Labour since 1983. It is spliced north to south by the M62 motorway, which speaks to its split identity. The constituency has grave health issues: depression, obesity, diabetes and high blood pressure are all several points above the national average.[1] Twenty-one per cent of the constituency is classified as highly deprived.

I began in Middleton, a town on Manchester's periphery. Having boarded no buses on this journey so far, I hopped on the 163 from Piccadilly Gardens to the town's bus station. The mid-century shopping centre was moderately busy, masked shoppers weaved in and out of Costa, the WH Smith newsagent and vitamin outlet Holland and Barrett. Underneath a community sculpture called *The Moonraker* – not related to the James Bond film, but local poachers – Chris Clarkson was waiting.[2] The thirty-eight-year-old Tory is a former member of Salford Council and was working as part of Virgin's corporate development team when he took the seat in 2019 with a mere 663-vote majority. He did not believe he was going to win. 'I didn't quit work. I was expected to go in on the Tuesday. I actually had to ring my boss to tell her what had happened,' he said. Clarkson was a Brexiter on 'strictly constitutional grounds', matching his constituency, which voted 62 per cent to leave the EU.

We set off on a walking tour of Middleton. Judging by the range of shops, Middleton is well stocked for the local residents but does not have enough to entice other people here – particularly with Manchester centre six miles away. Clarkson's first point of note was that the two towns of the seat are very different. Middleton is larger, with more of a high street and affluence – both due to its size and its Manchester-facing status. Clarkson explained the differences in the seat: 'Middleton is historically Manchester, it is an M postcode, 0161 dialling code and a Mancunian accent. If you talk to people around here, they sound like they're from Manchester. But you cross the motorway to Heywood and it's entirely different. Proper East Lancashire.' There are tensions between the two towns too: 'There's a perception that if one gets something the other doesn't.'

He felt the transport links were 'utterly crap' – noting the bumpy bus ride takes forty-five minutes. It is the same distance again across the M62 to Heywood. 'It's really poorly served for an area that is so well geographically located.' He is hopeful that better links could make the seat more akin to leafy Altrincham, which is linked to the city centre via tram. He hopes the light rail network would be extended to his constituency and 'didn't mind' Andy Burnham's plans to take full control of Greater Manchester's buses.

We wandered out of the town centre and into the streets of terraced housing, where Clarkson set out why he disagreed with Burnham's idea of a conurbation identity. 'There is a natural area of Greater Manchester in terms of economic area and all the rest of it,' he admitted. 'But I don't think anyone would say on holiday they're from there.' In a sense they are both right: the simplest answer about identity can be the one people most immediately grab. We reached the beautiful Warwick Mill building, an expansive red-brick factory overlooking Middleton. Some of the windows were intact, but many were shattered or boarded up. Clarkson was hopeful that the building can be restored to flats, but the process was bogged down in planning disputes. Pointing at the mill, he said 'It's frustrating, because in Middleton, there are lots of people who want to do stuff. It's just giving them the tools to do it. This is an area where people want to improve things.' As with the other red wall seats, skills and education are top of his levelling up priorities. 'The reason big firms don't relocate here is the wrong skilled or trained workers.' Looking at more deserted buildings, he reflected on how the reason for Middleton's existence has changed. 'The employer was based in the town, the workforce came from the town. Now the economy has changed. Most of the jobs are in Manchester, so this either becomes a dormitory town, not properly connected, or a destination.' Heywood and Middleton's weekly pay is £87 below the national average; its out-of-work benefits claimant rate is almost two percentage points higher.[3]

Next we came to leafier streets – 1930s detached houses with smart front lawns, with two cars in each driveway. Julie Grainger, a local housebuilder, has noted that the growth of such a place has overall made Middleton more middle class: 'Ten to fifteen years ago it was quite a rundown area. But now there has been an injection of cash with new bars and cafes, it's much better.'[4] Yet the socioeconomic mix of Middleton appears stark to the casual visitor. 'Conservative seats in the past didn't have that mix, they tended to be homogenous. The middle class is now effectively made up of well-paid public-sector workers with two Audis who are committed socialists,' Clarkson said. 'They aren't coming back, whereas the bloke with the white van and the England flag hanging out of his window is very much open for business with us.'

Middleton is not awaiting grand infrastructure projects, but Clarkson was hopeful for 'bread and butter stuff', the 'small fixes that make things work properly'. He is not looking for a revamped shopping centre, for example. 'You don't know if they're actually going to be useful and they could take years to build. If you want to demonstrate actual change you want to be able to say to people, "Does this work better than it did three years ago?"'

Our tour finished on the Langley housing estate – tightly packed council housing, lined with dark-green metal fences. This is where Clarkson made his largest gains in the 2019 election. 'We would normally find one in every 20 voters was Conservative. Last time, we were probably pulling even with Labour.' The main cause was Jeremy Corbyn. Almost every other house has a giant red poppy on the brickwork, commemorating the armed forces. 'The patriotism angle was strong; they didn't like or trust Corbyn. You had a lot of people staying at home, which is why the numbers went down.' Clarkson departed for home himself, to hop onto the latest of the endless Zoom calls that dominate the lives of the red wall Tories.

Still without the Mini, I went back on the 163 bus over the M62 to explore Heywood. As the bus trundled out of Middleton, it soon entered open countryside. The Scout Moor Wind Farm of twenty-six turbines glared over Heywood, which bore few remnants of being a Lancashire mill town. Heywood overlooks the moorlands of Rochdale and the dramatic peaks of the Cheesden Valley. Much of the town is populated by council estates built in the 1950s and 1960s, when the slums of central

Manchester were cleared out: one estate alone, Darnhill, housed 5,000 former city dwellers from Manchester. The traditional industry of the town, cotton, was in steady decline by this time. Back in 1833, the town had twenty-seven mills, creating 'an influx of strangers causing a very dense population'.[5] Rochdale had a brief moment of national political infamy during the 2010 election, when an irate life-long Labour voter, Gillian Duffy, confronted Gordon Brown about the influx of Eastern European migrants to the UK. As he darted away from the confrontation in his ministerial car, the then prime minister was inadvertently recorded describing her as 'that bigoted women'. Brown was forced into a grovelling apology, with his head in his hands, highlighting the party's challenges with its traditional supporters.

Alighting from the bus in Heywood, I found a barren town with almost no pedestrians. On a solo walking tour, I discovered a range of housing that reminded me of Newcastle upon Tyne's suburbs. From small terraces to spacious detached homes, Heywood's housing stock caters for all middle-class needs. The civic centre around the church and town were well-kept, with a black metal outline of a kneeling soldier to pay tribute to the armed forces, another sign of the area's deep patriotism. The old police station and post office buildings were abandoned, empty and to let. Even with lockdown restrictions allowing for shops to trade, almost everything was closed.

Heywood's last mill closed in the 1980s, with the town's economic activity dominated by the 200-acre Heywood Distribution Park. Opposite the site, surrounded by barbed fences and CCTV, was a McDonald's bakery for the fast food chain, its intoxicating presence permeating the air with the faint smell of yeast mixed with the diesel from the trucks.

After learning little from Heywood itself, I followed Chris Clarkson's advice to make the hour-long walk to the village of

Bamford. Coming out of the town and into the countryside, the classic traditional kind of Conservative prosperity started to emerge. The cars became more opulent, the houses larger. Google Maps guided me through a 1970s housing estate – the sort that proliferated in North East Derbyshire. As I trudged up Bamford Way, there was an unbroken row of five detached houses with a Mercedes parked in each driveway. When this estate was built, I doubted this level of prosperity existed.

At the end of a country lane, I came to the Bamford Barista. His name is Philip Beal. His quaint cottage on the edge of Bagslate Moor park – home to Rochdale's rugby union and golf clubs – became a takeaway cafe during the pandemic. Beal, fifty-two, repaired espresso machines for Starbucks as his day job. With coffee shops closed, he set up spare machines in his kitchen. His wife baked cakes and his family helped with the brewing and running the till. A steady stream of well-to-do families passing with assortments of dogs and children stopped en route for treats and flat whites. When the queues subsided, I asked Beal about where the idea came from.

'I used to leave books outside for people to pick up on their way to the moor,' he said. 'It was very successful, so I opened this.' His porch makes for a convincing cafe, the half stable door is his till. Beal followed politics 'a bit' and was wholly unsurprised when Heywood and Middleton elected its first Conservative MP in 2019. 'I was never a Labour man. It's good, it feels like we needed a bit of change.' He made an explicit point of saying that his wife 'doesn't like Keir Starmer much'. Beal did not have much to say about the Labour leader, but conceded 'he's better than the last bloke, Corbyn'. He mentioned that Clarkson had dropped by a handful of times and praised the new MP for 'getting well-known locally', something that is seen as 'pretty important'. There are few problems in the Heywood area. 'People are fairly easy-going, there are no troubles.' Beal reckoned most of his customers either run small businesses or work for Rochdale council. And when he goes on holiday, he would tell people he is from Rochdale. Not Manchester? 'Certainly not.' I understood Clarkson's point that Heywood is where the Tory support began and Middleton was where the seat was seized.

Far away from public transport, and missing the car, I headed out of the village via taxi. There is one major unknown factor for the next UK election: boundary changes. Every five years, constituencies are examined, redrawn and rebalanced based on their population changes. Heywood and Middleton is oversized, which means it is likely to be split. If Heywood becomes a separate seat, it will likely end up taking in parts of the Rochdale constituency, which would push it back towards Labour. Half of Middleton, on the other hand, will be subsumed into Manchester and be reunited with its Labour-leaning, city identity. The city was where I returned.

Aside from its split personality, Heywood and Middleton is politically significant for another reason. In 2014, the incumbent Labour MP Jim Dobbin unexpectedly died in office and a by-election was called. Polling day came when UKIP was on the rise and concerns about immigration were dominating the national debate. The party, then led by Nigel Farage, increased its vote by thirty-six percentage points and ended up a mere 617 votes away from winning the seat. Their candidate was John Bickley, a former music industry executive turned games developer (he played a role in creating the first PlayStation), who had stood in a by-election earlier that year in nearby Wythenshawe and Sale East. Bickley was judged to be one of the party's most effective campaigners with a real chance of making UKIP's first parliamentary gain.

Speaking from his home in Cheshire, Bickley, sixty-eight, spoke of his Labour-supporting family background: growing up on a council estate, reading the *Daily Mirror*, imbibing a strong Christian spirit. Despite his traditional working-class background, he voted Conservative all of his life until David Cameron became Tory leader and set about his modernizing mission. After Cameron didn't pursue a referendum on the EU's Lisbon Treaty, Bickley joined UKIP in 2011 and was soon encouraged to stand for parliament. In Heywood and Middleton, he found 'a lot of traditional Labour supporters were fed up with the way they saw the Labour Party not representing the working class anymore', particularly on the issue of immigration. Such voters found no home in Cameron's party either. Bickley said for these people, mostly found on the council estates around Heywood, the thinking was, 'Maybe we vote for UKIP as a means to express our disgust at the two-party cartel system?' He defined an imagined biography of the typical disaffected Labour voter: 'Your dad is Manchester-born. Your dad supports Manchester United and guess which team you end up supporting all your life? Man United. If my dad had supported Man City, I'd be a Man City supporter. That gets ingrained on the political side as well with Labour and the Tories.'

Two issues dominated that campaign, both of which were sensitive topics. The first was immigration and its impact on public services. Bickley said, 'a lot of people were seeing their jobs threatened, lost their jobs or had to take reduced wages' following the rapid rise in migrants from the EU's eastern expansion. These concerns were not xenophobic, he argued: 'Let's not blame these people. If I was in Eastern Europe, you know, on five hundred quid a month and I can get on a bus and come over to Britain and get fifteen hundred quid a month, I'd be on the first bus.'

The second issue was child sexual exploitation gangs. Bickley distributed a leaflet during the by-election that claimed 'Labour's betrayal is no more apparent than with the young white working-class girls of Rotherham and Rochdale where rather than upset immigrant communities, years of abuse were ignored and complaints swept under the carpet'. This issue, and sensitivities discussing it, affirmed a sense among traditional Labour supporters that the party was out of touch. 'A lot of people said "I'm not surprised, reading the report [into CSE], we've been concerned about that for a long time and Labour had seemed to ignore it." I think that fuelled even more the idea the Labour Party no longer represents the working class.'

During the campaign, Farage visited four times and Bickley was given solid financial support. Had it not been for the Clacton by-election on the same day – when Douglas Carswell was elected as the first UKIP MP – also using up campaign resources, he felt the extra heave could have seen him over the line. Had he won, Heywood and Middleton 'would have been a bigger result and had a greater impact on politics.' Despite the Tories moving in a direction that has swept up UKIP voters, Bickley remained disaffected and unconvinced by both sides. He quit UKIP when it took an increasingly far-right direction after Farage stepped away from the leadership. 'I look at the British political class and I'm afraid I have nothing but disdain for them. I think back to the old Labour Party, the front bench did seem to be populated by people who'd done proper jobs, people who had some substance to them, and some intellect. It's the same for the Tory Party. I look around now and see career politicians. I don't see a level of intellect, commitment to principles.'

I next went around to the other side of Manchester city to find the only prominent Labour figure who put serious thought into the plight of towns like Middleton and Heywood. Indeed, Lisa

Nandy's love of towns spawned a series of internet memes when the MP for Wigan ran for the leadership in 2019.[6] Nandy was first elected to parliament in 2010 and rose to become shadow foreign secretary under Keir Starmer. Although she came third in the 2020 leadership contest with 16 per cent of the vote, her presence in the race meant that the future of constituencies such as Wigan, and whether the party could win the red wall back, received due prominence.[7]

My first encounter with Nandy was back in 2017, when we appeared on BBC's *Question Time* beside each other. She was exceedingly friendly – I was a bag of nerves, all too aware that a wrong sentence on a prime time political debate can end a career. Chatting in the front garden of her suburban home, Nandy explained that she started the Centre for Towns think tank as a response to Westminster's reaction to the Leave vote in the 2016 referendum: 'We were hearing so much of the commentary and many politicians telling us that towns that voted to leave the EU in relatively large numbers were the people who didn't want to play any role in the world order. They wanted to stop internationalism. They wanted to stop the world, we want to get off. We're told equally that people were just too stupid to understand the question. We were told these people are xeno-phobic, they were racist. Or we were told that people were just in so much despair about how terrible their communities were that they had nothing left to lose. All of which is deeply offen-sive and completely wrong.'

The think tank aimed to focus the political agenda on the places that had faced decades of economic decline. Nandy agreed that the New Labour's intense focus on cities led to a brain drain. 'What we've seen in places like Wigan is that young people who want opportunities will go off to university, often in the cities. And when they look for good, well-paid jobs back home, they find quite often that those opportunities just aren't there. So we've lost our working-age population.' She went on to explain the consequences: 'The scars are visible on our high streets, we've got a crisis of loneliness among our older people who are growing old alone, hundreds of miles away from children and grandchildren. Almost every problem that I've been dealing with as a constituency MP over the last decade, you can trace back to that economic model and a political system that just wasn't responsive.' With the Tories engaging with this agenda before Labour, it was frustration that prompted Nandy to stand for the party leadership. 'Voters in places like Wigan, Leigh, Bolton and right across the country had to look at the Labour Party and see a party that understood that [change was needed].'

There was no doubt in Nandy's mind that Labour has been growing apart from the residents of Wigan for quite some time; with its interests being too theatrical. 'People often feel that we're quite obsessed in the Labour Party with being radical and we certainly have been in recent years. But what we often aren't is relevant. That very much came to the fore at the last election with all the manifesto pledges. There are a lot of pledges that people couldn't understand the relevance to their own lives.' She cited the example of Leigh, Andy Burnham's former constituency on the outskirts of Manchester, where campaigners were ordered on a particular day to talk about trains. 'Leigh doesn't have a train station, and it's a source of real frustration locally. Buses would have been far more relevant, to bring it back to my favourite theme. We needed to be much more relevant to people's lives and the only way that really happens is being far more rooted in communities, and decisions have to be driven locally.' With Jeremy Corbyn's retirement from front-line politics, Nandy admitted to feeling 'quite optimistic' about Labour's future, believing that 'it is actually walking the walk in terms of wanting to hand people real power in their lives and leading by example where we have the power to do that.'

'Levelling up' is a not a term Nandy uses, but she is pleased that the debate has brought the economic issues of towns to the front of the political agenda. 'It's a recognition that for a very long time, communities like mine have seen relative economic decline. We used to have large numbers of young people and working-age people forty years ago when we had the coal mines, we had mills. There were factories dotted around the outskirts of Greater Manchester in many of those towns similar to ours. And for the last forty years, we've seen that steady process of decline so that now the inequalities between parts of the country like mine and parts of the country like Manchester, which is only a few miles away, are very vast indeed.'

She does not, however, think that places such as Wigan are eager to return to the industries of the past; it is implausible to imagine its teenagers wanting to go down the coal mine, even if they still existed. 'We're very proud of the role that we played empowering this country and building the country's wealth and influence. But we don't want to see a return to that sort of work.' Many residents in her patch commute into larger settlements – Manchester, Salford or Bolton. She was hopeful that the rise in home working during the pandemic could give more purpose to places. 'Two thirds of my constituents have to commute out of the borough for work because the work isn't available in Wigan. And yet we've seen that quickly change with lots of people working from home or working locally . . . the new normal may well look a lot more like this, where our high streets will start to be boosted by the fact that people are working locally again and so they're spending locally again.'

Her prescription for towns includes significant investment in regional transport, especially buses and local train services. 'I know I talk about policy so much that it's become a running joke,' she smiled. 'But actually, I'll keep talking about buses until I see some of this start to change.' Nandy believed that decisions on infrastructure spending must be taken locally. 'If you'd asked people in the north of England how they wanted transport spending allocated, they wouldn't have started with High Speed 2. Now I'm not knocking High Speed 2, this country needs proper transport infrastructure. But before you can get any kind of political buy-in from the public for a project like that, you've got to sort out our regional trains.' Although more money is key, she believed power is just as important. 'The only way in the end it's going to start to change is if those decisions are made far closer to home.'

When I put to her the vision of the Northern Powerhouse – linking together the great northern cities to counter the economic might of London – I wondered whether this was compatible with her ideas for towns. Manchester has thrived in recent decades, but can towns and cities economically do well at the same time? She argued that the current model of life being increasingly based around cities is broken. 'Take a walk down my local high street and you'll see why that doesn't work, because people will commute into Manchester, they'll spend in Manchester, and then they'll come back. They sleep here, they see their families, maybe have their evening meal, but they're not spending on the local high streets and not spending in the local pubs. And then the whole social fabric starts to fall apart and people feel that very keenly. That's why we've had these big political upheavals in recent years and we've got to start paying attention.'

Nandy's priority is reimagining high streets for small towns, recalling the rise and fall of tower-block housing in city centres. 'I grew up in Manchester in the 1980s, when they were busy detonating tower blocks in the next community to mine, Moss

Side and Hulme, because they built them in the 1960s, largely for single parents with young kids and older people, who'd told them at the time that they didn't want to live twenty storeys up without access to a garden and without seeing their neighbours. And yet they didn't listen, so they had to tear them down all those years later. I think the debate about high streets has been really similar.' She wants high streets to be 'places to go where people can see each other and have that social fabric.'

Although Nandy did not win the 2019 leadership race, she is upbeat that the plight of towns such as Wigan is now at the forefront of the political agenda for the first time since she arrived in Westminster. Soon after Keir Starmer was elected Labour leader, he went on a virtual tour of the country, starting in Greater Manchester. 'He asked local people to set the agenda and spent several hours listening to what they had to say and talking to them on their own terms about their priorities.' She is deeply sceptical of whether the Johnson government can 'provide those opportunities' but acknowledged, 'I do think there's an element of the Conservative Party that really does understand this.' Above all, she is just relieved. 'It feels to me that this is now a very mainstream part of the political agenda and the prospects for people in towns, therefore, are much brighter than they would have otherwise been.'

The counter to Nandy's view on the importance of towns is embodied by George Osborne, who proposed the Northern Powerhouse concept in 2014: pursuing more devolution with more mayors, extra funding for these conurbations to encourage investment and improved transport links. 'Not one city, but a collection of northern cities – sufficiently close to each other that combined they can take on the world,' the former chancellor said.[8] He did not hide his belief either that cities were the economic unit of the future. 'In a modern, knowledge-based economy, city size matters like never before.' After being the second-most powerful man in the country during David Cameron's Conservative governments, Osborne's politics career came to an shattering end after the 2016 referendum. He exited parliament and, after a spell editing the *Evening Standard*, has started a third act in banking. Throughout lockdown, he has resided in the bucolic Somerset village of Bruton, where I spoke to him from my Manchester hotel about the towns versus cities debate.

His enthusiasm partly came from being a northern MP – Tatton in Cheshire – for sixteen years. 'I was someone who had been born and brought up in London. I'd always thought that this simplistic view in London, which is that nothing of any interest happens outside the M25, was wrong. Equally wrong, this view around the north-west of England that all the action was being sucked out of the north, down to London. Both were false and I was in a position as Chancellor and as a northern Tory MP to address it.' Osborne noted that successive efforts had been made since Harold Wilson's governments of the 1960s to 'build up the rest of the country' by shuffling government departments around (exactly what Boris Johnson's government is doing by moving 20,000 civil servants out of Whitehall by the end of the decade). The idea of sending 'a few hundred civil servants to some town in the north of England in ten years' time' would not achieve much, Osborne argued, because a future government would relocate them back.

'There's nothing new about wanting to level up. The Northern Powerhouse is a solid economic theory that cities – particularly around the Pennines; Manchester, Leeds, Sheffield, Liverpool – could be brought more closely together economically because they're geographically actually quite close to each other. If you linked them with good transport links, if you empowered them by creating new city mayors, if you invested in the science and the universities and the teaching hospitals there, then the whole would be greater than the parts and you'd attract private investment.' This theory was the brainchild of Jim O'Neill, a leading economist from Manchester, Goldman Sachs banker and later a Treasury minister under Osborne.

Did Osborne have concerns that towns would be left behind with the economic success of cities? He pointed out that the cities of the north were 'economically devastated and city centres hollowed out' during the 1980s and 1990s and their 'incredible journey' is evidenced that other places aspire to be like Manchester. He is unwavering in his belief. 'All around the world, the evidence is that cities act as a kind of cluster for economic activity with their universities and their science, teaching and hospitality. What you then need to do is make sure that the suburbs and the towns around these cities have proper links into them and that activity can spill out.' He cited the example of Reading, a long-standing commuter town near London where global tech firms have now opened bases. 'The Boltons, the Rochdales of this world, the Wakefields of this world, they're not going to succeed if Manchester isn't doing well, if Leeds isn't doing well. But you've got to create two-way traffic between those towns and those cities . . . you start with the cities and then the towns will benefit.'

When I pushed Osborne on the issue of identity – how these smaller towns will feel about an economy and political leadership rooted in a nearby city – he pointed out that 'a central part of the Northern Powerhouse has been to empower the local communities such as Wakefield and the towns of South Yorkshire, like the towns of the Pennines.' Osborne revealed that there was much internal opposition from Cabinet ministers and Whitehall, particularly the Treasury, who 'did not want to hand power away'. He argued that Andy Burnham's mayoralty is proof that it works for the whole area. 'Greater Manchester is not just Manchester city centre. It includes Rochdale. It includes Wigan. It includes Bolton and Bury. And now you have in the great mayor of Greater Manchester, Andy Burnham, a recognizable public national voice for those communities. The idea that Manchester's gain is Rochdale's loss is a total zero sum game.'

Osborne also said some Tory Cabinet members were solidly opposed to creating mayors with powers that could create political headaches. 'I remember there were some very senior Conservatives, colleagues of mine in the Cabinet, who said "What's the point of doing that, George? You're just going to create Labour fiefdoms." To which my answer was, "Will you tell me what Manchester or Liverpool is at the moment if it is not a Labour fiefdom? It's not like the Conservatives have got a big foothold there." If you're just looking at it in policy, political terms, this is a way for us to get a chance for Conservatives to be represented there.' Osborne cited Andy Street of the West Midlands and Ben Houchen in Teesside as examples of 'capable Conservative mayors'.

Osborne may be praised by local government leaders for pushing devolution and delivering directly elected mayors to Manchester and Tees Valley, but he has also been severely criticized for the cuts he made to local-government spending. In the decade after 2010, the core funding to councils from central government was cut by £16 billion.[9] Council leaders have spoken of the devastation this has caused to local services, exacerbating existing challenges such as housing and social care. Did Osborne accept any blame for the political dislocation that came to the fore in the 2016 referendum due to these cuts? 'No, I don't at all,' he curtly said. 'Did the financial crisis have a big impact on communities around Britain? Yes, it did. Were communities that were already hard done by even harder done by? Yes, they were. That's what happens when the economy blows up. I was there afterwards to try and clear up the mess.'

Osborne did not think the revival in Tory fortunes in the red wall was people 'rebelling against austerity' because the party's reputation for fiscal discipline was strong. 'They came to understand that the Conservative Party had more to offer them than their traditional support for a Labour Party that really wallows in nostalgia for the mining movement, or the steel mills that disappeared over a generation ago. It's because, over a period of time, the Conservatives had something to offer – which I'd like to believe included the Northern Powerhouse – that political support in these communities started to swing towards us.'

The deindustrialization of many Western economies over several decades was particularly rapid in Britain. Osborne pointed out that similar collapses in industry have created the same political dislocation elsewhere: 'As you can see from the United States and the Rust Belt there, the effects are still being felt just as harshly. If you like, they've taken longer. It's been a massive challenge for Western democracies. These arguments about left-behind towns, left-behind communities, they're not unique to Britain and we should stop this kind of British exceptionalism disease. These are exactly the same issues that they faced in the US, France, Germany and Italy and other countries.' He characterized the approach of the past as 'let's get in a Japanese microchip manufacturer and let's move the Inland Revenue there, and ultimately it did not prove sustainable or allow business to invest on a much longer and more permanent basis.'

He argued that austerity happened in developed countries across the world, a response to 'the fact that the global economy collapsed'. Osborne brought out the argument that was heard wall-to-wall during the 2015 election campaign: 'Because of the Cameron coalition government, more jobs were created in the north than we'd seen under any previous government. And Britain recovered faster than any other comparable country. So our economic plan delivered for the north.' After the recovery, his hope was to have the northern cities 'think collectively about their economic future' instead of being competitive with each other (something the north has continually struggled with). 'Rather than thinking that if Liverpool won, Manchester lost. Of course there are strong regional and city identities there. But as a whole, you can make the Northern Powerhouse bigger than the individual communities.'

The Northern Powerhouse project drifted under Theresa May's leadership of the party, with a greater focus on the 'Midlands Engine', driven in part by her chief of staff Nick Timothy. Osborne is naturally thrilled that Boris Johnson has embraced levelling up. 'He is our first prime minister coming from being an elected mayor, so I think he understands the benefits of devolution.' But he did question whether Johnson's plans for a levelling-up fund – a big pot of government money for small infrastructure projects below £20 million – could lead to structural change. 'Proof will be in the pudding. Over the next eighteen months we'll see in budgets and spending reviews whether all we get is a kind of levelling-up fund, in which case I think the world will move on. Then we will wait for another government to come up with a serious long-term plan. Or the levelling-up fund is a bridge to a much longer-term approach, which is what this country wants.'

The idea of a levelling-up fund is something Osborne has

seen throughout his political career, starting in the early 1990s. 'I totally understand. I've been there.' While such small-scale investments are a 'temporary measure 'to help ease the issues, he was concerned there is not enough focus on longer-term policies to 'change a century-old force in our country.' During the Industrial Revolution, the economic settlement of the country reversed. 'It used to be the north that was the industrial and economic powerhouse of the country. And over the last century that has changed. To reverse that, it cannot be done with a levelling-up fund. You need serious long-term policy thinking underpinned by solid economic theory.'

He also criticized the New Labour governments for only delivering small-scale projects in places they were elected to. 'If that approach worked, then Labour would still be in charge of all these seats,' he laughed. 'If you go to Sedgefield, you would probably see a whole lot of projects with Tony Blair's name on the plaque as the local MP who opened them.' He was right on that: every Labour MP I spoke to could list small projects they had delivered which did little to save them in 2019. Osborne added, 'People are not dumb, they can see that approach is not going to deliver long-term changes in the economic prospects for them and their families.' He felt red wall voters would respect a government that proved it can work with businesses and local leaders to forge a more resilient local economy.

And what does success for levelling up and the Northern Powerhouse look like? Osborne concluded with a story: 'The great test will be that if you are born in a community where perhaps the coal mine closed thirty or forty years ago, or the steel mill shut, or the fishing industry, you really feel there's a future for you and your family in this town. The town feels like it's going somewhere. The city nearby feels like it's going some-where, new jobs, new activity, new industries are opening. And instead of kind of clinging to the nostalgia of the past, there's pride in the past. There's also enormous optimism about the future.' Manchester's success is evidence enough for Osborne that such a vision is achievable and can work.

My visit to Greater Manchester concluded exactly how it started: outside surrounded by people drinking beer. I met Jennifer Williams, political and investigations editor of the *Manchester Evening News*, to try and form a conclusion about Heywood and Middleton, the future of mayors and local identities. Before my road trip, I was a fevered advocate for more devolution, and such enthusiasm has not waned, but I can appreciate from Heywood and Middleton that towns need to have purchase on the agenda and retain an identity they feel comfortable with.

On a rare dry day, with thin rays of sunshine across in the Cathedral Gardens, Williams and I opened up a couple of beers and discussed Heywood and Middleton within the context of the mayoralty. She was scornful about the idea of Greater Manchester identity, but admitted that since Andy Burnham won the mayoralty, more people would describe it as the place they came from on holiday's overseas.

Her biggest concern is that the momentum will be lost locally and nationally. Howard Bernstein and Richard Leese, the council's chief executive and leader who oversaw the city's renewal, are both on the verge of retirement. 'There is no longer an obvious Heseltine-style [or, perhaps, Osborne-style] figure in government with whom to do business. The question then arises: who is the next generation and how do they see this agenda moving forward? Who is the intellectual driving force, both here and in Westminster?' She pointed out 'the political momentum that has propelled the city itself in recent times, and by extension Greater Manchester dates back to the same period, when the core group of people driving it were the new generation, working with Michael Heseltine when he was at his most influential.' I wondered whether she felt the city suffered from some nostalgia, when its music scene dominated the world. She agreed: 'Manchester is very good at self-mythologizing its 1980s and 1990s cachet – to the point of being irritating at times, even as someone who lives in and loves the city. But in fairness, that has served it pretty well during its years of reinvention.'

Boris Johnson pledged 'full devolution' across England in the party's 2019 manifesto, so 'every part of our country has the power to shape its own destiny.' Ironically, it was Burnham's success in negotiating with Whitehall during the coronavirus pandemic that has turned Johnson off handing over more powers. Williams said, '[the mayoralty] doesn't have as much power as it might appear to do on the outside. And I think actually a lot of its power has probably been shown in the first term of the mayoralty to lie in its soft power.'

Williams knows more than most journalists in the country about how local government operates. I asked her what the core purposes of the mayoralties are. 'There's the advocacy: campaigning and profile and championing of the region. And then there's the policy side, actually changing things on the ground. Obviously every mayor is going to define that in a different way.' Burnham was one of the first directly elected mayors and has had to make a lot of it up as he goes along. Her main criticism is the lack of transparency about who is doing what and why.

If there is further devolution, Williams thought there needs to be honesty about funding for local councils. 'The way it has been treated in the past decade has been scandalous, albeit a scandal central government correctly calculated would come at no political cost. It now means that if you are hoping for a transference of power and resource out of London, the structures you would theoretically transfer that to are weak. Much institutional memory has been lost through waves of redundancy, much experience has gone; it will take time to rebuild an entire strata of the state. That bleeds into scrutiny, standards and accountability too.' The corruption scandal enveloping the mayor of Liverpool is an example of what can go wrong when there is too much power without accountability.

I was curious to know what she felt about the seats like Leigh, Bury, and Heywood and Middleton that had voted Tory for the first time. She did not think they would be a pushover for Labour to win back. 'There were already more Tory voters than people thought; I mean, Graham Brady's got a seat here after all,' she said, referencing the impeccably tailored Conservative grandee. 'It's always been written about as though it's this immovable Labour stronghold. Andy Burnham has to some extent not helped [that image] – he was pretty much the only massive Labour success during the Corbyn years. But actually when you get beneath the surface, there are already more Conservative-leaning voters here than you might initially think.'

The sun was fully gone by the last of our drinks, the cold plaza empty. Williams went off to a barbecue and I returned to my hotel, wondering how I felt about the towns versus cities debate. Having grown up in a town close to a city, I never felt any animosity to Newcastle (I was actually born at the special care baby unit in its General Hospital, the result of arriving six weeks early), but was aware of the low-level resentment from Gateshead's people. That felt unhealthy. Perhaps towns have such a level of unease because they sense their future is innately tied to cities.

Howard Bernstein, chief executive of Manchester City Council for almost two decades, told me there was 'an inherent economic strength of Manchester' that makes it unique among England's cities. But he rightly argued that the quality of its local leadership was just as important. 'You've had two of the most successful local government leaders over the last thirty years in Graham [Price] and Richard [Leese] . . . our approach to convening institutions, residents and businesses to get behind the vision for the city has been very strong and very effective.'

He was chiefly concerned that Whitehall and the Johnson government has developed a 'basic mistrust' of local government that has undone the last decade of advancement for devolution. 'People are not looking at local government as engines of change. They are being looked at as inconvenient, and in some cases, inadequate partners.' The case about why a fully centralized model may need to be rethought. 'We need to start to rehearse the reasons why a centralized model can't work just by itself. With devolution, it's something perhaps around co-design, partnerships, new place-based deals where government are not seen to be taking all their accountabilities for programmes.'

Fundamentally, Bernstein said that residents of Manchester city and the towns around the conurbation want the same thing. 'Most people want to improve their life chances, most people want to be able to access a job, most people want to be able to look after their families. The problems in certain towns are still problems in certain parts of Manchester: there are too many people experiencing serious inequality, experiencing levels of deprivation, and in some cases, abject poverty. And they are not being supported in the way the state, whether it's local or national, is able to support them.'

His vision for the future of these towns is similar to the wider questions for cities: diversifying the business base and adapting to different ways of working, particularly after the pandemic. 'You go around different parts of Greater Manchester, which I'm most familiar with, and you see a whole bunch of creatives . . . what we need to do is better structure our workplace provision, we've got to obviously boost skills and productivity. We have to look at new forms of housing, in our town centres as well as our city centres.' Agreeing with Lisa Nandy, he felt that the town centres need to become 'more attractive places to visit'. 'There will be new perspectives around retail provision, it will be more experiential, rather than huge shopping malls where you can't distinguish one shopping unit from the other. There are opportunities for independent retailing.' As well as devolution, he argued that flexible planning laws will be vital.

George Osborne's argument about the economic pull of cities is hard to dispute. There are many improvements to be made for towns, which the Johnson government's small pots of money will help to address. Their high streets may feel better in the coming years, but the directly elected mayoral model of grouping together a critical mass into a conurbation remains the best way of creating economic resilience. Even without a city of global standing, there is room for improvements: Ben Houchen has shown in Tees Valley how groups of towns can be brought together under a united economic vision. Economic gravitational pull matters. Some places can be major employers, some can be great and comfortable places to live. Economic prosperity tied to political autonomy. Not every town will be the same; a lesson Whitehall should remember when figuring out how to deliver for hundreds of places that voted Tory for the first time in 2019. And finally, heading a little further north one last time, it was the last stop on the road trip: the old mill town of Burnley in Lancashire.

10. Burnley

And did the Countenance Divine
Shine forth upon our clouded hills?
And was Jerusalem builded here,
Amongst these dark satanic mills?

WILLIAM BLAKE

The first thing that struck me on my arrival in Burnley, forty minutes north of Manchester, were the chimneys. Dozens of them, sprouting from abandoned mills in the town that was the heart of Lancashire's cotton industry. In its Victorian prime, Burnley had 100,000 looms powered by vast engines belching out steam and smoke. Along the Leeds and Liverpool Canal – carried through the town on the magnificent Burnley Embankment – the warehouses and sheds are now deserted. The cotton industry is long gone and the remnants have become the area's foremost tourist attraction. The Weavers' Triangle commemorates the times when Burnley was the cotton-weaving capital of the world, before the influx of foreign imports made it uncompetitive. During the 1960s and 1970s, mills were closed across Lancashire at a rate of almost one a week.[1]

From the train station, the Manchester Road slopes into the town centre and over the canal. The Weavers' Triangle Visitors Centre is a small building overlooking the canal that commemorates the cotton industry. Brian Hall, a retired teacher, runs the trust. At eighty-three, he spoke in soft, delicate tones with a broad Lancastrian accent about his memories of the 'last days' of the coal mining and cotton industries. 'I had several members of my family who worked in the cotton industry. Over the years, that has completely disappeared, practically completely. When I was young, it was already on its last legs. It's been taken over by a number of other industries such as aerospace engineering. But engineering was always very important to Burnley, some of the largest mill steam engines ever made were made in Burnley.' The only remaining engine is the Queen Street Mill, the world's last surviving steam-driven weaving shed, that was converted into a museum in 1986.[2]

He likened these vast engines to cathedrals and recalled visiting the mill his family worked in. 'I do remember how dreadfully noisy it was. I'm sure lots of people did go deaf just because of it. The weavers had to learn to lip read.' Reflecting on the industry, Hall said there was a 'great camaraderie' among the weavers despite the conditions William Blake wrote about. 'We look back and think, *Oh, it must have been dreadful, they had long hours. It was noisy.* Quite a lot of the people now talk fondly of their times in the mills, including my relatives, who actually quite enjoyed it.'

When Burnley's weaving moved from an active industry to a historical artefact, Hall recalled there was resistance from residents, who believed the remains of the town's mills should be destroyed. 'When we started the Weavers' Triangle area – it was given that name in the 1980s – there were quite a lot of people who wanted to get rid of the chimneys and the mill.' He argued 'you can't get rid of history' and the chimneys remained vital to Burnley's identity.

After the collapse of its main industry, Burnley's town centre declined. The mid-century shopping centre is located awkwardly alongside the Victorian buildings. Hall cited the disappearance of two kinds of useful shop as problematic for older residents such as himself: 'When Burtons went, how many gent's outfitters were there in the town centre? I was just thinking if I want a new pair of trousers, where would I go in the town centre? There's only Marks and Spencer.' He also misses local produce. 'The market hall used to have three or four greengrocers and three or four butchers. Within the last twelve months, the last greengrocer closed down and there's one butcher.' He also said the local library had 'deteriorated immensely' and its once voluminous local history collection has shrunk.

Hall is proud of Burnley's history, and the place. 'Burnley dates back to the Middle Ages. We celebrated the eight hundredth anniversary of the market in 1994. The first mention of Burnley was a parish church in 1122, so we'll be celebrating its nine hundredth anniversary next year.' He acknowledged that the town has a slightly downtrodden image but felt it was misguided. 'I've always enjoyed living here. I've wanted to bring people here to show Burnley's best side. A large number of visitors say how surprised they are and how nice it is. I remember a visitor a few years ago, someone who wasn't from this area, who thought it was way better than Wigan.' The main draw for Burnley is its football club, based at Turf Moor stadium on the outskirts of the town, welcoming supporters from across Europe for matches.

Although not especially political, Hall recalled the town's history was with the Liberals 'for much of the nineteenth century. It eventually became Labour, but not always.' His impression is that the town places particular pride on having a local candidate. Julie Cooper, the Labour MP who represented the seat from 2015 to 2019, was Burnley born and bred. Her successor, Antony Higginbotham, was born in Haslingden, a town twenty minutes away. Hall noted he was not seen as local.

*

My walking tour of Burnley town centre started outside the visitors centre with Higginbotham. The thirty-one-year-old may not be a pure Burnley resident, but he exemplified the new breed of Tories. Born into a northern working-class home, he moved to London for work and, similarly to Lee Rowley in North East Derbyshire, returned home to Lancashire for family visits. He was selected to fight Burnley days after the 2019 election was called. Although he felt from the start his party had a 'genuine chance' of taking the seat, some of his colleagues thought otherwise and assumed it was a no-hope battle. On his first day of campaigning in the town centre, he donned a blue rosette and found a warm reception; even children wanted selfies. Higginbotham's bid was aided by the fact he was a passionate Brexiter – his anti-EU stance was well received on the doorstep.

As we entered the shopping streets of the town centre, Higginbotham pointed at the range of Union Jacks and St George's flags on houses and offices. 'Don't underestimate how patriotic many northern towns are. Burnley is a prime example – not only because we have a really strong connection to the armed forces, as many northern towns do, but it is your typical British identity.' It was one of the reasons Boris Johnson connected with Burnley's voters. 'Boris is from the south, but he still has appeal because he's got the same patriotism, he's not sneering at people who want to fly the flag.' As we came to his constituency office, housed in a smart old yellow-stoned building, a large Union Jack was hanging on the corner. The handmade bracket was shaped as the portcullis of Parliament.

Thanks to Burnley's location, slightly isolated from Manchester in the Lancashire countryside, a particular community spirit has developed (similar to Great Grimsby). 'Probably because of the football club,' he said. 'It's almost unique in that it is so small.

The population of Burnley could fit in some football stadiums, and yet it's still a huge Premier League football club.' Burnley FC is one of the best-supported sides in English football per capita, with average attendances of 20,000 in a town of approximately 73,000 inhabitants.

As we walked away from the shops toward a series of small warehouses and workshops, Higginbotham explained Burnley is still an 'archetypal manufacturing northern town', despite the closure of its mills and mines. 'If you look at aerospace in the UK, it's hugely clustered around places like Burnley because of the ingenuity.' Safran Nacelles, a large French engine company, is one of the town's largest private sector employers.[3] Rolls-Royce has a factory nearby. Velocity Composites, another grandly titled aerospace company, employs 130 people.[4] In 2013, the town was named Britain's most enterprising place, thanks to its commitment to small- and medium-sized businesses.[5] The Burnley Bondholders scheme has brought together a hundred local firms to raise £10 million for improving the town and promoting local enterprise. The empty mills may be eerie, but looking beyond the decay of the past, in the new small and smart industrial parks, you can spot an economic revival similar to Consett in County Durham.

The health service is also a major employer: the second-largest hospital in East Lancashire is here. In turn, the University of Central Lancashire, known as UCLan, has a sizeable and expanding modern campus near the Weavers' Triangle. As we gazed admiringly at the buildings, yet to be occupied, Higginbotham explained there were mock wards for training midwives, producing a medical ecosystem he hoped will encourage more students to the town after the pandemic. 'That's already been accelerated by Covid and will no doubt continue.' Higginbotham, however, was eager to ensure that any new jobs are split between the private and public sector. Many of the red wall seats were improved during Labour's time in office thanks to an expanding public sector, which was later pruned back during the financial crisis and the Tory governments. 'My focus has to be on making sure that's balanced with equal private-sector growth so we don't become imbalanced and end up with a huge public sector and a very small private sector. If that happens, you become very reliant on the economic cycle of government investment.'

The town centre is in better shape than many others in the red wall, with few empty outlets and plenty of midday shoppers milling around. Burnley does not have a Debenhams or John Lewis department store, which may explain why the smaller shops on the high street continue to thrive. Higginbotham expressed surprise that so many of the bars and businesses have survived throughout the coronavirus pandemic. 'We've been through the most difficult period, but everybody's actually quite optimistic that when we get through it, it'll be fine.' The shopping centre was mostly dominated by older shoppers; it was obvious that not many people live or walk to the town centre.

The inclement weather that dogged me through the trip became too much, again, so I darted into a coffee shop for warming beverages. When I returned, Higginbotham introduced me to a local character. Charles Briggs was the former leader of the council, a disaffected Labour and Liberal Democrat councillor who broke away to form the Burnley and Padiham Independent Party. Informed that I was writing about Labour's troubles, Briggs explained he left the party because of the Iraq war, in which his son served for two years. 'On my bucket list, I want to get Tony Blair in a room and I'll kick seven bells out of him. What he did was to send lads and got them killed in Iraq so the Americans could get oil. That's how I took it. But I think he's a war criminal.' Briggs thought such feelings were likely shared with others in the town. 'The British Army is built on the north,' he claimed. 'It's northern men and women that make up all the infantry regiments and stuff like that. There is an incredibly proud connection.'

Higginbotham and I continued on our walk with our coffees, towards the bus station and the shabbier side of town. He admitted that Burnley suffered from a reputation problem – highlighted nationally in 2001 when riots caused £1 million of damages.[6] 'Burnley has not been without its problems over the last twenty or thirty years . . . it's consistently felt in the doldrums and feels like the poor relation to Manchester or Leeds,' he said. One of the biggest challenges is social drug use. 'It's not your well-off middle classes as it is in the cities, it's now a normal part of going to the pub,' he said. Police regularly discover greenhouses used for giant cannabis farms, which encourages gangs. 'You can buy a house in Burnley for £40,000 – there's no better place to put it.'

Warily, he added, 'we had someone shot the other week, it's few and far between. But anti-social behaviour is the biggest actual crime.' There are also racial overtones to some of the civic unrest. Higginbotham had to deal with a 'White Lives Matter Burnley' banner being flown over the Etihad Stadium in Manchester during a Burnley away game. 'Are there tensions? Yes. Do they bubble over? Rarely.' Tackling these issues is crucial for Higginbotham's re-election hopes. 'We're still in the top ten for deprivation across the country, which is a challenge.' He was typically critical of Labour for failing to address these problems. 'They've had decades of a Labour approach of putting more money into welfare. It's not worked for the unemployment rate, which has still been higher than the national average.' His message during the 2019 election was 'turbocharging businesses'.

Higginbotham was eager to show me Padiham, a smaller market town in his constituency. After a short ride in his Mercedes coupé, we arrived at a giant Tesco supermarket in the centre of town. 'This is the most Brexity part, there's a uniqueness to Padiham.' He hoped to reinvent it as a market town, encouraging shops and restaurants to have more outdoor seating. One of his most immediate levelling-up projects is to deal with flooding. The River Calder flooded in 2015 and 2020, with hundreds of homes and livelihoods destroyed.[7] Around £9 million is required for flood defences and improving bridges with £2 million coming from the government since the election. On the former gasworks and a disused coal mine, Homes England is preparing the groundwork for a vast new housing estate. Padiham was certainly less urban than Burnley.

At the end of our walk, I asked him about his vision for the future of jobs. One of Burnley's biggest employers is Boohoo, the online clothing retailer, which has a distribution site on the outskirts. By 2021, 3,500 people were employed in their warehouse with further expansion planned. But the company has stoked controversy: the warehouse was reported to be a 'breeding ground for coronavirus', which caused consternation among residents.[8] Higginbotham admitted 'they employ a big chunk of people, but it's a bone of contention'. He did not feel they had done enough to integrate with Burnley's people. 'Normally if you've got a company that size, they're part of the community, they do things. They sponsor events, they pay for nice things. Boohoo has never done that. It is just this giant grey box that employs thousands of people who read about it in the news. It's terrible.' He has urged them publicly and privately to improve their image in the town, to little avail.

Burnley's job market is stronger in some aspects than other red wall seats, but still has issues with skills. Before coronavirus, unemployment was 5.6 per cent – significantly above the national average.[9] The number of people with no qualifications is double the national average. It also suffered particularly during the austerity years: Burnley council saw 9 per cent knocked off its budget; charges were introduced to visit the town hall and a 3 per cent tax rise was introduced. Despite Higginbotham's cheerfulness – and that of several residents we met during the walk – funding is at the forefront of questions of how to provide a better, more secure social contract for red wall voters.

The issue of where Labour fits into the new jobs market – praised by the Tories for its flexibility, criticized by Labour for its lack of security – first came to the fore in the 2015 election, when Ed Miliband pledged to ban zero-hours contracts, claiming they were 'undermining family life'.[10] When he took over the party in 2010, his efforts to reconnect Labour with towns like Burnley were made through economic arguments, not emotional. In his first and only general election, the party's vote share declined in the red wall areas.

Miliband's leadership of the Labour Party is not widely remembered as a success. He had the unenviable job of forging a new path after the New Labour years in government and following the memories of the financial crisis. He never recovered from its inception: Miliband's older brother David was widely seen as the heir apparent and Ed's decision to enter the contest, and emerge victorious, was a spectre over the 2015 election. But the relevance of his economic pitch is stronger as time passes. Miliband's focus on inequality pushed it to the fore of political debate, although his nerdy, policy-wonk demeanour failed to connect with middle England and their vision of what a prime minister should sound like.

Miliband retreated to the backbenches after losing the 2015

election and devoted his energies to podcasting and book writing throughout Jeremy Corbyn's leadership. He has spoken infrequently about his time leading the party but with his return to the shadow cabinet as Keir Starmer's shadow business secretary, Miliband opened up about what went wrong for the party. We conducted a virtual interview, me in my cosy room in Burnley's Premier Inn, him in his North London home. He was enthusiastic about the 'big and interesting questions' about the changing jobs market with the example of Burnley and Boohoo, and how it affected Labour's standing.

'It's not simply about saying, "we're going to change every job people have", because it's not like warehouse jobs will suddenly disappear or that we should want that,' he said. 'We have to improve terms and conditions in these jobs and it's about new jobs we can create. The obvious area is around the whole Green New Deal. There are masses of jobs, some in manufacturing and some not, to be done as part of this revolution.' Unlike the Tories, Miliband thinks trade unions still have a significant role to play in this new flexible environment. 'We operate with very deregulated labour markets, people's work is incredibly insecure. What rights do they have? Do they have the ability to be part of a trade union? What engagement are those trade unions doing? Those questions are really important because we are dealing with an insecurity–power deficit.'

That insecurity fed into the 'take back control' message during the 2016 referendum. He concluded that too much risk has been put on individuals, away from the state. When I referenced the deep funding cuts made to Burnley Council and whether this had affected the services, Miliband thought, 'the welfare state, as we've seen in the crisis, is incredibly full of holes. It's not enough to live on. Fundamentally, you've got to act on the working conditions people have, and the rights and power they have at work. You've got to act on the risk question: what the welfare state is and where business responsibility lies.' He felt that the post-war social contract is too often dismissed as 'nostalgia', as it ultimately offered housing, job security and pensions. 'It's not that people want to go back. People in Doncaster North don't just say "let's have lots more coal mines". But it does mean recovering something that has been lost. It goes back to my overall belief: if you think about Trump, if you think about Brexit, if you think about some of the things that Jeremy was talking about, in very different ways they were all talking to the same deep economic discontent, in a way the mainstream right and left had not been doing.'

Miliband drew much ire inside his party for criticizing the New Labour project. He continues to believe 'there was too much complacency that people in the red wall seats weren't going to vote for anyone else'. He insisted that New Labour's investment in public services, the Sure Start programme and tax credits were all 'excellent' but noted 'good things doesn't necessarily mean it was a) enough or b) it is not right to say "this economic settlement question is really important".' Particularly on the issue of the labour market, he felt 'exploitation persisted in the Labour government', and deeper questions should have been asked about how the economy is run and how the growth gains were distributed.

Much of the economic reassessment mooted during his five years was later adopted by the Conservatives, yet the electorate rejected Miliband's world view by handing the Tories their first parliamentary majority in twenty-three years. Miliband theorized that he lost the election because his pitch was 'not primary-coloured enough' compared to Jeremy Corbyn's offer to the electorate two years on:

'What 2017 had over 2015 was that it was painted in bolder,

more vivid strokes and I do think that had an impact. I was too reassuring for the people who want radicalism, and too radical for the people who wanted reassurance,' he said, in a soundbite worthy of Tony Blair in his prime. 'Plus, we had also had a shorter period of austerity. And in the end, people wanted David Cameron and not me. I'm sure there were better ways that I could have put across what we were proposing.' At the time, Miliband said that observers thought he 'overestimated people's desire for change'. But on reflection from Brexit and the Corbyn years, he believed that he underestimated it. 'The Brexit referendum, a year later, was based on a lot of the things that I campaigned on, like stagnant wages, loss of good jobs and so on.'

He agreed that the Tory campaign was 'very rubbish' in 2017 but he thought it is 'too easy' for those who were critical of Jeremy Corbyn to pin all of the blame on the opposition. 'There is a danger that people want to write their version of history which is most convenient. For some, 2017 was a rather inconvenient election.' He saw the Brexit vote in 2016 as a vote for 'big economic change', as many others, including myself, do. 'You have got to think Corbyn's unexpectedly good performance was due to a desire, including in constituencies like mine, for big economic change. People were coming over to us because of the primary colours offer. There's no explanation about 2017 which does not incorporate that thesis.' In Burnley, Labour added nine percentage points to its vote in 2017, only for it to collapse by ten points in 2019.

Miliband felt vindicated that he was right in speaking about a need to 'reshape the condition of Britain'. But he felt he failed in his lack of boldness – something where he suggested Jeremy Corbyn bettered him with his policy solutions. 'They weren't equal to the scale of the crisis. And that isn't necessarily why I lost the election but it didn't help. Hence why I didn't get whatever enthusiasm that Corbyn got in 2017 in winning people back.'

Miliband insisted he took full responsibility for his failure to win in 2015, but argued that the disaffection with Labour went deeper. 'If you look from 1997 onwards, where the [voting] gap starts to close actually, what people say to me in my constituency is that they got disaffected with Labour in government. Not because Labour in government didn't do good things, but I don't think it fundamentally changed some parts of the economic settlement.' Although reforms such as the minimum wage and tax credits to help working families helped the poorest in society, he felt New Labour 'didn't fundamentally change the deep question' about insecurity and wages. He also struggled with moving on from the New Labour era. 'Coming out of thirteen years of government was always tricky. But I am not making excuses, I take full responsibility for all the decisions I took. I lost, it's my responsibility for having done so.'

But he felt there had been too much focus on the growth of the whole economy and not enough on the actual experience of people's lives. 'It's hard to remember now, but it was controversial to be saying at the Labour Party conference "the rising tide just seems to lift the yachts." The notion that we were deeply unequal; that there was a cost of living crisis; that more of the next generation would be worse off than the last.'

Reflecting on 2019, Miliband's analysis of what went wrong for Labour followed mainstream thinking of the left. He argued industrial change was significant in breaking the ties with the party. 'I don't think anyone can underestimate the extent to which, in a constituency like Doncaster North or Burnley, the combination of industrial jobs, unions and the sense of community was so significantly tied to Labour.' He also felt that the

policy changes made by the coalition and Conservative governments had failed to shape the new job markets. 'I am struck by
the insecure jobs, temporary agency work, zero-hours contracts
and warehouse jobs which all have issues versus the old mining
jobs. Those mining jobs, not to romanticize, had a very different
social contract. The current economic settlement is quite repu-
diated in the minds of a lot of people, especially after the 2010
election.' The final issue, of course, was Brexit, which became a
'lightning conductor for those deep issues'. In his constituency,
voters told Miliband they were voting Leave out of a desire for
a fresh start. 'There was a deep aching desire for something
better. Of course, for some people it was about immigration and
discontent with the EU, but it went much deeper.'

The campaign itself was 'really hard' for Miliband, who saw
his majority in Doncaster North drop from 14,024 to 2,370.
Had it not been for the Brexit Party, he would have almost
certainly lost his seat. 'It was really hard watching lots of people
who were really angry.' He put 'quite a lot' of the outcome on
Brexit, but also confirmed, 'Jeremy wasn't popular. For a lot of
people, it was very painful to think they were not going to vote
Labour.' Yet despite Corbyn's unpopularity as leader, Miliband
still felt he was 'on to something' with his slogan 'for the many,
not the few' – its origins in Shelley's poetry following the Peterloo
Massacre. Miliband said, 'I remember this conversation in my
local miners' welfare with somebody who was not voting for us.
"Well, I initially thought Corbyn was quite good actually." But
then they went onto Brexit. I'm not saying that Brexit was
Jeremy's only problem, because I know that it was also about
defence and other things.'

Ideologically, however, he believed the Tories will struggle
with their new voting base. He does not think the Johnsonite
Tories are reborn interventionists, 'that is not their fundamental

belief', and that will harm them in delivering on the levelling-up agenda. 'If you take someone like Kwasi Kwarteng or Rishi Sunak, that is fundamentally not their belief. Johnson is more of a shapeshifter. They're not doing a green stimulus at anything like the level of Biden or even the French or the Germans. They're good at talking the talk on this stuff, but they're not really good at walking the walk.' On the issue of zero-hours contracts and workers' rights, he does not think the Conservatives have fundamentally changed. 'Are they really going to say "we do think deregulated labour markets have gone too far". I don't think they're going to be able to solve these big problems that people face.'

Miliband still doesn't think seats like Burnley will 'automatically' come back. He felt Labour needs a compelling offer – although, like many others in the party, he did not define what it was – but felt that voters are impressed by Keir Starmer. 'People are more positive towards him than they were towards Jeremy. He's started to build the foundations. Some people went to the Brexit Party, not the Tories – you can overestimate the extent to which people in the red wall just went to the Tories. Quite a lot splintered from Labour or abstained. But they've got to be won back, because it's not just "well they've voted Labour before and they'll carry on voting Labour."' Labour must think big to tackle these issues. 'The challenge for Labour in the red wall is: can we make a sufficiently compelling offer of change for these deep-rooted issues? It's what Biden is trying to do. That is the way you unite the Labour coalition, because both metropolitan and red wall voters want economic change.'

Miliband's criticisms of the Tony Blair era deserved a response from one of its leading lights. And it is hard to think of a more assuredly New-Labour politician than Alan Milburn. Always cogently and clearly spoken, with only a soft hint of his County Durham background, the former Darlington MP was at the top of the New Labour project: first as Chief Secretary to the Treasury, later as Health Secretary and Cabinet Office Minister. After leaving Parliament, he served as the head of the government's Social Mobility Commission – based out of the Department for Education – which looked at the structural issues that limit aspiration. He resigned in 2017, blaming Theresa May's government for failing to commit enough support to tackling unfairness.[11] Whereas many key figures from that era remain prominent in British political life, Milburn has taken a much lower profile; he is not often seen in newspaper columns or on Sunday talk programmes. He feels almost a lost figure from the New Labour era, despite embodying all of its professionalism, pragmatism and ideological flexibility.

Milburn splits his time between London and Northumberland. Speaking on FaceTime while he walked through the countryside with his dog, he did agree with Ed Miliband's critique that New Labour had not been bold enough when it first entered government. 'I think in the early phase of New Labour that's a very fair criticism,' he said, breaking off to dodge a tractor. 'We were probably more frightened of Labour's gulf than necessarily we should have been. We probably didn't quite realize, post 1997, how much permission publicly there was for change.' Arriving in Parliament in 1992, he was closely tied to Tony Blair's rise to the leadership and concluded that the desire for change may have gone too far. 'We obviously chose to accentuate the "New" and not so much the "Labour". I do think that changed over time and I think it was a learning journey.' He pointed out that he had never been a minister prior to the 1997 victory; Blair and most of his Cabinet were novices in running a country. 'But as time went on, the argument about Blair and New Labour changed . . . at the end it was too much boldness – whether that was on public service reform or in Iraq.'

New Labour was about slaying ghosts that were deemed to be part of party's ineluctability; whether that be tax and spend, softness on crime, not being patriotic, weak on defence. Milburn believed that created an atmosphere that meant 'New Labour were defined more by our past'. Those policies may have been right for the period of 1994 to 1997, when the party was preparing for power, but failed to adapt in office 'The old bastions of support over time have crumbled. It's no longer – and it was no longer true then – that if you own a council house, you automatically voted Labour, any more than if you own your own home, you necessarily voted Tory. The trick in political strategy was about how you could straddle these constituencies, north and south, middle class and working class, in order to have a decent chance of winning.' New Labour, in his view, did a 'pretty awesome job' at that straddling, evidenced by the three large parliamentary majorities.

Milburn laughed it was 'objectively bollocks' to say that New Labour did not deliver enough in office for the red wall constituencies for towns like Burnley. But he was aware, through his experience in the trade unions, that bigger economic forces were at play. Before entering Parliament, one of Milburn's first major campaigns was to save the Sunderland shipyards. He recalled it as 'the epitome of the fight against deindustrialization under Mrs Thatcher', with 1,000 jobs on the line and more in the attendant industries. It was 'the finale' of what had been happening across the north of England over many decades. 'Purpose disappeared from these places, and particularly for young men, because all of the anchor points of their lives – whether it was an apprenticeship, or membership of a trade union, disappeared. At the same time you had these sweeping forces of globalization that were disrupting and disrespecting the veneer of these places.' The collapse of high streets was just as damaging to the local psyche as the end of the factory, he argued. 'It was very acute in towns, because something profound was happening in the labour market. Skills were being punished in crude terms and, as a consequence, [there was] wage stagnation.'

Whereas the cities of the north reinvented themselves, the towns did not have the scale to do so. New Labour, in its inherent eagerness to push forward, left the party's traditional supporters behind in such places. 'What people were hearing was "the Labour Party are talking about this stuff in the future and mean- while my present doesn't seem to have a place in the world anymore. And maybe there isn't an understanding about my past."' He did not think this was a policy failure the party could have dealt with: 'Was there a way of saving the shipyards or the steelworks? Was this something clever that we missed in policy terms? I think the answer to that is probably not. I don't think there probably was a way, in a globalized world, short of a "fortress Britain" approach to saving those industries.' But the failure, Milburn posited, was one of empathy to those who had suffered through deindustrialization. 'What they heard was that we were not fully respecting that past and we didn't understand the pain of the present. And that all we were focused on was a future that was out of reach.' That created a perfect storm for the likes of Boris Johnson and Nigel Farage, who put empathy and emotion at the centre of their message. Labour too often offered rational analysis without an emotional answer.

With the thoughts about jobs and skills in my mind from Burnley, I asked Milburn about his views on the trade union movement that brought him into politics. Throughout his eight years as a minister, his view remained that the UK needed 'strong and sensible' unions. 'The problem is that they're neither strong nor sensible. What you had was this dreadful structural need for trade unions to act as a counterweight to what was happening in the labour market – an increasing proportion of national wealth in developed economies going to capital, rather than going to labour – and at the same time you had trade unions who hadn't come to terms with that. And who frankly decided that they were going to be a complete pain in the arse to a Labour government.' That created a stand-off between the Labour government and union leaders. Again, he wondered if the party had got that aspect of its time in government wrong. He put the problem down to a 'failure of storytelling' needed to convince voters that the party cared about the market.

Did he feel that New Labour did not change enough while in power? He recalled a saying of Blair's – 'you can't keep selling the same product five or six times over' – and pointed to the challenges social democracy is facing in other countries. 'The crisis is fundamentally a crisis about what is the project for social democracy in a globalized world. Tony had an answer to that, but the way that was heard did not necessarily translate.' He was critical of both Gordon Brown and Ed Miliband for exacerbating the disconnect between the party and its traditional base. 'It's no longer good enough just to have the smarts, you've got to have the connection. You've got to be emotionally able to relate.' He recalled that Blair used to constantly tell Milburn he should move his family to London, but he insisted on staying in Darlington. 'I used to say to him, "No, we won't, because this is our place." And it's still my place. Here I am' – he turned his iPhone around to show me the countryside he was walking through – 'I'm literally twenty miles from where I grew up. We have a house in London, my work is in London, but we're grounded in this place. What people felt with Ed [Miliband] is that he may be the smartest guy in the world, but he certainly doesn't get my life.'

The combination of being a rational public policymaker, while having the necessary emotional skills, is essential for a politician but one that Milburn thought the generation of Labour politicians after his have struggled with. 'People underestimated Boris Johnson, because he's mercurial, to put it politely. Somehow or other, he has a point of connection. It doesn't matter he's from Eton. He is able to translate belief into emotional connection and that, in today's world – as Trump so amply demonstrated – is an extremely potent force, particularly if you have these structural changes, making the landscape ripe for [someone offering] an answer.' For politicians that deemed themselves as 'hyper-rationalist and highly technocratic', the struggle to form an emotional connection is their greatest challenge.

You will not be surprised to hear that Milburn was no fan of Jeremy Corbyn's leadership, but he felt that the schism with working-class voters began with the Brexit referendum. '2016 was the moment where people got to the edge of the cliff and decided they were going to jump. Once that happens, it's quite hard to claw your way back.' The main problem of the Corbyn leadership in the red wall was highlighted in Burnley and beyond: a sense of patriotism. 'The critical thing that Jeremy and his contingent can never understand is what I call the innate patriotism of working-class voters. If you want to single out a factor that wasn't Brexit, it was the fact that you had a guy who was soft on defence, who was soft on international terror.' Corbyn's reaction to the Salisbury poison attack, where the opposition leader was seen to give Russia the benefit of the doubt, was toxic in northern towns. 'The poisoning in Salisbury is seared in people's minds. One thing that people can remember is the sense he had no respect for our armed forces, flirted with the idea of separating from NATO. All of these things are part and parcel of the complex emotional map that people have, which they construct to make meaning in their lives.'

Milburn had arrived back at his countryside home by this point and settled into an armchair in his conservatory, the dog barking in the garden. As well as the problems with emotional connection, he felt the greatest challenge for Labour to over-come today is language. 'It is no coincidence, in my view, that the two most successful electoral prime ministers in twentieth-century history, Mrs Thatcher and Mr Blair, have one thing in common: an absolute understanding that the language of aspir-ation is a language that unites voters, whether they're north or south, middle or working class, because that's effectively what people are looking for in their lives.' Milburn, who grew up in the shadow of the Consett steelworks and could see the red embers burning over the County Durham sky from his bedroom window, feels this is what is missing the most from political discussion. 'This is the thing that so pisses me off about a lot of the debate around social mobility. It isn't about the low aspirations of working-class kids or working-class parents. You've got to be kidding! If you're of that class, of course you have aspirations.'

As with many of the other interviewees, he concluded Keir Starmer still had to find a vision to define both his leadership and the purpose of the Labour Party. 'Churchill's project was to see Britain through the war. Attlee's project was to rejuvenate Britain after the war. Thatcher's project was to liberalize the economy and society. Blair's project was to modernize Britain. They had lots of policies, and they had values that informed their policies.' Boris Johnson was successful in his first project, Brexit, but Milburn was less sure about whether levelling up, his second, would be as successful. 'Keir has to define what his project is. Without a project, you simply don't cut through and you don't get the golden thread that allows the emotional conversation. He needs a story to connect with the public.'

The economic story of what has happened in Burnley and other places in the red wall has best been told by Diane Coyle, economics professor at the University of Cambridge. In her public and academic writing, she has long argued that the UK requires a new economic model. She put forward that the issues began with deindustrialization in the 1970s and 1980s, 'when in those formerly strong industrial areas, a lot of economic and social problems got embedded because of long-term unemployment, poor housing and underinvestment.' This cycle became vicious for towns such as Burnley, but also for economies around the world, as work based on knowledge came to the fore. 'Intangible assets have become more important, so that people who have a high level of education who are working in advanced engineering or software or the other professions have gathered together increasingly in London.' This shift, as I have seen throughout my travels, has created resentment – below and above the surface – and a belief that some people are becoming better off all the time, while others are not.

Coyle has repeatedly argued that long-standing economic policies of successive governments have made the situation worse, by encouraging investment in particular parts of the country that are 'already productive and already have high land values'. For prospective investors, London and the south-east is always the natural draw, as these areas are the most productive. 'That too has contributed to these vicious and virtuous cycles that have exacerbated the divergences between fortunes in different parts of the UK.' She has campaigned for reforms to the Green Book – the guidance used by the Treasury in assessing value for money in infrastructure projects. She found that the current system meant that the unevenness in the amount of public money put into different parts of the country has increased over time. Chancellor Rishi Sunak listened to Coyle, and has replaced the Green Book with a greater focus on place. 'As well as looking at the hard numbers about where productivity is the highest, they will be looking at how investments align with the ambition to level places up . . . raw economic efficiency is not the only criterion for making an investment decision in future.'

The other campaign Coyle has waged is against the metropolitan mindset of decision-making in the UK – namely that policymakers in all of the major government ministries are based in ornate palaces off the same road in central London. The dominance of Whitehall as a place and as a mindset has been 'incredibly damaging' to policymaking because 'decisions have been made among a not very diverse group of people living in the same part of the country.' She cited transport infrastructure as the classic example: the per capita investment is often the same in parts of the north of England as the south, but the infrastructure base was so low that the lived experience was vastly different. 'These were people who had never had to take the train from Liverpool to Manchester and didn't know how overcrowded and unreliable it was. Or the fact that many of the trains were buses on tracks, literally [the maligned Pacer trains, finally discontinued in May 2020].'[12] She argued that policymakers need to better understand the fabric of life of people who are not professional civil servants and live in different places.

The UK economy is one of the most unbalanced and unequal of advanced countries. Coyle described it as 'flying on one engine', in this case London. And when there is overreliance on one engine, as has been witnessed in recent decades, problems emerge. 'You're limiting your capacity to grow as a nation if you're only doing it in one place. That's the hard economic reason for it [rebalancing the economy] but it matters for political reasons, too. We've seen those very clearly in voting patterns and discontent in recent years.' Until the Brexit vote in 2016, she believed Tory and Labour governments were not paying enough attention to regional variations, which in turn played into the Leave argument. 'It's a combination of places around England – and around the rest of the United Kingdom – not having any control over their own destiny or political accountability for decisions. The consequences of that fed through to a weaker economic performance, and a lower increase in living standards over time compared to London and the south-east.'

Coyle agreed that skills, along with infrastructure, are vital. 'People need to develop skills that will suit them for higher wages and more productive jobs. And you've got to align that with bringing in the kind of employers who want those kinds of workers.' Britain's economy suffers from what is called a 'long tail' on productivity: the top end is very efficient, but it trails off quite rapidly and large parts are lagging behind. Coyle noted that all advanced economies have seen this tail grow but it's a particular issue in Britain, because the whole range of smaller productive firms have struggled. Better access to finance is one example she cited of how to improve this. And again, skills and training are crucial.

On the debate between cities or towns as the economic focus of the future, Coyle is firmly on the side of cities. 'I'm in the cities camp, because of the way that advanced economies have become much more dependent on knowledge . . . people have been congregating in cities because of the way you can exchange and build supply chains.' She agreed with Lisa Nandy that working from home post-pandemic may 'change it a bit', but differed in thinking it would not be in a significant way. The successive lockdowns during 2020 and 2021 have acted as an 'X-ray on society', highlighting the existing problems and making them worse. 'Because of all the disadvantages that certain places have accumulated over the past thirty years, it's places with poor housing or crowded housing or poor air quality where the impact of the pandemic has been worse in terms of health. And it's the vulnerable economies where the shutdowns have made things even worse.'

What does success in levelling up look like in Coyle's view? Although investments in physical infrastructure are important, she believes it is still about the whole package of jobs, economic resilience and a palpable sense that life is improving. 'I think of it in a broader way as people's lives are getting better wherever they are. Some of that will be high-skill jobs, high pay and the productivity growth that shows up in the statistics.' The country is never going to be completely and wholly equal, nor does she think these challenges can be rapidly resolved. 'We have a big gap, a big challenge . . . we ought to be thinking about a minimum offer for everybody around the country, no matter where they live, in terms of public services, transport, access to nature and a sense that things are getting better, because that's what we've lost.'

And does she think that Boris Johnson is serious and can deliver, despite the reservations of some Labour politicians? 'From all the conversations I've had with Treasury officials and ministers, I think they do take very seriously the need to deliver on levelling up. But expectations have been raised now, it's a big challenge. And I'm not sure anybody has really got their minds around the scale of the challenge that we face and also the interaction between the economics and the politics of it.' Crucially, Coyle agreed with Andy Burnham, George Osborne,

Michael Heseltine and almost every other political figure that more devolution is needed in decision-making. We concurred that levelling up cannot be done from Whitehall.

My visit concluded near the train station at Burnley College, whose origins were as a mechanics institute 150 years ago; it now has over 7,500 students on a gleaming new campus that speaks to the importance the town puts on further education.[13] Karen Buchanan has worked at the college for twenty-seven years and has been principal for the last three. In her spacious office, she defined the mission for upgrading the town, trying to improve its skills offering and taking some on to university level education. 'Our students, a lot of them come from families where no one had been to university before, they are the first generation to go to university.' Her push has seen some Burnley students go to Oxford and Cambridge, but there are also 2,000 apprentices studying at the college, many going into the town's manufacturing sector.

More than half of the college's students are aged sixteen to eighteen, recent secondary-school leavers. For those who have left school with inadequate maths or English qualifications, the aim is to make the subjects 'fun and enjoyable' to achieve a basic level of proficiency. Buchanan is also closely involved with the college's programmes to help adults reskill after they have been made redundant, so they 'fit into other companies whose order books are thriving', whether that be in aerospace or solar panels. She likened her role to a recruitment agency, ensuring there are local skills to match local jobs. Employers are even involved in the college's curriculum.

Her aim is to ensure that every adult who enrols in the college has a guarantee of a job at the end. 'The whole premise of that is reskilling local adults, so that they can stay living where they are but bring in an income for their family.' One macabre example of this adaptability came during the coronavirus pandemic, when there was a greater need for black rubberized body bags due to the huge number of deaths. One company that works closely with Burnley College, specializing in composite materials, had to diversify rapidly. 'They've been able to use some of our kit and trial prototypes before they change their equipment to make sure they're producing the right things.'

Although the college had 3,500 sixteen- to eighteen-year-olds – its core demographic – the town's birth rate has recently declined. They have attempted to make up the gap by encouraging students from elsewhere: Manchester, the Lake District, Yorkshire and elsewhere in Lancashire. The college is on track for another major building expansion and is hopeful of expanding its adult education facilities. Buchanan said that the future will be based on expanding its higher education offering that provides university degrees. 'We've got a clear vision and plans for how we want to grow university offers, as well as, obviously, everything else.' She is hopeful that they will encourage more students to Burnley, which in turn will boost the shopping centre and the town's wider economy.

Jayne Wynee, who oversees marketing for the college, also joined our discussion, and I asked her about her feeling of the place. Before I arrived in Burnley, I was expecting to find somewhere a little tetchy, yet everyone I met was warm and welcoming. 'There's a real pride in Burnley. For us as an organization, with the campus being so close to the town centre, it feels like it's an extension of the college. There's been a huge focus with the council on it becoming a university town,' she said. Having spent most of my time in the town on foot, it feels compact and united. Wynee agreed, 'Everybody is kind of connected and they're proud and really wanting to share in the successes of Burnley.

That absolutely comes from the football club.' The college also hosts lots of free events to encourage people from the town to visit its campus, and holds an annual science festival to encourage interest in STEM subjects and promote the town's engineering prowess. 'We wanted to support our local schools in terms of getting kids excited about science, engaging parents with science.'

Both Buchanan and Wynee praised Antony Higginbotham for his eagerness to improve the college. 'Since becoming an MP, he's been brilliant for the college and for the town. He's brought a youthful vitality and energy that we've not seen before and he's been here to talk to the students about politics,' Buchanan said. Several government ministers have virtually visited the town and she was hopeful that Boris Johnson would come soon. She added, 'We did a presentation to the whole of the Department for Education – not the politicians, but the civil servants who are there all the time. There were 180 of them online. I've worked here for eighteen years and have never had such a good day as I had virtually touring Burnley College.'

The last stop on my road trip prompted the greatest surprise. Burnley, in many respects, is a model of how former industrial towns can be revived. Small pieces of infrastructure investment can go a long way to boosting their connectivity – like the reinstatement of the Todmorden Curve. The 500 metres of railway track directly link Burnley to Manchester for the first time since the 1960s Beeching cuts, and cut half an hour from journey times when it reopened in 2015.[14] The Johnson government's pledge to 'reverse' the closure of rural railways is unlikely to see swathes of new stations and lines opened, but small strategic improvements like this can be made. Burnley College is an example of how employers, the community and businesses can integrate better. A new £18 million shopping complex will provide the town centre with a new cinema and restaurants, which residents hoped would appeal to the student population.[15] I left feeling a great sense of optimism for Burnley's future.

But I was also aware of the biggest challenge in levelling up is going to be structurally improving jobs and skills. Burnley needs to give its young people a reason to stay, if they want, to do the kind of work that is also available elsewhere. Rob Halfon, the Tory MP who chairs Parliament's Education Select Committee, has plenty of ideas about how this could be done. Inspired by the work of the college in Burnley, he believes every town should have an Adult Community Learning Centre, to encourage people of all ages who lack the confidence to enrol in a further education college. He also believes the government should offer a 'lifelong learning account', where every eighteen-year-old is given an account with credit they can spend on adult learning of their choice. The Johnson government announced this policy in May 2021, to his delight. Halfon also believes that companies should be given skills credits from the government to improve workers.

The stigma that further education is inferior to university education also needs to be addressed. Halfon set out to me what he calls the 'dinner party test'. When this is cracked, then he believes the long-lasting struggle with skills will be addressed: 'Let's say you invited me to dinner and there was a young person there. That young person says, "I'm going to Oxbridge." Everyone will go, "Wow, how amazing!" If someone next to them said, "I'm doing an apprenticeship in engineering at Jaguar", I'd bet you hardly bat an eyelid about it. That is what's wrong with our system. What it should be is when someone who is doing an apprenticeship at a dinner everyone starts to ask them, "Oh, that's incredible! What do you have to do? How did you get that?" We have a complete contrast, but I've seen myself how German and Swiss businesses train their workers because they believe it's their duty to do so. They believe vocational education is prestigious and important.' The emphasis New Labour put on university education was key to Blair's grand vision for renewing the country, but it also had the impact of pushing anyone to apply – regardless of grades – with little thought given to whether academic study was the right path for them.

There is no doubt that life is still a struggle for too many in Burnley, but the town has many of the qualities needed to improve its future: a high-skilled engineering base; a positive collective attitude in its community. Nearly all of the red wall seats have distribution warehouses, like Boohoo, and they do provide valuable employment. But such jobs are unlikely to deliver on the hopes of the levelling-up agenda. There is a danger that, without intervention from government, these places will drift into an economic base that does not provide stable employment and a resilient local economy.

After hearing the complaints about Boohoo, I spoke to two policy experts who have pondered how to balance the benefits of a flexible labour market with the blight of insecure work. James Bloodworth, author of *Hired: Six Months Undercover in Low-Wage Britain*, spent time working in an Amazon distribution warehouse and discovered a similar dislocation among their new employees. Bloodworth found that the enthusiasm for an alternative to life on benefits soon disappeared with the reality of working for a big multinational, without trade unions and without security.

When Amazon built a new warehouse in Rugeley, north of Birmingham, the local authority constructed the building and built special roads with a certain type of tarmac to cope with the weight of the lorries. The same was true in Swansea, with millions invested to encourage the company to locate there. With some longer-term thinking, Bloodworth argued that the same investment could eventually reap improvements for other sectors. 'Do we want twenty-first century employment in Britain in these communities to be all Amazon warehouses? This is not really a short-term solution but if we build up the skills base, it's going to be more likely that we attract those companies.'

Much of Bloodworth's research has focused on the isolated new communities among migrants that have emerged in these towns, which do not imprint themselves on political debate. 'They often can't vote, they don't appreciate the job protections.' He found that many of the new jobs in these towns had limited career progression. 'The problem with some of the jobs like Amazon is that there is no real advancement unless you can go directly into management.' Bloodworth believes trade unions need to be strengthened to tackle the individualistic economies that are found in towns such as Burnley.

Matthew Taylor, head of the Number 10 policy unit under Tony Blair, was commissioned by Theresa May to review the nature of work with a particular focus on the gig economy. He praised the benefits of a flexible labour market – something the economy will 'always need' – but similarly to Bloodworth, he believes that workers need to be empowered. 'Trade unionism is actually an aid to effective staff engagement and even assists productivity because you hear your workers' voices complaining about things which adversely affect them.' He argued in his Good Work report that workers' rights should be strengthened and the thresholds for giving more rights to casual workers be lowered.

Taylor was enthusiastic for expanding the higher education sector, and growing the UK's 'export-focused, high tech, high investment sectors'. During his research for the report, he found the biggest distinction between England's towns was whether they had a student economy or academies. 'If they haven't, then unless they've got another significant employer of skilled labour, you're talking about a mixture of public sector work, relatively poorly paid service economy work including gig work, casual work, zero-hours work. And then you have obviously a smattering of the professionals that you have in any town such as estate agents and dentists.' For those who stay in those places, the state of work has deteriorated. 'The sense of the paternalistic employers, the notion of a job for life, that has obviously declined, and it does feel for people more insecure. And for many people, it's very difficult to support a comfortable lifestyle on the basis of their employment.'

But Halfon also believed that central government action needs to be taken on further education. 'I would create individual learning accounts, for example, so I would give everybody a lump sum of money which they can only spend on education, that they can spend at any point in their lives, so it's not just graduates who keep on learning.'

Taylor also believed that devolution and local power is crucial. 'All the evidence in the world is that you don't achieve levelling up unless you devolve serious power.'

Having clocked up 6,000 miles on the Mini – desperately in need of a wash and a service – my six-month long, U-shaped tour of the red wall was complete. I was ready for the four-hour drive south, back to Westminster, to meet Michael Gove and Keir Starmer, who will be among those to define the future of the red wall. But an unexpected by-election in a part of northern England that had many traits of Labour's former heartlands necessitated a detour eastwards, to meet another two key players in the future of the red wall. So instead of heading south, I took a two-hour drive across the Yorkshire Dales and back to the north-east, to Hartlepool, a remote northern port town in the Tees Valley, for the beginning of the end of this road trip.

The extra miles were worth it: 6 May 2021 produced a seismic result that challenged even Boris Johnson's election victory of 2019 for its significance and shock.

Conclusion –
Hartlepool and Westminster

'Boxing in Hartlepool started on the beach at
Seaton Carew, where the fighters fought bare
knuckle.'

STEPHEN RICHARDS, AUTHOR OF *BORN TO FIGHT*[1]

The seafront of Seaton Carew on the County Durham coast was
more than bracing. Over the May bank holiday weekend, it was
cold, overcast and wet. The promenade was littered with police
protection officers, Conservative party activists and perplexed
bystanders enjoying an early fish and chip lunch. Three days
before the people of Hartlepool voted to choose their next MP,
Boris Johnson made his third sojourn to the industrial town to
campaign in a by-election that helped answer the question posed
at the start of this journey: was the collapse of the red wall a
confluence of Brexit and Jeremy Corbyn? Or was it reflecting a
structural change in how England votes?

Hartlepool was not on the Tories' radar during the 2019
election; it was deemed 'too far out of our reach', according to
one strategist. Yet Labour's majority still dropped to 3,595, and
had it not been for the 10,603 votes taken by the Brexit Party,
the Tories might have taken it. Peter Mandelson, who served as
its Labour representative from 1992 to 2004, told me he felt it

would have gone blue had it not been for their presence. The resignation of Mike Hill as the incumbent MP on 16 March prompted one of the most closely watched by-elections in years. Such contests are either local knife fights or a barometer of the national mood. Hartlepool had the honour of being both: its remote location – thirty minutes' drive from the nearest large settlement – creates a sense of disconnection from the rest of the Tees Valley and County Durham, never mind the rest of the country. The national significance of the campaign was in what it might tell us about the future of the red wall.

At midday, the prime ministerial motorcade pulled into the car park, Range Rovers with blue sirens, and Johnson leapt out onto the campaign trail. With Jill Mortimer, the Tory candidate, he paced up the seafront in his trademark blue suit – sans coat, despite the weather. He was mobbed. Soon, the traffic piled up as every car stopped to point and shout, 'Boris!' He was the Pied Piper in the middle of a hurricane. He asked each voter he stopped to talk to if the party could count on their support. Bar some who were uncertain, every one answered in the affirmative. No one said they were backing Labour. The response was unlike any I have seen to any politician on the campaign trail, in any election: dozens of Hartlepudlians wanted selfies and elbow bumps with the prime minister. You cannot imagine David Cameron or Theresa May eliciting such a response.

A little later, Johnson arrived at the Surfside Fish Bar, a short drive away, for a quick-fire round of interviews. Throughout these, he downplayed expectations for polling day – pointing out that no Tory had been elected in Hartlepool since 1959. When quizzed as to why he was back here if there was little chance of winning, he joked, 'Unless you hear otherwise, assume I am in the north-east.' He'd been dogged by a series of headlines about donations to redecorate his Downing Street flat – but Johnson told the collected journalists he thought voters had more important priorities. He was in a chipper mood. As we sheltered from the gale with Americanos for our one-on-one interview, he launched into his own explanation about what happened in 2019. 'There is a change, I hope that there is a long-term change, because people understand that the Conservatives are now on the right agenda.'

That agenda is levelling up, a term that Johnson started to use the morning after his election victory in 2019, but one that has remained a source of confusion in Whitehall. Civil servants, ministers and even some close to the prime minister were uncertain about what it meant. He admitted, 'I've got lots of people in Downing Street for two years saying, "Levelling up? Nobody understands what that means."' Yet his experience on the doorsteps suggested people are starting to appreciate it. 'I think people do intuitively understand it. It doesn't mean you don't think that London isn't the greatest city on Earth. I do. But it means that you go for the whole thing.'

Johnson harked back to his pre-parliamentary roots as Mayor of London as the inspiration for tackling regional inequality. 'Of course I'm a believer in the City of London.' He reminded me that throughout the financial crisis, he supported the sector 'through thick and thin', once going as far as to declare nobody 'stuck up for the bankers as much as I did.'[2] He went on, 'I also think that the agglomeration effects of London – the mass transit systems, all those are amazing – we've got to keep investing in them.' For the first and not last time in our conversation, he expressed his dissatisfaction with his Labour successor, Sadiq Khan. 'I think it's a disgrace that the mayor hasn't done Crossrail Two, his performance on Crossrail has been abysmal. He's done no new river crossings, he's done virtually nothing.' Voters seemed to disagree – Khan was re-elected with a thumping mandate in May 2021.

One of Johnson's notable traits is a desire to be liked, and to be a unifier. It was striking how often he mentioned his love of cities and delivering for the red wall did not require zero sum decisions. 'I'm a believer in a giant metropolitan economy, I love it and I'm a creature of it. The insight that I had when I was running London was that politicians can drive change. You can and it takes leadership. It won't just take national leadership, it's going to take local leadership.' With passion rising, he stressed the importance of mayors. 'When you have a visionary local leader, who is running an operation that has got to be clean, it's got to be fair and it's got to be progressive, but when it's passionate about that area, nothing can stop it.'

By far the most notable statement the prime minister made was on economics. Zarah Sultana, the left-wing Labour MP for Coventry South, was criticized by her party colleagues in January 2020 for decrying 'forty years of Thatcherism', which piled together the New Labour years with the Conservative governments that came before and after.[3] Yet Johnson offered a similar criticism: the UK's economic model since Margaret Thatcher came to power has not worked and needs refreshing. 'The Treasury has made a catastrophic mistake in the last forty years in thinking that you can just hope that the whole of the UK is somehow going to benefit from London and the south-east. There is potential for everyone, but there isn't the same opportunity.'

Levelling up is the new model, but how exactly would he define it? Johnson, once again in full rhetorical flow, said it was about 'unleashing the potential of everybody in the whole country', especially the 'brilliant kids growing up across the whole of the UK, who simply don't have the same quality of education or opportunity as other kids.' He felt that such inequality was not only 'unjust' but also 'economically dumb'. 'That's why as a free-market conservative I object to it so much. It's just stupid. This place, Teesside, is bursting with ideas – it's the same for everywhere else in the UK. But you look at the attainment gap, it is huge.'

Johnson conjured up a verse from the Bible, St Mark's Gospel, about the importance of creating the right conditions for learning: 'For he that hath, to him shall be given: and he that hath not, from him shall be taken even that which he hath.' If this gap is not changed, he described the UK's economy as 'solar systems moving in different directions' that will result in a 'total waste.' Again, he returned to how he believes he delivered change in East London following the 2012 Olympics, even if some of the gentrification priced out poorer residents. 'Look at what we did with the Olympic Park in East London. You know where had the fastest rise in property values in London when I was mayor? It was Walthamstow, it was Waltham Forest, East London, it was Stratford. It's all about giving people the belief that they can make a change. That's what I hope that the people of Hartlepool want.'

Is he at all concerned that the pandemic, which occupied much of his first eighteen months in office, has neutered his aspirations for the red wall? And did it expose greater problems in the fabric of British society than we knew existed? Johnson said it had 'made some things easier' in the sense that issues were 'revealed more clearly' – such as social care and the need to reform the NHS. Coronavirus also proved costly to the whole economy, with an additional £300 billion added to the public debt by May 2021.[4] Yet the prime minister felt it would not temper levelling-up ambitions: 'I don't think so and I don't think it should.'

Johnson did not think the Tories will have to make a choice between holding their new seats in the north and traditional leafy strongholds in the south. 'We will be fighting for every seat' – as you would expect him to say. He argued that levelling up is important for the whole nation. 'The level-up agenda is right for the seats in the south. If you're a liberal, relatively affluent, one-nation Conservative, do you think your long-term prosperity is going to be more effectively secured by building a country where people across the whole of the UK feel happier, more involved, with better life chances? Or do you think it's going to be better if you just continue with the current approach of the last forty years, or the post-war approach?' He said bankers and financiers were 'brilliant' and 'clever' people who realized that 'the long-term health of our economy depends on us changing now'. Johnson returned to his core theme of economic change. 'We cannot continue with this model; it's not right and [change] will bring greater prosperity to the south-east, not less.'

He will measure success in levelling up by three metrics. 'It is skills. It's going to take a while, it will take ten years, but it's skills. It's quite a lot of infrastructure. And you've got to find local leadership. That is [Ben] Houchen not [Sadiq] Khan. You need local leaders who take responsibility, don't blame and who have pride.' His peroration on his successor as London mayor continued. 'I mean, when do you ever hear Sadiq Khan say that London is the greatest city on earth? When do you ever hear him say what a great, fantastic place London is?' Khan does actually talk up London in his own way. Days after he was re-elected as the city's mayor, for example, he said, 'London is in my blood: and it's a privilege to serve the city that has given me everything'.

The red wall Tories I met on my journey are not your typical free-market Tories, who worship the economic policies of

Margaret Thatcher. Yet Johnson said he did not see an ideological clash ahead, insisting his free-market credentials were as strong as ever. 'The freak that I am, because I want people to have agency, I want people to have control, I want people to be able to run their own businesses and run their own lives.' He added that he was still eager to pursue deregulation. 'There's lots of regulations we can do better with and have less of.'

Did Johnson feel that the Tories are unnecessarily stoking 'culture wars', turning movements such as Black Lives Matter into wedge issues to create a dividing line between Labour and its traditional voters? He certainly did not think that, but described the idea of challenging Britain's history as 'totally bananas'. Banging the table hard, he said, 'I believe in putting statues up, not tearing them down. I think on statues . . . it's so ahistorical and so barbaric. It's iconoclastic and dumb. Why would you do that? I get very impatient with this stuff and I think it's fundamentally bollocks.' Instead, what he felt mattered more was 'opportunity'.

Recalling the scenes on the beach front, I asked why he felt he was so personally popular with working-class voters, despite his Eton and Oxford background. Was it that he was seen as an unconventional political insurgent? After running his hand through his mop of hair several times, Johnson said, 'Look, it beats me.' He appeared to be on the cusp of revealing more, before restraining himself. 'It's not about me, this is about this country.'

Outside the black door of Downing Street after his 2019 victory, Johnson proclaimed of the first-time Tory voters, 'Those people want change. We cannot, must not, must not, let them down.' He intended to demonstrate that trust had not been misplaced with tangible changes to public services. 'I'm going to show that we did build forty hospitals, that we did recruit

20,000 more police, that we did recruit 50,000 more nurses,' stressing each area of spending. He went on, 'But much more profoundly than that, I'm going to show that we got Brexit done and we delivered the change that we thought we could, through a £640 billion infrastructure programme. We're revolutionizing skills. We're going to tackle social care. We're going to do all the big things that the government set out to do.' He admitted that 'some of it won't be at all easy' to deliver on, but he felt that by 2024 – confirming that he had no intention of calling an early poll, as some in Westminster have predicted – 'people will be able to see a great project of uniting and levelling up is underway.'

Johnson also fleshed out the argument of what could be his 2024 re-election pitch: vote Labour and the UK will slide back towards EU membership. 'I'm going to level with you,' he said firmly. 'We've got to keep it going because I do think the risk is if we were to be stopped, if we [the Conservatives] were to be pushed out, the whole thing will slump back . . . we will be back into half of the things of the European Union before we could say it. I'm serious about things we've been able to do: the freeports, the vaccine rollout, scuppering the Super League' – a reference to several English football clubs ill-fated plans to join a European Super League, which collapsed under pressure from fans, his government and beyond – 'I can tell you this: those European clubs, as soon as they heard of the UK government's new powers of visa and curbs. Game over. We couldn't have done it in EU law.'

Shelley, Johnson's harried operations manager, appeared smiling over his shoulder – our time was up. Johnson drained the last of his coffee, donned his black face mask – complete with Number 10 logo – and re-entered the media scrum outdoors. After more selfies and arm bumps with the bemused lunchtime diners of the fish bar, the prime ministerial motorcade whizzed off to his next stop: the market village of Yarm in Stockton, where he paced the slippery cobbles to campaign for Ben Houchen, the mayor of Tees Valley. Another traffic jam was caused on the high street as the pair scuttled from pavement to pavement under umbrellas.

On 6 May, the voters of Hartlepool confirmed they wanted the change Johnson spoke of. Jill Mortimer was elected as the first Tory to represent the town in a generation, with a landslide victory. It marked only the second time in forty years that a sitting government won a by-election. Thanks to another brick out of Labour's red wall, Johnson's working majority rose. And Ben Houchen, who delivered the first indication the red wall was collapsing in 2017, was re-elected as metro mayor in the first round with a remarkable 73 per cent of the vote. If there was any further evidence that a structural realignment in British politics was taking place, albeit aided by a successful vaccination programme, these two results were it.

After leaving the prime minister's entourage, I walked back through Hartlepool town centre to the Roker Street car park for another wind-blown conversation with one of his foes. Angela Rayner was notionally in charge of Labour's campaign for the 2021 local elections, and is a rare example of an authentically northern working-class voice in the party's upper echelons – the sort of figure they lacked during Ed Miliband's leadership years. Rayner made her national reputation during Corbyn's leadership as an effective shadow education secretary and stood for the deputy leadership when he exited the stage. Although she endorsed Keir Starmer's left-wing rival Rebecca Long-Bailey for the leadership, the pair appeared to be the perfectly matched duo: north and south, clipped tones and broad Mancunian, male and female, university and further education.

In an enthusiastic chat, Rayner painted the duo as one unit, waging an intense battle for the party's future. During the 2021 election, she reported that voters were pleased with the progress under Starmer's 'New Management slogan', but felt they still had 'a long way to go'. She continued, 'The truth of it is, me and Keir took over just a year ago. If you look at where our results were in 2019, it's very clear that people were angry, the core Labour vote.' In what she called the party's foundation seats – its former heartlands – some progress in rebuilding its reputation had been made, despite the pandemic. 'A lot of people are starting to give us the opportunity to speak to them again,' she said. Although Rayner was re-elected comfortably in her Ashton-under-Lyne constituency in Greater Manchester, her majority dropped from 11,295 to 4,263 votes. She recalled the campaign, 'Sadly, I got a grilling on the doorstep. It was not just specifically Jeremy [Corbyn] or Brexit, it was all of those things accumulated, so people said, "You're just not listening to us."' Addressing those feelings that Labour wasn't listening was the focus of her efforts around the country during the local elections.

Much of Rayner's conversation with me was dominated by her assiduous loyalty to Keir Starmer and praising how he had moved the party on since 2019. She spoke warmly of his 'strong Labour values', defined as 'principles of fairness, principles of a hard day's work for a good day's pay, all of those things that bind us together.' She praised his work as opposition leader throughout the pandemic, especially for 'pushing the government on things like making sure that we've got the support for business and furlough, making sure our kids have got the support they need in education. He's been constructively trying to make the government better and improve things.' Although her job and the opposition leader's were 'very difficult' in the circumstances, she felt Starmer had proved 'he wants to govern in the interest of the whole country.'

Just days after we conducted our interview, she was abruptly sacked by Starmer as party chair for her role overseeing the 2021 local elections, where the Tories scored a hat-trick of Hartlepool, Tees Valley and the West Midlands mayoralties – as well as picking up control of dozens of councils, unheard of for a party a decade into power. Labour made some gains, including the directly elected mayors in West Yorkshire, the West of England and Cambridgeshire, but they were overshadowed by yet another internecine war over who was to blame for the party's problems in the red wall.

Rayner used Starmer's name twenty-one times during our chat and consistently praised the Labour leader, arguing that his stature would counter the 'strong personality of Boris Johnson after the public had more opportunities to know him. I've got a huge amount of respect for Keir.' The pair were not close before 2020, despite being elected to Parliament in the same year and concurrently serving in Corbyn's shadow cabinet. But once he became leader and she was elected deputy, Rayner was won over by his 'very strong, very dependable' personality. It may be the opposite of Johnson's emotional image, but she argued Starmer could be trusted by voters of all ages and demographics, as well as having a personality she felt 'needs to come out. Keir's not the oversharing type and I think that, as the public get to know Keir, they will fall in love with him. They'll feel he's the sort of guy that you definitely want running the country.' Despite the abrupt demotion, she remained Labour's deputy leader, with her own mandate from the membership.

Labour's biggest challenge, in Rayner's view, is to earn the respect of the electorate and rebuild the lost 'emotional connection' that she sensed had disappeared in 2019. 'We've got to the point now where people are saying, "Okay, we'll let you in the room", and it's a question now of tentatively proving that we've got the right answers.' She also felt that the party was too self-critical and wasted its energies on critiquing the New Labour years. 'I refuse to condemn the Blair years when they gave us education, Sure Start centres. Gordon Brown helped many single parents like me when I was growing up.'

Some in Labour have exhausted themselves trying to argue that Boris Johnson's Tories have been in power for a decade and should shoulder the blame for the changes in society. Rayner has picked up on this and put it down to 'very different' messages. 'The Conservatives have been in power since 2010, yet they reinvent themselves every couple of years. Every time they get a new leader, it's like "nothing to see here". Boris Johnson is going around the country saying "we're putting 20,000 police on the street"; they literally took 22,000 police officers *off* the street! We're the complete opposite of that. We tend to beat ourselves up about the things that we wanted to achieve or that we haven't achieved.' In too many instances, she thinks the Labour movement 'set the standard and bar so high that sometimes even our membership can't reach it.'

I put it to Rayner that, based on her background, she would now demographically most likely be a Conservative voter. How did that make her feel? She responded, 'I don't blame the voters for going Tory', and attacked those in the party who argue 'it's the voters that are the problem'. But nor does she think people in the red wall are now automatically Tory supporters. 'I think the voters want to come to us, it's that we prevented them from doing that. I don't think they've all suddenly just switched to the Conservatives.' When quizzed on what will draw these people back to Labour, Rayner said it would not be a platform of slogans and platitudes. 'It'll be a programme that will change things the way the Labour movement did after the war; in the way that the Tony Blair government did in the late 1990s . . . raising the country all together and making sure that education is important, that business and prosperity across the whole of our country is important, and bringing people together.'

Rayner, who has vied with Boris Johnson at the parliamentary dispatch box, thought that voters would punish the prime minister on his handling of the coronavirus pandemic and Brexit. 'He's had the slogans, but at the end of the day, we're seeing the situation in Northern Ireland, which is very worrying and concerning. Ask any business that works across the EU and they'll tell you that the promise the government gave is not what they're currently delivering on. This is not about whether you agree with Brexit or not, this is about the genuine promise that was made to the people in this country and the inadequate way in which the government has been able to perform.' Although many of the effects of Brexit had yet to kick in by May 2021, there was no indication of a voter rebellion coming to pass.

The levelling-up agenda, which sees cash being pumped into seats like Rayner's, is not something she is concerned about, dismissing the spending efforts of the government as 'jam tomorrow' that would not tackle the structural issues. 'You can say you're going to give a little bit of money here. But if that money, like the Towns fund, doesn't actually come down to people being able to get the skills, get those jobs, then people in the north, those towns and cities will get more and more frustrated.' She is especially concerned that social mobility will be hampered until such reforms take place. Rayner cited the example of Durham University, and asked me how many working-class kids from the city attend. Having spent three years there, I can confirm the answer was very few. She cited the same problem with the BBC's relocation to MediaCity in Salford. 'That's wonderful it came to Salford, but how many people move from London to work in MediaCity versus how many of the kids from Oldham got jobs in MediaCity? Unless you deal with a structural inequality, which we've seen grow, then actually all you're doing is putting a nice shiny building in a town for people that are already doing well and will continue to do well.'

The overwhelming sense I had of Rayner was a politician especially hungry for the power to change people's lives. 'I'm not in this to lose the next general election. I have watched over the last ten years – and certainly since I've been in Parliament – time and time again the government does things that damage the area that I grew up in,' she said, with passion rising in her voice. 'That has rolled back the opportunities for the kids, put kids in poverty again. I used to be on free school meals, I used to sit on the kerb and wait for my mates to come out after they had their dinner. And over summer, I was so upset.' Rayner was reprimanded for calling her fellow Greater Manchester MP, and fellow interviewee in this book, Chris Clarkson, 'scum' in a heated debate during the pandemic. She did not think the language was un-parliamentary, and was upset. 'I thought we're going back there again and leaving kids starving. I don't want to watch that anymore. I do not like being in opposition and I'm not in this now to be the deputy leader of the Labour Party in opposition. I mean to be the deputy prime minister.'

Rayner concluded by reiterating her core message: 'What myself and Keir have been very clear on is that the number-one priority for us is the voters. We want to be in power, we want to change people's lives for the better.' Whether the Rayner–Starmer coalition continues until the next polling day will be the test of that. Hopping back into the Mini for the last time, I left Rayner to return to the campaign trail and made the journey south to the place where Rayner dreams of holding power: Westminster.

*

It was time to meet two final figures, among the most prominent in British politics, and who will both be key protagonists in the fight over whether the red wall stays blue, or whether Labour can rebuild it and reconnect to its lost heartlands. The first stop was a building I spend a lot of time thinking and writing about in my role as the Whitehall Editor of the *Financial Times*: the Cabinet Office. By far the most inscrutable Whitehall ministry of the British state, it emerged a century ago out of a necessity to connect the more established ministries – it's the lubricant for the machinery of government. Based in a grand white building on the corner of Whitehall and Downing Street, its physical location symbolizes its power and importance. Its chief occupant under Boris Johnson's government, Michael Gove, is crucial to his government's mission. As well as delivering the UK's full exit from the EU, his department was tasked with reforming the civil service and overseeing the shift of 20,000 officials out of Westminster within a decade. The parts of levelling up that require the British state to function better were entirely in his purview.

In his large office, decorated with a handful of ornate oil paintings and white armchairs that could have belonged in a charity shop, I reminded Gove of a conversation we had at the start of the 2019 election campaign. On a train back from Birmingham, where the Conservative Party had launched its election campaign, I was collecting beverages from the buffet car after an extremely long day. I was greeted by heckling from the other end of the carriage, and found the source to be a third of the Cabinet. One of those present was Gove, who was especially excited about the impending campaign. I asked him then which seat I should look out for that no one was watching. 'Redcar' was his response, which duly went Tory for the first time in 2019. When I reminded him of this, he confessed it was mostly a fluke guess. In his quirky Scottish accent, he described the 'euphoria' of the 2019 election night results. 'I was sitting next to Dawn Butler [a Labour shadow minister] in the ITV studio when I heard the news, so I had to maintain an impassive facade. But I could just see out of the corner of my eye the spad team dancing in the corridor outside. I didn't quite believe it. I only really believed it was true when I had the Blyth Valley result.'

Gove did not spend much of the campaign in the north of England, but recalled a remarkably warm response in the East Midlands seats of Chesterfield and Bolsover. 'The doorstep conversations were almost exactly what you might have dreamed of; in attitudes towards Corbyn, in attitudes towards Brexit, in attitudes towards Boris.' He felt they were so positive that it could have been a set-up. 'I wasn't sure whether or not I could believe that it was true, because it seemed as though I walked into a stylized voxpop designed to boost our morale.' He put Brexit as the primary issue that drove voters towards the Tories, but argued it was tightly linked to Jeremy Corbyn's leadership. 'While the [Westminster] bubble knew about Corbyn's real views in 2017, it wasn't sufficiently credible with voters. When we were critical of Corbyn for IRA links people thought, *That's ridiculous, that's incredible, no Labour leader would do that, this is clearly made up*. Then, by 2019, there was more than enough information about the type of leader he was for people to think he's not really Labour.'

The difference between 2017 and 2019, for Gove, was the Labour Party's unstable Brexit position. Whereas in Corbyn's first election the party was 'skilful' at not presenting itself as seeking to overturn the result, while also being 'a vehicle for Remainer anger', it was not able to strike such a delicate position two years on. 'The twists and turns of everything that had happened in Parliament meant that Labour's role, collectively through Corbyn's position, was seen as enigmatic. It was impossible to see Labour as anything other than seeking to block and frustrate.' The Tory message that people 'just wanted it done' was crucial, in his view. The recurring view Gove heard was '"We've given our views, we've explained what it is that we wanted, and you're just not listening." But again, I think it's impossible to disinter the importance of each specific thing.'

Much of the Cabinet Office's capacity in 2020 and 2021 was dominated by the coronavirus pandemic. Gove was one of the Cabinet ministers involved in the key decisions about lockdowns, procurement, vaccine passports and equipment. He was often seen as one of the more pro-lockdown voices in the Johnson government, with some of his more authoritarian instincts contrasting with the prime minister's innate libertarianism. The experience of the pandemic made Gove believe that the state needs to be more ambitious in tackling inequalities. 'I think, if anything, the ambition is sharper because of the need to demonstrate in short order that a difference is being made. I wouldn't say that it's easy, quite the opposite,' he said. 'What Covid has also done is draw even sharper attention to some of the inequalities in society, and therefore placed more of an onus on the government to address them.'

I put to Gove the economics question raised throughout the road trip: has the liberalism of the David Cameron–George Osborne era disappeared? And, similarly to Boris Johnson, does he believe that the Thatcherite consensus of the last four decades has ended? His response was as stark as his party leader's: 'I think we've got to focus upon fiscal prudence, but what we can't do is pursue an ever smaller state.' Keeping the state small has defined the Tory Party in recent history. He put forward the view that Johnson will be 'a more traditional Tory' in his economic thinking. 'For quite a lot of the Tory Party's twentieth-century – and indeed nineteenth-century – existence, it had close links with business but it wasn't a purist economic Liberal Party. Obviously we've got to do lots of stuff to bring the budget into balance over time, but I don't think that we will be pursuing a Thatcherite federal economic reconstruction.'

His view on delivering 'levelling up' mirrors that of many Tory MPs: small, tangible changes in people's lives will be proof that the Johnson government is delivering for them. 'A little can go a long way,' as he put it. 'The most important thing is care and attention to the specific concerns of those communities. That doesn't necessarily require massive investment, but it does require thoughtful investment and working with businesses and individuals in those communities.'

As the Cabinet minister for education and justice, as well as a brief spell as chief whip, Gove was a core part of the project to modernize the Tory Party, until he fell out spectacularly with Cameron over Brexit. With hindsight, and the party's newfound ability to win majorities after the election, he felt that an image problem developed during its return to government in 2010. 'One of the things that was more harmful for the Tories was not necessarily trying to bring the budget under balance per se, it was the perception that we were a party of the rich and the south.' He added, 'The point was made that the people who had missed out from Tory modernization were the working classes, however they're defined. And Brexit provided an opportunity for that breach to be healed.'

With the next election in Johnson's eye for 2024, Gove suggested that the cultural split is going to create significant structural issues for Labour in the future. Although 2019 was 'a uniquely capricious set of circumstances', he argued, 'I think parties of the left across the Western world risk a preoccupation with identity politics and risk being the echo chamber for a particular alliance of academics, public-sector professionals, human rights lawyers etc. And so it has proven more difficult for parties of the left to combine a working-class base with a traditional social democratic intellectual element.' He rightly noted that the traditional left-wing parties in France and Germany are suffering from the same issues in keeping their traditional working-class base on side, while seeing the 'hipster intellectual' element of the party's agenda being taken over by the Greens. 'My hunch is that, while Keir Starmer understands much of this intellectually, and many people in his team do, they don't appreciate this in the way that Blair did; that you have to reorient your party until it hurts.'

Gove was also disparaging about Keir Starmer's efforts to keep both sides of the Labour coalition happy. 'I think if he attempts to square the circle, he won't succeed. It's the lesson of all oppositions, that you always have to go further in renovating your party than you think.' He also argued that the Joe Biden example, which has been mentioned by several Labour figures during my journey as an aspiration, does not translate to figures within the party. 'Notwithstanding everything, [Biden] has authenticity because of his background. The squad [a reference to four especially liberal congresswomen who have campaigned to take the Democratic Party leftwards] – Alexandria Ocasio-Cortez etc – didn't dominate the [2020 US election] campaign in the way that they might have done. And then Trump was Trump. So the irony is that he assembled a particular coalition that perhaps the other Republicans wouldn't have been able to.'

Along with Johnson, Gove was the central figure in the Vote Leave campaign, the spokesperson who gave the cause more intellectual authenticity. With the UK having formally exited the bloc in January 2021, he believed that the identity divide would last, even if the particular issue of Brexit had less significance.

'One of the problems that Labour has with Keir – as he was an obvious standout candidate – is that he was someone who was so clearly and strongly identified with the battle against Brexit.'

Whitehall is one of London's most famous roads, separating Parliament from the civil service, MPs from officials, and power from opposition. On the Embankment overlooking the River Thames, Norman Shaw South stands as one of the grandest buildings in the Palace of Westminster. Once home to Scotland Yard, it was converted into offices in the 1970s for MPs, with the second floor dedicated to a hallowed suite known in Westminster jargon as Loto, or the Leader of the Opposition's Office. It is a place where many Labour leaders have devoted decades to plotting a path across the road to Downing Street, only to find their plans thwarted by the small matter of the electorate. The corridor to the conference room overlooking the River Thames was lined with mid-century election posters. 'Let's go with Labour and we'll get things done', one proclaimed. Another screamed out 'You know Labour government works'. Nostalgia, perhaps, for an era when the party won elections.

Sitting opposite me at a long oak table, Keir Starmer launched into his reflections on what went wrong for the party in 2019. Freshly out of Prime Minister's Questions, his tie was gone and a pair of grey glasses were balanced on top of his iPhone. As one would expect of a former head of the Crown Prosecution Service, he was clear and articulate in talking about his despair at the result. 'We'd lost heavily to everyone everywhere – including seats that were held for many, many years – so I thought it was devastating for our party and our movement.' Unlike some in the party, he appreciated the size of its trials. 'As the days and weeks emerged after that election, I began to appreciate the scale and extent of the challenge that we had ahead.'

Starmer was not surprised by the result, but was taken aback by the scale of the party's collapse. 'We were behind at the polls and it was always a challenge and we had real issues on the doorsteps. But the scale of it was a shock . . . for the Labour Party to have the worst result since 1935 should be and was a shock.' Although we were speaking primarily about the red wall, he was eager to point out his party 'lost everywhere across the United Kingdom' – in the east, south, south-east, Wales and Scotland. Labour 'lost heavily and badly' and his chief concern was that the party should not turn inwards. 'One of the things that it's very important for a party to do when you lose that badly is not look at the electorate and say "what do you think you were doing?" but to look at your own party and say "what were *we* doing?"'

During the 2019 campaign, Starmer visited over forty constituencies and found four 'strong themes' on the doorstep that were to blame for the 2019 result: 'Jeremy, as leader of the party; Brexit; the manifesto, which people felt was overloaded, promised too much which couldn't be delivered; and antisemitism.' In some parts of the country, concern about antisemitism was more prevalent than in others, but he said there was 'no denying' those issues dominated the campaign. 'If anybody says they weren't the four issues I'd question how many campaign doorsteps they actually went to. Because whether they're fair or not is secondary. We've got to be honest about what the issues were.' He acknowledged that factions have their own reasons for emphasizing different parts of what went wrong. 'People will have their battles as to whether they think it was Brexit more than it was Jeremy, whether it was antisemitism more than it was the manifesto. Actually, it was probably all of them taken together, where there was a quite a deep sense of "you're not listening to us", and "you're not presenting us with a credible offer for the future."

We have got to recognize that defeat in 2019 was down to us, not the electorate, and therefore that listening needs to be good and hard.'

But Starmer agreed there were structural and deeper issues that contributed to the party's failure to win in 2019. He argued that the slightly longer-term view of the decade since Gordon Brown was ejected from office was crucial. 'I'm very mindful that we've lost four elections in a row. This was not an election where everything had been going fine for a decade and suddenly we were confronted with this inexplicable election defeat.' He rightly identified that around the red wall constituencies, there were harbingers of seats that flipped. 'Even within those seats, our vote had been declining, although there was a bit of that up to 2017. But the bigger political questions are: what's happened over that ten-year period? What have the changes been? How's the Labour Party responded or not responded to them? While we can have our internal battles about what the primary factor was in 2019, that's probably not as important a question as what's been going on over the last decade.'

Although he used 'red wall' frequently in our conversation, Starmer said Labour had to be careful in using catch-all terms. 'Whenever I've tried to get underneath the skin of what the change is, what the political issue is, then I see in those seats something that I also see, actually, in other parts of the country. If you go to eastern England, if you go to some of the coastal towns, go to Plymouth and places like that, the emotion that I think was driving certainly the 2019 election and the referendum is not dissimilar across the country.' I pointed out to him the clear demographic and political trends that separate the red wall from the rest of country, but he felt that Labour's problems needed to be seen in a national context. 'I think it is probably wrong to say, "here's a band of seats which are unlike other areas in the United Kingdom". Certainly, when you look at other towns around the United Kingdom, southern England, coastal towns, parts of Wales, arguably, the same emotion is there.'

There was much of Ed Miliband's view of the world in Starmer's outline of what produced their defeat in 2019, and why people voted for the Conservatives as their route for change. 'One [factor] is, very strongly, Britain isn't working for us, and you're not listening. That is a very, very strong driver – whether it's the economy that's not working for people – we've got a short-term economy, low wage, low standards, low productivity, low investment, not working for millions of people – whether it's public services, which aren't working for people, whether it's the health service. There's a strong sense of "it isn't working for me", and "you're not listening to me", a frustration, almost, of "I can't influence this".' That feeling manifested itself during the referendum, where Starmer was firmly on the Remain side. But he explained, 'I never underestimated the power of the phrase "take back control" and the emotion that that triggered. Because obviously there was the referendum question, which was membership of the EU or not, but there was the deeper question, which is almost a referendum on the state of Britain.'

During the Brexit wars, Starmer was seen within the party as one of the chief proponents of adopting a second referendum. Does he offer a *mea culpa* for a policy position that, judging by almost every conversation I had during the tour, played a major part in the party's 2019 defeat? 'There's no question that came up in the red wall. It was one of the issues on the doorsteps,' he said wearily. 'It's fair to point out that it came up differently in different parts of the United Kingdom. You didn't have to campaign for very long in Scotland to realize there was a different read out there, or in other parts of the country.' That may be true, but the explicit issue of Brexit was problematic for the red wall.

He admitted, 'Was it a factor? Yes. Did it impact on the result? Yes, it did. Do we need to accept that Brexit has happened? Yes. We do.' He explained this was why he whipped Labour MPs to support Boris Johnson's withdrawal deal after the 2019 election. 'I was not so much thinking about the election result in 2019, I was thinking about the election in 2024 or 2023, whenever it may be . . . it is very important for the Labour Party to be able to speak to the country then and say, "If you vote Labour, it will make for a better Britain and therefore we will make whatever this arrangement with the EU is work."'

After his election as Labour leader in April 2020, Starmer had intended to travel the country to the areas where the party lost. He did the same after the 2016 EU referendum, visiting Hull several times. With a sly dig at his predecessor Jeremy Corbyn, who gathered thousands of eager young supporters to his rallies, he said, 'Whereas some Labour leaders like to go to places and be surrounded by Labour supporters, I wanted to go to places where people were going to say, "I did vote Labour and don't vote anymore." We tried, by and large, to make sure that we didn't have too many Labour voices. Unfortunately, due to the coronavirus pandemic, these visits had to be virtual.' He was eager to hit the road in the summer of 2021 to do these exercises in person, but even through Zoom he was struck by the emotion of those speaking to him on these calls. 'I could almost see them asking the question, "Is he listening to me?" It wasn't fierce arguments about Brexit, or the manifesto or even the Labour Party. It was a raw thing: "Is this fella now leading the party listening to me?"'

I put to Starmer that many of the red wall seats do not resemble a scene from *Billy Elliot*. The rise in private housing that I saw in North East Derbyshire, or the new industries in North West Durham, has made them structurally more favourable to the

Tories. He agreed there had been a significant economic transformation since deindustrialization and that Labour had to find
ways of connecting with these voters. 'It is certainly true that
people [in these parts of England] have got good jobs in manufacturing or whatever it may be; highly skilled, good jobs and
some increasingly decent housing. But there are those that haven't
and they sit side by side, you can almost see it in those communities.' Labour's standard message appeals to those who have not
benefited from the changing nature of these seats, but Starmer
is also set on winning over those who are better off. 'For those
that have got a good job, are skilled, have aspiration – real aspiration for themselves and their family, which is a great thing – I
feel the Labour Party hasn't been talking to them for the last
five years. In other words, we have not been clear enough that
we are a party of aspiration and opportunity, and that aspiration
and opportunity are a good thing.'

Starmer referenced his personal backstory as an example of
what that message should look like: 'Look at me. My dad worked
in a factory, my mum was a nurse. And it was their greatest pride
that their son went off to university and became a lawyer and
then ran the Crown Prosecution Service, now an MP. That is
the story of Labour.' He went on to cite how Labour's three
successful periods in power were defined by such a message:
'1945 was aspiration, opportunity, building a better Britain. Then
you had the 1960s with Wilson, and when he was talking about
a better Britain he was saying "the white heat of technology is
all about how Britain can be better", once we understand and
harness this technology. Blair, as well, was saying, "Britain can
be different, it can be better", and we're only going to win if we
are able to say we're optimistic about the future.'

This tied into Starmer's view on patriotism, and why he has
embraced Tony Blair's stance on the issue. 'People seem surprised

when I say I'm patriotic, but actually it is a belief that your country is fantastic and can be better that lies deep within politics.' I took the opportunity to put to Starmer two comments about Labour's cultural split with the red wall. First, I recalled the two men in the Doncaster pub who said the image of him taking the knee in solidarity with the Black Lives Matter movement was proof that 'he hated white people'. Starmer's response was to decry the 'characteristic' of the last decade of looking at politics through what divides people. 'What's the difference between the town and the city? What's the difference between urban and rural? What's the difference between black and white? What's the difference between old and young? What's the difference between the manu-facturing and the service worker? And you see in it America, you've seen it here, and it's toxic.' Instead of being split on cultural issues, he said that what most people were seeking to hear from Labour was about economics. 'They wanted an economy that works better than the one we've got. Almost everybody agrees with that. And they want quite big changes to the economy. So there are really uniting factors. And if you look at the last twelve months of the pandemic, what we've seen there – not much good comes out of a pandemic – but one thing is the solidarity, the looking out for each other, the empathy, the values and emotions that have been buried pretty deep in the last ten years.' I pointed out that trying to win elections with emotion alone, as Alan Milburn argued in Burnley, is impossible. He disagreed. 'I do think there is a stand-back moment where we say, if all we do is pick away at what divides us, what makes us different, this group over that group, then we're going nowhere.'

The second cultural point I put to Starmer was Tony Blair's argument that Labour, while still supporting the sentiment, should not subcontract policies to movements such as Black Lives Matter, Extinction Rebellion, MeToo and trans rights groups.

His curt response was, 'I certainly don't think we should outsource anything to anyone as the Labour Party; we have confidence in our own arguments and have confidence that we're a party that can pull people together.' But he went on to say that Labour under this leadership would never ignore injustices and inequalities. 'If we shut our eyes to that, we'll be making a huge mistake. The question is, how do we make that a unifying argument and an argument about a better future for all of us? That is the single biggest challenge that we face as the Labour Party.'

Starmer will face a formidable opponent at the next election. Boris Johnson has moved the Conservative Party into new terrain that will see government spending and investment on a scale Labour would traditionally propose. His belief is that the government will fail to deliver on levelling up – or to use a phrase he trotted out at PMQs in the early months of 2021, 'the mask will slip'. The prime minister's words and actions 'don't very often match up', and Starmer thinks this will provide Labour with an opening. 'What people are hearing about levelling up is a big agenda that will genuinely level-up people and communities and Johnson will not deliver on that.' For emphasis, he said it again: 'He will not deliver on that.'

Why not? 'If you're going to level up, you've got to tackle the difficult issues in the economy, you've got to be prepared to tackle the short-termism of the economy head-on. People say "Oh, well, isn't there a bit of big economics going on?" What the government's done in the pandemic is, understandably, put quite a lot of money into supporting businesses. That wasn't a change of ideology. That was a necessity caused by a pandemic. You've seen that across the world, including across Europe, in the sort of global ideological shift that happened in about March, or on 23 March in this country last year – this was the economics of necessity.'

But what if Johnson does deliver? What if the first-time voters in the red wall do feel their lives have been improved by voting Conservative? Is it not a high-risk strategy to base your chances of electoral success on someone else's failure? 'Now, obviously, we'll see how that plays out over the next few years. But with Johnson, it's action versus words. Words are easy.' He pointed to how the government has looked to wind down the state's largesse as the pandemic has seemed to ease. 'The chancellor's first question is, "How quickly can we withdraw the support that we've got?" Compare it with other countries, where the support is going on for longer. The uplift in Universal Credit isn't going to be there, the council tax for families is going to be imposed, the pay freeze for those in the public sector. These are not the hallmarks of a government that's had an ideological shift towards changing the fundamentals of our economy.'

With the loss of the Hartlepool by-election, the wolves on the Labour left began to circle and doubts were raised about whether Starmer would even make the next general election. When I departed from Loto, with Starmer off to a Zoom call with activists, he insisted that the party's direction would be entirely set by him. 'Going back, whether it's Tony Blair, Gordon Brown, or all past leaders – and I talk to them all, it's important to talk to them all – what happens next in the next few years is down to this Labour Party, this leadership and the team that I'm leading. We've got to do this from first principles, going forward.' As I walked back through the Norman Shaw building to my desk in the parliamentary press gallery, I wondered if I had just met the next prime minister, or another Labour leader who would try and fail to get his party back into power. After 6,000 miles, over 120 interviews and dozens more conversations, plus three coronavirus lockdowns and one bout of the virus, the latter felt more likely than the former.

*

Before I set off on this journey, I had a few preconceived ideas about how permanent the electoral changes in 2019 would be. I would not have devoted almost two years to researching this book if I assumed the Tories' triumph reflected a one-off fluke, contingent on a very particular set of circumstances in which Britain found itself in December 2019. Without a doubt, a structural change has taken place in how England votes, and it is not yet over. As politics continues to polarize, reflecting the Remain–Leave lines, more potential gains will open up for the Tories, while the identity challenge for Labour will become even trickier.

The strength of these factors is abundantly clear throughout the ten constituencies on my journey. In every place, in almost every single conversation, Labour's stance on Brexit and the unpopularity of Jeremy Corbyn were top of the list of why the party lost its fourth election in a row. Combined, they handed Boris Johnson his eighty-seat majority, aided by a particularly effective Conservative campaign and a chaotic Labour one.

Had Labour taken a different stance on Brexit, entering the 2019 election without a second referendum attached to the party's manifesto, Johnson's message of 'get Brexit done' would have been far less effective. And had Labour not entered the campaign with a leader who failed to connect with most of the electorate, voters would have been less open to Boris Johnson. These contingent issues, however, are structural too. Jeremy Corbyn's leadership was delivered across the Labour movement – MPs, activists and trade unions all endorsed him to be the leader.

It is impossible to separate out the issues of Brexit and Corbyn, as the two became intertwined in voters' minds. Corbyn's equivocation on the EU question was one of the most notable examples of his poor leadership. Alan Johnson was correct to argue that the greatest missed opportunity for Labour was after the 2017 election. Within the disrupted, uneasy parliament that followed, there was a majority for a softer Brexit, but the circumstances never existed for it to emerge. Labour MPs in pro-Brexit seats professed publicly to be committed to delivering on the referendum result, but the majority, in the backs of their minds, still harboured hopes Brexit could be stopped. Had senior Labour figures all firmly committed to delivering on the referendum result, I remain convinced Theresa May would have done a deal. There would have been a terrific political fallout: ardent pro-EU campaigners in Labour may have split off into the Liberal Democrats; some hardline Brexiters in the Tories may have gone the other way and formed a new force with Nigel Farage. But it may have propped up the red wall for a little longer, and given Labour the opportunity to rebuild its standing.

The prevarication was disastrous. The intellectual vacuum around Corbyn's Brexit policy paved the way for the People's Vote campaign. After the referendum, Labour's initial message to its pro-Brexit voters was the right one: it would implement the result and campaign on their behalf for the best deal. Further back, however, there is little doubt that the referendum itself was very damaging for Labour. The disconnect that grew between the party leadership and its traditional supporters – starting with the rise of UKIP – was forced into the open. The 2016 referendum was the first time that millions of the party's traditional supporters went against their historic family attitudes towards politics. In many ways, the referendum acted like a bleach on their prejudices towards the Conservative Party.

When the furore of the Brexit years has settled and the events of 2016 to 2020 can be reflected on from a distance, the referendum will be seen as more disastrous for Labour than the Tories. The collective nervous breakdown of the Conservative parliamentary party during the Theresa May years was acute and very public, but it was rapidly resolved. Under Boris Johnson, the party has become *the* Brexit party and its voting coalition has reflected that. What happens to the pro-Remain Tories, especially those in the south-east of England, could be the next major story in English politics. The policies Johnson will have to enact to deliver on his pledges of delivering fundamental change to the red wall will cause consternation in what could be termed the 'blue wall' – the Home Counties. The Liberal Democrats are the natural force poised to seize this opportunity; their combination of pro-EU attitudes and social liberalism are ripe for progress. But whether their leadership and political nous are up to beating the Tories in Tunbridge Wells is unclear.

My road trip across the red wall could not possibly cover every inch or speak to an equal sample of voters. But thanks to the pollsters Opinium, I conducted a comprehensive survey of forty first-time Tory constituencies – including Hartlepool – to examine the themes of the road trip, and my sense of structural change was reflected in a wider analysis of how voters feel. The data affirmed the feedback and overall conclusion of my journey: the parts of England that voted Tory for the first time in 2019 have no regrets and, in some parts, have become more Conservative.

Conducted at the end of May 2021, as the country was emerging from the third coronavirus lockdown, the poll put the Conservatives on fifty per cent of the vote share in the red wall – twelve per cent ahead of Labour and up three percentage points from their nationwide result in the 2019 election. There was no indication of voters changing their minds since the last general election: eighty-six per cent of Tory voters from 2019 election said they remained happy with how they voted.

Fifty-nine per cent of those polled had voted Labour in the past and we probed why these former supporters had gone elsewhere. Jeremy Corbyn was the most common reason (which should be heeded by his supporters who claim that the leader was actually popular in the country), followed by Labour's stance on Brexit – both for its lack of clarity and for being seen as anti-democratic. But the variety of other responses are telling about Labour's challenges in winning back these voters, particularly on the issue of leadership. This is a selection of the comments from the 800 voters polled:

- *'At the moment, they are not credible. I dislike the stance they seem to have taken of just disagreeing with everything the government does during the pandemic. It seems to just be for the sake of it.'*
- *'Became too left-wing, London-centric, youth-focused and spending policies became truly crazy.'*
- *'Didn't like the way they were going. Didn't like the party leaders or their policies.'*
- *'They have lost touch with what they stand for and they do not represent my own views any more.'*
- *'They no longer represent people like me. They are a joke.'*
- *'My political beliefs have changed since I was a teenager.'*
- *'They are woke and racist against the white people of the UK and want to replace us with ethnic minority groups.'*
- *'They do not like anyone who is employed.'*
- *'The way they spent money I felt was wrong.'*
- *'No leader of the party [was] strong enough or who I trusted enough to deliver.'*
- *'I got more for my money with a Conservative government.'*
- *'How Labour ran the country.'*
- *'Distrust in their ability to run the country.'*
- *'Party values, permitting terrorism/terrorists.'*
- *'They have lost their direction and connection to the working classes.'*
- *'Weak policies on immigration, human rights, judicial system. Inability to balance the books.'*

The number one reason that would persuade voters to back Labour again was a 'better connection with working people', cited by twenty per cent. Fourteen per cent said they would back Labour again if it dropped some of its more left-wing policies, such as widespread nationalization of industries, while an equal number said they would never vote for the party again. Thirteen per cent said that new leadership or a 'greater emphasis on British values' would entice them back to the party.

Tony Blair was right in his deduction that a lack of leadership on cultural issues has created a consensus that is not reflective of where the party's voters are. Half said that historical statues of those involved in activities such as the slave trade should remain standing. A quarter felt that plaques should be added to explain their links to the slave trade, with only eleven per cent supporting their total removal. But Labour's schism is that while a clear majority of Conservatives want statues left as they are, a third of Labour agreed with them and another third wants plaques added. And sixty-two per cent stated the Conservative Party was patriotic compared to just thirty-seven per cent for Labour.

On the question of leadership, Boris Johnson outstripped Keir Starmer in every category – often with substantial leads. Overall, the prime minister had a +18 net approval rating for his leadership while the Labour leader was -18, a large gap that Starmer will have to reverse if he has any hope of winning the next election. Forty-eight per cent said that the Tories under Johnson are better at 'standing up for Britain' compared to twenty-three per cent Labour under Starmer. Thirty-nine per cent back the Tories for 'representing your values' compared to twenty-eight per cent for Labour. Johnson's Conservatives had a twenty-six-point lead ahead of Starmer on running the economy. The parties came closest on the issue of improving the NHS, where the Tories are five points ahead of Labour.

Despite the missteps of 2020 and 2021, the government emerged with a positive rating for handling of the pandemic in the red wall: fifty-four per cent state their approval. Twenty-nine per cent also said that coronavirus has improved their view of Boris Johnson, although forty per cent said it has not changed their past views. Unsurprisingly, the UK's vaccination programme has emerged with a glowing endorsement: three quarters approve, including two thirds of Labour voters. All of the positive endorsements of Johnson and the Tories should be viewed through this lens, the glow of the vaccine programme will eventually subside.

Emerging from the pandemic, the top priority for the red wall was more job opportunities. The second priority was better local health services and tackling crime. The other issues – improving high streets and better skills and retraining – were cited as lower priorities. But there was widespread pessimism about the economic progress in the past and future. Over the last decade, forty-three per cent think their area has become poorer but only twenty per cent think their area will become richer over the next five years, although the numbers are significantly higher for Conservative voters. Remain supporters are also more downbeat about the future. And overall opinion on Brexit was balanced: thirty-five per cent think it will not make their local area better off, but forty per cent think it will – including six in ten Conservative voters. Nonetheless, a mere seven per cent felt that leaving the EU has already made them better off.

The most fascinating responses were on the question of which prime ministers have had a positive or negative impact on the respondent's local area. Given that he is fresh in voters' minds, it is no surprise that Boris Johnson emerged as the figure having the most positive impact on a local area – the only individual to have a net positive rating. The two least popular figures were the least charismatic prime ministers: just ten per cent felt John Major had a positive effect on their area and fourteen per cent for Theresa May. Gordon Brown did not fare much better either, with only fifteen per cent believing he had a positive impact on their area.

Strikingly, red wall voters jointly placed Tony Blair and Margaret Thatcher in second, with twenty-three per cent believing they had a positive impact on their area. But the divisive qualities of Thatcher persist: many felt she did good things for their communities but a significant part of the electorate felt otherwise, including thirty-two per cent of current Conservative voters. The party that adored Thatcher as a modern-day icon is not the party's voting base today, which explains why Boris Johnson has had no qualms about forswearing her free market outlook and defined a levelling up mission to tackle some of the long tail effects of her deindustrialization policies.

A structural change has taken place. The Hartlepool by-election was evidence that the Tories could indeed win once Brexit was delivered and Jeremy Corbyn was no longer leader (or even in the Labour Party). It is important to recognize that the collapse of Labour in these seats did not suddenly arrive in 2019. In some the erosion of those massive majorities from 1997 has been gradual. In others, a wave started in 2010 and grew in each election over the coming decade. First it touched the classic marginal seats in the Midlands, like Nuneaton. Then it was the more rural Labour-aligned seats, such as Morley and Outwood in 2015. Then, prompted by Brexit, the specific red wall effect kicked in in 2017, with the first four constituencies collapsing. And by 2019, the trend was clear: Labour's support in the larger cities grew at almost the same rate of its decline elsewhere in England. Gain after gain, the Tories were winning places that had the demographic profile of a traditional Labour stronghold.

There are, however, two clear categories of red wall seats. Some of the first time Tory areas are more urban – centred around larger towns like Blyth and Wakefield – while others are more rural, made up of lots of smaller settlements. The more prosperous ones, such as Sedgefield, will be easier for the Tories to hold. They have been marginal for longer and the structural changes will help Johnson hold onto them. Changes have taken place in the poorer ones too, but in a less pronounced way. The upcoming boundary changes, which will redraw the political map based on population moves, could hand the Conservatives another ten or so seats based on their 2019 polling, but it will also mean others will disappear. The shift in population towards cities means that some seats, such as Blyth Valley, will be subsumed. When the redrawing is complete, only then can the specific impact be seen.

Despite their thumping victory, the boundary commission will highlight a clear demographic trend that should worry the Conservatives: Britons are moving increasingly towards cities. Many of the red wall seats have declining populations that are becoming increasingly older. Over time, this is going to create more electoral challenges if the Tories cannot find a way of winning again in cities. Boris Johnson was clearly aware of this, hence his emphasis in our fish-bar conversation on his love of London and cities. Ever the shape-shifter, he will no doubt seek to pivot back to his roots and look to expand the party's appeal again in the country's great metropolitan areas.

There is a case to be made that Labour's problems will prove existential. The party came into existence at the beginning of the twentieth century based on a specific set of circumstances: the prominence of socialist intellectuals combined with the eman-cipation of the working class – overwhelmingly white men working in manual jobs. While the intellectuals continue to be prominent in society, mostly found on social media, universities and in newspaper columns, the working class has changed beyond recognition. As Phil Wilson put it in Sedgefield, the world has changed and the Labour Party has not changed with it. Too often in elections, it is focused on the arguments of the past and the present instead of the future. The most needing in society are now those working in the Boohoo warehouse in Burnley. Yet Labour has failed to find a way of engaging with these residents, despite campaigning against zero-hours contracts for a decade.

Robert Oliver, a Conservative councillor in Sunderland who has campaigned for the party in the north-east for over two decades, thought the passing of time has been crucial for the change in the party's fortunes. 'Young people were not alive when the last mine closed in Sunderland in 1990, but they use it as a reason to hate the Tories. Whereas people who were alive at the time have possibly moved on a bit, they can see the sense in letting it go. They're not blaming people who were not responsible for it at the time. Once Thatcher and Major had gone, you're blaming people who had nothing to do with it.' Oliver noted that in Jarrow, on the banks of the River Tyne, Labour continued to use the Jarrow March in their election campaigns. 'It's approximately a hundred years after it happened! For some people it will rouse up passions and feed the anti-Tory vote, but I think a lot of people are saying, "It's too long ago".'

The Tories' biggest challenge, however, is combating the structural changes. Skills and education are by far the most important public-policy challenge for the government. A better life in every red wall seat is about a more resilient local economy. I was surprised in every place I visited at how well they have recovered from deindustrialization (once you look beyond the decaying buildings), and the new, more diverse economic bases that have emerged. The collapse of the red wall has demonstrated the long-tail effects of Thatcherism. The decline of Britain's unproductive heavy industries created years of economic problems, yet it also laid the foundations for the rebirth happening today. Until Labour appreciates how much these places have changed, it will not make inroads.

Labour's long-standing Hampstead-to-Humberside alliance has been destroyed by Brexit and it cannot be rebuilt on the old foundations. Neil Kinnock's narrative of security is the strongest I've heard, and may be able to bridge that gap once again. Keir Starmer has made a solid start to regaining the trust of these voters, but he still has far to go. Labour is further away from power than it has been at almost any time in its existence. Barring an economic, political or constitutional upheaval, the default assumption has to be that the next election will be an uphill battle for the party. The Labour Party could gain one hundred seats at the ballot box in 2024 and still not have enough MPs to form a majority.

For the Conservatives, holding onto the red wall has been complicated by the pandemic. Lost time and money has meant their ambitions for the levelling-up agenda have been curtailed. At the time of writing, the phrase continues to baffle people in government and it is surprising that not a single minister or Whitehall department has been devoted to the most crucial factor in the government's hopes for re-election. In the 2021 Queen's Speech, Johnson set out some of the policy areas that will define what the agenda should look like – house building and adult education to name two – but how much he can achieve before returning to the polls is doubtful. Instead, he is likely to be inspired by the message of Tees Valley mayor Ben Houchen: 'a record of delivery, a promise of more'. If the prime minister can tour the country and point to physical, tangible improvements in people's lives by the next election, voters may feel rewarded.

Johnson should not underestimate the scale of the challenge. Cracking the nut of productivity has vexed British politicians for generations. Although it rose consistently after the war, the long tail of poor productivity is not quick to fix and there is no guarantee of success. The UK's economy is imbalanced; as Johnson argued in Hartlepool, it is in the interests of the whole country to tackle that. Many of the most immediate fixes are small policy tweaks – better training for small businesses in using accountancy software, for example – that will take time to have an impact. The construction of new further education colleges and the adjustment of the national curriculum to give equal balance to technical education will again take some years. The best that the Tories can hope for is to put these ideas in motion, acknowledging their completion may not be seen until the election after next, which would be 2029 at the latest – almost twenty years since the party returned to power.

And finally, there is character and charisma. Whether you like him or not, Boris Johnson is the most effective campaigner of his generation – and arguably beyond that. He has never lost a major election: the London mayoralty in 2008 and 2012, the 2016 EU referendum and the 2019 general election. He wears his ideology lightly, but as John Gray argued, his instincts have landed him in what is the new centre ground of British politics. By taking the Tory Party leftwards on economic issues and remaining centre-right on social and cultural ones, he has found a formula that can span most of England. In this respect, he is the real heir to Tony Blair. It is forgotten how media-savvy and combative the latter could be in his prime – Noel Gallagher visiting Downing Street, front pages of the *Sun* bashing Brussels, his tough stance on migration. Johnson is more Eurosceptic than Blair, but on domestic policy, his agenda is essentially an updated version of New Labour's.

Barring a catastrophe, he is the favourite to win again in the next election. He is often described as a 'formidable campaigner', but that does not tell the whole story. Johnson is an international celebrity, who could walk down the streets of most capital cities and be recognized. Keir Starmer cannot match that, nor any of the other figures prominent in the Labour Party today. Only Tony Blair from its recent history comes close. Johnson has been in the public spotlight for two decades, his strengths and flaws are well known to the country. If Labour wishes to beat him, they will need to find a fresh emotional message that can counter the long-held feelings many have about Johnson.

Across the spectrum of those I have interviewed, there is a clear consensus about what needs to be done for the people of the red wall. The majority of interviewees have highlighted that the issues are primarily economic, not cultural. While identity will continue to provide headaches for Labour – and the Tories will no doubt continue to push them now and during the next election campaign – the Tories will have to counter issues created by their economic agenda of the last decade. The structural, economic and societal changes have made these parts of England more Conservative, but there is no doubt that reform is needed, hence Boris Johnson's levelling-up agenda. Johnson has made a clear break on the orthodoxy of the austerity years; the gap between Labour's 2017 manifesto and the Tories' agenda in government is surprisingly small.

Johnson's leftward nudge on spending and the role of the state leaves little room for Labour to define an alternative, except by veering further into radicalism. The decades of underinvestment on infrastructure needs to be righted – especially on local bus and rail services. The nostalgic pull of reversing the Beeching Cuts to the railways warms the cockles of the heart of older voters, recalling their childhood memories of steam trains. But better connectivity from towns and cities, and between cities, is critical for tackling the productivity gap.

It will cause headaches in the south of England where land is tighter and nimbyism is more potent, but an aggressive house-building programme is also important for providing the red wall with better housing stock to encourage aspiring families to move there. The liberalization of planning laws will also help to get rid of the old derelict warehouses, but there is an absence of strong economic visions on a local level. Central government cannot decide what each town should look like.

On skills, there is full agreement about more emphasis on non-university education and the plans set out in the 2021 Queen's Speech go some way to achieving that if the promise is fulfilled. Other towns should follow the example of Burnley College: a strong further education college that works with central government, the county council and local employers to ensure it is training up the right people with the right skills. With a relentless focus on the benefits of further education, the snobbish attitude to technical advice will begin to wane.

The towns I have visited suffered from a poor physical environment in places, and allocating small pots of money to improve the feel of these places will help. Rachel Wolf, who wrote the 2019 Tory manifesto, will be delighted to see more hanging baskets in the coming years. Local councils and their leadership, however, need to be more empowered to craft individual visions of what these places look like. The shells of some town centres can be filled with independent retailers and boutique shops; others will be wholly leisure-focused with pubs and restaurants dominating. But, again, the key is localism: the future of Grimsby will be nothing like Middleton, and Whitehall should not define it.

For me, the success of levelling up cannot be purely measured in metrics, but in a palpable sense that life is getting better. For an eleven-year-old child, growing up in a northern town who started secondary school in 2019, their life chances should be better when they leave seven years later. His town should have better further education opportunities, a stronger local economy, new businesses opening, better connections to neighbouring settlements as well as cities. He should not feel disconnected from the national debate or disenfranchised by Britain's institutions. Crucially, it should be recognized that parts of the south of England are as poor as the most deprived in the north. This continued divide in how we think about the country is unhelpful. There is also not enough political leadership and grip on the machinery of government to achieve this currently. Levelling up poses as big a challenge, if not greater, to the British state as Brexit, which had a cabinet minister, a series of junior ministers and hundreds of civil servants to deliver it. Yet there is not a single member of the government specifically responsible for it. If Johnson is serious about this agenda, he should designate a 'Secretary of State for Levelling Up' who sits across the Cabinet Office, the Treasury and the Ministry of Housing, Communities and Local Government. Taking inspiration from civil service delivery expert, Sir Michael Barber, that minister should start every day with an overview of the key metrics for delivering on the agenda, the status of all the major and minor infrastructure projects and assess which is on track and those that are behind. This minister needs the full backing of the prime minister's office and the authority to intervene in other government departments. Without a ruthless focus on delivery, the project will drift into the ether of Whitehall and risks becoming another failed political slogan.

Above all, what the red wall needs is empowerment. The votes of 2016, 2017 and 2019 were a cry to be listened to. Our national spending and policy decisions will always be taken in Whitehall, but devolution is going to be critical to rebuilding England after the pandemic into a better society. As well as pumping more money into local government, there needs to be more power to accountable figures. Bluntly, there needs to be more directly elected mayors, with more powers and more authority to shape their communities. They also need more resources and improved capacity to fulfill their roles.

Whether it is Andy Burnham, Andy Street, Ben Houchen or Tracy Brabin, some of the most impressive politicians in the UK today are not found in Westminster for good reason. They recognize that real power lies in being able to wield the most direct influence on people's lives. The model should be replicated elsewhere, even if it causes central government some uncomfortable moments when the political priorities do not match. This is something voters can decide on at the ballot box.

Mayors can also solve the English question. The rise in the angry English identity that Nigel Farage highlighted came in part due to the rise in Scottish and Welsh nationalism, reinforced by the devolved parliaments. David Cameron's half considered English Votes for English Laws (EVEL) programme has little connection to voters. Something far more radical is required.

The House of Lords needs to be scrapped. I adore an archaic institution as much as anyone, but it is living on borrowed time and is a symbol of all that voters dislike about Westminster. The only reason it has not been dramatically reformed so far is that no politician is willing to squander the political capital to do so. Tony Blair's efforts to rid the upper chamber of hereditary peers in the late 1990s ended in a half-finished job.

My solution would be to form a new chamber, still with the intent of revising legislation instead of creating it, with say two hundred members. Half of this new body would be made of legislative experts, serving up to two five-year terms and therefore avoiding the 'job for life' accusations peers currently face. They would be appointed by an independent panel with a fair mix of party representation, backgrounds, locations, gender, ethnicity. This component would ensure that the second house still fulfils its main objective of making better legislation.

The other half would be formed of the directly elected mayors and representatives from the devolved parliaments. The fracturing ties of the United Kingdom and the British identity, since the 2016 referendum, mean that something urgently needs to be done to better integrate the parliaments of Scotland, Wales and Northern Ireland into the national debate while also giving due balance to England. The pandemic has proved that virtual representation is possible, so these members would not be required to spend their lives on trains and planes to be part of the Westminster debate.

Reforming the House of Lords is one of the most complex constitutional questions facing the UK over the next decade – one that I believe Boris Johnson intends to grapple with. A whole book could be dedicated to the intricacies of what and how it would work. But a clear signal is needed to Britons who feel disconnected from the political process. A new architecture has already emerged through devolution and this should be seized on.

But whether the red wall stays blue or begins to revert back to its original form, what I have found most uplifting about these years in British politics is the focus on places that were politically forgotten. Economically, Labour did aid its traditional seats while in power, but politically they were taken for granted. They may have been 'our people', but the New Labour project was focused on the marginal seats it had to win to stay in office. The 2016 referendum brought these corners of England to the fore of political debate, which I have found a fulfilling and much-needed phenomenon. The distrust many former Labour voters have towards the party is deep, but there is also a brittleness of new Conservative support. They may like Johnson now, but they still do not wholly trust him. The pressure to deliver for these people is huge, and one of the greatest challenges Johnson faces is to prove that levelling up is more than a slogan. Voters will be unforgiving if he fails. From Blyth to Burnley, these places feel less abandoned than at any time in recent political history. They are the new battlegrounds. Whether the Conservatives remain in power, or Labour takes over soon, the political incentive to win the voters of these places means that the 2020s will be the decade when my personal heartlands will begin to feel less broken.

Epilogue –
Esher and Walton

Claygate is not the red wall. The Surrey town is as far from the pro-Brexit band of first-time Conservative constituencies further north as is possible. The Esher and Walton constituency, where it lies, has backed the Tories throughout its history. A majority within the seat voted Remain. It is wealthy, with excellent employment options and housing, as well as superb road and rail links. In short, it is the inverse of the red wall. Hence why I visited: to explore one of the Tories' happier heartlands, and whether they can still win here, while also in Labour's more broken ones.

The Parade and Albany cafe, on Claygate's smart run of shops, was packed with mothers mulling over their life woes. School fees, the average speed limit on the M4 motorway, the predilections of their husbands – the middle-class chatter was apt for these well-heeled surroundings. At one of the scrubbed wooden tables, Monica Harding waited patiently as I weaved through West London's terrible congestion in the red Mini. The fifty-year-old mother of four slotted into the Thursday morning scene, with neat hair, professional work attire and an enthusiastic demeanour. Over a pair of coffees, Harding took me into her latter-day political odyssey, beginning when she joined the pro-EU Liberal Democrats in the 2016 referendum after feeling 'fed up' with the state of politics.

Harding and I chatted during the disconcerting times of March

2022. The war in Ukraine dominated all of the news; hours were squandered on doom-scrolling the conflict playing out in real time on social media. The war exacerbated the so-called 'cost of living crisis' at home. Inflation and interest rates were rising; the cost of food, energy, petrol and bills spiralling. March also marked one year since the conclusion of my red wall road trip around England's north and Midlands.

Boris Johnson was still prime minister, albeit significantly less popular than in spring 2021. The blistering 'Partygate' scandal involving a series of illicit gatherings in Downing Street that broke coronavirus restrictions nearly led to his defenestration as Conservative Party leader. The war in Ukraine, however, handed the prime minister a domestic reprieve, although his survival until the next election in 2024 appeared uncertain. Fears were especially rife among senior Tories that he could lose the next time the nation went to the polls – not only due to much of the red wall flipping back to Labour, but also the potential loss of a 'blue wall' of traditional Conservative heartlands. Places like Esher and Walton.

Harding moved to the constituency fifteen years ago, when house prices in this suburban corner of the Home Counties were more manageable than London's. Similarly to many of the professional classes who dominate this patch, Harding was politically attuned but had little desire to enter the arena – until the Brexit referendum. Whereas the first-time Tory voters in the north were drawn to Johnson for his advocacy of leaving the bloc, she was repelled. Locally, she was disgruntled at the disconnect between the pro-Leave stance of Dominic Raab, Esher and Walton's Tory MP since 2010, and the 58 per cent of the seat that voted Remain, ten points above the national average. She termed her rival 'one of the bogeymen of Brexit', adding: 'People here were pretty appalled that they weren't being listened to.'[1]

Her relationship with the local Lib Dems led to her being selected as their parliamentary candidate in her home seat. The traditional third party of British politics trailed here in third place behind Labour in the previous two elections, where Raab returned mighty majorities: 28,616 in 2015 (63 per cent of the vote) and 23,298 in 2017.[2] What appeared an initially thankless electoral task turned out to be an extraordinary opportunity. Harding almost ended Raab's political career, shrinking his majority to a mere 2,743 votes. She was aided by the fifteen-point collapse in Labour's vote, which resulted in the party losing its deposit. Yet it was the rapid bounce in the Lib Dem fortunes, in a seat that was always true blue, that troubled Tory high command.

Recalling the 2019 campaign, Harding said she was entirely focused on her opponent. 'It was less about being Lib Dems and more the anti-Raab thing.' She benefited from the endorsement of Ian Taylor, Raab's Tory predecessor in the seat for twenty-three years and an ardent pro-European.[3] However, limited resources and the slow realization that the seat could be winnable resulted in voters sticking with the incumbent when the postal votes landed. 'We met lots of people on the doorstep who said, "If only I had known earlier I would have switched the other way." There was a period when we were getting a lot of press attention' – including from this reporter who visited the seat for a *Financial Times* column – 'I thought we had a real chance of winning. And he was certainly scared [of us].'[4]

She put the Lib Dem failure to win Esher and Walton down to a deep fear of one person: the then Labour leader Jeremy Corbyn. 'One lady had a Lib Dem sign stapled in her garden and we asked her, "Have you voted yet?", and she burst into tears. She said, "I couldn't do it because of Corbyn."' When the campaign entered its final days, the Tories found an attack line to dampen the Lib Dems' momentum and tip them over the edge. 'It was all "vote for Monica, you'll get Corbyn in". It had cut through and people were really worried.'

Come the next election, Esher and Walton's voters are set to face the less fearful prospect of Sir Keir Starmer as their alternative prime minister: a fifty-nine-year-old, successful, if dry, lawyer who reflects the look and feel of its residents (he grew up in the town of Oxted, just over twenty miles away and reached via the M25 from Claygate). Labour's desultory standing in the Home Counties means it has little chance of making gains – Harding mooted that voters find Labour 'scary' – but her campaigning in local elections suggested that Starmer 'takes away the Corbyn factor'.

Raising her family in Thames Ditton, a village on the London-facing east side of the constituency and once home to the Milk Marketing Board, Harding has seen two demographic shifts that have softened the natural Conservative vote. 'House prices are too high. I came here when my kids were small and we could just about afford to live here. Prices are now so high that the thirty-year-olds have stopped coming.' If that traditional life journey of urban metropolitan liberals morphing into comfortable middle-income suburban conservatives has indeed dried up, the natural Tory vote will do the same.

The second change is in public services, which Harding called 'just dreadful', especially following the coronavirus pandemic. Her experience is that GP appointments cannot be sought, crime is rising – '85 per cent of burglaries in Surrey are unresolved' – and the community fabric is being stretched. Claygate town centre oozes prosperity, with not a single empty shop, yet Harding senses voters are not happy. 'You've got a constituency, which is the biggest single contributor to the exchequer in the country, where people can't get appointments and don't have policemen on the beat.' And, ominously for Johnson, she noted that all the talk of the prime minister's flagship 'levelling up' agenda to tackle regional inequality was not well received on the door step; voters see it as a zero sum game.

Our coffee chat was peppered with her brusque anger about Brexit and how it has shifted the window of discourse. She was incensed at Johnson's decision to cut overseas aid. For a corner of England full of professionals, she stated curtly that 'managerial competence is really important', something that few punters would dispute Johnson has struggled with. Her target voters have mixed views on how he has handled the pandemic. 'Amongst those people that we wished had voted for us and would have got us over the line, he [Johnson] wasn't liked, though during the pandemic there was a sympathetic "he's doing as best he can".' Events have changed that perception, including the UK's botched withdrawal of troops from Afghanistan, of which Raab as foreign secretary was at the forefront; plus Partygate. As she put it, 'this kind of steady drip of sleaze and corruption'.

Harding is standing again for Esher and Walton at the next general election. Without Corbyn and Brexit, does she still have a chance at taking the seat on a second run? Raab has certainly woken up to her threat, hiring extra staff and raising his local profile. But she, in turn, is hopeful that the seat's symbolism will motivate activists. 'Everybody wants a scalp,' she smiled widely. 'Our work will be around telling voters that you're free to change the direction of the UK and that change starts here.' Her message will be one of 'your local mother who is not particularly ambitious about politics but sees it going in the wrong direction, versus a super ambitious sitting MP who's not that interested in the constituency, plus is propping up Boris Johnson'.

With the coffees drained and the morning gaggle of mums being replaced with older patrons seeking chunky lunchtime sandwiches, she leaned in to ruefully sum up why Esher and

Walton matters for the politics of the next election: 'that kind of unholy coalition that you had in 2019 – between the red wall conservatives and that one nation conservative – is coming unstuck here.'

That dichotomy makes Esher and Walton politically significant for the first time. The constituency lies along the Thames Valley, between the western fringes of London and the rolling hills of Surrey. It is a land of Aston Martins, mock Tudor mansions and mellow riverside pubs. Londoners who want more space escape here. It is commuter land: the seat has nine train stations, most of them less than a forty-five-minute journey from the capital. There is palpable prosperity: Weybridge, in the next constituency along, is where John Lennon and Ringo Starr decamped to escape their vast fame and fortune. Elton John still resides nearby.

It is not an especially coherent constituency. After circling round the key settlements in my car, it can be summarized in two parts. The towns of Claygate, Molesey and Thames Ditton are occupied by those who came from London for spacious houses and well-rated schools. Those I met here mostly maintain the sensibilities of the capital; their typical worldview is liberal but fiscally conservative. Out to the west of Esher and Walton, however, Cobham has an older, less metropolitan demographic. Its high street is larger than the parades closer to London. Esher itself is dominated by Sandown Park racecourse and the type of mansions that are popular with footballers.

Ian Taylor, its MP from 1987 to 2010, believed that the flow of Londoners had risen gradually, which in turn changed the community spirit. 'It became much more segregated, but harmonious in a way.' Some major employers like Procter & Gamble mean that not everyone here is reliant on London for work.

Much of the area is protected by the Metropolitan Green Belt, to curb the urban sprawl of the capital. Driving through some of the more rural villages, the prosperity is palpable. Waitrose is the dominant supermarket chain. Jaguars seemingly sit in the driveways of every detached house. Almost three-quarters of the constituency is designed as the ABC1 socioeconomic group, compared to 55 per cent across the country. The average house price is £790,786, nearly triple the national average.[5] The *Financial Times* reported in 2015 that, thanks to the many footballers who lived in Esher and Walton, it topped the national average earnings for the country.[6] It was almost a different country to many of the northern towns that I visited on my road trip around the red wall.

Were it not for Monica Harding's near miss at winning the seat, Esher and Walton would be a typical Tory shire safe seat of little interest. Taylor's majority dipped to 7,727 in the 2005 election, with the Lib Dems riding high on their opposition to the Iraq War.[7] Yet even in the 1997 Labour landslide, he returned a healthy 14,528 majority.[8] Throughout my travels across the red wall, one question dominated: was the last election a blip? I concluded the fall of the red wall and the size of Johnson's majority was primarily due to Brexit and Jeremy Corbyn, but the decline in Labour's standing was decades in the making. The question was the same here: was the Lib Dem surge a one-off? Or the fall of a new blue wall of old Tory heartlands?

Since the morning after the 2019 election, Johnson and his party have been dogged not only by the question of whether he can hold onto the red wall, but whether the natural shift towards the north and pro-Brexit voters would have consequences else-where. In short, can their 2019 voting coalition hold across England? Can they continue to win in both Guildford and Grimsby? Does the post-Brexit political realignment mean

Johnson and his successors will be forced to choose one or another?

The term 'blue wall' surfaced when newly elected Tory MPs used it to describe the seats they seized in 2019 (it failed to catch on). But after two striking by-election wins by the Liberal Democrats in 2021, it became a byword for places that felt out of sync with the post-Brexit direction of the Conservatives. As Johnson shifted the party's policies and attitudes to target their new electorate in the north and Midlands, it is understandable that their own blue heartlands may feel slighted. While Westminster might have had enough of 'walls' to describe seats – one Tory strategist bemoaned the first edition of *Broken Heartlands* as 'they're all just seats, labels aren't helpful' – there is a debate about whether there is a blue one.

The first thesis on the blue wall was set out by Steve Akehurst, a campaigns strategist who has worked a lot on housing and climate policy.[9] He defined a bucket of forty-odd Conservative-held seats that could be at risk at the next election with a mix of Labour and Liberal Democrat challengers. His core criteria for the seats were:

- *Held by the Conservatives since at least 2010 (although in many cases long before).*
- *Where Labour or the Lib Dems have overperformed their national swing versus the Conservatives in both 2017 and 2019.*
- *Where, as a result, the Conservative majority now stands at under 10,000 votes – such that either Labour or the Lib Dems, or both, are within striking distance.*

Akehurst's definition captured some of the Tory Party's most prominent seats, including former leader Sir Iain Duncan Smith's constituency Chingford and Woodford Green, and Johnson himself in Uxbridge and South Ruislip. There is one final criteria that I would add that defines such areas: a significant Remain vote, say above 50 per cent. On these metrics it appears to be the simple opposite of the red wall.

Akehurst and I debated his thesis over beers in Westminster during one of my return trips from Esher and Walton. The concept originated from his childhood home of Hove, on the south coast, and how he saw the area evolve. 'It was once a fairly solid Tory seat, then it became a swing seat, and out of nowhere, it became pretty rock-solidly Labour. That is to do with the realignment in British politics but also lots of interesting things to do with the housing market.' He cited the rise in private renting among 'nice young couples under forty, graduates who are settling down but not massively well-off', as those floating away from the Tories.

We agreed such voters and seats hold clear policy differences with red wall voters: climate change, foreign policy and taxation are all potent issues, as well as the difference on Brexit. Many of the seats he identified as blue wall were Labour-facing but, with Esher and Walton in mind, I was chiefly interested in those where the Liberal Democrats are the challengers. This spoke to why the blue wall concept was not as convincing as the red wall: the crucial thing was the contiguous nature of those northern seats and their similar economic and social profiles. Winning one means a good chance of winning them all.

Yet something was changing. In 2021, the Lib Dems showed signs of being able to knock down some of this wall. The Chesham and Amersham by-election, held on 17 June, should have been an easy win for the Tories. Represented for many years by the popular MP Cheryl Gillan, the party's strategists had few qualms about holding it – despite the 55 per cent of its voters who backed remaining in the EU – and instead poured resources into the Batley and Spen race in West Yorkshire, which they failed to take.[10] On polling day the Lib Dem candidate pulled off a shock. With a 25 per cent swing, the party won the seat for the first time.[11] Sir John Curtice, the polling supremo, put the loss to local unease about planning reform combined with the Johnson government's focus on the 'levelling up' agenda to address regional inequality.[12] Both policies were direct results of the red wall focus.

The second shock came in December, when the Liberal Democrats took the seat of North Shropshire for the first time with a 34 per cent swing away from the Tories.[13] The party was particularly to blame in this instance: the by-election was prompted by the resignation of disgraced ex-minister Owen Paterson, who was found guilty of breaching parliamentary rules on lobbying. A botched ruse to reform the standards system to let Paterson off the hook backfired and he was forced out of public life. In a very tried and tested manner for the Lib Dems, they ran on a successful anti-establishment, anti-politics platform.

Privately, the Liberal Democrats are hopeful of a seat total in 2024 beginning with a 2, a significant rise from their current tally of thirteen.[14] The party believes that the national focus on the fight for the red wall will help them. 'One reason for Lib Dem optimism is that the general election for both Labour and the Tories is fought elsewhere – not only geographically, but by appealing to the least liberal aspects of their voting coalitions.' The official noted that whether it is on immigration, civil liberties or Europe, the Lib Dems feel there is a significant intellectual vacuum to be filled.

Those two blue wall by-elections are a bad sign for the Tories, but by-election wins rarely translate into similar gains at the next general. It may be all Panglossian campaigning talk from the Lib Dems, but the structural questions posed by Steve

Akehurst deserve further scrutiny. Not least as every commentator in 2024 will be talking about a blue wall with little concept of what it means. It was therefore back to the car and a drive to Esher, the heart of the seat, to see if the incumbent Tory MP had a plan.

Hummings on Esher High Street styled itself as a cafe by day, bar by night. Dominic Raab warmly greeted its proprietor, Ramon Mullan, who moonlights running the town's chamber of commerce. He informed his pal, the deputy prime minister and justice secretary, that the glitzy cafe-bar had recovered its weekend and evening trade from the pandemic, 'but the daytimes are proving difficult'. He continued: 'We need to get people in who are still buying Tesco meal deals for their lunch.' The pandemic was difficult for Hummings, Mullan told me, but his business had mostly recovered – much in part thanks to the economic support from the government.

Raab and I settled into a window seat overlooking a rainy bus stop, after he had spent the morning on constituency work followed by a trip to the swimming baths. Raab has a stern public persona in Westminster, yet I have always found him engaging one to one. That day in typical Tory casual wear – blue shirt, blazer and chinos – we discussed Esher and Walton. 'In lots of small ways, this is a crossroad seat between London and the shires,' he said. 'For some people here in Esher, people lay their head on the pillow but really consider themselves Londoners.'

During his twelve years as its MP, he has witnessed the continued 'shift of middle classes out of London', not a trend he thought was especially new. Over that period, the average age of the seat's occupants has increased from forty-one to forty-three. Raab described the demographic as 'very well-educated middle class; a well-to-do, well-heeled constituency' that is full of informed voters who engage with the news. 'That gives you a great opportunity to have genuine conversations on the doorstep.'

Raab has lived here since he was first selected to fight Esher and Walton before the 2010 election – 'even when I was foreign secretary, I didn't move out', he noted. He disagreed with Ian Taylor about the decline of community spirit, pointing to life during the pandemic. 'You've got many small towns and villages here. The community spirit is very strong and we definitely saw that during lockdown. I remember through the pandemic mass volunteering. I would go out volunteering with a local food bank. There were also other charitable groups that delivered furniture to the homeless.'

When Raab first entered Parliament, the tenor of Tory politics chimed well with his seat. The huge majorities he returned in 2015 and 2017 spoke to what he called the 'small liberal conservative values' that define the seat. Voters are not tribal, in the way Labour's supporters were in the red wall, he thought, but they are transactional. 'Above all it's quite consumerist, in the sense that my constituents ask, "What is a party going to do for me?"' He admitted there are 'a whole load of other micro trends' that have impacted the Tory vote, with one in particular. 'Brexit has obviously shaken things up a little bit but I don't get it raised a lot with me now' (contradicting what Harding suggested). Raab did not play a prominent role in the 2016 referendum but argued that his 'outward focus' for the UK was going down well, even with those who backed Remain. 'The one thing we've demonstrated in the last two years is whatever else people might feel about Brexit, if you look at Ukraine, we're leading the way. We lead the way in the BNOs visas [British National Overseas] in Hong Kong.' The government's approach to small boats and its initially stingy approach to Ukrainian refugees might suggest otherwise.

His loss of 21,000 votes was down to 'a whole range of things' in Raab's view, such as a chance to exercise a protest vote.[15] Brexit was a 'one-off lightning strike' issue that defined the election in his patch and he was eager to suggest voters have moved on. With the referendum fading into history, Raab hoped the next election would be 'more business as usual' for his party. 'This is a seat where the Conservative message on the economy is about encouraging entrepreneurs like Ramon here,' he gestured at the proprietor, back behind the counter with his large dog.

Since his 2019 near miss, the pandemic has demonstrated the awesome power of the state. Esher and Walton received £49 million in grants, 21,000 people used the furlough scheme and £220 million was dispersed in bounce-back loans. Raab said this 'huge agility' in how the government operated has gone down well, despite the contradictions between the rhetoric on cutting taxes, while raising the overall burden to its highest in six decades. 'There is a very strong sense in this constituency that for all the Thatcherite credentials, the government was also there when they needed it.' He echoed a line of Johnson's that voters can expect to hear over and over in the next election: the government 'made the calls of the pandemic right'. Every specific decision may not be defensible, such as the delay going into the first lockdown, but the broader narrative on vaccines and easing measures may be.

The general election of 2024, however, is unlikely to be fought on Covid. Raab outlined a typical Conservative message similar to 2015: the economy and jobs, with a dash of environmentalism thrown in. 'What we're doing on net zero, what we've done on COP26, as well as being the only party consistently standing up for the green belt, puts us in the driving seat. Of course, the cost of living is going to be a big challenge, but fundamentally, we've got a positive offer.' He is hopeful that his track record, including several new secondary schools, will find favour. 'Whether it's cost of living, crime – which is increasingly going up people's list of concerns – the Conservatives are the ones with a really clear, intelligent, positive message.' Yet the widespread scepticism to chancellor Rishi Sunak's efforts to deal with rising inflation suggests Raab's upbeat attitude has yet to be matched with policy substance.

But what about Boris Johnson personally, whom the Lib Dems plan to put front and centre of their blue wall campaign? 'I don't think voters will be theological about this,' he said carefully. 'They will want a thriving economy, they'll definitely want to see that we're keeping their taxes down, but they'll also want decent schools for their kids . . . the message on the green belt is also critically important.' Raab claimed that if his voters can move beyond 'the superficial caricature' of the prime minister, he will have a strong resonance. 'The prime minister's values are perfectly well placed for a seat like his because he's socially liberal. He's strong on human rights. We introduced the Magnitsky sanctions [on human rights abusers]. He has led on the issue of net zero; that's very important around here.' He failed to note that Johnson's focus on so-called 'culture war' debates may find less favour.

Raab was fairly dismissive about the appeal of Sir Keir Starmer in Esher and Walton. 'To the extent that he's resonated at all, he is in the same economic place as Gordon Brown. He's to the left of Tony Blair but he's very careful, in the lawyerly-like way, in avoiding articulating what he's going to stand for.' To dampen Labour's appeal here, however small it may be, he pointed back to the 2015 election when his party 'flushed out' Labour's economic policies, which he characterized as 'you're going to get taxed to the hilt; you get taxed on your income, you get taxed on your property'.

Throughout our conversation, Raab did not hold back his contempt for the Liberal Democrats, arguing several times they have a poor record on delivery since they went into coalition to run Elmbridge Council, which encompasses his seat. He dismissed their appeal as nothing more than a 'negative protest vote', suggesting 'they make a lot of promises and they criticize a lot. If they offer Keir Starmer, then you are back to 2015.'

On economics, Raab stated the Tories were 'the party of low taxes', and he hoped this would come to fruition by the next polling day (a 1p cut in income tax has been pencilled in for April 2024). 'I'm sure that by the time we get to the next election, we will have made the difficult decisions and be able to demonstrate that.' With the significant rise in national insurance due to be introduced in April 2022, Raab felt Esher and Walton would welcome the fact that social care was being dealt with, despite the effective cut in people's pay packets. 'It is probably the single biggest social issue here because of the high property prices and the ageing population. We have now gripped that issue and we're the first government in a generation to talk seriously about this.'

With constituency events pressing, Raab wrapped up our conversation with some optimism. 'We've got to spend two years delivering and demonstrating that and if we do and we get our vote out, I'm confident we will win.' Raab reiterated his framing of the race: 'Do you want to vote for a party polling on 10 per cent to get a Brownite prime minister?' The right moment, therefore, to hop back in the Mini to leave Esher and Walton behind for the arduous drive into Westminster to find out whether there is more to the Lib Dems than Raab's downbeat imagery of negative campaigners.

Sir Ed Davey is well positioned to cause the Tories pain in their blue heartlands. Representing the South London constituency of Kingston and Surbiton since 1997, he has an innate feel for the very voters he must win over. He became party leader after his predecessor embarrassingly lost her seat in the 2019 election, when their strongly Remain message failed to find an electorate. Davey was part of the 2010–2015 coalition government with the Tories, serving as Climate Change Secretary for the final three years of the brief blue–yellow bromance. After the coalition fell apart, the party went through every variety of leader: chirpy Tim Farron, staid Sir Vince Cable and pugnacious Jo Swinson. There is little to say about Davey's persona: he is professional and serious. He is never going to excite voters, but if my travels in Esher and Walton are anything to go by, that may not be what they want.

Perched in his parliamentary office overlooking Big Ben, Davey miraculously found a bright side to the last election where the Lib Dems returned eleven MPs, down one on their previous result. 'The evidence from the 2019 general election was that we came from third to second in a lot of places,' he said, with at least something to build on. 'More importantly, in the run-up to the local elections of May 2019 I talked about the blue wall then. We had a really good night in places like Oxfordshire, Cambridgeshire, Hertfordshire and Surrey – those sorts of places where we hadn't done that brilliantly for some time.' All of the areas he is hopeful for gains in 2024.

Both of the Lib Dems' 2021 by-election victories under the blue wall umbrella happened under Davey's leadership. In Chesham and Amersham, he cited a demographic change that is reflected in his Kingston constituency and Esher and Walton that has benefited the party. 'You could really feel that it was a different demography from twenty years before . . . it's young families, so education is much more important.' He also noted the rise in diversity in these suburban seats, noting the Korean, Sri Lankan and Tamil communities in Kingston.

Among the Tories' core voters Davey cited 'two quite big' shifts that are hurting the party. First is the apathy of the professional classes who have solidly voted Conservative since the 1970s. They hold centre-right economic values on business and the economy, but also a more liberal mindset. 'For some reason, we've never managed to persuade that we're the right party for them. We haven't changed our values; we've always been pro-market, pro-economy, pro-small business, pro-free enterprise. There's a clue in our name, liberal, and I do think people have recognized that.'

Davey naturally cited the economic impact of Brexit, but he generally felt the Tories' lack of interest in enterprise would harm them. 'They haven't really shown they're listening to businesses, professionals or farmers – that's what we saw in North Shropshire. These voters feel taken for granted, that the Tories don't care about us.' He reeled off a host of examples: the focus on levelling up, Brexit (again), Johnson's infamous 'fuck business' remark, the Partygate scandal. 'These people feel really embarrassed about Johnson. Johnson absolutely is a negative.'

The 2019 election was still sore for Davey. It led to him taking the party leadership, but his predecessor lost her seat. It saw Brexit delivered. The Lib Dems abysmally failed to capitalize on the groundswell in some parts of the country for a second referendum. He echoed the sentiment of Monica Harding that Jeremy Corbyn was the cause. 'Last time, we had so many people who were desperate to vote Lib Dem. They were Remain who hated Johnson. They liked what we were saying, mostly, but they could not get over Corbyn.'

Yet Davey is hopeful that, as well as the presence of Starmer as an alternative prime minister, the backdrop is 'much tougher' for the Conservatives. 'Forget the Corbyn issue; Brexit has happened, Covid has happened. I mean if you listen to Johnson, the economy is all fantastic. But interest rates are going up, inflation is going to continue to rise, taxes will continue to rise. The economy is in a pretty disastrous place in terms of core voters.' In the respect of voters' perception, he thinks Johnson is the mirror image of Corbyn: populist but increasingly unpopular.

Much of the Liberal Democrats' success in Esher and Walton was due to their pro-Remain stance. But according to the pollster YouGov, there is little appetite to re-join the bloc (even if a small majority suggest they would vote to stay in the EU if the referendum was held now).[16] Nor is the party planning to fight the next election on a manifesto of going back in. In typical verbose Lib Dem style, the party was producing a policy paper on how to take UK–EU relations forward. Davey had travelled widely across the Continent to figure out where the party should land. 'What we're hearing people saying is "we want you to fix the problems of the Brexit deal".' It does not excite in the same way as the primary colours pitch of re-joining the bloc, but instead triangulates around the centre ground. The party's eventual strategy will be focused on a move away from what he described as 'megaphone diplomacy' and deeper collaboration with EU partners:

'People want a period where we build back those relations and so do the Europeans. They do not want to hear we're on our way back into the EU. They're not ready for it; they are bruised, they're pretty fed up and they think it's not credible. I want us to be in an area of credibility to show it will work. The question is dealing with the costs of Brexit, the bad Brexit deal. Our policy paper is quite chunky because it sets out all the problems and the practical ways you can deal with them. But you can't help reading evidence and not say it's going to take a little while.'

Davey and Starmer have acquired the sobriquet of 'the two knights', a reference not only to their knighthoods but also their ideological symmetry. As well as being of a similar age and disposition, they are both on the centre-left and it is not hard to imagine them in the Cabinet room together. To gain a majority of one, Labour would need to gain 121 seats in 2024 – barring some kind of disaster, an impossible feat. Much of the next campaign will be dominated by talk of pacts and coalitions. Unless the Conservatives win an outright majority, or come within the margin to strike a pact with Northern Ireland's unionist parties, they will be out of office. Collaboration between Labour and the Liberal Democrats therefore appears natural, or 'Lib-Labbery' to use its nickname in Westminster.

In the duo of blue wall by-elections, the parties worked together. Labour stood candidates in Chesham and Amersham and North Shropshire, yet activists in both parties confirm that Labour held back resources. Were such an approach to be used in a general election, it has the potential to pose Johnson a real headache, albeit if voters do not think they are being played. Davey suggested such collaboration merely was down to 'the practicalities' of running a political party. 'We have limited resources and therefore have to make choices about where we put our resources. Even a big party like Labour has to make choices. The general election is 650 by-elections. You have the same calculation just writ large.'

If Lib-Labbery happens, publicly or privately, the election can be carved up simply: Labour focusing on the cities and winning back the red wall, the Liberal Democrats on the leafy suburbs. Aside from the exception of Sheffield Hallam, where the parties are head to head, and East Dunbartonshire in Scotland, where the Lib Dems hope to take on the SNP, it fits neatly. And given the scale of electoral challenge facing both sides, it would be madness for them not to try it. Davey conceded that the 'vast majority' of their target seats face the Tories as their main competition. 'We have thirteen MPs: nine of them have the Tories in second place, four of them it's the SNP. In the next thirty seats I think they all have the Tories in first place . . . you can draw your own conclusions.'

Come 2024, Davey said his party has two tactics for making blue wall gains. 'We have to squeeze the Labour vote, saying you can't win here – that's quite simple because it's true. But then you've got to switch those Tory voters, which is actually much more difficult. We've got to persuade those Tory voters that actually we share their values in many ways.' He is hopeful that many such target voters are already biased against Johnson and the Conservative Party as it currently stands. 'If that wasn't the case, it'd be far more difficult. We're building on a really strong foundation; it's much stronger than the voting figures suggest.'

And what does success for him look like? Davey will not be the next prime minister – and will not make the mistake of Jo Swinson by claiming he might be – but he has the potential to double the party's seat count. 'This isn't a prediction or target, but if you take the long view of our party, being at twenty seats would be seen as a good place.' Indeed, it would be their best showing since 2010 and Brexit. To make that happen, Davey wanted a relentless focus on Tory–Lib Dem switchers. 'What I have been doing as leader is making sure the party listens and gives a liberal response to their concerns, not tell them what we think is important.' He smiled at the prospect. 'There's a lot of short-term political trends that are all very positive for us. There is massive potential.'

At this juncture, I had hoped to speak to Labour and find out where Sir Keir Starmer's leadership see the red and blue wall battles one year on. Unfortunately the party was more hesitant to engage than during my first road trip with a newfound message discipline to ensure not too much is given away. Instead I spoke to four members of the shadow Cabinet off the record, plus a similar number of party officials, to gather a sense of the party's standing.

Off the record, these Labour figures were increasingly optimistic the party may now have a shot at winning the next election – post Partygate. Yet victory may come in many forms: Labour needs to gain 121 seats to govern with a majority of just one, meaning that some form of coalition or alliance is more likely. One senior member of the shadow Cabinet remarked, 'I feel it's more doable now than certainly when your book was first published. Back then [September 2021], I was much more pessimistic about Labour's chances.' This senior MP felt Partygate – which Labour has made much hay over – had inflicted 'serious core brand damage' on the prime minister and meant 'there's no doubt in my mind that Boris Johnson has lost the benefit of the doubt with voters'.

As Labour's standing has risen in the opinion polls, Starmer has increasingly focused on the character of the Tory leader, accusing him of 'lying through his teeth' and being a leader who has 'degraded the office of Prime Minister'. The savvier members of the shadow Cabinet realize Johnson was not elected based on his virtue – that he frequently gets into scrapes is part of his honed public image. 'No one voted Conservative thinking Boris Johnson was an angel, but he has shown a level of disrespect for the voters that will not easily be forgotten,' one said. 'There's also a degree of incompetence across the government and it provides some encouragement for a Labour revival.'

Those who are preparing Labour's next election campaign think the character of Johnson versus Starmer is 'solid ground to fight an election on'. The risk, however, is that voters view all politicians with a level of contempt, and attacks on the Tory leader fail to land – a point that Dominic Raab made when I visited him in Esher and Walton. Within the shadow Cabinet, there is an acceptance that Starmer will lead the party into the next election, despite his struggles to land blows on Johnson at prime minister's questions and his failure to define a compelling public persona.

One of the leader's allies, however, pointed to how much the party has changed since April 2020. They said Starmer's 'lack of complacency' was reassuring because he has worked ceaselessly to change the party from the Corbyn years: 'What Keir does an awful lot of is saying, "Don't look at this through rose-tinted glasses; we are not going to win the next election because of Tory failure." The polls are soft for Labour. We're drawing people across from the Conservatives, but we need more of them. Those we are drawing across could easily go back.'

There was growing confidence among Labour MPs that the Tory Party's England-wide coalition would struggle to hold without Brexit and Jeremy Corbyn. One, who represents a southern constituency, remarked that the Conservative electorate 'seems to me to be very fragile' and unusual. 'I'm not sure it's one that hangs together and there are not enough common concerns and interests across the breadth of their coalition, which will start to pull in different directions; you can see that in the parliamentary party, when I look across the House of Commons.'

Some I spoke to in the Parliamentary Labour Party were hopeful there were some blue wall seats where the party could be competitive, not purely leaving it to the Liberal Democrats. Sir Iain Duncan Smith's outer London constituency seat Chingford and Woodford Green is one of the party's core targets, given that he held on with a mere 1,262 votes in 2019. Worthing West, on the south coast, is another example where it has made gains. One party figure representing such a seat said, 'There's a suburban commuter belt around London that is increasingly filling up with Londoners fleeing the high cost of living in the city, starting families. Those people will have a natural predisposition towards us.'

Almost immediately after Starmer became leader, he began to change Labour by marginalizing Corbyn supporters and other internal left-wing opponents – with a clear eye on southern voters – as well as winning back the crucial red wall. Those who have spoken to Starmer about his strategy argued that 'wholesale change' is both necessary and possible due to the scale of their 2019 election defeat. 'It's bizarre, but one of our opportunities is that we've got a problem everywhere,' one party insider said. 'There's been an understandable focus on the red wall seats because it was such a shock. But we've also got to win back seats in Scotland, we've got to win back those seats in our traditional heartlands. We also need to win in the south. And we've got real challenges in the Midlands, real challenges in north Wales. It's everywhere.' Doing that requires Labour to ruthlessly focus on what it usually struggles with in opposition, which is the hopes and desires of middle-class England.

Throughout these furtive conversations, in corners of Westminster's Portcullis House, over lunches and through WhatsApp messages, one phrase cropped up several times that highlighted what Labour fears the most in 2024: 'long Corbyn' (a play on 'long Covid', used to describe the long-term health effects of coronavirus). Starmer may have done everything in his power to move the party on from the 2015–2020 leadership, but he served in the Corbyn shadow Cabinet and twice supported his candidacy for prime minister. The same is true for many of his allies, such as Angela Rayner, Emily Thornberry and David Lammy. He insists the party is 'under new management', but the

Tories argue it is not and will do so in increasingly vigorous terms. This is how one shadow Cabinet minister summed up their view of the party's challenge:

'The biggest challenge for us is Corbyn and Corbynism. The Ukraine crisis has shown the real contrast between Keir and Corbyn; there's no doubt where Labour stands at the moment. We are proud of our role in creating and founding NATO. We've been standing by our armed forces to support Ukraine – not just in terms of humanitarian aid, but lethal aid. The "long Corbyn" issue is real and a big problem. That's why we have to constantly remember that as much as we're trying to set out a positive vision for the future, we also need to reassure voters that we're not going to swing back to where we've been in the recent past. That's why so many of the things that Keir has been doing are really important.'

Many of Starmer's allies are pugilistic about purging memories of the Corbyn years. They are helped by the fact that the former leader is helping make the case. 'To some degree, Jeremy Corbyn and his followers have helped because a whole bunch of them have walked out and are now trying to publicly trash the Labour Party, saying, "You can't trust this, this is no longer the great left-wing socialist party of Jeremy Corbyn." The more Jeremy Corbyn and company say, "This is not the party that we led into the 2019 general election" the better. I mean, knock yourself out!'

Starmer's allies were pleased with their progress in reshaping the party. 'We've got a clear strategy and so far the signs are it's working. The first couple of years have been about trying to detoxify and decontaminate the Labour Party and to show it has changed, that we got the message from the voters at the last election.' But its policy agenda is still mostly void. Beyond pledging a windfall tax on the big energy companies to deal with the post-Ukraine cost of living crisis, its offer remained thin.

Rachel Reeves, shadow chancellor, has attempted to make much out of her analysis that Britain risks becoming a 'high-tax, low-growth economy'. But her response to the Tories' fiscal plans has sounded little more than reheated rhetoric from the Miliband years. As one senior Labour figure summed up, 'The challenge for Labour is that we can't just go into the next election saying, "We're the party that spends more." We've actually got to go into the election saying, "We're the party with a plan that will actually work." And so it's investment and reform to get results.'

Starmer's core message has been captured in three words: security, prosperity and respect. His colleagues admit they are 'not ones that voters skip into the polling stations shouting from the rooftops' and may be dropped before the election. But the leader hopes they can provide something of an underpinning. The 'security element' speaks to the need to reassure voters, which I explored during my visit to Great Grimsby. As one strategist said, 'It speaks to the part of Labour's coalition that worries about where we are literally on defence and security, but also those who seek security for their families, they have precarious incomes and want to feel settled; want to feel they are able to enjoy life comfortably without worrying.' The prosperity element is naturally the economy – not just individual wealth but the aspirational part of Labour's electorate that it often struggles with.

Respect is the most interesting. As witnessed in a series of increasingly bombastic speeches by senior Tory figures – such as party chairman Oliver Dowden – cultural issues will play a major role in the next election campaign. Be it on trans rights, statues or free speech, the Tories will use it to draw further 'long Corbyn' parallels, but also to attempt to paint the party as run by extremists. One person who has spoken to Starmer about his attitude on cultural issues said he seeks to rise above it: 'We need to avoid any temptations to get into the culture wars, which is not the same as abandoning our principles and not being a party that believes in equality and social justice; quite the opposite. It does mean approaching it with more care and sensitivity and more adeptly than the left has traditionally done.'

Above all, Labour's greatest challenge for the next election is ensuring it is engaged in a dialogue beyond its own members. One senior MP said the biggest barrier to beating the Tories will be 'whether we are willing to anchor ourselves in the concerns of voters or whether we're a party that's dominated by the Twitter conversation rather than the doorstep.' He added that 'all of us MPs should spend less time on Twitter and spend more time knocking on doors in marginal seats.'

Despite how much the party has changed, some of its most senior figures remained downbeat about its prospects. Two people in Starmer's shadow cabinet predicted their gains could be as low as twenty or thirty seats, noting that the party has struggled to rebuild in Scotland; it had yet to resolve its cultural divide in the red wall; and was being outgunned by the Liberal Democrats in the blue wall. 'Superficially we are making progress, but our support is wide but not very deep,' one Starmer ally said. Another added, 'The country is falling out of love with Johnson, but it's far from clear they are loving us. I still don't know if we can fix all of our problems with two years to go.'

It was a year since I sat down with the two Tory strategists who will likely run the next election campaign. Isaac Levido and Michael Brooks have remained in the shadows, focusing on their political consultancy, Fleetwood, that advises private-sector clients. At a pertinent moment in 2023, the pair are likely to return to work for the Conservative Party. That is the moment when Johnson's re-election campaign will officially begin. At

Soho's swish Ham Yard Hotel the pair of thirty-somethings were happy to chat once more about the findings of my latest mini road trip and how the political landscape had changed.

Michael Brooks, now sporting a post-lockdown beard, concurred with every other interviewee that the departure of Jeremy Corbyn had heightened the Tories' political challenge. 'A lot of the headline danger associated with Labour has dissipated with Corbyn going – and that leaves voters at risk of the negative consequences of a Starmer Labour government.' With an eighty-seat majority, the southern voters may think that the party is 'locked in' for another five or ten years, which Brooks thought could give them a licence to vote Lib Dem. 'They think they can get both a Tory government without actually voting for it, and make a point about whatever local issue concerns them.'

As we moved on to discussing where the Liberal Democrats could make gains, Isaac Levido (also bewhiskered) chimed in his clipped, curt tones about the voters they are thinking about for 2024. 'They still live a lot of their social life in London,' he mulled. Brooks went on to paint his picture of Esher and Walton's typical voters and, crucially, how they think about the British state:

'They're the ones for whom the government actually touches their life in the most impactful ways; they tend to be in that middle age bracket, where their kids are still in school or about to head to university. Housing tends to be a big issue for them; a lot of their wealth is tied up in their home. Their parents are probably thinking about social care options. Therefore, it's very much about communicating how the government improves their lives.'

Similarly to Dominic Raab, Brooks said the yellow peril is based on feelings. 'The Lib Dems are making a values-based argument at the moment combined with local performance. For a lot of their target voters the Lib Dems don't even need an issue; they just need to not be the Tories and not be Labour.' All three of us agreed that 'wall' analogies are not always especially helpful, but Levido added that the Lib Dems' southern hopes are 'confirmed to a certain type of seat' due to only having thirteen MPs. 'They don't hold more blue-collar, lower socio-economic places out in the south-west like they used to. They don't hold seats in some of the suburban areas around Birmingham and Manchester and that limits their appeal somewhat.' Brooks added that it is in these suburban areas the argument about the economic and financial impact of a Labour government can cut through. 'They don't see any risk of Labour winning at the minute at all.'

I took this cue to move on to the question of Labour and how Levido-Brooks saw their improved polling standing in 2022. Brooks responded with an existential question: 'You have to ask: what is the purpose of Labour? Who are they? Who are they there to represent?' It is a question Starmer has yet to answer successfully during the first two years of his leadership, and the dilemma he will have to face when drawing together the framework of his election campaign. He summarized, 'They have ended up being torn between their metropolitan base and the traditional base. The idea of "labour" in the name has changed completely. They're struggling to be relevant, but to identify a purpose and struggling beyond "Okay, we're a sort of more competent version of the Tories, then", what do they offer? What is it that voters want?'

Levido tackled Starmer's personality and how it contrasts with Johnson, reflecting on Labour's equivocal stance on the Remain/ Leave question. 'He apparently believed so profoundly in remaining in the European Union, in reversing Brexit. But when he was the shadow Brexit Secretary going into the last election, for some reason he and his party couldn't take a stance. The official position was neutral.' But has the Partygate scandal caused terminal damage for Johnson's personal ratings? Levido argued forcefully that he can recover. 'Of course he can, because of the time there is between now and the next election to demonstrate those crucial leadership qualities. Of course there was a drop in ratings because of a perception, by big chunks of the public, that he wasn't demonstrating those qualities. But he's got two years to demonstrate those.'

The two-year countdown to the election was obviously at the front of Brooks and Levido's minds. With the Brexit crisis followed by the Covid crisis followed by the Ukraine crisis, the Johnson government's capacity to deliver their election pledges to tackle inequality have been stunted. Levido argued that levelling up was still crucial for their next election hopes. 'If Labour's message is that these Tories don't care about certain parts of society, I think they're going to have a bit of a problem,' he extolled. 'If they're going to try and position the Tory Party as some sort of far-right wing force, they're not going to have much evidence to base that on – look at the levelling up agenda. By definition, the absolute centre ground of politics is picking people up in neglected areas, focusing on investment and policies to improve their lives and the circumstances around them for the long term.'

Brooks confirmed the thesis at the end of my initial road trip that 2019 represented 'a very particular set of circumstances' that handed Johnson such a significant majority. 'If you look at the two biggest reasons people voted Tory, as your book outlined, it was Brexit and Corbyn. And at the next election, both of those are gone,' he noted. Levido was hopeful, however, that the tranche of red wall Tories elected for the first time 'have a very good shot' at winning re-election after getting stuck into their constituencies. 'A lot of those MPs will hold on because they've worked very hard in the subsequent five years since the election to establish themselves, raise their profile and do good work as a new hardworking MP in that constituency.' Even if they have gone cool on the prime minister, he felt that a reason to vote Conservative may be simply to keep a good local MP.

Considering the framing of an election campaign two years away may be fruitless. So much has happened in the year since our first chat, not least the war in Europe. Brooks explained: 'The context of the next election could change massively. Take Ukraine, for example. Who knows what's going to happen? If that escalates in a way that I don't think anybody wants it to, then the issues at the next election could be fundamentally different to those we are considering now.' But Levido-Brooks had some clear contours in mind. Just as one of their most effective party-political broadcasts in 2019 focused on getting politics out of people's lives, 2024 will likely feature the same.

Brooks said Brexit was a 'done issue' and the majority of voters were misanthropic towards politics. 'They're sick of talking about political stuff. They had the Scottish independence referendum, and they had a general election campaign, then they had a referendum campaign, then they had another general election campaign, and they had two years of wrangling over Brexit and had another general election campaign. And then they've had two years of politicians on their TV talking about Covid. They're just sick of the whole lot of it. They want all of them to go away.'

He went on to say that the overall context was that people are refusing to pay attention to Westminster politics, which makes fluctuations in opinion polls meaningless. 'The really big emotional context at the moment is that people just don't want to engage. And I can only imagine that this situation in Ukraine is simply going to heighten that fatigue.' The Ukraine crisis has highlighted the volatility: Johnson's unpopularity plummeted to new lows after the Partygate scandal in early 2021, yet recovered within weeks of the Ukraine war. Brooks put it down to apathy. 'This creates a situation where the status quo remains broadly stable as people are disengaged and then changes very quickly as people engage. But until voters are in the position of being asked to make a decision at an election, any changes in public polls are just surface-level commentary.'

The pair insisted that the next election will still be in spring 2024. The UK has not experienced a normal election cycle since 2015 – my debut as a political journalist – when the campaign began at the start of the year. Brooks thought the 'media focus' would commence then. Although, the actual campaign will begin in March, he expects voters will engage nearer polling day.[19] 'The voting focus – where voters start to recognize their role in the process – which I think is much more interesting, can be anywhere from ten days to three months. It's rarely more than three months out.'

What might the message and campaign look like? Given the trauma of Brexit and Covid, the Conservatives will naturally want to look forward. 'Electorates care about the future not the past,' Levido said. Brooks elaborated: 'It's about setting out a clear vision of the future and how these communities are going to be better off under a Tory government, and the ways in which a Labour government will leave them worse off. I fundamentally think it's that simple. [Regarding] the exact mechanism and devices for doing that [it] is too early to say. But a lot of these [red wall] places we're talking about are very sensitive to economic and financial events.'

It was palpable that the pair hope to return to the 2019 themes. 'People are sick of politics,' Levido reiterated. 'We've come through a period with Covid where people have experienced the awesome power of the state to reach and affect people's lives. It is just right in front of your face all the time for the first time in a way that no one has experienced since arguably the Second World War.' And what about the other theme of 2015: vote Liberal Democrat, get the Scottish National Party? With such a high bar for Labour to win a majority, could the (much-parodied) message of a 'coalition of chaos' return? With a gentle smile and nod, Brooks concluded: 'Imagine another three years of all your politicians on your telly every night arguing about a referendum, about whether or not the country should stay together? Doesn't sound very attractive, does it?' Whether it is a believable scenario will decide how much of the blue wall the Tories will secede.

At the end of my red wall road trip, concluding that a structural realignment in British politics had taken place after Brexit was clear. Boris Johnson had just smashed Labour once again in the 2021 local elections, won the historic Hartlepool by-election, and his personal ratings were higher than ever. The legacy of Brexit and Jeremy Corbyn continued to bedevil Labour; Keir Starmer's 'new management' had failed to make much headway and the party was behind in the polls. After my blue wall trip, however, the political scene is far murkier and the future almost entirely uncertain.

My scepticism about whether there is such a thing as a consistent blue wall remains. There is undoubtedly a band of seats in which the Liberal Democrats will target the Tories, but they are mostly classic marginals than a wall that collapses as a whole. This is how they will fight the incumbents: digging in at a local level, focusing on small-scale concerns, while making cultural attack points about the Johnson government. Some losses are inevitable: Dominic Raab faces a huge challenge holding onto

Esher and Walton. After my road trip, one senior Tory party advisor, who declined to be named, told me, 'He's probably fucked.'

The biggest challenge for the Liberal Democrats is presence. Each time the party has a good showing, they do so thanks to a major national issue and a moderate Labour leader. In 2005, it was the Iraq War and Tony Blair. In 2010, it was tuition fees and Gordon Brown. This time, it may be Keir Starmer, but the issue is less clear. Neither Monica Harding, nor Ed Davey, nor anyone else I spoke to in the party, could highlight what topic will give them airtime. The Lib Dems briefly achieved some media cut-through by opposing vaccine passports, but the issue fell away as with the pandemic. It is not going be the EU question: none of the three parties can see any mileage in bringing it to the fore.

Rising from thirteen to twenty-odd seats seems entirely achievable for the Liberal Democrats, but, as Michael Brooks highlighted with relish, they will be squeezed by the prospect of a Labour-led coalition involving Scottish nationalists. Such messaging was effective in 2015 for the Tories, if not the union of the United Kingdom, and there is no doubt it will be used again. Social media will be entertained by the return of the 'coalition of chaos' line and the Scottish Conservative Party will face an even greater challenge in holding onto their six seats. If the message connects in the south, however, marginal voters may indeed become fearful about more political instability.

Labour is undoubtedly in a stronger position across the whole of England than in 2021. Keir Starmer has radically changed the party in ways not even his fiercest supporters believed plausible. After the 2019 election, Jeremy Corbyn's supporters controlled every part of its infrastructure. Three years on, the shadow Cabinet, national executive committee, parliamentary party and nearly all of the membership are behind the new leader. This unity forms the bedrock of what Starmer's allies talk of as 'the return of proper Labour'. They are aware that when the 2024 campaign begins, the Tories will hit the party with every piece of evidence to build the case of 'long Corbyn'; that the party has not really moved on from its left-wing bent and many of its key figures – including Starmer – wanted Corbyn to be prime minister. To stave off such attacks, Starmer and his team are severing possible ties with those years. With Corbyn's refusal not to resile from a letter by the Stop the War campaign group that partially blamed NATO for the Ukraine war, his return to the party seems inconceivable. More of his comrades may find themselves out of the party in the coming years.

Starmer is aiming very high. He is attempting to condense Neil Kinnock, John Smith and Tony Blair's transformation of the party from fourteen years into five. Those around him are betting that the electorate's volatility makes victory possible and he can seize on Johnson's chaos to gain a fresh hearing in 2024. It is unclear whether those internal changes are translating into support from the electorate. Labour may be two to five points ahead in the opinion polls at the time of writing, but MPs and members of the shadow Cabinet are fearful that Starmer's favourability has struggled to rise to high enough levels. Others point to how his steady and gradual rise has seen him eclipse Johnson on all the key polling metrics that typically decide election winners. One of his closest shadow Cabinet allies admitted to me that the party may struggle to gain more than twenty/thirty seats in 2024, which would keep Johnson in power.

And what of the red wall that gave Johnson his thumping majority? According to Chris Curtis at the pollsters Opinium, the biggest losses in his party's standing over the Partygate scandal have come in those constituencies that voted Tory for the first time. Labour's line that there is 'one rule for them, one rule for the rest of us' was wielded initially for the Barnard Castle scandal, but has been adapted to every subsequent alleged abuse of power by the government. Some pollsters, such as Theresa May's ex-strategist James Johnson, think the prime minister can never recover from the Partygate scandal. The argument goes that his ratings are too low, trust too busted and his true character exposed. The prospect of a leadership challenge before the Ukraine war was precipitated by the 'pork pie plot' of 2019 MPs, led by Alicia Kearns of the Rutland and Melton constituency where the famous pies are baked. They were fearful that Johnson would lose them their seats and urged a new leader.

But as the prime minister's rapid change in fortunes following the war suggests, it can be a mistake to write off Boris Johnson too soon. Multiple times throughout his career, he has beaten conventional wisdom. After his first time as Mayor of London concluded, few thought he could win re-election. After the Brexit referendum, it was assumed he would never be prime minister – ditto when he flounced out of Theresa May's government against her softer Brexit deal. And yet, he is still in Number 10. The chaos of his first term in Downing Street has significantly damaged his standing, but Isaac Levido is right: delivery and a better track record hands him the chance to win again.

Without Johnson, there is a danger for the Tories that much of the red wall flips back to Labour. Rishi Sunak, the chancellor, polls better than any of the other contenders in the red wall. But his personal ratings in these seats still rank behind the prime minister and questions about the tax status of his family will dog him into the next election. Any new leader would still face the problem that the pandemic means there has not been enough time or capacity in Whitehall to level up. With Johnson, the party has a battle to hold it – his unique standing with the electorate means he has a small window to persuade voters that another five years can see his initial vision fulfilled.

When Tory MPs decide his fate over Partygate, they have to consider whether a tarnished leader is better than an untested one. The Ukraine war means he may never be challenged, despite becoming the first prime minister to have been found to have committed a criminal act while in office (Johnson was fined for a lockdown-busting party in April 2022). If he is, electability will be at the top of MPs' worries after twelve years in power. Above all, Tory MPs always want power and will choose the most viable route to it. Johnson's allies hope that if any serious challenge emerges, they will make the case he has never lost a national election. 'He's won London mayor twice, the referendum and a general election. Would they really want to swap him out for someone else?' one asks.

With two years until the next polling day, the tolerance for any further mistakes from the prime minister is finished, and his time to deliver on the 2019 election pledges is dwindling. Whether in the red or blue wall, his future will rest on whether England's voters opt for change or more of the same. Johnson, and no one else, can prove whether the latter is the country's best future. But from both road trips, I am sure that, post-2016, values are now central. Whether in the red or blue walls, the commonality is that culture is of equal – if occasionally greater – importance than economics and the traditional metrics of competency. The Liberal Democrats' overperformance in the south and the Tories' in the north, both with their potent Brexit messages, speaks to this. All three parties believe this is a structural change; none believe it will have gone by 2024. And, as witnessed during the Brexit wars, the result is division and combative discourse. When the Conservatives are eventually turned out of office and the Brexit era comes to close, this will be the legacy of the most tumultuous years in modern British history.

Notes

Introduction: Gateshead

1 J. B. Priestley, *English Journey*, Penguin Books, London, reissue 1977, originally published 1934

2 Sebastian Payne, 'Seb Payne's schooldays', *Spectator*, 14 May 2015, https://www.spectator.co.uk/article/seb-payne-s-schooldays [accessed 19 March 2021]

3 'Revised estimates of leave vote in Westminster constituencies', https://docs.google.com/spreadsheets/d/1wTK5dV2_YjCMsUYlwg0l48uWWf44sKgG8uFVMv5OWlA/edit [accessed 20 March 2021]

4 Peter Moore, 'How Britain voted at the EU referendum', YouGov, 27 June 2018, https://yougov.co.uk/topics/politics/articles-reports/2016/06/27/how-britain-voted [accessed 20 March 2021]

5 'YouGov/The Times/Sky Survey Results', https://d25d2506sfb94s.cloudfront.net/cumulus_uploads/document/df8cjzcpgw/TheTimes_Sky_VI_191106_w.pdf [accessed 20 March 2021]

6 'Survation Final General Election 2019 Poll Results', Survation, 11 December 2019, https://www.survation.com/final-general-election-2019-poll-results-a-preview/ [accessed 20 March 2021]

7 'ICM Voting Intentions - General Election 2019: Poll 6', ICM Unlimited, 6 December 2019, https://www.icmunlimited.com/our-work/icm-voting-intentions-general-election-2019-poll-6/ [accessed 21 March 2021]

8 Conservatives, 'End the argument. Get Brexit done. Vote Conservative.', YouTube, 7 December 2019, https://www.youtube.com/watch?v=FPjkTCQh3RM [accessed 21 March 2021]

9 Sarah Provan et al, 'London terror attack: man shot dead by police after stabbing — as it happened', *Financial Times*, 29 November 2019, https://www.ft.com/content/421bb4a8-5b84-3882-a1a2-0ef4216e5251[accessed 22 March 2021]

10 Rob Merrick, 'London Bridge attack: Jeremy Corbyn says terrorists can be

released early if they have been "rehabilitated"', *Independent*, 1 December 2019, https://www.independent.co.uk/news/uk/politics/london-bridge-attack-jeremy-corbyn-terrorist-release-boris-johnson-stabbing-a9227971.html [accessed 22 March 2021]

11 'Corbyn: I'm "seven out of 10" on EU', BBC News, 11 June 2016, https://www.bbc.co.uk/news/av/uk-politics-eu-referendum-36506163 [accessed 22 March 2021]

12 Alain Tolhurst, 'Jeremy Corbyn "most unpopular opposition leader of past 45 years", says poll', *PoliticsHome*, 20 September 2019, https://www.politicshome.com/news/article/jeremy-corbyn-most-unpopular-opposition-leader-of-past-45-years-says-poll [accessed 22 March 2021]

1: Blyth Valley

1 'Hartley Colliery disaster remembered 150 years on', BBC News, 15 January 2012, https://www.bbc.co.uk/news/uk-england-tyne-16494120 [accessed 23 March 2021]

2 'Blyth Market', https://web.archive.org/web/20070201210208/http://blyth-market.com/ [accessed 23 March 2021]

3 'Alcan Lynemouth smelter: Landmark day as closure starts', BBC News, 29 March 2012, https://www.bbc.co.uk/news/uk-england-tyne-17545827 [accessed 24 March 2021]

4 Edward Milne, 'Port of Blyth', Commons and Lords Hansard, the Official Report of debates in Parliament, 9 December 1963, https://api.parliament.uk/historic-hansard/commons/1963/dec/09/port-of-blyth [accessed 23 March 2021]

5 Edward Milne, 'Blyth Shipyard (Closure)', Commons and Lords Hansard, the Official Report of debates in Parliament, 20 December 1966, https://api.parliament.uk/historic-hansard/commons/1966/oct/20/blyth-shipyard-closure [accessed 24 March 2021]

6 Ben O'Connell, 'Government confirms £34million for Northumberland Line - Rail Minister says he's "lucky to be reopening train lines"', *Northumberland Gazette*, 23 January 2021, https://www.northumberlandgazette.co.uk/news/politics/council/government-confirms-ps34million-northumberland-line-rail-minister-says-hes-lucky-be-reopening-train-lines-3110263 [accessed 24 March 2021]

7 Peter Campbell and Chris Tighe, 'UK's first gigafactory to provide £2.6bn boost for "red wall" town', *Financial Times*, 11 December 2020, https://www.ft.com/content/010aabf1-9728-4171-8f39-f2cb4b2d6193 [accessed 24 March 2021]

8 Tony Henderson, 'Gateshead National Garden Festival: 25 years since the event on Tyneside', *ChronicleLive*, 13 May 2015, http://www.chroniclelive. co.uk/news/north-east-news/gateshead-national-garden-festival-25-9240847 [accessed 24 March 2021]

9 'Britishvolt enters exclusive technology collaboration with Siemens UK', *Automotive World*, 15 January 2021, https://www.automotiveworld.com/ news-releases/britishvolt-enters-exclusive-technology-collaboration-with-siemens-uk/ [accessed 24 March 2021]

2: North West Durham

1 'Which political party would be the best at handling defence and security?', YouGov, https://yougov.co.uk/topics/politics/trackers/defence-and-security [accessed 24 March 2021]

2 'Jeremy Corbyn: "You can't protect people on the cheap"', BBC News, 4 June 2017, https://www.bbc.co.uk/news/av/uk-politics-40154309/jeremy-corbyn-you-can-t-protect-people-on-the-cheap [accessed 24 March 2021]

3 Gavin Havery, 'Eden Pit in Leadate [sic] closed 40 years ago on Saturday', *Northern Echo*, 13 July 2020, https://www.thenorthernecho.co.uk/news/ 18578964.eden-pit-leadate-closed-40-years-ago-saturday/ [accessed 25 March 2021]

4 'Steel Towns – From Boom to Bust', BBC http://www.bbc.co.uk/nationonfilm/ topics/steel/background.shtml#:~:text=In%201980%20the%20death%20 knell,the%20national%20average%20at%2015%25 [accessed 25 March 2021]

5 The genesis of Consett, *Northern Echo*, 12 March 2005, https://www. thenorthernecho.co.uk/news/6958789.genesis-consett/ [accessed 25 March 2021]

6 Ibid.

7 'Derwentside Directory 06/07', Informnorth, http://www.informnorth.com/ images/testimonials/directory.pdf [accessed 25 March 2021]

8 'In at the rebirth of forgotten town', *ChronicleLive*, 13 September 2008 [updated 27 February 2013], https://www.chroniclelive.co.uk/news/local-news/rebirth-forgotten-town-1474679 [accessed 25 March 2021]

9 Lanchester Wines, 'Entrepreneur of the Year 2019 - Tony Cleary of Lanchester Group, YouTube, 26 September 2019, https://www.youtube.com/ watch?v=7mJsPgcAdZ4 [accessed 26 March 2021]

10 Kelley Price, 'KP Snacks to close Consett site: Third of staff could be redeployed to Billingham', *TeessideLive*, 20 November 2014, https://www.gazettelive.co.uk/ business/business-news/kp-snacks-close-consett-site-8139768 [accessed 26 March 2021]

11 Alain Tolhurst, 'Jeremy Corbyn "most unpopular opposition leader of past 45 years", says poll', *PoliticsHome*, 20 September 2019, https://www.politicshome.com/news/article/jeremy-corbyn-most-unpopular-opposition-leader-of-past-45-years-says-poll [accessed 22 March 2021]

12 'Social Grade', Market Research Society, https://www.mrs.org.uk/resources/social-grade [accessed 27 March 2021]

13 Judith Woods, 'Alan Johnson: Blair told me, 'Gosh, you really are working class, aren't you?', *Telegraph*, 4 May 2013, https://www.telegraph.co.uk/news/politics/10036814/Alan-Johnson-Blair-told-me-Gosh-you-really-are-working-class-arent-you.html [accessed 26 March 2021]

14 '"He couldn't lead the working class out of a paper bag" - Alan Johnson launches fierce attack on Corbyn and Momentum', ITV News, 13 December 2019, https://www.itv.com/news/2019-12-13/alan-johnson-momentum-jeremy-corbyn-itv-news [accessed 26 March 2021]

3: Sedgefield

1 Paul Stokes et al, 'Bush (and 1,300 police) pop into Blair's local for fish, chips and mushy peas', *Telegraph*, 22 November 2003, https://www.telegraph.co.uk/news/uknews/1447381/Bush-and-1300-police-pop-into-Blairs-local-for-fish-chips-and-mushy-peas.html [accessed 27 March 2021]

2 'Sedgefield Community College', World Class Schools, https://www.worldclass-schools.org/our-schools/sedgefield-community-college/ [accessed 27 March 2021]

3 'Trimdon Colliery', Durham Mining Museum, http://www.dmm.org.uk/colliery/t023.htm [accessed 27 March 2021]

4 Martin Wainwright, 'Trimdon Labour Club falls victim to budget', *Guardian*, 27 June 2010, https://www.theguardian.com/politics/2010/jun/27/trimdon-labour-club-closes-down [accessed 28 March 2021]

5 'Election 2019: Sedgefield', BBC News, https://www.bbc.co.uk/news/politics/constituencies/E14000915 [accessed 28 March 2021]

6 'Revised estimates of leave vote in Westminster constituencies', https://docs.google.com/spreadsheets/d/1wTK5dV2_YjCMsUYlwg0l48uWWf44sKgG8uFVMv5OWlA/edit [accessed 20 March 2021]

7 Nick Gullon, '"I am for Labour not for Corbyn" - Sedgefield election candidate's bid to distance himself from party leader", *Northern Echo*, 22 May 2017, https://www.thenorthernecho.co.uk/news/15300397.i-labour-not-corbyn---sedgefield-election-candidates-bid-distance-party-leader/ [accessed 28 March 2021]

8 'Trimdon Labour Club closed', *Northern Echo*, 22 July 2010, https://www.

thenorthernecho.co.uk/news/8286065.trimdon-labour-club-closed/ [accessed 29 March 2021]

9 Christian Dustmann et al., 'The impact of EU enlargement on migration flow', Home Office, 25 March 2003, https://www.ucl.ac.uk/~uctpb21/reports/ HomeOffice25_03.pdf [accessed 29 March 2021]

10 Prof. John Salt, 'Report of the United Kingdom SOPEMI Correspondent to the OECD, 2015', University College London, https://www.geog.ucl.ac.uk/ research/research-centres/migration-research-unit/pdfs/Sopemi_UK_2015. pdf [accessed 29 March 2021]

4: Wakefield

1 'More funding pledged for £35m Hepworth gallery', *Yorkshire Post*, 29 July 2014, https://www.yorkshirepost.co.uk/news/more-funding-pledged-ps35m-hepworth-gallery-1837580 [accessed 30 March 2021]

2 Yorkshire Sculpture International, https://yorkshire-sculpture.org/about/ [accessed 30 March 2021]

3 BALTIC, https://baltic.art/about/baltic-history [accessed 30 March 2021]

4 'Council to discuss future support to the Hepworth Wakefield', Wakefield Council, 23 July 2014, https://www.wakefield.gov.uk/Pages/News/PR4656. aspx [accessed 30 March 2021]

5 Yorkshire Sculpture Park, https://ysp.org.uk/about-ysp/heritage [accessed 31 March 2021]

6 Nick Frame, 'Green light given to convert former campus near Yorkshire Sculpture Park into hotel', *Wakefield Express*, 7 May 2020, https://www. wakefieldexpress.co.uk/news/people/green-light-given-convert-former-campus-near-yorkshire-sculpture-park-hotel-2845893 [accessed 31 March 2021]

7 Tom Ravenscroft, 'Feilden Fowles unveils The Weston visitor centre at Yorkshire Sculpture Park', Dezeen, 4 April 2019, https://www.dezeen. com/2019/04/04/yorkshire-sculpture-park-weston-visitor-centre-feilden-fowles/ [accessed 31 March 2021]

8 W.E. RAWSON LIMITED, D&B Business Directory, https://www. dnb.com/business-directory/company-profiles.werawson_limited. 616b121798cbc88c974200450f7a2b09.html [accessed 1 April 2021]

9 John Gaunt, 'Bringing Yorkshire's disused mills back to life could create 27,000 homes - John Gaunt', *Yorkshire Post*, 10 March 2020, https://www.yorkshirepost. co.uk/business/bringing-yorkshires-disused-mills-back-life-could-create-27000-homes-john-gaunt-2444883 [accessed 1 April 2021]

10 'Denby Grange Colliery', Hansard 1803–2005, 2 July 1990 vol 175 cc832-

40, https://api.parliament.uk/historic-hansard/commons/1990/jul/02/denby-grange-colliery [accessed 1 April 2021]

11 South Elmsall & South Kirkby, Wakefield, http://www.halinaking.co.uk/Location/Yorkshire/Frames/Places/W%20Yorkshire/Wakefield/Wakefield.htm [accessed 1 April 2021]

12 Terry Macalister, 'Selby closes with loss of 5,000 jobs', *Guardian*, 16 July 2002, https://www.theguardian.com/business/2002/jul/16/globalrecession [accessed 2 April 2021]

13 'UK's last deep coal mine Kellingley Colliery capped off', BBC News, 14 March 2016, https://www.bbc.co.uk/news/uk-england-york-north-yorkshire-35803048 [accessed 2 April 2021]

14 'First Arrivals in Wakefield', My Learning, https://www.mylearning.org/stories/the-story-of-the-pakistani-community-in-wakefield-west-yorkshire/1165 [accessed 2 April 2021]

15 Ibid

16 Patrick Wintour, 'British barrister Karim Khan elected ICC's new chief prosecutor', *Guardian*, 12 February 2021, https://www.theguardian.com/law/2021/feb/12/karim-khan-international-criminal-court-prosecutor [accessed 2 April 2021]

5: Don Valley

1 'Doncaster Sheffield voted the UK's Best Airport by Which? Magazine three years in a row', *Doncaster Echo*, 23 October 2019, https://www.doncasterecho.co.uk/doncaster-sheffield-voted-the-uks-best-airport-by-which-magazine-three-years-in-a-row/

2 'Amazon now employing more than 1,000 people in Doncaster', *Yorkshire Post*, 4 December 2017, https://www.yorkshirepost.co.uk/business/amazon-now-employing-more-1000-people-doncaster-1766537

3 Chris Hanretty, 'Most Labour MPs represent a constituency that voted Leave', Medium, 30 June 2016, https://medium.com/@chrishanretty/most-labour-mps-represent-a-constituency-that-voted-leave-36f13210f5c6

4 'Church of St Lawrence, Station Road, Hatfield – Doncaster', https://historicengland.org.uk/advice/heritage-at-risk/search-register/list-entry/16726

5 'History of Conisbrough Castle', https://www.english-heritage.org.uk/visit/places/conisbrough-castle/history/

6 'Samuel Smith Old Brewery', https://www.samuelsmithsbrewery.co.uk/pubs/

7 'The "Blair babes": Where are they now?', BBC News, 8 May 2007, http://news.bbc.co.uk/1/hi/uk_politics/4698222.stm

8 Helen Pidd, '"She has listened to us": constituents back Labour rebel Caroline

Flint', *Guardian*, 20 October 2019, https://www.theguardian.com/politics/2019/oct/20/she-has-listened-to-us-constituents-back-labour-rebel-caroline-flint

9   George Torr, 'Doncaster "very much in running for new hospital" says Prime Minister' *Doncaster Free Press*, 17 March 2021, https://www.doncasterfreepress.co.uk/health/doncaster-very-much-in-running-for-new-hospital-says-prime-minister-3169167

10 Patrick Maguire, 'Robert Kilroy-Silk: the godfather of Brexit', *New Statesman*, 18 September 2019, https://www.newstatesman.com/politics/brexit/2019/09/robert-kilroy-silk-godfather-brexit

11 Boris Johnson, 'Keep calm everyone – now is not the time to do a Nicolas Cage', *Daily Telegraph*, 28 April 2013, https://www.telegraph.co.uk/news/politics/UKIP/10024202/Keep-calm-everyone-now-is-notthe-time-to-do-a-Nicolas-Cage.html

12 Andrew Sparrow, 'Labour delegates vote overwhelmingly for Brexit motion backing second referendum as option – as it happened', *Guardian*, 25 September 2018, https://www.theguardian.com/politics/blog/live/2018/sep/25/labour-conference-brexit-debate-starmer-increasingly-likely-to-vote-down-mays-brexit-deal-starmer-says-politics-live?page=with:block-5baa2770e4b0a9b9706792e0#block-5baa2770e4b0a9b9706792e0

13 Caroline Wheeler and Gabriel Pogrund, 'Starmer calls in Mandelson to inject a dose of New Labour's "winning mentality"', *Sunday Times*, 4 February 2021, https://www.thetimes.co.uk/article/starmer-calls-in-mandelson-to-inject-a-dose-of-new-labours-winning-mentality-wr0w25jpb

14 Malcolm Pithers, Keith Harper and Peter Hetherington, 'From the archive, 6 March 1984: Colliery closure reversed in crisis coalfield', *Guardian*, 6 March 2015, https://www.theguardian.com/politics/the-northerner/2015/mar/06/miners-strike-1984-num-yorkshire-archive

6: Great Grimsby

1   Samira Shackle, 'Fishing After Brexit: Grimsby Awaits a New Economic Reality', CIGI, 19 June 2018, https://www.cigionline.org/articles/fishing-after-brexit-grimsby-awaits-new-economic-reality

2   Walker Mills, 'The Cod Wars and Today: Lessons from an Almost War', Center for International Maritime Security, 28 July 2020, https://cimsec.org/the-cod-wars-and-today-lessons-from-an-almost-war/

3   'Fishing for Leave Campaign Launched', *Fishing News*, 15 May 2016, https://fishingnews.co.uk/news/fishing-for-leave/

4   Boris Johnson, 9 December 2019, https://twitter.com/borisjohnson/status/1203981568055947264?lang=en

5 'Tony Blair's Speech in Full', BBC News, 28 September 1999, http://news.bbc.co.uk/1/hi/uk_politics/460009.stm

6 https://www.rightmove.co.uk/house-prices/west-marsh-82274.html [accessed 22 April 2021]

7 Dawn Foster, 'Interview with Melanie Onn', *Guardian*, 26 July 2017, https://www.theguardian.com/society/2017/jul/26/big-ambitions-tackle-housing-shortage-national-problem

8 Jim Pickard and Leslie Hook, 'UK prepares to set out steeper climate targets', *Financial Times*, 19 April 2021, https://www.ft.com/content/a8c749b1-35fe-4613-a9b8-45688177843c

9 Rob Norris, 'More than 69,000 jobs and £60 billion private investment in UK offshore wind by 2026', RenewableUK, 24 March 2021, https://www.renewableuk.com/news/557871/More-than-69000-jobs-and-60-billion-private-investment-in-UK-offshore-wind-by-2026.htm

10 Roger Harrabin, 'Cumbria coal mine: What is the controversy about?', BBC News, 1 March 2021, https://www.bbc.co.uk/news/explainers-56023895

11 'MP changes name to Haddock', BBC News, 1 October 2002, http://news.bbc.co.uk/1/hi/england/2290283.stm

7: North East Derbyshire

1 Barratt Developments, 2018, https://viz.tools.investis.com/Barratt/flipbook/v2/files/assets/common/downloads/publication.pdf [accessed 2 May 2021]

2 http://www.killamarsh.org/ [accessed 29th April 2021]

3 Jim Packard, 'Party pollsters chase after Motorway Man', *Financial Times*, 21 January 2021, https://www.ft.com/content/2c5b66b6-06c4-11df-b426-00144feabdc0

4 Bob Cooper, 'General Election: Who is target voter Workington Man?', BBC News, 30 October 2019, https://www.bbc.co.uk/news/uk-england-cumbria-50239341

5 'The truth behind the Tories' northern strongholds', *The Economist*, 3 April 2021, https://www.economist.com/britain/2021/04/03/the-truth-behind-the-tories-northern-strongholds?giftId=056e96d9-d4f5-44d9-8cb3-f5545439d12e

6 Andrew Gimson, 'How Macmillan built 300,000 houses a year', Conservative Home, 17 October 2013, https://www.conservativehome.com/thetorydiary/2013/10/how-macmillan-built-300000-houses-a-year.html

7 Rajeev Syal, 'Jeremy Corbyn vows to take on exploitative landlords if elected PM', *Guardian*, 24 November 2019, https://www.theguardian.com/politics/2019/nov/24/jeremy-corbyn-vows-to-take-on-exploitative-landlords-if-elected-pm

8 Harriet Agerholm, 'Jeremy Corbyn was just 2,227 votes away from chance to be Prime Minister', *Independent*, 9 June 2017, https://www.independent.co.uk/news/uk/politics/corbyn-election-results-votes-away-prime-minister-theresa-may-hung-parliament-a7782581.html

9 Nick Gullon, 'I am for Labour not for Corbyn' – Sedgefield election candidate's bid to distance himself from party leader', *Northern Echo*, 22 May 2017, https://www.thenorthernecho.co.uk/news/15300397.i-labour-not-corbyn---sedgefield-election-candidates-bid-distance-party-leader/

8: Coventry North West

1 Office for National Statistics, https://www.ons.gov.uk/peoplepopulationand community/populationandmigration/populationestimates/bulletins/annualmidyearpopulationestimates/mid2018 [accessed 2 May 2021]

2 Jennifer Harby, 'The Coventry Blitz: "Hysteria, terror and neurosis"', BBC News, 13 November 2015, https://www.bbc.co.uk/news/uk-england-coventry-warwickshire-34746691

3 Joshua Chaffin, "We need change': why an old Labour city is looking right in UK election', *Financial Times*, 6 June 2017, https://www.ft.com/content/de01a2ae-4609-11e7-8d27-59b4dd6296b8

4 'English Indices of Deprivation 2019 – Coventry summary report', Coventry City Council, https://www.coventry.gov.uk/downloads/file/31860/english_indices_of_deprivation_2019_-_coventry_summary_report [accessed 1 May 2021]

5 'Populations and Demographics', Coventry City Council, https://www.coventry. gov.uk/info/195/facts_about_coventry/2435/population_and_demographics/3 [accessed 3 May 2021]

6 Gerald Eve LLP, 'Examination in Public of Coventry Local Plan: Hearing Statement in respect of Hearing Session 7 – Employment, On behalf of Jaguar Land Rover', https://www.coventry.gov.uk/download/downloads/id/21763/lp220_jlr_hearing_statement_session_7.pdf [accessed 30 April 2021]

7 'Surprise in Coventry North West as members select Taiwo Owatemi', LabourList, 3 November 2019, https://labourlist.org/2019/11/surprise-in-coventry-north-west-as-members-select-londoner/

8 Simon Heffer, *Like the Roman: The Life of Enoch Powell* (London: Faber and Faber, 1998)

9 Zubaida Haque, 'The "BME" vote is up for grabs in the general election 2017 – who will capture it?', *New Statesman*, 1 May 2017, https://www.newstatesman. com/politics/june2017/2017/05/bme-vote-grabs-general-election-2017-who-will-capture-it

10 'Runnymede Trust briefing: Ethnic minorities at the 2017 general election',

Equally Yours, 4 March 2019, https://www.equalyours.org.uk/runnymede-trust-briefing-ethnic-minorities-at-the-2017-general-election/

11 'Social background of Members of Parliament 1979–2019', House of Commons Library, 27 March 2020, https://commonslibrary.parliament.uk/research-briefings/cbp-7483/

12 Sajid Javid, Twitter, 19 October 2018, https://twitter.com/sajidjavid/status/1053336915850739714?lang=en [accessed 2 May 2021]

9: Heywood and Middleton

1 Gregory Robinson and Helen Pidd, 'How deprivation in the north has led to a health crisis', *Guardian*, 25 February 2020, https://www.theguardian.com/society/2020/feb/25/how-deprivation-in-the-north-has-led-to-a-health-crisis

2 Jennifer Williams, 'Rochdale council bids to end Middleton Moonraker art confusion', *Manchester Evening News*, 1 April 2011 [updated 11 January 2013], https://www.manchestereveningnews.co.uk/news/local-news/rochdale-council-bids-to-end-middleton-857649

3 'Labour Market Profile – Heywood And Middleton Parliamentary Constituency', Nomis, https://www.nomisweb.co.uk/reports/lmp/wpca/1929380058/printable.aspx [accessed 5 May 2021]

4 Dominic Smithers, 'Is now a good time to buy a home in north Manchester?', *Manchester Evening News*, 9 April 2017, https://www.manchestereveningnews.co.uk/news/property/north-manchester-now-good-place-12862438

5 'Heywood grows as Darnhill rises', *Manchester Evening News*, 1 June 2005, https://archive.is/20130420231101/http://menmedia.co.uk/heywoodadvertiser/news/s/388016_heywood_grows_as_darnhill_rises

6 Hannah Al-Othman, 'Lisa Nandy Saying "Towns" Has Become A Meme', Buzzfeed News, 18 December 2019, https://www.buzzfeed.com/hannahalothman/lisa-nandy-towns-memes

7 'Leadership and Deputy Leadership election 2020 – Results', Labour, https://labour.org.uk/people/leadership-elections-hub-2020/leadership-elections-2020-results/ [accessed 4 May 2021]

8 James Ashford, 'What is the Northern Powerhouse?', *The Week*, 27 August 2019, https://www.theweek.co.uk/102951/what-is-the-northern-powerhouse#:~:text=The%20Northern%20Powerhouse%20is%20the,can%20take%20on%20the%20world%E2%80%9D [accessed 1 May 2021]

9 'Local government Funding: Moving the conversation on', Local Government Association, June 2018, https://www.local.gov.uk/sites/default/files/documents/5.40_01_Finance%20publication_WEB_0.pdf

Notes

10: Burnley

1 Andy Phelps et al, 'The Textile Mills of Lancashire: The Legacy', Oxford Archaeology North, https://historicengland.org.uk/images-books/publications/textile-mills-lancashire-legacy/textile-mills-lancashire-legacy/

2 'Queen Street Mill', Engineering Timelines, http://www.engineering-timelines.com/scripts/engineeringItem.asp?id=957 [accessed 7 May 2021]

3 'Safran Nacelles in the United Kingdom', Safran Narcelles, https://www.safran-nacelles.com/country/safran-nacelles-united-kingdom [accessed 7 May 2021]

4 'Velocity Composites', Zoominfo, https://www.zoominfo.com/c/velocity-composites-plc/356916709 [accessed 7 May 2021]

5 'Burnley named most enterprising place in Britain', Department for Business, Innovation & Skills, 27 August 2013, https://www.gov.uk/government/news/burnley-named-most-enterprising-place-in-britain

6 Paul Burnell, 'Burnley riots: Town "moves on"', BBC News, 23 June 2011, https://www.bbc.co.uk/news/uk-england-lancashire-13889160

7 'Padiham Flood Risk Management Scheme', The Flood Hub, https://thefloodhub.co.uk. [accessed 8 May 2021]

8 David Collins, 'Boohoo warehouse was "a breeding ground for coronavirus", said staff at distribution centre where 25 caught Covid-19', *Sunday Times*, 12 July 2020, https://www.thetimes.co.uk/article/boohoo-warehouse-was-a-breeding-ground-for-coronavirus-said-staff-at-distribution-centre-where-25-caught-covid-19-j5jltklpl

9 'Labour Market Profile – Burnley', Nomis, https://www.nomisweb.co.uk/reports/lmp/la/1946157091/report.aspx?town=burnley#tabempunemp [accessed 6 May 2021]

10 'Labour will end "epidemic" of zero-hours contracts', BBC News, 1 April 2015, https://www.bbc.co.uk/news/election-2015-32147715

11 Alan Milburn, 'The government is unable to commit to the social mobility challenge', *Guardian*, 2 December 2017, https://www.theguardian.com/commentisfree/2017/dec/02/alan-milburn-government-not-comitted-to-social-mobility

12 Nathan Hyde, 'Northern are finished with Pacers and now they could be bought by taxpayers', LeedsLive, 12 December 2019, https://www.leeds-live.co.uk/news/leeds-news/northern-finished-pacers-now-could-17405200 [updated 16 December 2019]

13 'Burnley College', Further Education Funding Council, October 1995, https://core.ac.uk/download/pdf/4152944.pdf

14 'Todmorden Curve railway line opens for the first time in 40 years', *Global*

Railway Review, 18 May 2015, https://www.globalrailwayreview.com/news/23825/todmorden-curve-railway-line-opens-for-the-first-time-in-40-years/

15 Bill Jacobs, 'Burnley's Pioneer Place gets projected opening date as 120 jobs announced', LancsLive, 14 February 2021, https://www.lancs.live/news/lancashire-news/burnleys-pioneer-place-gets-projected-19819322

Conclusion: Hartlepool and Westminster

1 Richy Horsley and Stephen Richards, *Born to Fight*, John Blake Publishing, London, 2005

2 Nick Duffy, 'Boris Johnson says nobody "stuck up for the bankers as much as I did" when asked about "f**k business" jibe', iNews, 22 June 2019, https://inews.co.uk/news/politics/boris-johnson-says-nobody-stuck-up-for-the-bankers-as-much-as-i-did-when-asked-about-fk-business-jibe-305412

3 Dan Bloom, 'Labour MP, 26, demands end to "40 years of Thatcherism" in first speech attack', *Mirror*, 15 January 2020, https://www.mirror.co.uk/news/politics/labour-mp-26-demands-end-21286565

4 George Parker et al, 'After the Pandemic: Sunak signals the UK's return to fiscal conservatism', *Financial Times*, 25 February 2021, https://www.ft.com/content/4e7a8fc1-f505-4545-9c2e-b9e9bcfc0aaa

Epilogue: Esher and Walton

1 'Revised estimates of leave vote in Westminster constituencies', https://docs.google.com/spreadsheets/d/1wTK5dV2_YjCMsUYlwg0l48uWWf44sKgG8uFVMv5OWlA/edit?usp=sharing [accessed 20 March 2022]

2 'UK 2019 Election Results: Esher and Walton', BBC News, https://www.bbc.com/news/politics/constituencies/E14000697 [accessed 20 March 2022]

3 Matt Honeycombe-Foster, 'Dominic Raab's Tory predecessor urges voters to back Lib Dems as he blasts Boris Johnson's Brexit plans', Politics Home, 25 November 2019, https://www.politicshome.com/news/article/dominic-raabs-tory-predecessor-urges-voters-to-back-lib-dems-as-he-blasts-boris-johnsons-brexit-plans [accessed 20 March 2022]

4 Sebastian Payne, 'Signs of shifting allegiances in Surrey's Tory heartlands', *Financial Times*, 3 December 2019, https://www.ft.com/content/1679ca82-152c-11ea-9ee4-11f260415385 [accessed 20 March 2022]

5 'Esher and Walton: Seat Details', Electoral Calculus, ttps://www.electoralcalculus.co.uk/fcgi-bin/seatdetails.py?seat=Esher+and+Walton [accessed 20 March 2022]

6 Roger Blitz, 'Esher and Walton residents top average earnings table', *Financial*

Times, 13 April 2015, https://www.ft.com/content/4e4100c4-e10c-11e4-8b1a-00144feab7de [accessed 20 March 2022]

7 Electoral Calculus, https://web.archive.org/web/20111015054249/http://www.electoralcalculus.co.uk/electdata_2005ob.txt [accessed 20 March 2022]

8 Electoral Calculus, https://web.archive.org/web/20111015054424/http://www.electoralcalculus.co.uk/electdata_1997.txt [accessed 20 March 2022]

9 Steve Akehurst, 'The "Blue Wall"', Strong Message Here, Substack, 15 April 2021, https://strongmessagehere.substack.com/p/the-blue-wall?s=r [accessed 21 March 2022]

10 'Revised estimates of leave vote in Westminster constituencies', https://docs.google.com/spreadsheets/d/1wTK5dV2_YjCMsUYlwg0l48uWWf44sKgG8uFVMv5OWlA/edit#gid=893960794 [accessed 21 March 2022]

11 'Chesham and Amersham: Lib Dems overturn big Tory majority in by-election upset', BBC News, 18 June 2021, https://www.bbc.co.uk/news/uk-england-beds-bucks-herts-57472032 [accessed 21 March 2022]

12 'John Curtice: By-election result is "warning for Conservatives"', GB News, YouTube, 18 June 2021, https://www.youtube.com/watch?v=Awpkga FPZnU&t=294s [accessed 21 March 2022]

13 'North Shropshire parliamentary by-election', Shropshire Council, https://shropshire.gov.uk/elections-and-electoral-registration/election-results/north-shropshire-parliamentary-by-election/ [accessed 21 March 2022]

14 'MPs', Liberal Democrats, https://www.libdems.org.uk/mps [accessed 21 March 2022]

15 '2019 general election results: Esher and Walton', UK Parliament, https://electionresults.parliament.uk/election/2019-12-12/Results/Location/Constituency/Esher%20and%20Walton/ [accessed 21 March 2022]

16 Adam McDonnell, 'Britons would vote to Remain but are less sure about re-joining', YouGov, 2 February 2021, https://yougov.co.uk/topics/politics/articles-reports/2021/02/02/britons-would-vote-remain-are-less-sure-about-re-j [accessed 22 March 2022]

17 Toby Helm, 'Jeremy Corbyn "failed to reply" to Israeli Labour on fears of antisemitism', *Guardian*, 28 May 2016, https://www.theguardian.com/politics/2016/may/28/jeremy-corbyn-failed-reply-israel-left-antisemitism-ken-livingstone [accessed 22 March 2022]

18 'Revised estimates of leave vote in Westminster constituencies', https://docs.google.com/spreadsheets/d/1wTK5dV2_YjCMsUYlwg0l48uWWf44sKgG8uFVMv5OWlA/edit#gid=893960794 [accessed 22 March 2022]

19 'General Election 2015 timetable', UK Parliament, http://www.parliament.uk/about/how/elections-and-voting/general/general-election-timetable-2015/ [accessed 22 March 2022]

Acknowledgements

When this book was envisaged at the start of 2020, coronavirus was an unknown word to a country unprepared for normal life to abruptly cease. Forging a road trip across England during three lockdowns, with social distancing, was almost impossible at times. But I did not want this to be a pandemic book, so despite the logistical challenges of immersing myself in the places I have written about, the final story is hopefully close to what it would have been without the virus.

Broken Heartlands came to fruition thanks to my two wonderful mentors who have guided the project: Matthew Cole, my learned editor at Pan Macmillan, and David Evans, my ever-supportive agent at David Higham Associates. The pair have expertly chaperoned the project from inception to publication, tempering my verbosity and offering unfailing support and imaginative ideas. At Pan Mac, thanks to James Annal for a cover that captured what the journey was about, Fraser Crichton for his astute copy-editing and Charlotte Wright, who saw the project over the line. Caroline Murray's careful reading was most welcome and without the early backing of Andrew Gordon at David Higham, none of this would have happened.

I have been blessed with three fantastic researchers who slaved through Hansard, endless interviews and statistics to complement my travels. While finding time to stand as a local councillor, Nathan Boroda's dedication to the *Broken Heartlands* project was a feat to behold. Amy O'Brien and Gabe Milne diligently worked through interviews, and researching the ten stops. A special thanks also goes to Chris Curtis at the pollsters Opinium, who led the survey of the red wall.

I interviewed over 120 people and I am grateful to every one of them for their time. The cast list makes *Broken Heartlands* what it is. And for those who wanted to remain in the shadows: thank you, you know who you are.

For their hospitality during my travels, I am grateful for the company of Joe and Heather Brooke, Ed Leech, Joshi Hermann, Julian Glover and Matthew Parris. *Broken Heartlands* would not have been completed without writing sessions at the bucolic Lookout Tower on Aldeburgh Beach – with a special thank you to Caroline Wiseman and Derek Wyatt for always going above and beyond with their hospitality.

In February 2020, I presented a BBC Radio 4 documentary, *England's Level Best*, examining what Boris Johnson's 'levelling-up' agenda is. If you enjoyed this book, then please do dig it out. Some of the interviews from the programme also feature here: thanks to Ellie Clifford and Robert Nicholson at Whistledown Productions, and Imogen Walford at the BBC.

Throughout this project, Patrick Maguire has been a rock. Following his own superb book on Labour's troubles under Jeremy Corbyn, he has been a much-needed sounding board. Jonathan Derbyshire and Daniel Finkelstein were also incredibly helpful with their thoughts on the final manuscript.

I am indebted to Fraser Nelson, Lionel Barber and Roula Khalaf for the opportunities they have given me throughout my career. My colleagues at the *Financial Times* have been fantastically understanding as I have juggled writing a book with my reporting job. I could not ask for better comrades than those in Westminster's finest political reporting team: George Parker, Jim Pickard,

Acknowledgements

Robert Shrimsley, Jasmine Cameron-Chileshe and Laura Hughes. Anna Dedhar and the team behind *Payne's Politics* podcast kindly adapted to a presenter darting around the country. And for everyone at *Financial Times* HQ, who suffered from late copy, thank you. Andrew Parker and the rest of the UK desk will be relieved I can answer the phone more often.

A book is a shared experience, and my friends have lived the whole thing. To Elizabeth Ames and Chris Murray, Katy Balls, Toby Coaker, Lucy Fisher, Ed Macdonald, Luke McGee, Matt and Sarah McGrath, Alex Wickham and Rhiannon Williams, thank you for all the supportive drinks and dinners. The key workers, Van Mildert and Suffolk gangs also know who they are.

To my family and friends in the north-east: Richard Bruce, Judith and Martin Davis, Christine and Andrew Lawlan, Jonathan Goodfellow and Frank and Irene Tatoli – thank you for everything, then as now. The Gastons, Budds and Bozzis have also been joyful additions to family life. My mother, Bronwen, raised me in a single-parent household from the age of eight and gave me the best start in life anyone could ask for. With unfailing support, love, and her astute teachers' eye on the manuscript, the realization of this book is thanks to her.

But above everyone else, you have read *Broken Heartlands* thanks to my wife, Soph. Throughout my long absences and writing into the early hours, her understanding and advice was unfailingly brilliant. She nursed me back to life after I contracted coronavirus, while still performing at 150 per cent in her own demanding job. Her renowned social research has informed so much of my thinking, and her love of good prose has pushed me to make this the best possible read. Thank you for everything and our wonderful life together.

– *Sebastian Payne*
Westminster, June 2021

Index

Page references in *italics* indicate images.

453

Praise for *Broken Heartlands*

The Times Political Book of the Year
A *Daily Telegraph*, *Guardian*, *Daily Mail* and *FT* Book of the Year

'Immensely readable. Labour's crisis in the red wall . . . will shape the future of English politics. This engrossing, warm and insightful work is an indispensable guide to how it came about' – *The Observer*, Book of the Week

'Reminiscent of Orwell's *The Road to Wigan Pier*, Payne travels around Labour's former red wall to paint a stark picture of those left behind' – *The Daily Telegraph*

'First class political reportage . . . should be considered required reading for anyone interested in British politics' – *Mail on Sunday*

'Compelling, authoritative but human . . . the book will inevitably become an important resource for historians' – *The Sunday Times*

'Nuanced take on Labour's lost strongholds. Raised in Gateshead, Payne brings intimacy and depth' – *The Guardian*

'Payne's entertaining and insightful book is essential reading' – *Evening Standard*

'*Broken Heartlands* is the product of rich reporting on the ground . . . Payne tells many stories of many places and people with affection and respect, to weave a picture of the changing political fabric of England' – Laura Kuenssberg

'A compelling chronicle of why English politics is undergoing such fundamental change. A must-read for anyone who wants to understand England today' – Robert Peston

'The p[. . .]onsequential electio[. . .]rew Neil

'A really fascinating and surprisingly moving book. Payne takes us on a journey that feels personal as well as political and helps us better understand what the red wall really is, who its voters are, and what politics has meant to them over the past few tumultuous years' – Isabel Hardman, author of *Why We Get the Wrong Politicians*

'A must-read for all those who want to learn the lessons of Labour's 2019 defeat' – Paul Mason, author of *PostCapitalism*

'Sebastian Payne demolishes the clichés that smother debate about the north of England and provides a simultaneously tender and acute guide to the land that London forgot' – Nick Cohen

'Part travelogue, part *Question Time*, Payne interviews pretty much everyone. This is a first draft of history as first drafts of history should properly be written' – Tom Holland

'One of the book's many strengths is its precision . . . Payne's book examines the narratives on red wall constituencies like the layers of an onion: starting with superficial readings, before peeling them back to reveal greater complexity' – Stephen Bush, *New Statesman*

'Entertaining political travelogue . . . plenty of insights . . . Payne is a guide without any trace of snobbery' – *Financial Times*

'The most revealing book about politics just doesn't happen to come from America: the United Kingdom's red wall, Albion's version of the Rust Belt, is the subject of *Broken Heartlands*' – *The Washington Post*

'*Broken Heartlands* digs into the fabric of the post-industrial communities that only make headlines at election time and challenges received wisdom and lazy myths' – *Literary Review*

'Payne, who grew up in Gateshead . . . has an instinctive rapport with people who feel overlooked and abandoned by Labour' – *The Week*